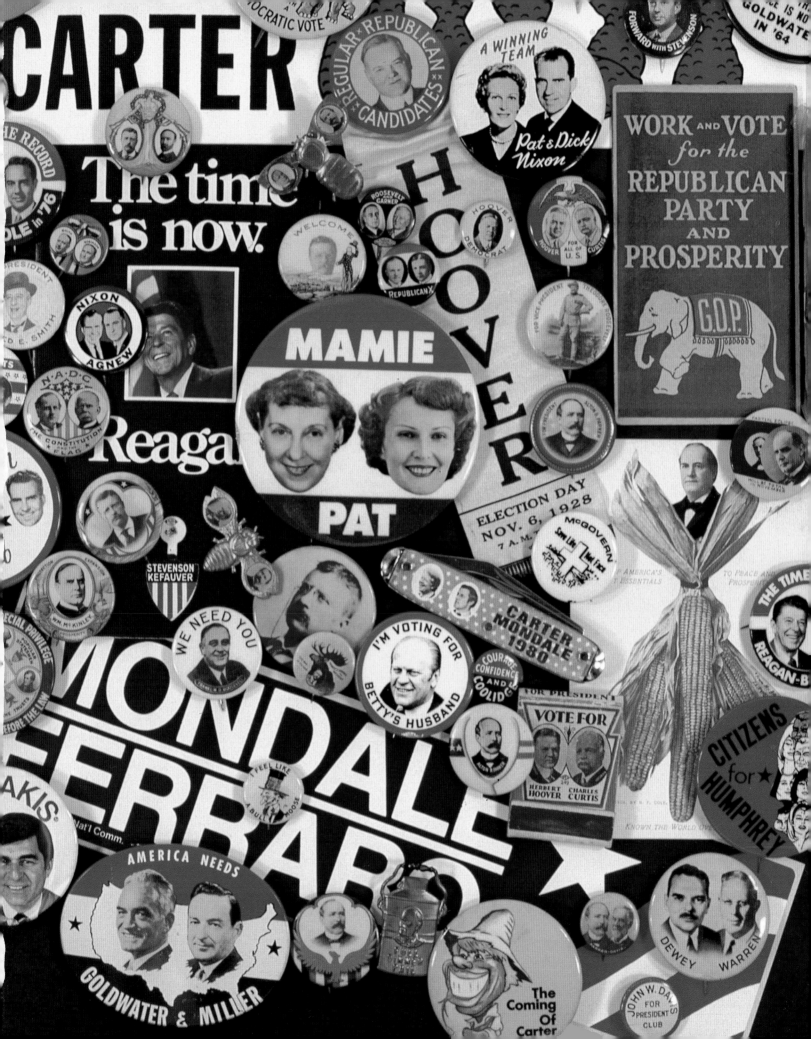

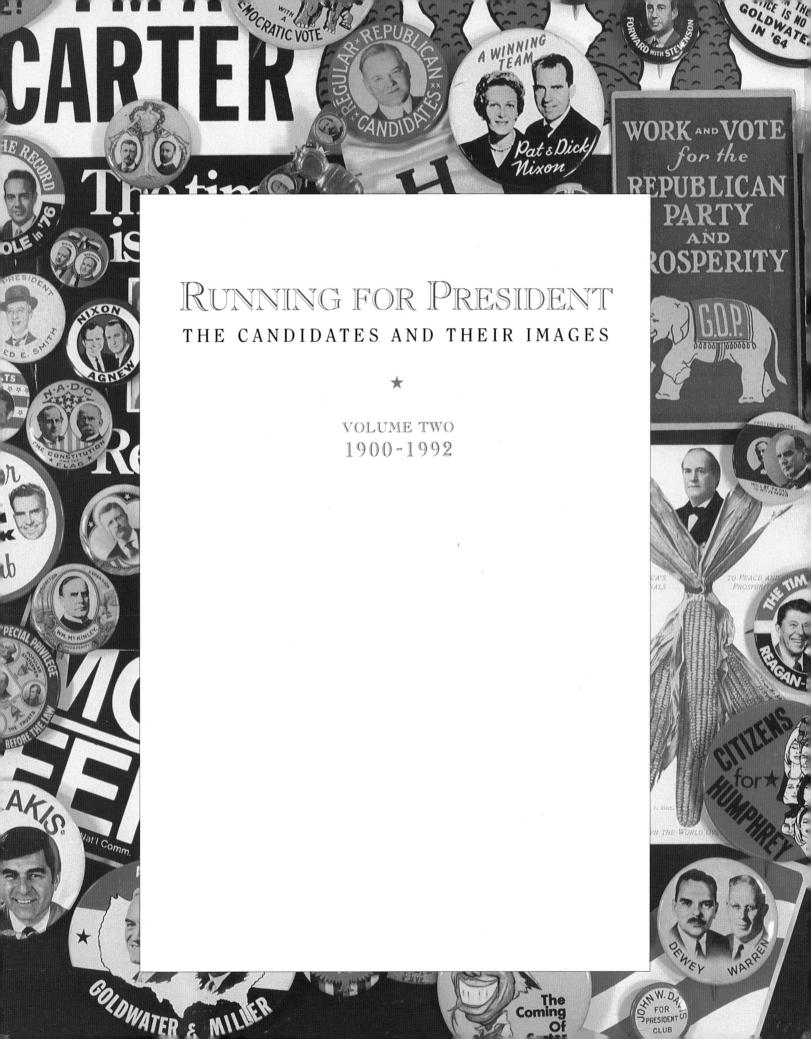

# Running for President

## THE CANDIDATES AND THEIR IMAGES

★

VOLUME TWO
1900-1992

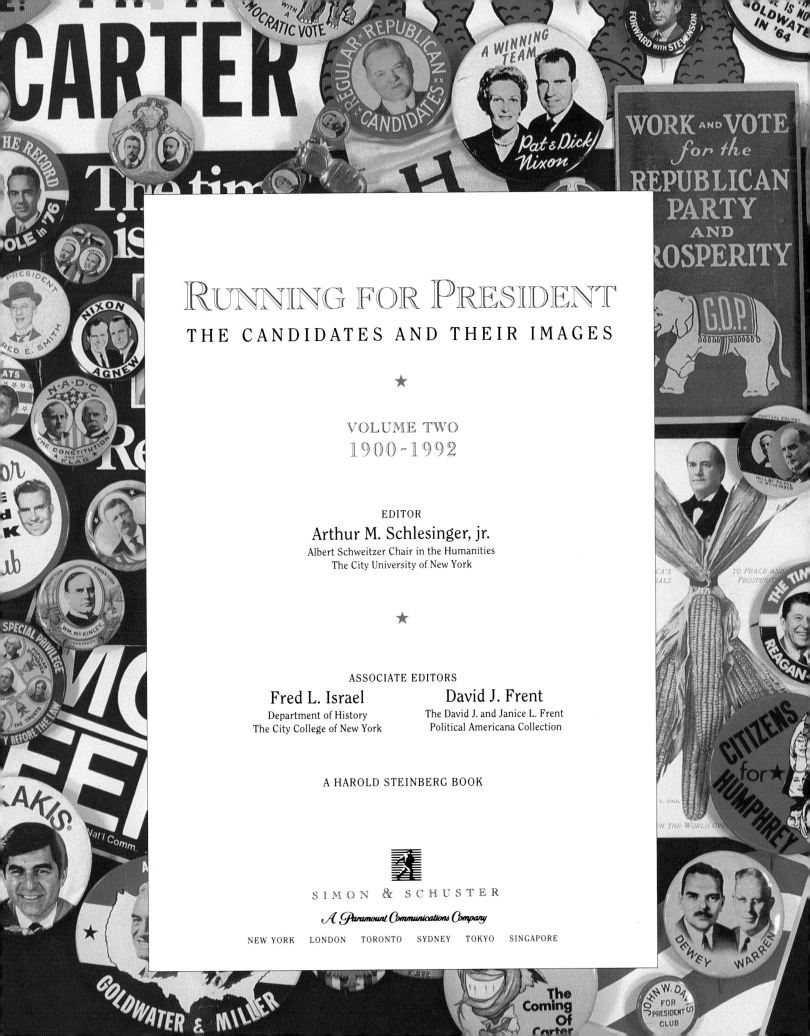

# RUNNING FOR PRESIDENT
## THE CANDIDATES AND THEIR IMAGES

★

### VOLUME TWO
### 1900~1992

EDITOR
## Arthur M. Schlesinger, jr.
Albert Schweitzer Chair in the Humanities
The City University of New York

★

ASSOCIATE EDITORS

### Fred L. Israel
Department of History
The City College of New York

### David J. Frent
The David J. and Janice L. Frent
Political Americana Collection

A HAROLD STEINBERG BOOK

SIMON & SCHUSTER
*A Paramount Communications Company*

NEW YORK   LONDON   TORONTO   SYDNEY   TOKYO   SINGAPORE

RUNNING FOR PRESIDENT was originated and prepared by Harold Steinberg and his associates. Grateful acknowledgment to: caption consultants Jonathan H. Mann and Rex Stark; the editorial assistance of Jo-Anne Elikann, Mary McCarthy Steinberg, Barbara Raynor, James Uebbing; photography of the David J. and Janice L. Frent Collection by Jim Dorn; cover photograph of the Jonathan H. Mann Collection by Fred Robertson.

Designed by Susan Lusk

Academic Reference Division
Simon & Schuster
15 Columbus Circle
New York, New York 10023

Printed in Hong Kong

printing number
1 2 3 4 5 6 7 8 9 10

Library of Congress Cataloging-in-Publication Data
   Running for president: the candidates and their images / editor Arthur M. Schlesinger, Jr.;
    associate editors Fred L. Israel, David J. Frent.
      p. cm.
     "A Harold Steinberg book."
     Includes index.
     Contents: v. 1. 1789–1896 — v. 2. 1900–1992.
     ISBN 0-13-303371-6 (2 v. set : acid-free paper) — ISBN 0-13-303355-4
    (v. 1 : acid-free paper) — ISBN 0-13-303363-5 (v. 2 : acid-free paper).
     1. Presidents—United States—Election—History. 2. United States—Politics and
   government. I. Schlesinger, Arthur Meier, 1917– . II. Israel, Fred L. III. Frent, David J.
    E183.R96 1994
    324 .97309—dc20
                  93-46386
                  CIP

The paper in this publication meets the requirements of American National Standards for Information Sciences — Permanence of Paper for Printed Library Materials ANSI Z39.48-1984.

## Volume Two
### 1900-1992

PREFACE

IN HIS PREFACE to the first edition of *History of Presidential Elections* (1884), Edward Stanwood modestly noted that his 407-page volume "professes to be little more than a record of the circumstances of such elections, and of whatever had an appreciable influence upon the result." In the ensuing 109 years abundant monographs have been written dealing with presidential elections. The Library of Congress catalog lists hundreds of titles under the entry "Presidents–U.S. Elections," and it would take a volume larger than Stanwood's just to list the scholarly articles on this subject.

In 1971, Professor Arthur M. Schlesinger, jr. edited a four-volume *History of American Presidential Elections, 1789–1968* and I served as associate editor (a fifth volume followed in 1986). Our goal then, as now, has been to provide a comprehensive history of American presidential elections written by prominent historians and political scientists. This current study is not the definitive word, such a task would be impossible. In a sense, however, we have aimed, like Stanwood, to document the circumstances and effects of such elections.

The emergence of the two-party system by the late 1830s, along with the extension of the franchise, made it necessary for candidates to convey their message directly to the voter. Until the mid twentieth century when television and the print media dictated the form, campaign artifacts, such as banners, posters, and buttons, were limited only by their makers' imaginations. But each election is a referendum whereby the nominees must demonstrate that they favor peace, prosperity, and progress while combining these and other goals with a carnival atmosphere. Our contributors, then, had two assignments: to analyze an election and to focus, wherever possible, on the diverse styles, tactics, and techniques used by presidential candidates and their parties to woo the electorate.

In organizing this project, Professor Schlesinger and I have incurred many debts of gratitude. Our first is to our contributors who graciously agreed to participate in this study. We also gratefully acknowledge the assistance of David J. and Janice L. Frent, whose outstanding collection of American campaign artifacts has been the primary source to illustrate this work. Such artifacts are ephemeral, meant for a specific use and then to be discarded. Mr. and Mrs. Frent have helped to preserve a unique aspect of Americana. It is hoped that this study will contribute to bridging the gap between the academics who write the scholarly interpretations and the collector who gathers and saves the physical relics of campaigns.

Harold Steinberg, founder and former president of Chelsea House Publishers, encouraged and reassured us, as he has for so many creative projects throughout the years. To him, Professor Schlesinger and I owe a very special thank you. Susan Lusk served as the art director and her talent, patience, and professionalism enabled us to complete this complex undertaking. The high standards which she maintained made working with her a special pleasure. In writing the captions for the illustrations, I was assisted by Jonathan Mann, a collector of political memorabilia, Rex Stark, a foremost dealer in Americana, and Mr. Frent.

We in academe depend upon publishers who convey our thoughts to the printed page. Professor Schlesinger and I are indebted to Charles E. Smith, president of the Academic Reference Division of Simon & Schuster, whose capable staff, and professional and personal guidance overcame the many obstacles presented by this complicated project.

From the inception of this project, Professor Schlesinger has been inspirational. This outstanding historian was always available for advice and assistance. His editing of each essay without missing a deadline was an impressive feat. I have known Professor Schlesinger for twenty-five years, and my admiration for this brilliant man increases each year.

*Fred L. Israel*
*The City College of New York*
*December 1, 1993*

## THE EDITORS

**ARTHUR M. SCHLESINGER, JR.** holds the Albert Schweitzer Chair in the Humanities at the Graduate Center of The City University of New York. He is the author of more than a dozen books including: *The Age of Jackson; The Vital Center; The Age of Roosevelt* (3 vols.)*; A Thousand Days: John F. Kennedy in the White House; Robert Kennedy and His Times; The Cycles of American History;* and *The Imperial Presidency.* Professor Schlesinger served as Special Assistant to President Kennedy (1961-63). His numerous awards include: the Pulitzer Prize for History; the Pulitzer Prize for Biography; two National Book Awards; the Bancroft Prize and the American Academy of Arts and Letters Gold Medal for History.

★

**FRED L. ISRAEL** is the senior professor of American history at The City College of New York. He is the author of *Nevada's Key Pittman* and has edited *The War Diary of Breckinridge Long* and *Major Peace Treaties of Modern History, 1648-1975* (5 vols.). He holds the Scribe's Award from the American Bar Association for his joint editorship of *The Justices of the United States Supreme Court* (4 vols.). For the past 25 years Professor Israel has compiled and edited the Gallup Poll into annual reference volumes.

★

**DAVID J. FRENT** is the president of Political Americana Auctions, Oakhurst, NJ. With his wife, Janice, he has assembled the nation's foremost private collection of political campaign memorabilia. Mr. Frent has designed exhibits for corporations, the Smithsonian Institution and the United States Information Agency. A member of the board of directors of the American Political Items Collectors since 1972, he was elected to its Hall of Fame for his "outstanding contribution to preserving and studying our political heritage."

## INTRODUCTION

ARTHUR M. SCHLESINGER, JR.

AMERICA SUFFERS FROM A SORT OF INTERMITTENT FEVER—WHAT ONE MAY CALL A QUINTAN AGUE.
EVERY FOURTH YEAR THERE COME TERRIBLE SHAKINGS, PASSING INTO THE HOT FIT OF THE PRESIDENTIAL
ELECTION; THEN FOLLOWS WHAT PHYSICIANS CALL "THE INTERVAL"; THEN AGAIN THE FIT.
—JAMES BRYCE, *THE AMERICAN COMMONWEALTH* (1888)

RUNNING FOR PRESIDENT is the central rite in the American political order. It was not always so. *Choosing* the chief magistrate had been the point of the quadrennial election from the beginning, but it took a long while for candidates to *run* for the highest office in the land; that is, to solicit, visibly and actively, the support of the voters. These volumes show through text and illustration how those aspiring to the White House have moved on from ascetic self-restraint to shameless self-merchandising. This work thereby illuminates the changing ways the American people have conceived the role of their President. I hope it will also recall to new generations some of the more picturesque and endearing dimensions of American politics.

The primary force behind the revolution in campaign attitudes and techniques was a development unforeseen by the men who framed the Constitution—the rise of the party system. Party competition was not at all their original intent. Quite the contrary: inspired at one or two removes by Lord Bolingbroke's British tract of half a century earlier, *The Idea of a Patriot King*, the Founding Fathers envisaged a Patriot President, standing above party and faction, representing the whole people, offering the nation non-partisan leadership virtuously dedicated to the common good.

The ideal of the Patriot President was endangered, the Founding Fathers believed, by twin menaces—factionalism and factionalism's ugly offspring, the demagogue. Party competition would only encourage unscrupulous men to appeal to popular passion and prejudice. Alexander Hamilton in the 71st Federalist bemoaned the plight of the people, "beset as they continually are . . . by the snares of the ambitious, the avaricious, the desperate, by the artifices of men who possess their confidence more than they deserve it, and of those who seek to possess rather than to deserve it."

Pervading the Federalist was a theme sounded explicitly both in the first paper and the last: the fear that unleashing popular passions would bring on "the military despotism of a victorious demagogue." If the "mischiefs of faction" were, James Madison admitted in the Tenth Federalist, "sown in the nature of man," the object of politics was to repress this insidious disposition, not to yield to it. "If I could not go to heaven but with a party," said Thomas Jefferson, "I would not go there at all."

So the Father of his Country in his Farewell Address solemnly warned his countrymen against "the baneful effects of the spirit of party." That spirit, Washington conceded, was "inseparable from our nature"; but for popular governments it was "truly their worst enemy." The "alternate domination of one faction over another," Washington said, would lead in the end to "formal and permanent despotism." The spirit of party, "a fire not to be quenched . . . demands a uniform vigilance to prevent its bursting into a flame, lest, instead of warming, it should consume."

Yet, even as Washington called on Americans to "discourage and restrain" the spirit of party, parties were beginning to crystallize around him. The eruption of partisanship in defiance of such august counsel argued that party competition might well serve functional necessities in the democratic republic.

After all, honest disagreement over policy and principle called for candid debate. And parties, it appeared, had vital roles to play in the consummation of the Constitution. The distribution of powers among three equal branches inclined the national government toward a chronic condition of stalemate. Parties offered the means of overcoming the constitutional separation of powers by coordinating the executive and legislative branches and furnishing the connective tissue essential to effective government. As national associations, moreover, parties were a force against provincialism and separatism. As instruments of compromise, they encouraged, within the parties as well as between them, the containment and mediation of national quarrels, at least until slavery broke the parties up. Henry D. Thoreau cared little enough for politics, but he saw the point: "Politics is, as it were, the gizzard of society, full of grit and gravel, and the two political parties are its two opposite halves, which grind on each other."

Furthermore, as the illustrations in these volumes so gloriously remind us, party competition was a great source of entertainment and fun—all the more important in those faraway days before the advent of baseball and football, of movies and radio and television. "To take a hand in the regulation of society and to discuss it," Alexis de Tocqueville

observed when he visited Americas in the 1830s, "is his biggest concern and, so to speak, the only pleasure an American knows. . . . Even the women frequently attend public meetings and listen to political harangues as a recreation from their household labors. Debating clubs are, to a certain extent, a substitute for theatrical entertainments."

Condemned by the Founding Fathers, unknown to the Constitution, parties nonetheless imperiously forced themselves into political life. But the party system rose from the bottom up. For half a century, the first half-dozen Presidents continued to hold themselves above party. The disappearance of the Federalist party after the War of 1812 suspended party competition. James Monroe, with no opponent at all in the election of 1820, presided proudly over the Era of Good Feelings, so called because there were no parties around to excite ill feelings. Monroe's successor, John Quincy Adams, despised electioneering and inveighed against the "fashion of peddling for popularity by travelling around the country gathering crowds together, hawking for public dinners, and spouting empty speeches." Men of the old republic believed presidential candidates should be men who already deserved the people's confidence rather than those seeking to win it. Character and virtue, not charisma and ambition, should be the grounds for choosing a President.

Adams was the last of the old school. Andrew Jackson, by beating him in the 1828 election, legitimized party politics and opened a new political era. The rationale of the new school was provided by Jackson's counsellor and successor, Martin Van Buren, the classic philosopher of the role of party in the American democracy. By the time Van Buren took his own oath of office in 1837, parties were entrenched as the instruments of American self-government. In Van Buren's words, party battles "rouse the sluggish to exertion, give increased energy to the most active intellect, excite a salutary vigilance over our public functionaries, and prevent that apathy which has proved the ruin of Republics."

Apathy may indeed have proved the ruin of republics, but rousing the sluggish to exertion proved, ironically, the ruin of Van Buren. The architect of the party system became the first casualty of the razzle-dazzle campaigning the system quickly generated. The Whigs' Tippecanoe-and-Tyler-too campaign of 1840 transmuted the democratic Van Buren into a gilded aristocrat and assured his defeat at the polls. The "peddling for popularity" John Quincy Adams had deplored now became standard for party campaigners.

But the new methods were still forbidden to the presidential candidates themselves. The feeling lingered from earlier days that stumping the country in search of votes was demagoguery beneath the dignity of the presidency. Van Buren's code permitted—indeed expected—parties to inscribe their creed in platforms and candidates to declare their principles in letters published in newspapers. Occasionally candidates—William Henry Harrison in 1840, Winfield Scott in 1852—made a speech, but party surrogates did most of the hard work.

As late as 1858, Van Buren, advising his son John, one of the great popular orators of the time, on the best way to make it to the White House, emphasized the "rule . . . that the people will never make a man President who is so importunate as to show by his life and conversation that he not only has an eye on, but is in active pursuit of the office. . . . No man who has laid himself out for it, and was

unwise enough to let the people into his secret, ever yet obtained it. Clay, Calhoun, Webster, Scott, and a host of lesser lights, should serve as a guide-post to future aspirants."

The continuing constraint on personal campaigning by candidates was reinforced by the desire of party managers to present their nominees as all things to all men. In 1835 Nicholas Biddle, the wealthy Philadelphian who had been Jackson's mortal opponent in the famous Bank War, advised the Whigs not to let General Harrison "say one single word about his principles or his creed. . . . Let him say nothing, promise nothing. Let no committee, no convention, no town meeting ever extract from him a single word about what he thinks now, or what he will do hereafter. Let the use of pen and ink be wholly forbidden as if he were a mad poet in Bedlam."

We cherish the memory of the famous debates in 1858 between Abraham Lincoln and Stephen A. Douglas. But those debates were not part of a presidential election. When the presidency was at stake two years later, Lincoln gave no campaign speeches on the issues darkly dividing the country. He even expressed doubt about party platforms— "the formal written platform system," as he called it. The candidate's character and record, Lincoln thought, should constitute his platform: "On just such platforms all our earlier and better Presidents were elected."

However, Douglas, Lincoln's leading opponent in 1860, foreshadowed the future when he broke the sound barrier and dared venture forth on thinly disguised campaign tours. Yet Douglas established no immediate precedent. Indeed, half a dozen years later Lincoln's successor, Andrew Johnson, discredited presidential stumping by his "swing around the circle" in the midterm election of 1866. "His performances in a western tour in advocacy of his own election," commented Benjamin F. Butler, who later led the fight in Congress for Johnson's impeachment, " . . . disgusted everybody." The tenth article of impeachment charged Johnson with bringing "the high office of the President of the United States into contempt, ridicule, and disgrace" by delivering "with a loud voice certain intemperate, inflammatory, and scandalous harangues . . . peculiarly indecent and unbecoming in the Chief Magistrate of the United States."

Though presidential candidates Horatio Seymour in 1868, Rutherford B. Hayes in 1876, and James A. Garfield in 1880 made occasional speeches, only Horace Greeley in 1872, James G. Blaine in 1884, and most spectacularly, William Jennings Bryan in 1896 followed Douglas's audacious example of stumping the country. Such tactics continued to provoke disapproval. Bryan, said John Hay, who had been Lincoln's private secretary and was soon to become McKinley's secretary of state, "is begging for the presidency as a tramp might beg for a pie."

Respectable opinion still preferred the "front porch" campaign, employed by Garfield, by Benjamin Harrison in 1888, and most notably by McKinley in 1896. Here candidates received and addressed numerous delegations at their own homes—a form, as the historian Gil Troy writes, of "stumping in place."

While candidates generally continued to stand on their dignity, popular campaigning in presidential elections flourished in these years, attaining new heights of participation (82 percent of eligible voters in 1876 and never once from 1860 to 1900 under 70 percent) and new wonders of pyrotechnics and ballyhoo. Parties mobilized the electorate as never before, and political iconography was never more ingenious and fantastic. "Politics, considered not as the science of government, but as the art of winning elections and securing office," wrote the keen British observer James Bryce, "has reached in the United States a development surpassing in elaborateness that of England or France as much as the methods of those countries surpass the methods of Servia or Roumania." Bryce marvelled at the "military discipline" of the parties, at "the demonstrations, the parades and receptions, the badges and brass bands and triumphal arches," at the excitement stirred by elections— and at "the disproportion that strikes a European between the merits of the presidential candidate and the blazing enthusiasm which he evokes."

Still the old taboo held back the presidential candidates themselves. Even so irrepressible a campaigner as President Theodore Roosevelt felt obliged to hold his tongue when he ran for reelection in 1904. This unwonted abstinence reminded him, he wrote in considerable frustration, of the July day in 1898 when he was "lying still under shell fire" during the Spanish-American War. "I have continually wished that I could be on the stump myself."

No such constraint inhibited TR, however, when he ran again for the presidency in 1912. Meanwhile, and for the first time, *both* candidates in 1908— Bryan again, and William Howard Taft—actively campaigned for the prize. The duties of the office, on top of the new requirements of campaigning, led Woodrow Wilson to reflect that same year, four years before he himself ran for President, "Men of ordinary physique and discretion cannot be Presidents and live, if the strain be not somehow relieved. We shall be obliged always to be picking our chief magistrates from among wise and prudent athletes,—a small class."

Theodore Roosevelt and Woodrow Wilson combined to legitimate a new conception of presidential candidates as active molders of public opinion in active pursuit of the highest office. Once in the White House, Wilson revived the custom, abandoned by Jefferson, of delivering annual state of the union addresses to Congress in person. In 1916 he became the first incumbent President to stump for his own reelection.

The activist candidate and the bully-pulpit presidency were expressions of the growing democratization of politics. New forms of communication were reconfiguring presidential campaigns. In the nineteenth century the press, far more fiercely partisan then than today, had been the main carrier of political information. In the twentieth century the spread of advertising techniques and the rise of the electronic media— radio, television, computerized public opinion polling—wrought drastic changes in the methodology of politics. In particular the electronic age diminished and now threatens to dissolve the historic role of the party.

The old system had three tiers: the politician at one end; the voter at the other; and the party in between. The party's function was to negotiate between the politician and the voters, interpreting each to the other and providing the link that held the political process together. The electronic revolution has substantially abolished the sovereignty of the party. Where once the voter turned to the local party leader to find out whom to

support, now he looks at television and makes up his own mind. Where once the politician turned to the local party leader to find out what people are thinking, he now takes a computerized poll.

The electronic era has created a new breed of professional consultants, "handlers," who by the 1980s had taken control of campaigns away from the politicians. The traditional pageantry—rallies, torchlight processions, volunteers, leaflets, billboards, bumper stickers—is now largely a thing of the past. Television replaces the party as the means of mobilizing the voter. And as the party is left to wither on the vine, the presidential candidate becomes more pivotal than ever. We shall see the rise of personalist movements, founded not on historic organizations but on compelling personalities, private fortunes, and popular frustrations. Without the stabilizing influence of parties, American politics would grow angrier, wilder, and more irresponsible.

Things have changed considerably from the austerities of the old republic. Where once voters preferred to call presumably reluctant candidates to the duties of the supreme magistracy and rejected pursuit of the office as evidence of dangerous ambition, now they expect candidates to come to them, explain their views and plead for their support. Where nonpartisan virtue had been the essence, now candidates must prove to voters that they have the requisite "fire in the belly." " 'Twud be inth'restin," said Mr. Dooley, " . . . if th' fathers iv th' counthry cud come back an' see what has happened while they've been away. In times past whin ye voted f'r president ye didn't vote f'r a man. Ye voted f'r a kind iv a statue that ye'd put up in ye'er own mind on a marble pidistal. Ye nivir heerd iv George Wash'nton goin' around th' count  distributin' five cint see-gars."

We have reversed the original notion that ambition must be disguised and the office seek the man. Now the man—and soon, one must hope, the woman—seeks the office and does so without guilt or shame or inhibition. This is not necessarily a degradation of democracy. Dropping the disguise is a gain for candor, and personal avowals of convictions and policies may elevate and educate the electorate.

On the other hand, the electronic era has dismally reduced both the intellectual content of campaigns and the attention span of audiences. In the nineteenth century political speeches lasted for a couple of hours and dealt with issues in systematic and exhaustive fashion. Voters drove wagons for miles to hear Webster and Clay, Bryan and Teddy Roosevelt, and felt cheated if the famous orator did not give them their money's worth. Then radio came along and cut political addresses down first to an hour, soon to thirty minutes—still enough time to develop substantive arguments.

But television has shrunk the political talk first to fifteen minutes, now to the sound bite and the thirty-second spot. Advertising agencies today sell candidates with all the cynical contrivance they previously devoted to selling detergents and mouthwash. The result is the debasement of American politics. "The idea that you can merchandise candidates for high office like breakfast cereal," Adlai Stevenson said in 1952, "is the ultimate indignity to the democratic process."

Still Bryce's "intermittent fever" will be upon us every fourth year. We will continue to watch wise if not always prudent athletes in their sprint for the White House, enjoy the quadrennial spectacle and agonize about the outcome. "The strife of the

election," said Lincoln after his reelection in 1864, "is but human-nature practically applied to the facts. What has occurred in this case, must ever recur in similar cases. Human-nature will not change."

Lincoln, as usual, was right. Despite the transformation in political methods there remains a basic continuity in political emotions. "For a long while before the appointed time has come," Tocqueville wrote more than a century and a half ago, "the election becomes the important and, so to speak, the all-engrossing topic of discussion. Factional ardor is redoubled, and all the artificial passions which the imagination can create in a happy and peaceful land are agitated and brought to light. . . .

"As the election draws near, the activity of intrigue and the agitation of the populace increase; the citizens are divided into hostile camps, each of which assumes the name of its favorite candidate; the whole nation glows with feverish excitement; the election is the daily theme of the press, the subject of every private conversation, the end of every thought and every action, the sole interest of the present.

"It is true," Tocqueville added, "that as soon as the choice is determined, this ardor is dispelled, calm returns, and the river, which had nearly broken its banks, sinks to its usual level; but who can refrain from astonishment that such a storm should have arisen?"

The election storm in the end blows fresh and clean. With the tragic exception of 1860, the American people have invariably accepted the result and given the victor their hopes and blessings. For all its flaws and follies, democracy abides.

Let us now turn the pages and watch the gaudy parade of American presidential politics pass by in all its careless glory.

# RUNNING FOR PRESIDENT
## THE CANDIDATES AND THEIR IMAGES

**1900**

45 STATES
IN THE UNION

\*REPUBLICAN\*

# William McKinley

ELECTORAL VOTE 292, POPULAR VOTE 51.7%

DEMOCRAT/POPULIST

# William J. Bryan

ELECTORAL VOTE 155, POPULAR VOTE 45.5%

PROHIBITION

# John C. Woolley

ELECTORAL VOTE 0, POPULAR VOTE 1.5%

JOHN MILTON COOPER, JR.
is the William Francis Allen Professor of History
at the University of Wisconsin, Madison. He is
the author of *The Warrior and the Priest* (1983)
and *Pivotal Decades* (1990).

I f the presidential election of 1900 had been a piece of music, critics would have had to choose between calling it a repeat performance or a theme with variations. Repetitious features dominated, at least at first glance. Both the major players (the presidential candidates) and the results (which pitted sections of the country against each other) repeated the characters and events of 1896. The Republicans once more nominated William McKinley, and the Democrats chose William Jennings Bryan. McKinley won again, by slightly increased margins in the popular vote—7,219,530—almost 52 percent of the total, up more than 100,000 votes and one percentage point from 1896; his electoral vote was 292, an increase of 21 votes over his earlier showing. Bryan similarly clung to his constituencies in the South, where he carried every state below the Potomac and Ohio rivers, and to a lesser extent in the West, where he carried five fewer states than in 1896, losing even his home state of Nebraska. The Commoner's popular vote fell by slightly more than 150,000 to give him 6,359,061, or 45.5 percent. Voter turnout declined six points from 1896 to 73.2 percent of the electorate, beginning a trend that would continue more or less steadily in the next century. In fact, this would be the last presidential election to witness a turnout as high as 70 percent. Congressional contests in 1900 came out virtually identical in both years, with the Republicans winning 197 seats in the House of Representatives (down

seven from 1896) to the Democrats' 151. (In the Senate, which was not popularly elected, the Republicans increased their majority to 55, over the Democrats' 31.) Withal, the 1900 contest fitted the term used by a later generation of political writers—it was a "confirming election."

N ot everything, however, followed the script of 1896. In personnel, in methods of campaigning, and especially in the mixture of themes and issues, the election of 1900 contained significant variations from its predecessor. The changes in personnel came in the second spots on both parties' tickets, and each embodied a bow toward altered political circumstances. The less weighty shift occurred on the Democratic ticket. In a gesture designed simultaneously to placate the dethroned Grover Cleveland wing of the party and to ratify the dominance of the free silverites, the delegates to the Democratic convention in Kansas City, who were left uninstructed by the easily renominated Bryan, overwhelmingly chose as their nominee for vice president Adlai E. Stevenson of Illinois. As both vice president in Cleveland's second administration and a silverite who had backed Bryan in 1896, Stevenson could legitimately pose as all things to all Democrats. The Illinoisan took gamely to the hustings and often stressed foreign policy issues, but he excited little enthusiasm and made little impact on the campaign. This Adlai Stevenson remains a notable historical figure primarily because he was the grandfather and namesake of the Illinois governor and two-time Democratic presidential candidate of the 1950s, who was born in 1900.

Far more significant to that year's election and to the course of American history was the new Republican vice presidential candidate, Theodore Roosevelt. Every circumstance—from the death of the incumbent vice president, to the patriotic afterglow of the Spanish-American War and Roosevelt's well-publicized heroism in it, to his governorship of New York—seemed to thrust this nomination upon him. Both because he relished the challenges of his state office and because the New York governor's chair was the best springboard to a presidential nomination, Roosevelt discouraged friends and well-wishers from pushing him for a place on the national ticket. But his desires did not deter the surreptitious machinations of Senator Thomas C. Platt, the boss of the state's Republican machine, who wanted to kick the independent-minded,

obstreperous governor upstairs. Still, more than Platt's skulduggery secured Roosevelt's nomination. Rank-and-file Republicans around the country yearned for a dynamic presence on the campaign trail, to match Bryan's, even though they knew that they could win without exploiting new techniques of popular politics. The only reservation about Roosevelt's nomination came from McKinley's erstwhile right-hand man, Senator Mark Hanna of Ohio, who warned his fellow party barons, "Don't any of you realize that there's only one life between that madman and the Presidency?" But intimations of presidential mortality could not keep glamour-hungry Republicans from their heart's desire in 1900.

Roosevelt's presence on the Republican ticket made personal campaigning a two-sided major party affair for the first time in a presidential election. Financial and organization necessity again fused with personal yearning to speed Bryan out on marathon swings around the circle by railroad. As in

*Stereoscopic card of President McKinley in San José, California. McKinley began an extensive rail tour of the United States on April 29, 1901.*

Underwood & Underwood, Publishers, New York, London, Toronto-Canada, Ottawa-Kansas.

Works and Littleton, N.H. Arlington, N.J. Studios Washington, D.C.

President McKinley speaking near the scene of the Alamo massacre, San Antonio, Texas.
Copyright 1901 by Underwood & Underwood.

*Stereoscopic card of McKinley in San Antonio, Texas. Part of a set of cards chronicling the President's cross-country tour.*

1896, his typical day on the hustings stretched to sixteen and seventeen hours, featured over a dozen speeches, and averaged six hours of speaking. At first, as he had done four years before, Bryan concentrated his efforts on his native Midwest, where he believed he had a better chance to take votes away from McKinley. In October, however, he followed the advice of Democratic leaders and made more extensive forays into the "enemy's country," the Northeast. The Commoner's chances had improved there, those advisers maintained, provided he downplayed free silver and concentrated on anti-imperialism. The candidate tried hard to oblige them, but he could not change his inflationist spots. "All ye can say about William Jennings Bryan's recayption," wrote Mr. Dooley, "is that he got by Wall street without bein' stoned to death with nuggets from the gold resarve." He also besmirched his crusader's image in the eyes of many observers by appearing in public with the bosses of Tammany Hall. "Bah! Wasn't it awful!" snapped his uneasy anti-imperialist supporter Carl Schurz.

The Republican vice presidential candidate matched his party's main rival in energy and persistence, but, deliberately, not in platform polish. Roosevelt often boasted of his lack of training in forensics, which he likened to highflown chicanery, and he left his party's oratorical forays to such recognized stars in the supporting cast as Senators Jonathan P. Dolliver of Iowa and Albert J. Beveridge of Indiana. Actually, Roosevelt had little need for expository skill. He drew and swayed crowds through the vividness of his personality. Nor did this candidate have to confine his impact to those who heard and saw him. Instead, Roosevelt pioneered in developing the techniques for dominating the news that twentieth-century leaders, particularly Presidents, would later regularly exploit. His nicknames of "Teddy" and the "Roughrider" preceded him, and the impressions he made spread after him, mainly through newspapers and magazines. Radio and television lay far in the future, and newsreels remained nickelodeon novelties in 1900, but photographs and cartoons augmented written descriptions to invest Roosevelt with the sort of public recognition that would later characterize and bedevil American politics.

Notwithstanding the Democratic challenger's and Republican vice presidential newcomer's high public profile, real mastery of the campaign never departed from the front-runner, President McKinley. He honored the taboo against incumbents participating openly in the campaign, and he made only two public statements. The first came in July with the speech accepting renomination delivered from his front porch in Canton, in an exact reenactment of the ceremony four years before. The other utterance came in his separate acceptance letter, a ponderous but comprehensive document that amplified the party platform and set forth campaign themes. As in 1896, McKinley's apparent repose masked careful direction of an exquisitely coordinated effort at targeting appeals to potential waverers and converts. Industrial workers again got special attention, including the President's and Senator Hanna's quiet but by no means unsung pressures on coal mine owners to end a big strike by meeting some of the miners' demands. Hanna broke the pattern of 1896 by campaigning himself. Overruling near unanimous protests of Republican leaders, the national chairman invaded the Commoner's home turf. Hanna made an unexpected hit on the Great Plains, thanks to his blunt manner and the disarming ploy of praising parts of Bryan's "Cross of Gold" speech before lambasting the Democrat's domestic poli-

cies as threats to the nation's newfound, hard-won, Republican-induced prosperity.

Hanna's stress on domestic concerns—encapsulated in the Republican slogan, "the full dinner pail"—represented a deliberate repetition of 1896. The Republican national chairman stood foursquare with most party leaders and pro-business conservatives in wanting to downplay any other issues, particularly the foreign policy questions that had arisen out of the Spanish-American War and the acquisition of colonial possessions in Puerto Rico, Guam, and, most controversially, the Philippines. When Bryan stuck to his inflationist guns, one leading Republican reportedly chortled, "Silver, silver, silver! Now we've got him where we want him!" Warmed-over passions from the earlier Battle of the Standards almost surely played a big part in determining how people voted. The striking similarities in outcomes in 1896 and 1900, especially Bryan's unyielding grip on credit-starved southern and silver-producing mountain states, strongly suggested continuity in loyalties forged over the money question. But it would be a mistake to dismiss the impact of other concerns at home and abroad.

1900 witnessed the first presidential election since 1844 to feature foreign policy as an important issue. The debate over the new colonies presented both parties with opportunities and troubles. Besides their vote-getting potentials, imperialism and anti-imperialism offered politicians in each party chances to affirm loyalties in the face of past or present domestic deviations. Rallying to the cause of retaining the Philippines, especially after American forces started to fight against native *insurrectos,* furnished many Silver Republicans of 1896 (such as

Idaho's future Senator William E. Borah) with a bridge back to their partisan home. Wisconsin's 1900 Republican gubernatorial candidate, Robert M. La Follette, was an insurgent against the party hierarchy and a critic of business influences in politics, but he conducted a jingoistic campaign on the Philippine issue that aped the outpourings of vice presidential candidate Roosevelt. Anti-imperialism assumed an even larger place for Gold Democrats of 1896, who persuaded themselves that the issue could eclipse their conflict with Bryan and the silverites. Moreover, because far more Republicans and independents had opposed the Philippine venture than Democrats had supported it, the out party entertained high hopes for making inroads in McKinley's majorities.

Their hopes went aborning. Instead, like the 1844 contest earlier and several of those later in the twentieth century, the 1900 election demonstrated how unsuitable an American presidential election is as a foreign policy referendum. That unsatisfactory performance did not happen because candidates on both sides shied away from these issues. On the Republican side, not only did Roosevelt dwell on little else as he worked the hustings, but McKinley devoted the bulk of his acceptance speech and much of his acceptance to a defense of his diplomacy. On the Democratic side, Bryan called imperialism the "paramount issue" in his acceptance speech, and he hammered away at the sins of Republican colonialism throughout the campaign.

What was lacking was genuine debate. Bryan and the Democrats hit hard at the choice between what the candidate called "Republic or Empire?"—the contradiction

The Union League were patriotic organizations during the Civil War. After the war, they became social and political groups, invariably backing Republican candidates.

*McKinley- Roosevelt pierced-tin lantern in the shape of the "Full Dinner Pail."*

between the Declaration of Independence and colonial rule. They also argued that foreign adventures distracted attention from domestic concerns, and they occasionally invoked America's tradition of diplomatic isolation from overseas entanglements. All would be important recurring themes in twentieth-century foreign policy debates.

The 1900 presidential campaign failed to stage the first of those debates mainly because the Republicans declined to answer their opponents' charges. Rather, they set future patterns of their own with evasion, manipulation, and emotion. The more thoughtful Republican imperialists, particularly Roosevelt and his friend Senator Henry Cabot Lodge of Massachusetts, favored a global reach for the nation's power, abandonment of traditional isolation, vast expansion and modernization of the armed forces, and military training for American youth—in sum, wholehearted participation in the game of great power politics led by the Europeans. They justified such a role as proof of national maturity and fulfillment of their party's Hamiltonian heritage of nationalism and centralized power, which had been hardened in the fires of the Civil War, and they denounced the Democrats for clinging to Jeffersonian legacies of small government, state rights, pandering to selfish interests, and international timidity. But few of those arguments found their way into public discussion in the 1900 campaign. Nearly all Republicans fudged on questions about eventual Philippine independence, ignored charges that they were breaking with isolation, and resorted to patriotic bombast. Short-run prudence prevailed over considerations of long-run enlightenment in foreign policy.

Some Democratic conservatives then and afterward faulted Bryan for not subordinating his domestic views totally to anti-imperialism. Those criticisms were both unrealistic and unfair. The Commoner possessed many faults as a politician, but temporizing was not among them. Neither his own convictions nor his followers in the South and the West would have allowed him to shelve his inflationist and anti-big business views. One story out of the campaign recounted how some farmers listened to a Democratic speaker warn of the dangers of Republican imperialism and shouted back, "Well, I guess we can stand it so long as hogs are twenty cents a hundred." Such lukewarm responses allegedly impelled Democratic candidates to soft-pedal anti-imperialism. In fact, Bryan himself did no such thing. He kept denouncing McKinley's foreign policy and Republican jingoism right down to election day. What really galled his conservative party cohorts was that he persistently mixed those denunciations with fervent attacks on the administration's pro-business domestic policies.

The concern that the Democratic challenger emphasized most was neither anti-imperialism nor monetary inflation. Instead, it was the explosive growth of big businesses—"the Trusts"—and what he decried as Republican subservience and favoritism toward them. In his acceptance speech, Bryan declared that "the contest of 1900 is a contest between Democracy on the one hand and plutocracy on the other." The Commoner cited well-known facts about the massive proliferation of business combinations since McKinley took office in 1897, and he arraigned his opponents for aiding and abetting this cancerous growth, not only with the gold standard but also through protective tariffs, nonenforcement

An "eclipse" button inspired by the May 28, 1900, solar eclipse. Both Republicans and Democrats used this motif.

of the Sherman Anti-Trust Act, labor injunctions, lack of real railroad regulation, deafness to pleas for corporate and income taxes, and generally fawning indulgence toward their plutocratic allies and patrons. In all, Bryan brought in a powerful indictment of Republican policies, and he established the dominant themes of domestic political debate for the next two decades.

Not all Republicans were impervious to public disquiet about big business, either. As governor of New York, Roosevelt had made a few stabs at corporate regulation. Such efforts had helped to convince Senator Platt to ease him out of the gubernatorial chair and into the supposedly safe haven of the vice presidency. Wisconsin's La Follette meanwhile was rhetorically pitting the "People" against the "Interests," in accents that sounded strikingly like the talk of Bryanite Democrats. Insurgent movements like his were also springing up elsewhere in the Midwest, especially in neighboring Iowa, where party dissidents would soon assail the most sacred cow of Republican domestic policy, the tariff. Even President McKinley privately worried about the trusts, and he included a brief anti-trust remark in his acceptance letter. Still, such discordant notes on the trust issue were few, far between, and generally ignored among Republicans in 1900. Such scanty notes made a stark contrast with the Democrats' fulsome and widespread, though not unanimous, endorsement of anti-trust, anti-plutocratic, and governmentally interventionist ideas and attitudes. The positions of the two parties on economic issues in 1900 fleshed out the opposing tendencies that they had shown in 1896. The contrast foreshadowed the courses that both would pursue in these areas with remarkable consistency throughout the twentieth century.

When the voters went to the polls on November 6, continuity and majority contentment prevailed. No surprises were anticipated, and none occurred. A popular President with a fresh new face for a running mate enjoyed all the advantages of incumbency, a largely prosperous economy, and the afterglow of easy victory in what his secretary of state called "a splendid little war." For the winners, repetition enhanced the result, and theme overshadowed variations. For the losers, whose efforts at raising new issues fell short, repetition sealed their fate. Still, although the prospect could offer no consolation at the time, Bryan had solidified his stature as one of the most important political leaders not only of his generation but in all of American history. Moreover, he had set the terms of public discourse for years to come. Splinter parties also pointed to the future, although they made scant impact in 1900. The Populists were reduced to a splintered shell, contributing to Bryan's total through a variety of joint arrangements and attracting 50,373 votes to a separate ticket. The Socialist party mounted its first presidential campaign and thereby introduced a vibrant, appealing figure in Eugene V. Debs, who polled 87,814 votes. The single-issue Prohibition party, dedicated to the eradication of alcoholic beverages, racked up 208,914 votes. As always, the present was pregnant with future actors and concerns. Yet it was fitting that the new century did not formally open until 1901, because this election savored more of the end of the nineteenth century than the beginning of the twentieth.

A 1900 campaign poster contrasting economic desolation, fiscal chaos, and Spanish tyranny in Cuba under the Democrats with American prosperity and Cuban liberty under McKinley.

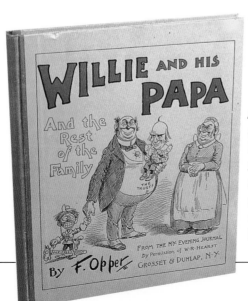

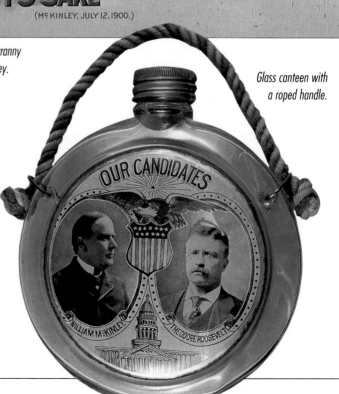

Anti-Republican cartoon book by Frederick Opper showing McKinley and Roosevelt as unruly children controlled by big business.

Glass canteen with a roped handle.

Advertisement poster for Scribner's magazine by Howard Chandler Christy. Roosevelt organized the 1st U.S. Volunteer Cavalry ("Rough Riders") and as its colonel led the charge up San Juan Hill, Cuba, on July 1, 1898, during the Spanish-American War.

COL. ROOSEVELT

Tells the story of THE ROUGH RIDERS in Scribner's Magazine. It begins in January and will run for six months, with many illustrations from photographs taken in the field.

JANUARY SCRIBNER'S

NOW READY   PRICE 25 CENTS

Cotton banner from Roosevelt's 1900 vice presidential campaign.

Brass shell badge urging "Vote with the Rough Riders."

Celluloid button with Roosevelt in his "Rough Rider" uniform.

Embossed celluloid-covered photographic album.

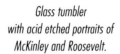

Glass tumbler
with acid etched portraits of
McKinley and Roosevelt.

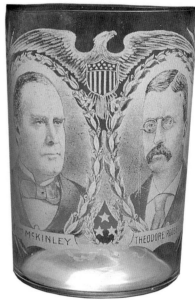

Royal Vienna
porcelain plate
with a hand-painted
portrait of McKinley.

Opposite:
Lithographed
tin trays with
portraits of
the candidates
were popular
campaign items
between 1900
and 1908.

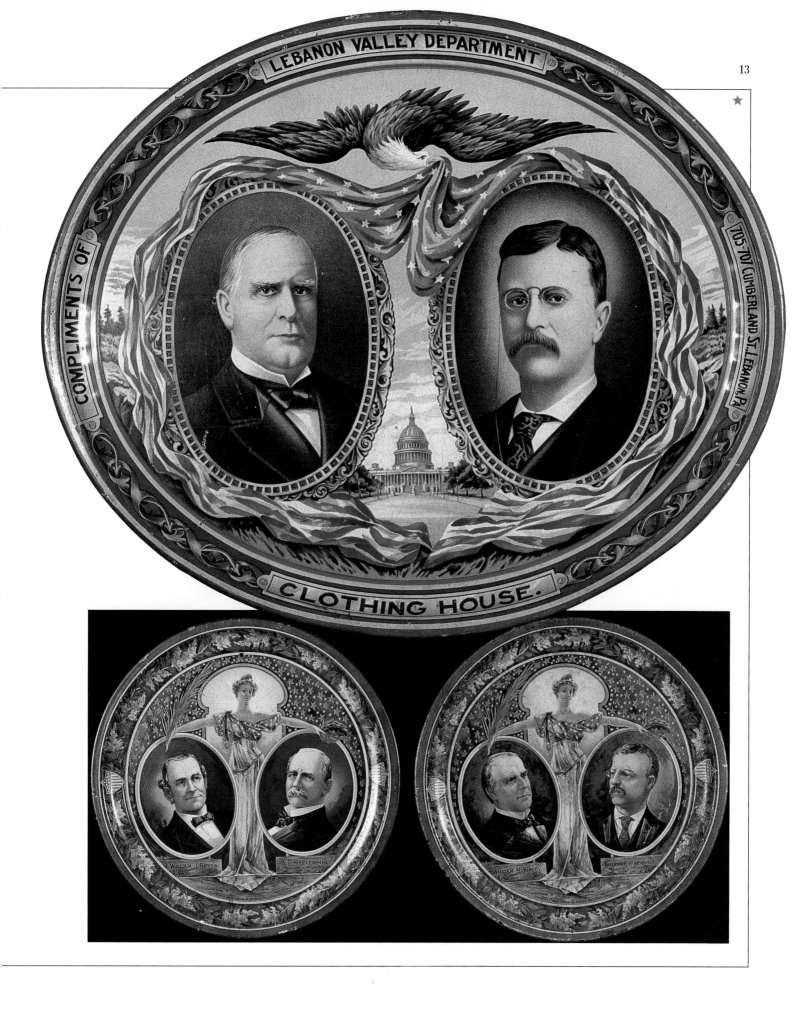

Celluloid button of
McKinley and Roosevelt
evoking the Civil War
theme. McKinley was the
last President to be a
Civil War veteran.

A combination of traditional and modern decorative
styles emerged in the artifacts of the 1900 campaign.

McKinley ribbon badge with celluloid attachment.

McKinley poster. He is standing victorious on a "SOUND MONEY" platform.

Celluloid button showing a prosperous farm and booming industry.

McKinley is linked with John C. Frémont and Abraham Lincoln.

*Photograph of a group of young women showing their support for Bryan. They wear a variety of campaign buttons, badges, and bandannas.*

*Celluloid button of Bryan.*

*This anti-Bryan celluloid button associated him with Philippine resistance leader, Emilio Aguinaldo and with Tammany boss Richard Croker. His name is misspelled.*

*Bryan-Sewell celluloid button with a cornucopia of silver dollars.*

*Bryan ribbon with an interesting slogan.*

*From 1896–1912, William Jennings Bryan was virtually the undisputed leader of the Democratic party. He advised Senate Democrats to approve the peace treaty with Spain (1899) but fought the 1900 presidential campaign on the issue of anti-imperialism.*

*1900 Bryan poster depicting him as an apostle of free silver and an opponent of imperialism. The trust octopus is engulfing American farms and factories.*

Celluloid buttons featuring the "Full Dinner Pail" and the Republican prosperity design.

Miniature wooden dinner pail probably used as an inkwell. The 1896 and 1900 Republican "Full Dinner Pail" campaign slogan called attention to the Republicans' perennial advocacy of full employment and prosperous factories.

Covers from Judge magazine endorsing McKinley and his policies.

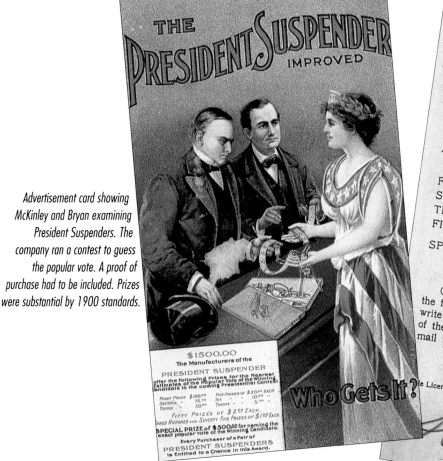

Advertisement card showing McKinley and Bryan examining President Suspenders. The company ran a contest to guess the popular vote. A proof of purchase had to be included. Prizes were substantial by 1900 standards.

Selection of specialized celluloid buttons.

Graphic 1900 McKinley and Roosevelt campaign umbrella.

Silk bandanna with portraits of Lincoln, Garfield, and McKinley. Scenes under each portrait bear the name of the assassin and date.

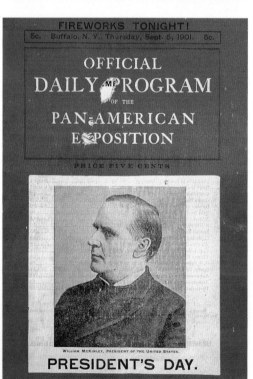

Items commemorating McKinley's visit to the Pan American Exposition in Buffalo, New York.

Where our President fell
Sept. 6th 1901

*A 6" stand-up celluloid of the Temple
of Music building, where McKinley was shot on
September 6, 1901.*

IN MEMORIAM

*McKinley memorial celluloid buttons. The
President died on September 14, 1901.*

## 1904
45 STATES
IN THE UNION

*REPUBLICAN*
# Theodore Roosevelt
ELECTORAL VOTE 336, POPULAR VOTE 56.4%

DEMOCRAT
# Alton B. Parker
ELECTORAL VOTE 140, POPULAR VOTE 37.6%

SOCIALIST
# Eugene V. Debs
ELECTORAL VOTE 0, POPULAR VOTE 3.0%

PROHIBITION
# Silas C. Swallow
ELECTORAL VOTE 0, POPULAR VOTE 1.9%

JOHN MILTON COOPER, JR.
is the William Francis Allen Professor of History
at the University of Wisconsin, Madison.
He is the author of *The Warrior and the Priest*
(1983) and *Pivotal Decades* (1990).

*Brass stickpin fashioned after Roosevelt's pince-nez eyeglasses. Celluloid portraits are of Roosevelt and Fairbanks.*

lmost everything important about the election of 1904 can be summed up in two words—"Theodore Roosevelt." No other presidential contest in American history has revolved nearly so completely and exclusively around the personal qualities of one man. "TR," as he was already known in 1904, did not win the biggest landslide, arouse the greatest fervor, or put together the most committed winning coalition. Such emotions and interests are the necessary stuff of turning a presidential contest into a great political mandate, and their absence underscores how little else besides this one man mattered in this election. From preelection preludes and planning to outcome and long-running consequences, 1904 belonged to Roosevelt.

His dominance became clear from the beginning of the campaign, but it could not have been forecast much earlier. For one thing, Roosevelt was breaking an historical jinx on the vice presidency. Before the twentieth century, the second-highest office in the land was no jumping-off place for the White House. Only one previous vice president (Martin Van Buren) had gone on to win the presidency, and he did not offer a hopeful precedent. Unlike Roosevelt (a fellow New Yorker of Dutch ancestry) in 1904, Van Buren had not already succeeded to the presidential office at the time of his election. Before Roosevelt, none of the four vice presidents who had succeeded fallen Presidents—John Tyler, Millard Fillmore, Andrew Johnson, and Chester Arthur—had been

elected to the top spot in his own right. None of them had even received his party's nomination, and only Fillmore had run for President at all, on a third-party ticket.

More than historical coincidence underlay Roosevelt's apparent weakness as a presidential aspirant for 1904. The case of the last President similarly situated, Chester Arthur, offered uncanny parallels. Almost twenty years apart, another New Yorker who had been chosen to give geographical balance to a Republican ticket headed by an Ohioan unexpectedly found himself in the White House only six months into his predecessor's term. Each of these successors also contrasted sharply with his predecessor in looks, background, personality, and reputation. Finally, each of these successors nominally headed a Republican party dominated by machines and bosses in the big states and by legislative barons on Capitol Hill and also superintended by the fallen President's closest friend, political confidant, and party manager. Where Arthur had had to contend with James G. Blaine, Roosevelt now had to face Mark Hanna, and few people forgot that Blaine had easily wrested the 1884 Republican nomination away from Arthur.

No one had appreciated such political liabilities of the vice presidency better than Roosevelt before his nomination for the office in 1900. He then held the best office from which to run for President, the governorship of New York. Since the Civil War, three of his gubernatorial predecessors had won presidential nominations, and one of

25

them, Grover Cleveland, had served two terms in the White House. In the first half of the twentieth century four more present or former governors of New York, including Roosevelt, would run; of these, the two who won would both be named Roosevelt.

TR's own preferred strategy would have been to serve two more two-year terms as governor after 1900 and run for President in 1904. It is interesting to speculate what might have happened if his wish had been granted. Had a different vice president succeeded McKinley, the dynamic, glamorous Roosevelt would have been a major contender for the nomination. Moreover, a reputation as an effective Republican reform governor, which he had begun to gain before 1900 and which Robert M. La Follette captured so dramatically in the meantime in Wisconsin, might have enabled Roosevelt to push his party in significantly different directions on the important domestic issues of the time.

Instead, the governor found himself trapped in the 1900 vice presidential nomination. The machinations of the state boss, Senator Thomas Platt, who wanted him out of New York, together with his immense popularity with rank-and-file Republicans throughout the country, had left him no choice. But Roosevelt's popularity pointed to the major political change that had broken the jinx on vice presidential successors' political fortunes. Nearly always before, vice presidential nominations had served as a means to pay factional debts and to assure geographical balance to the ticket—northeasterners coupled with midwesterners for the Republicans, and always a northerner for top spot and usually a southerner or Border State man behind him for the

Democrats. By contrast, Roosevelt brought political strengths of his own to the ticket as New York governor, and he injected the new public dimensions of personal public campaigning that the Democrats had enjoyed in 1896 and would enjoy again in 1900 with Bryan.

Roosevelt's vice presidential nomination really marked a premature leap forward in American politics, not a definitive break with the past. Plenty of lackluster candidates, including Roosevelt's own running mate in 1904, would grace party tickets in much of the twentieth century. Only occasionally would a person of independent strength and reputation get the nod for second place. Not until the second half of the twentieth century would vice presidential nominations like Roosevelt's become the rule rather than the exception. Only then would the office cease to be a jinx and become the most favored starting-point on the road to the White House.

At the century's beginning the vice president-become-President could only see handicaps to overcome. Securing the 1904 Republican presidential nomination became Roosevelt's highest, overriding priority during his first term. Partly out of the need to avoid rousing potential opposition, the new President proved exceedingly cautious in domestic affairs his first term. His most spectacular actions—modest enforcement of the Sherman Anti-Trust Act and mediation of the anthracite coal miners' strike in 1902—either carried out initiatives already begun or imitated moves earlier made by McKinley. In fact, Roosevelt's most important and controversial actions during this term were in foreign affairs, especially his interventions in the Caribbean and his role in the

1903 Panamanian revolt that secured the route for the Panama Canal.

In order to assure his nomination, the new President did not stop at policy appeasement of his party's dominant conservative factions. He also played one of their favorite games, spoilsmanship, with skill and gusto, and he exploited internecine rivalries among the business barons, even at the price of making some unsavory alliances. Roosevelt's own longstanding background as a civil service reformer notwithstanding, he used patronage to solidify his support, especially among rotten-borough southern Republican organizations. Because Mark Hanna was his greatest potential rival, the President consorted with Hanna's bitterest adversary in Ohio, Joseph B. Foraker. "Fire Engine Joe" was a mean-spirited machine politician who would later turn on Roosevelt before he was driven out of office after exposure of his shady dealings with John D. Rockefeller's Standard Oil Company. Yet Roosevelt made common cause with Foraker in their mutual desire to dish Hanna. Out of these patronage manipulations and factional intrigues, TR built a presidential "steamroller" that would fix presidential nominations for as long as Republicans occupied the White House in this era. Curiously, that steamroller gave Roosevelt the only Republican presidential nomination that he was ever able to win for himself.

Ironically, all this maneuvering was probably unnecessary. Neither publicly nor privately did any of the Republican bosses say anything about opposing Roosevelt's nomination. Why should they have? Even though some conservatives doubted TR's soundness on vital economic issues, he was far preferable to any Democrat. As their chief editorial mouthpiece, the New York *Sun*, put the

Silk ribbon appealing to the workingmen. It plays on the "Full Dinner Pail" theme.

*Monochrome campaign poster for Parker and Davis.*

matter in 1904, "We prefer the impulsive candidate of the party of conservatism to the conservative candidate of the party which the business interests regard as permanently and dangerously impulsive." More important, savvy Republicans of all persuasions recognized that Roosevelt's popularity, now so much magnified by his shrewdly publicized doings in the White House, was an inestimable asset with which it would be foolish to tamper, except under extreme provocation. His putative rival, Hanna, made no move toward running for the nomination. The Ohio senator's spirits never recovered from the loss of his friend McKinley, and he died in February 1904.

When the Republican convention met in Chicago in June, everything went smoothly, perhaps too smoothly. The speeches and the platform predictably lauded Roosevelt, although their content could as easily have described McKinley four years before. Apart from massive photographs, teddy bear emblems, and the slogan ("The Square Deal") the convention bore astonishingly little imprint of the President's vivid personality. Even the vice presidential nomination offered a stark contrast to Roosevelt's own four years earlier. The President went along with the congressional leaders' wish to nominate one of their own, Senator Charles W. Fairbanks of Indiana. Everyone agreed, evidently, that the top of the ticket supplied glamour to spare. Mr. Dooley captured the essence of the proceedings when he wrote:

> Th' raypublican convintion labored, too, like a cash register. It listened to three canned speeches, adopted a predigested platform, nomynated a cold storage vice president, gave three especially prepared cheers and wint home. The convintion's mind all made f'r it met.

Indeed, President Roosevelt had made its mind up, and for once in his life he wanted and he got no zest, no gusto, no excitement.

All those qualities in 1904 came from the Democrats. But, as is often the case in party politics, excitement can be a sign of sickness, not health. 1904 was, arguably, the low-water mark of Democratic party fortunes since the Civil War. Having lost twice in a row with Bryan, many party leaders, especially some southerners, wanted to give the deposed northeastern, Cleveland wing another turn at bat. But the aging Cleveland, the party's only President since 1861, refused to run, and his cohorts faced two problems—how to overcome Bryanite resistance and whom to nominate. Although the Commoner had likewise taken himself out of the running, he could have made life harder for his adversaries by backing the candidacy of William Randolph Hearst. But Bryan disapproved of the newspaper tycoon's "immoral" personal life, ties to Tammany Hall, and lavish campaign spending. Instead of settling on a candidate, Bryan labored at St. Louis on the convention floor and in the platform committee to produce a document that endorsed much of his earlier inflationist and anti-big business direction for the party.

As their candidate, Democratic conservatives picked possibly the darkest horse

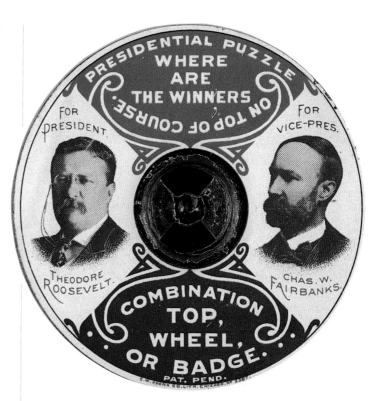

ever nominated by a major party. He was Alton B. Parker, a fifty-two-year-old New York judge. Parker had three claims to consideration. First, he had distinguished himself from other ranking New York Democrats by publicly supporting Bryan in 1896. Second, because he had unexpectedly gotten elected Chief Justice of the Supreme Court of Appeals in 1897, Parker was the only Democrat to win a statewide office in New York in a decade. Third, as a sitting judge, Parker had refused to comment on political issues for the past seven years, and he had reportedly swung majorities on his court to render pro-labor decisions. Not only did the whole business smack of crafty calculation, but the deal almost came unstuck when Parker telegraphed the convention that he would

*Lithographed toy spinning top with pictures of Roosevelt and Fairbanks. This item, which could also be worn as a badge, is the only one known to exist.*

not run if he had to accept the platform's quasi-inflationist currency plank. Over Bryan's strenuous opposition, the delegates voted to acquiesce in the nominee's insistence. Meanwhile, they had chosen as their vice presidential candidate, Henry Gassaway Davis, an octogenarian, multimillionaire former senator from West Virginia. Davis barely participated in the campaign, not even financially.

The campaign itself proved anticlimactic until near the end. Because Roosevelt, like McKinley four years earlier, was a sitting President, he honored the as yet unbroken rule against open presidential participation in the campaign. TR did busy himself behind the scenes directing organizational, financial, oratorical, and publicity efforts on his behalf. The financial efforts led him to commit a blunder that eventually stirred the only momentary excitement of the campaign. Worried by Parker's success in raising money on Wall Street, Roosevelt ordered his managers to hit a number of tycoons for big donations. Who said what to whom in shaking loose these funds remains unclear and controversial, especially about whether anyone made promises of favored treatment for big business in general or certain companies in particular. Afterward, the steel magnate Henry Clay Frick claimed, "He got down on his knees to us. We bought the son of a bitch and he did not stay bought."

Parker initially strove to contrast himself further with Bryan by imitating McKinley. For the first two months of the contest, he received delegations at his home, after the fashion of the 1896 Republican "front porch" campaign. The statements Parker made, by and large, castigated Roosevelt from a conservative Democratic, state rights standpoint. He accused the President of pow-

er-grabbing usurpation at home in economic affairs and abroad in Panama and the Caribbean. Inferior management and shopworn usage, as well as a much harder sell for Parker and against Roosevelt, made the front porch techniques much less effective than earlier. Finally, after repeated urgings, the challenger changed the tone and method of his campaign. In the last week before the election, Parker made one short speaking tour in New York, New Jersey, and Connecticut.

Meanwhile, the Democratic ticket received sorely needed assistance on the campaign trail from an unexpected source. The most energetic performer for the party in 1904 was, once again, Bryan. Incorrigible party loyalty and a yen for the hustings, burning convictions about the need to rebuild his influence in the party—all these motives combined to make the commoner campaign hard, even for somebody like Parker. The toughest anti-Roosevelt arguments emanated from Bryan, who assailed the President from nearly the opposite direction as the nominee. Bryan castigated Roosevelt as a tool of plutocracy, a sham reformer, and a militarist and imperialist. This was vintage Bryan, and the disparity between the advocate and his intended beneficiary was widely noted.

Parker embarked on his eleventh-hour campaign swing mainly because he had learned about Roosevelt's fundraising among the nation's richest businesses. Despite his lack of oratorical flair, the Democratic candidate fired up his audiences with the substance of his charges. At the President's direction, Parker asserted, the Republican campaign organization had engaged in "organized importunity" toward business leaders to raise money

Cotton sailcloth banner. Theodore Roosevelt acted as a mediator in negotiating the Treaty of Portsmouth (1905), which ended the Russo-Japanese War. He was awarded the Nobel Peace Prize in 1906. "Rough Rider" battle scene is at top.

and promised them protection from anti-trust suits and regulation. Soon, the Democrat used stronger language. Roosevelt had, he alleged, committed "blackmail." Parker's charges stung TR, who lashed back with verbal overkill, his typical response to a moral predicament. On November 4, the White House issued a press release that labeled Parker's contentions "monstrous" and "unqualifiedly and atrociously false." The statement also challenged Parker to name names and reveal his sources, something which he was not prepared to do. The incident came so late that it made no discernible impact

on the election. In the longer run, however, this flap over tycoons' contributions revealed an unheroic side of Roosevelt and disclosed flaws in his all-embracing campaign strategy.

On election eve, bookmakers were giving five-to-one odds on the President, and the results from the polling on November 8 vindicated their judgment. Roosevelt won handsomely, with 7,628,875 votes (or 56.4 percent) as opposed to Parker's 5,084,442 (or 37.6 percent). TR bettered McKinley's 1900 showing by 1.3 million votes and more than four percentage points. He fattened

*Ceramic Buffalo Pottery Company pitcher designed by Seymour Eaton, who popularized the "Roosevelt Bears" in books and illustrations. The Teddy Bear is named after Theodore Roosevelt who apparently spared or saved the life of a bear cub while hunting.*

the margin in the electoral college even more by carrying 33 states, 5 more than McKinley, with 336 electoral votes. Parker retained only 12 southern and border states, with 140 electoral votes. He lost another border state, Missouri, and he forfeited the gains Bryan had made in the West, where he won no states. Voter turnout continued the downward slide begun in 1900, declining over eight points to 65.2 percent. The congressional results gratified the Republicans almost as much as the presidential tri-

umph. Their majority in the House rose to 250, an increase of 53 over the 1900 margin, to mark the high point of Republican strength in that chamber until the 1920s. The Senate was likewise theirs by a whopping margin of 57 Republicans to 33 Democrats. Also, for the first time in a decade and a half, no minor party members were elected to either house.

The clearest message to be read from the returns was Roosevelt's overwhelming popularity. He ran ahead of Republican tickets in every part of the country, even in the South. He was, commented one magazine, "the most popular man that has come into public life within recent times. The people like his energy, his frankness, his robust way." Nobody was going to beat TR in 1904, and that was nearly all there was to it. But not quite all. An equally clear message from the voters went to the Democrats. They had only made matters worse for themselves by trying to forsake the policies and constituencies that Bryan had attracted to the party. Two facts left the message unmistakable. One was the disastrous showing in the West, and the other was the more than fourfold increase in the showing of the second-time Socialist presidential candidate. Eugene Debs polled 402,283 votes, up from fewer than 90,000 in 1900, and he got his best percentages in the West. The Prohibitionists likewise improved over their 1900 showing, to more than 258,536 votes. Even the Populists made a modest comeback, more than doubling their total, to give Tom Watson of Georgia 117,183 votes.

Fittingly for an election that had revolved around one man, its most important consequence also emanated from him. On election night, when the magnitude of his victory became apparent, President Roosevelt issued a statement thanking the people for their endorsement and pledging that he would not run again in 1908. Roosevelt's renunciation was not an impulsive or emotional gesture. It had been well thought out in advance, and it fulfilled his campaign strategy of winning by downplaying controversial issues and making the election a personal vindication. No better way existed to give the lie to allegations about his hunger for power and usurpation, which some Republicans also privately believed, than his voluntary future withdrawal. But this was another campaign blunder. Noble as the sacrifice might be, it helped rob him of the dynamic, great presidency that he craved. The first two years of his second term would witness exciting, significant departures in domestic policy. Once it became clear, however, that he meant to honor the pledge to quit in 1908, a stalemate quickly developed between the President and Republican congressional leaders.

The next two presidential elections likewise took their shape from the way TR won in 1904 and the way he interpreted his triumph. Deepening intraparty strife between Republican conservatives and insurgents, the trials of Roosevelt's successor, and his own later insurgency and party bolt—all flowed from the events of 1904. Moreover, in a supreme irony, even the Democrats' long sought restoration began then, too. Parker's drubbing did not convince all conservative Democrats that their cause was hopeless, especially if they kept seeking attractive new faces. One such potential savior surfaced in the unlikely person of a college president named Woodrow Wilson. Although Wilson

subsequently proved to be anything but a conservative, he got his start in Democratic politics as a possible successor to the mantle of Parker, who disappeared from national politics as suddenly as he had entered. Wilson's later emergence gave clearest testimony of all to the absolute centrality of Roosevelt's personal role in 1904—he would inadvertently spawn his own nemesis. In sum, this election was his, from start to finish, even in its aftermath.

Pair of advertisement postcards showing fashionable women cheering the candidates. Democrat: "Toot! Toot! Toot!/ Alton's a beaut!" Republican: "Boys get ready/ To cheer for Teddy!"

Cardboard advertisement promoting the Republican candidates.

Roosevelt and Fairbanks
campaign poster.

Rebus celluloid button
[rose+velt].

Monochromatic woven silk ribbons issued at the 1904 St. Louis Exposition.

Trio of lithographed tin trays. The value of
these beautifully colorful items is enhanced
when they also carry an advertising message.

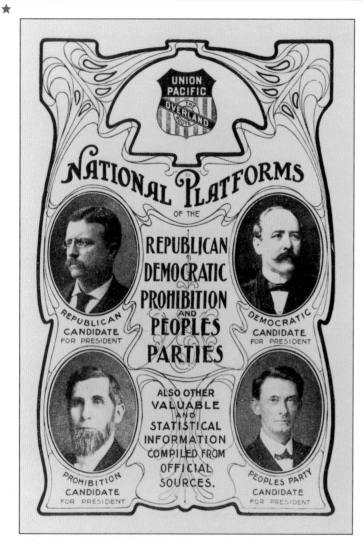

*Railroad advertising booklet distributed on the transcontinental route.*

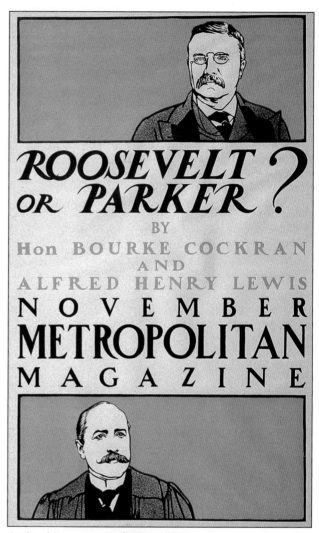

*Graphic advertisement poster for Metropolitan Magazine.*

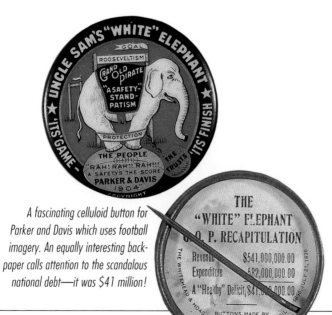

*A fascinating celluloid button for Parker and Davis which uses football imagery. An equally interesting back-paper calls attention to the scandalous national debt—it was $41 million!*

*Sepiatoned photographic portrait celluloid button of Alton B. Parker.*

1904 celluloid buttons. The brand on the steer (left) was the one used at Roosevelt's South Dakota ranch.

1904 campaign postcards. The most colorful political postcards date from 1900 to 1912.

Left: Bronzed-iron mantel clock
of Roosevelt, the Rough Rider.
Below: Figural caricature Toby mug. Theodore
Roosevelt was a popular subject for Tobies.

A game issued while Roosevelt was
governor of New York (1899–1901).

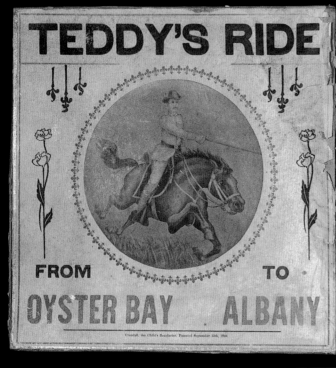

A TRUE AMERICAN ROUGH RIDER.

"Nothing could be more definite and emphatic than Mr. Roosevelt's reaffirmation of the Monroe doctrine. It is, he reminds the world, a declaration that there must be no territorial aggrandizement by a non-American power at the expense of any American power on American soil."—*Daily paper.*

Mechanical postcard game.

Left: Mechanical postcard with Roosevelt playing
with the famous "Teddy" bear, which is fur-covered.
Below: Plaster nodding caricature doll of Roosevelt.

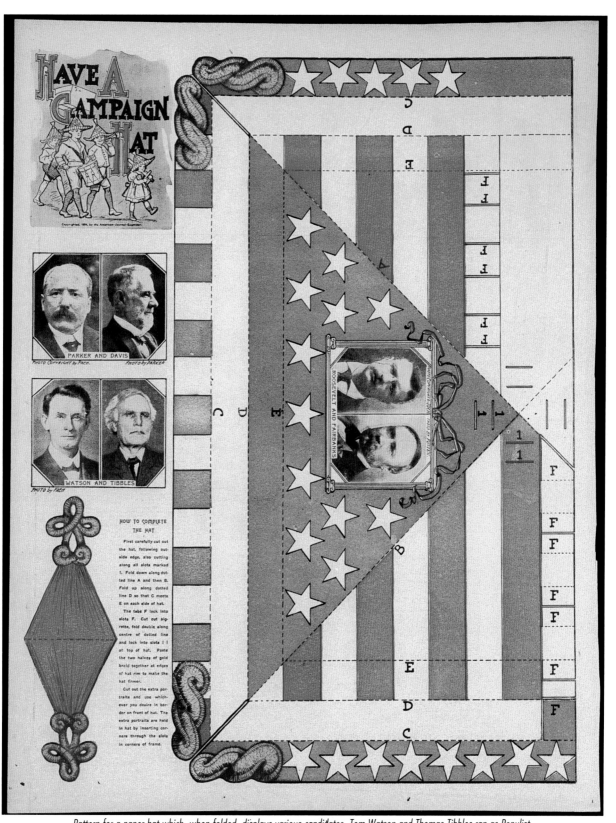

*Pattern for a paper hat which, when folded, displays various candidates. Tom Watson and Thomas Tibbles ran as Populist party candidates for President and vice president, receiving less than 1 percent of the popular vote.*

A July 1904 Judge
magazine cover endorsing
the Republican candidates.

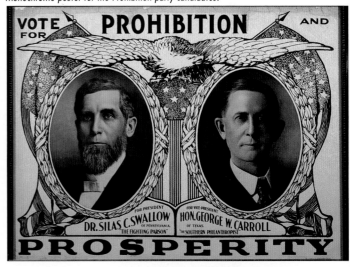

Monochrome poster for the Prohibition party candidates.

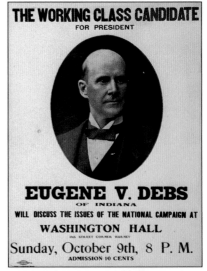

1904 broadside for Socialist presidential
candidate Eugene V. Debs.

Campaign poster for Parker and Davis.

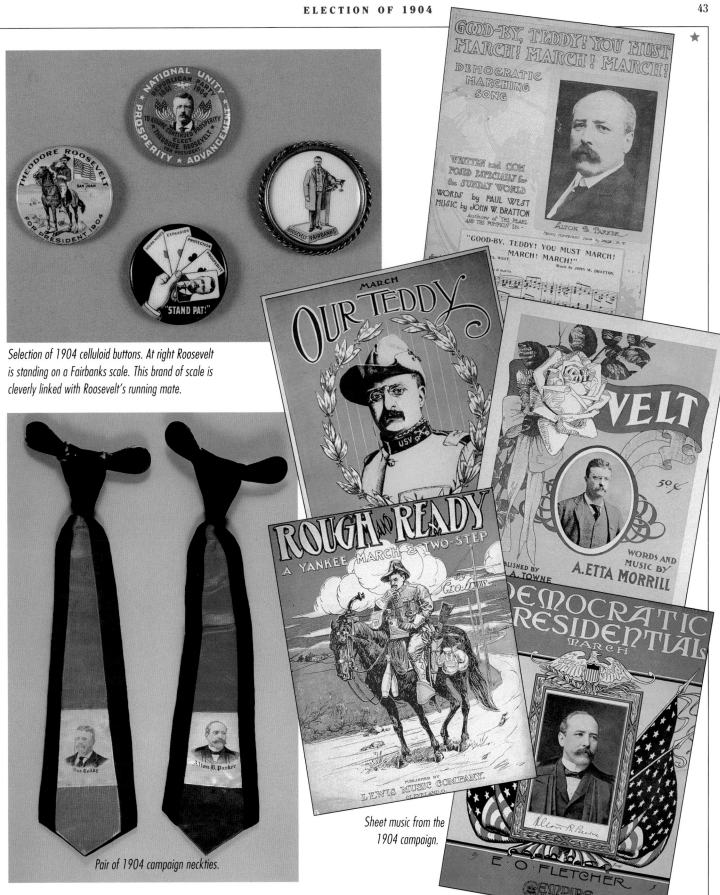

Selection of 1904 celluloid buttons. At right Roosevelt is standing on a Fairbanks scale. This brand of scale is cleverly linked with Roosevelt's running mate.

Pair of 1904 campaign neckties.

Sheet music from the 1904 campaign.

Selection of 1904 campaign celluloid buttons.

Three Roosevelt celluloid buttons. None were campaign items. Issued to welcome Roosevelt back from his African safari (1910), the center button shows him grinning atop an ark filled with animals headed to new homes in American zoos.

Large celluloid button—clear and to the point.

1905 inaugural badge.

DINNER GIVEN AT THE WHITE HOUSE BY PRESIDENT ROOSEVELT TO BOOKER T. WASHINGTON, OCTOBER 17th, 1901

Roosevelt was the first President to host a black American at the White House. His 1901 dinner with Booker T. Washington became an issue in the 1904 campaign. The lithographed print, with "Equality" inscribed on the tablecloth, was issued in 1903. In 1904, Democratic committees in border and southern states distributed buttons with the positions of the men reversed and Washington portrayed blacker and with more stereotyped negroid features.

Roosevelt autographed White House card.

★

**1908**

46 STATES
IN THE UNION

*REPUBLICAN*

# William H. Taft

ELECTORAL VOTE 321, POPULAR VOTE 51.6%

DEMOCRAT

# William J. Bryan

ELECTORAL VOTE 162, POPULAR VOTE 43.1%

SOCIALIST

# Eugene V. Debs

ELECTORAL VOTE 0, POPULAR VOTE 2.8%

PROHIBITION

# Eugene W. Chafin

ELECTORAL VOTE 0, POPULAR VOTE 1.7%

PAOLO E. COLETTA

retired from the Naval Academy as professor emeritus in 1983. In addition to several naval histories he has published *William Jennings Bryan* (3 volumes, 1964–69); *The Presidency of William Howard Taft* (1989); *William Howard Taft: A Biography* (1990); and some eighty articles on naval and political subjects.

Three of the five presidential candidates in 1908 were seasoned campaigners. In 1896, Democrat William Jennings Bryan had violated the century-old tradition that (with a couple of exceptions) presidential candidates do not campaign. Renominated in 1900, he lost again. Although overwhelmed by conservative forces in 1904, he quickly regained the titular leadership of his party and was easily renominated in Denver in July 1908.

Except for the years 1883-85, when he practiced law, Bryan's foremost opponent, Republican William Howard Taft, had held nothing but appointive offices after 1881, and hence never had to appeal to voters. Obese and cherubic, he was politically and socially conservative, yet by declining his life's ambition, a seat on the Supreme Court, offered to him three times by President Theodore Roosevelt, he had proved his devotion to the public service—and Roosevelt believed that he could control him. The party wanted Roosevelt, but after he chose Taft no other need apply. Taft would obtain many tips on campaign management and tactics from his benefactor, who also wielded the patronage and was expert in educating public opinion.

Taft's most important other advisers were his ambitious wife, Helen Herron "Nellie" Taft, a rich half-brother, Charles P. Taft, and brothers Henry and Horace. A major drawback was the enmity of labor, for as a judge he had opposed the labor boycott and issued injunctions against strikers, enough to prove that he sided with the corporation rather than the man. Another drawback was his dislike of politics and of campaigning, saying in one instance that "a national campaign for the presidency to me is a nightmare." Lastly, he was often charged with merely being an echo of Roosevelt. Yet he struck pay dirt by stating that he would seek the continuity of Roosevelt's policies.

The strongest of the minor parties—Socialist, Populist, and Prohibition—was the first. In his third campaign, Socialist nominee Eugene Victor Debs had organizations in thirty-nine states, sent out a great many reams of literature, and campaigned nationwide in his "Red Special" railroad train. He addressed about eight hundred thousand people who paid to hear him on the need to overthrow the capitalistic system. Few favored the single-issue Prohibition party. The Populist candidate, Thomas E. Watson, held Bryan to be an abomination and believed that Negroes should have no more political rights than the Indians or Chinese. William Randolph Hearst's Independence party named Thomas Hisgen as its candidate but campaigned only in the state of New York, its objective being to split the opposition to Taft and obtain revenge for Bryan's refusal to support Hearst as the Democratic presidential candidate in 1904 and for his *volte face* on the issue of the government ownership of public utilities (which he had endorsed in 1906).

Bryan's strategy for 1908 was again to concentrate upon such economic issues as tariff, currency, and banking reform; continue his anti-trust, "anti-government by injunction," and anti-imperialism campaign; and cement an eastern labor-western farmer coalition.

To achieve his goals, Bryan advocated the direct election of senators, limiting the powers of the Speaker of the House, adopting the initiative, referendum, and recall, and demanding the publication by candidates of their campaign contributions before an election. By omitting various old demands, he adjusted his program to the dynamics of American life. His most conservative platform to date was designed to complete the unfinished business of President Roosevelt's progressivism and draw conservative and progressive Democrats together.

With New England and the Pacific Coast states Republican and the South safely Democratic, Bryan would campaign in major cities in the East and Midwest. Unable to obtain a suitable eastern vice presidential candidate, he accepted John Kern of Indiana, who would stump the East and South. He was delighted when Samuel Gompers, head of the American Federation of Labor, said he would campaign for him.

Bryan charged Roosevelt with using the patronage to get Taft nominated and elected. He would not accept contributions from corporations, would publish the names of donors of $100 or more by October 15, and by raising money by dollar subscriptions end the influence of wealth in politics. Under the caption of "Shall the People Rule?" he discoursed on his favored themes in his weekly journal, *The Commoner*. This lay leader of the Social Gospel also called for men to turn away from crass materialism and "love one another instead of running

riot after money and emulating men of wealth." He thus turned every public question into a moral one and let the full weight of his rhetoric fall upon the wicked who opposed his holy cause.

Bryan planned to establish Democratic clubs and a Democratic newspaper in every county, a Bryan Club in every voting precinct, Bryan and Kern Businessman Clubs, and Bryan Traveling Men Clubs. He could call for support from friends and politicians in his debt because of his continual campaigning. His headquarters, in Chicago, had a branch in New York City. Because of radio delivery, he intended to use the written word more than oratory. While he wrote a weekly letter to every Democratic precinct, he relied heavily upon such experienced editors on his press committee as Josephus Daniels, Henry Watterson, and Herman Ridder, of the New York *Staats Zeitung*. The last would try to win the foreign-born vote. Daniels loomed large in the preparation of a campaign textbook replete with data on trust prices, Taft's judicial record, and statistics on the Panic of 1907. He also fed material for Gompers to use in his *American Federationist* and on the stump. One of the few millionaires who supported Bryan, Colonel Moses G. Wetmore, chaired his finance committee. Support also came from George Fred Williams in Massachusetts, Ollie James in Kentucky, John E. Lamb in Indiana, and the blind Senator Thomas P. Gore in Oklahoma.

To win their states, Bryan must get rid of national committeemen Roger Sullivan, the political boss of Chicago; Thomas Taggart, who controlled Indiana; James Guffey, who ruled Pennsylvania; and oust or convert Charles F. Murphy, of Tammany Hall,

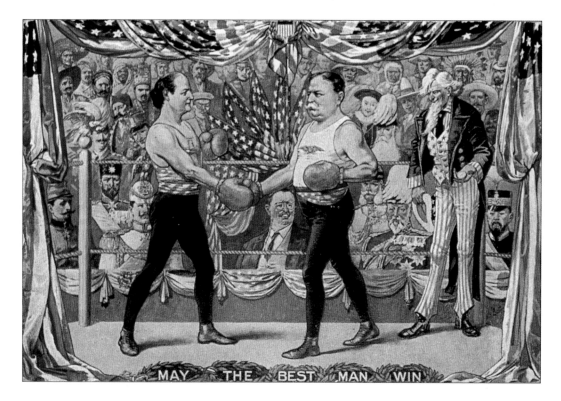

*Postcard of Bryan and Taft in a boxing ring. Theodore Roosevelt sits in the first row and Uncle Sam is the referee.*

and Patrick McCarren, the Democratic boss of Brooklyn. He got rid of Guffey and probably reached accommodation with Sullivan by softpedaling the initiative and referendum, but Murphy and McCarren remained noncommittal. Obtaining the election as national chairman of Norman Mack of Buffalo, New York, would help Bryan because Mack would try to win the state for him against Murphy and McCarren. Bryan recognized the West by choosing a Nebraska banker as the vice chairman of the national committee, and the South by designating Governor Charles H. Haskell, of Oklahoma, who had a business background, as his treasurer. He thus raised the awkward question of how he could support both business interests and labor.

Bryan alleged that Republicans were responsible for all abuses existing in government and were impotent to accomplish imperatively needed reforms. When offered a "deal" in New York City—New York City and State and the White House would be his if he promised to appoint only "safe" judg-

es to the Supreme Court—he refused. But since Roosevelt had in 1907 conceded that "about half of Bryan's views are right" and now also appeared as a political moralist, Bryan asserted that he, himself, rather than Taft, was his legitimate heir.

Bryan's most important campaign manager was his brother, Charles Wayland Bryan. Charles cross-indexed the country and not only managed *The Commoner* but enrolled its subscribers in a "Commoner Army." He hired a battery of secretaries to send out extra thousands of the journal, other literature, and answered wagonloads of mail each day. Yet he and other advisers faced a major hurdle in Bryan himself, for he was difficult to work with; maintaining that he was "always right," he branded any opponent a "tool of the interests" and refused to delegate responsibility.

Taft delivered his acceptance speech, edited by Roosevelt, on July 28, Bryan his on August 12. By answering Taft topic by topic in a tour of the Midwest rather than using a simple campaign theme, Bryan publicized his opponent. A novelty was the movie made of his Labor Day address in Chicago, later exhibited along with a phonograph record carrying his voice. A second tour, early in September, took him into the upper states of the Mississippi Valley; a third, in mid-September, from Rhode Island to Colorado. After invading the East, he spoke in the Midwest. With only a week's rest in Lincoln, he was off again until election eve for a total of sixty days on the stump during which he made as many as thirty speeches a day.

He hit hardest on the corrupt use of money and on underhanded election methods. His audiences being larger than ever before, he thought he had national support. An innovation, one followed by Woodrow Wilson and F.D. Roosevelt, was the special attention given to economic, social, and national differences in city groups while simultaneously stressing issues upon which urban and rural folk could agree. For exam-

*Needlework showing "Billy Possum," the pro-Taft emblem.*

ple, he praised the Irish and Jews for their contributions to American life.

Bryan erred in thinking he had national support and that his program differed greatly from Taft's. Taft agreed on the income tax, direct election of senators, and prohibition and differed little on the Philippines, although he would free them much later than Bryan. Taft was more conciliatory on the Negro question than Bryan, who risked losing the white vote of the South if he encouraged Negroes to join the Democratic voting coalition. Both men avoided religion, which Bryan could have used to his advantage because Taft was a Unitarian. Greater differences were over the tariff, guarantee of bank deposits, labor, and campaign contributions. But Bryan had to fight Roosevelt rather than Taft, and Hearst gave him a hard blow.

On September 17, 1908, by publishing letters John D. Archbold of the Standard Oil Company had written to various senators in 1905, Hearst alerted the nation to Archbold's attempt to kill "objectionable" legislation and defeat "dangerous men" and of checks totaling $29,500 that could be regarded as a bribe. Involved also, however, were not only Republican Senator Joseph B. Foraker of Ohio but Governor Haskell of Oklahoma, Bryan's campaign treasurer, who allegedly had stopped an antitrust suit against the company in his state and also engaged in sharp railroad practices in Chicago. Haskell vehemently denied Hearst's charge. While Taft ruined Foraker's career by cutting ties to him, Roosevelt directed Taft to "put some ginger into the campaign." He was to "smash and cut" Bryan via Haskell on the ground that excess funds in the Democratic treasury in 1904 meant Standard Oil money for Bryan.

Bryan had been told by an Oklahoma newspaperman in the fall of 1907 about Haskell's connections with Standard Oil. Disbelieving the stories, Bryan said he would support Haskell until Roosevelt provided proof. After Roosevelt replied that Haskell's connection with Standard Oil was of court record in Oklahoma and that Bryan's support for him was "a scandal and a disgrace," Josephus Daniels and others persuaded Haskell to resign. He was succeeded by Herman Ridder. When Bryan countercharged that Roosevelt had, during the Panic of 1907, permitted U.S. Steel to acquire the Tennessee Coal and Iron Company and thus obtain control of more than 50 percent of the country's steel production, Roosevelt pointed to his crusade against trusts and "malefactors of great wealth," said that he had violated no law, and held that the action had helped to check the spread of financial panic. He was rocked on his heels when John D. Rockefeller announced for Taft.

Finally aroused by Roosevelt, Taft lumbered forth to destroy Bryan's image, for image predominates over issues in a campaign. Bryan, he said, was merely an eloquent critic who had made a career of adroit protest but had never given practical demonstration of his ability to solve problems, a theorist and sophist whose election would mean financial panic. Moreover, Bryan had been inconsistent on issues and policies whereas Taft would continue Roosevelt's policies but administer them more equally, without so much disturbance to business. Bryan invited conflict; Taft, conciliation. In sum, Bryan was a demagogue. Taft erred in calling honest Bryan a demagogue but was correct in divining that he

sought economic as well as political equality via the ballot and, like Square Dealing Roosevelt, would have the national government control industrial and commercial interests whose unchecked power had enabled them to ignore the public interest.

A federal statute forbade contributions from corporations but not from their officers or directors. On October 15 Bryan published his roll of contributors. Most of the money had come in small sums and as of October 9 totaled $248,467.25. From national headquarters Daniels wrote Mrs. Daniels, "The work here is great and the *money is scarce*." Taft accepted contributions from corporation officers and said he would publish the list of his contributors *after* the election. He refused money from Standard Oil but accepted $20,000 from Andrew Carnegie, who had retired from the steel business.

Bryan was sure of the 120 electoral votes of the South and he would probably win 13 in Kentucky and 7 in Oklahoma. To win 107 additional votes he must carry New York (39), Illinois (27), Indiana (15), Missouri (18), and Nebraska (8). Taft took nothing for granted and directed his brother Charles "to fight as if he were making a losing fight, to contest every inch in the western states, and not to look on Ohio or any other state as certain."

During the first two months of the campaign the "Balding Boy Orator" appeared to be winning. Polls reported during the third week of October, however, put Taft ahead by 205 to 178 electoral votes. As he had in 1896 and 1900, Bryan now adopted fear and smear tactics: he charged Republicans with the "purchasing of the election," "the coercion of labor," offering of business contracts "conditional" upon his defeat, and ordering by Republican employers of their workers to march in Taft parades or be fired. There was truth in the second and third charges, but his wild allegation that the Republicans sought to purchase the election lost him many votes. His antitrust, tariff, and labor views drove business away from him, and he could not hide such skeletons in his closet as free silver and his previous demand for government ownership of railroads. Very important was his failure to win eastern labor, to whom Republicans still represented the party of prosperity.

Whereas the lethargic Taft preferred a front porch campaign, Roosevelt told him to stop saying what he had said in his judicial decisions and become an aggressive "leader." He must make his audiences see not an etching but a poster full of blue, yellow, and red to catch the eye. He advised, "Do not *answer* Bryan, attack him! Don't let *him* make the issues. . . . Hit them hard, old man!" He must "get up close to Bryan."

Taft's choice as chairman of the Republican National Committee was the assistant postmaster general, Frank H. Hitchcock. William Hayward, the Nebraska Republican state chairman, became the committee's secretary and was expected to keep Nebraska safe for Taft. Hitchcock opened offices in Chicago and Washington and operated nationwide. He used a filing card system for every caller and, without fully informing Taft, wielded the patronage power in his behalf particularly in capturing Republican votes in the South. In addition to help from a policy advisory committee of moderately to very rich businessmen and financiers and from a unified and disciplined party organization, Taft was aided by the National Association of Manufacturers.

Taft finally began to campaign seriously in September. From a swing from Indiana to Colorado between September 23 and October 8, he concluded that the West was safe. He told Roosevelt that Bryan's claim "to be the heir of your policies is now the subject of laughter and ridicule." As Bryan did, he concentrated on New York and the states of the Midwest during the last two weeks of the campaign. If no orator like Bryan, he grew into a capable campaigner and made no serious mistake. Moreover, he was aided by an interview in which Roosevelt praised him highly; speeches delivered by a number of senators, governors, former cabinet members, and, during the last week, by the entire Cabinet; by a revival of business activity; and by money from the business community.

Late on election night, November 3, Roosevelt repeatedly said, "We've beaten them to a frazzle." On the fifth, Bryan sent Taft congratulations. Taft won 321 electoral votes to Bryan's 162 and, with 7,679,006 votes, 51.58 percent of the popular vote to Bryan's 6,409,106, or 43.05 percent. Though pulling a million and a half more votes than Alton B. Parker, the Democratic candidate in 1904, Bryan suffered the worst defeat in his three presidential races, carrying only the solid South and a few unimportant states in the Midwest. Taft took the heavily urban states of New York, New Jersey, Ohio, Illinois, Indiana, three Pacific coast states, and New England. Gompers's support for Bryan notwithstanding, Taft obtained his largest vote where Gompers's membership was greatest. The third party vote totaled only 771,059, of which Debs received 420,793.

Unable to account for his defeat, Bryan publicly asked for information to clear up

"The Mystery of 1908." He concluded that neither party was ready to push for the reforms he still desired. However, Roosevelt's "lapses" into reforms had undermined the Democratic ticket, especially in the West, which gave Taft 60 percent of his electoral votes. Roosevelt had won Taft many votes by stating that the Republican candidate would continue his own policies—which was what the people wanted—whereas Bryan's painting of Taft as a mere Me Too for Roosevelt helped ensure his election. Conservative Democrats and Hearst had knifed him. Returns from his dollar subscription plan showed that few supported him. His party had raised $629,341, the Republican party $1,655,518. He had offered no plan for handling trusts other than extirpating them, and Taft appeared to many as the "advance agent of prosperity." He was too well-known to have the attraction of novelty. With few speakers supporting him, he again had to provide most of the oratory, and few important Democratic newspapers were on his side. He had to pay for "the sins of Grover Cleveland" (the great depression of the 1890s), could not hide such skeletons in his closet as "the ghosts of '96," and demand for government ownership of railroads. His friendship with Tammany, designed to win New York, lost him support in the West and South; by condemning conservatives he lost the states they controlled; the brewing and distilling interests opposed him, Hearst's "treason" cost him some votes in the East, and the Haskell affair raised the question of his sincerity in demanding stringent antitrust regulations.

Elihu Root was correct in saying that "it was a vote more against Bryan than for Taft," because Bryan but not his party had

The Republican Party is in Power

THE BOTTOM IS OUT OF THE "FULL DINNER PAIL"

COPYRIGHT 1908 J.M. ERMERINS DETROIT

Isn't a change desirable?

1908 Democratic postcard with the bottom falling out of the "Full Dinner Pail." Reference here is to the Panic of 1907 which saw a major drop in the stock market and many business failures.

been defeated. Democrats won more congressional seats than Republicans did, the congressional insurgent Republican bloc waxed stronger, and Democrats increased their strength in almost every state legislature and won eleven governorships to seventeen for the Republicans. Taft won the presidency and Congress was Republican, but the wind had shifted against the Republican party. In time, all of Bryan's reasonable reform demands would be fulfilled.

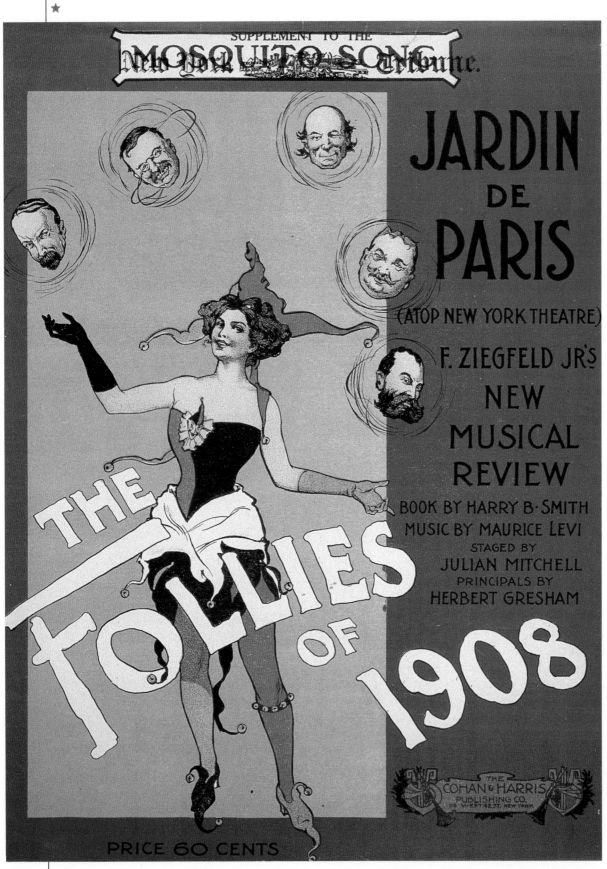

Satirical sheet music parodying the 1908 Ziegfeld Follies. The jester juggles (left to right) Vice President Charles Fairbanks, President Theodore Roosevelt, William Jennings Bryan, William Howard Taft, and New York State Governor Charles Evans Hughes.

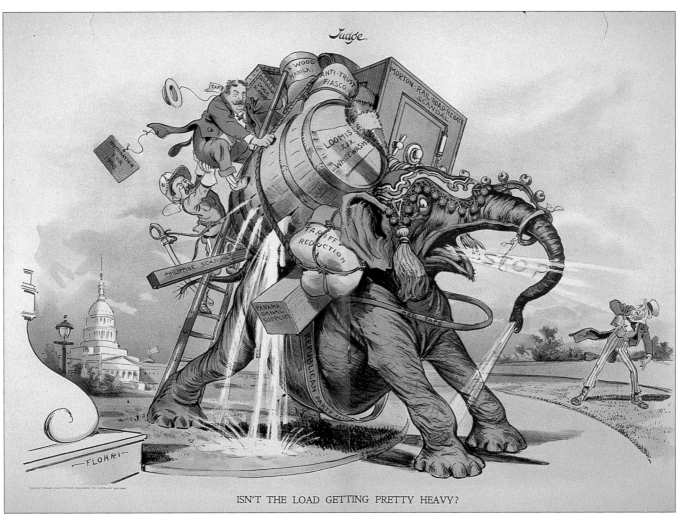

ISN'T THE LOAD GETTING PRETTY HEAVY?

Satirical cartoon from Judge magazine. Roosevelt is pushing Taft atop a scandal-burdened Republican elephant.

Postcard showing Roosevelt's support for Taft in 1908.

Set of four satirical postcards issued during the 1908 campaign. "THE TAILS GO WITH THE HEADS" refers to vice presidential candidates Republican James Sherman (top) and Democrat John Kern (bottom).

Lithographed tin caricature puzzles. The object of this game was to get the small metal balls to land in the candidate's eyes. Bryan is on the left, Taft on the right.

The 1908 campaign was outstanding for the variety
of items manufactured. Postcards, posters, and
buttons combined personality, politics, and satire.

Republican ribbon for Taft and Sherman
includes a list of candidates for local offices.

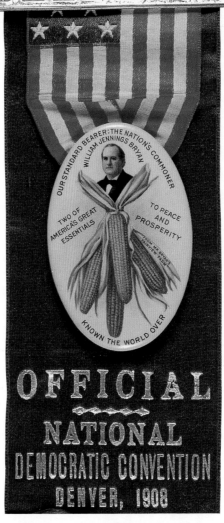

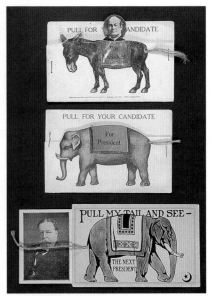

Above: Mechanical postcards.
When the string tails are pulled, the
candidate's face pops up.
Left: 1908 Democratic convention
badge with attached celluloid button
linking Bryan to his rural origins.

Above: U-N-I-TED reads, "You
and I, Ted." This expresses
1908 Republican unity which
would crumble by 1912.
Left: Postcard showing
Roosevelt leading Taft and
the Republican elephant.

*Right: Political postcards. Bryan is associated with Jefferson and Jackson, and Taft with Roosevelt. Below: Celluloid buttons. Bryan's slogan echoes his anti-big business rhetoric from past campaigns. The Taft statement reflects the playground movement supported by Republican social progressives.*

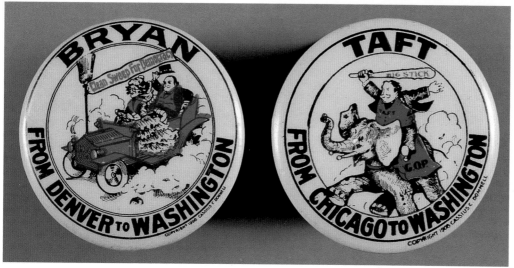

*Pair of 1908 caricature buttons showing Bryan and Taft traveling from their respective convention cities to the White House.*

*Bryan poster. Among Bryan's enemies in the background is "the corrupt and trust-dominated press."*

UNCLE SAM–MR BRYAN.YOUR ENEMIES ARE MINE ALSO.

*Salesmen's advertisement cards with designs for two 1908 campaign buttons. The scarcity of these buttons suggests that few orders were placed.*

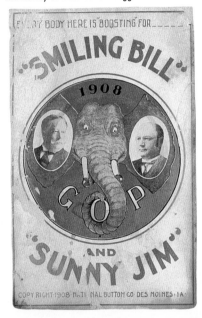

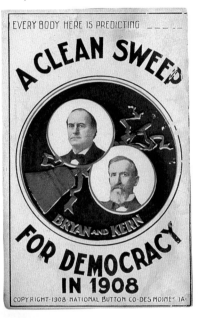

*Elaborately decorated covered box with copyrighted photographs of Taft and Sherman.*

*Glass paperweights with photographic portraits in the bases.*

*Painted plaster bust of Taft.*

Graphic celluloid button. Slogans are associated with Bryan, as is the connection with Jefferson and Jackson. Abraham Lincoln is a surprising inclusion.

Detailed tin tray with border portraits of every Republican presidential nominee. Taft and Sherman are in the center.

Many 1908 multicolor celluloid buttons utilized the art nouveau style, exhibiting aesthetic qualities rarely equaled on campaign items.

# PROHIBITION NOMINATIONS

**EUGENE W. CHAFIN**
**OF ILLINOIS**

**AARON S. WATKINS**
**OF OHIO**

## THE PROHIBITION PLATFORM

The Prohibition Party of the United States, assembled in convention at Columbus, Ohio, July 15-16, 1908, expressing gratitude to Almighty God for the victories of our principles in the past, for encouragement at present and for confidence of early and triumphant success in the future, makes the following declaration of principles and pledges their enactment into law when placed in power:

1. The submission by Congress to the several states of an amendment to the federal Constitution prohibiting the manufacture, sale, importation or transportation of alcoholic liquors for beverage purposes.

2. The immediate prohibition of the liquor traffic for beverage purposes in the District of Columbia, in the territories and all places over which the national government has jurisdiction, the repeal of the internal revenue tax on alcoholic liquors and the prohibition of interstate traffic therein.

3. The election of United States Senators by direct vote of the people.

4. Equitable graduated income and inheritance taxes.

5. The establishment of postal savings banks and the guaranty of deposits in banks.

6. The regulation of all corporations doing an interstate commerce business.

7. The creation of a permanent tariff commission.

8. The strict enforcement of law, instead of the official tolerance and practical license of the social evil which prevails in many of our cities, with its unspeakable traffic in girls.

9. Uniform marriage and divorce laws.

10. An equitable and constitutional employers' liability act.

11. Court review of postoffice department decisions.

12. The prohibition of child labor in mines, workshops and factories.

13. Legislation basing suffrage only upon intelligence and ability to read and write the English language.

14. The preservation of the mineral and forest resources of the country and the improvement of the highways and water-ways.

Believing in the righteousness of our cause and in the final triumph of our principles and convinced of the unwillingness of the Republican and Democratic parties to deal with these issues, we invite to full party membership all citizens who are agreed with us.

THE NATIONAL PROHIBITIONIST, CHICAGO
Weekly · One Dollar per Year

This Poster will be supplied at the following prices: Per 1,000,
$5.00; 500, $3.00; 100, $1.00; per dozen, 25 cents.

*Although the Prohibition party received less than 2 percent of the popular vote in 1908, the first statement of their platform will become the Eighteenth Amendment to the Constitution in 1919.*

*Gold-embossed lithographed campaign postcards.*

*Cardboard campaign fan listing the Presidents of the United States with Bryan and Taft within the question marks.*

*Castiron Democratic donkey and Republican elephant with celluloid portrait inserts. By 1908, the donkey had replaced the rooster as the Democratic party symbol.*

**1912**

48 STATES
IN THE UNION

*DEMOCRAT*

# Woodrow Wilson

ELECTORAL VOTE 435, POPULAR VOTE 41.9%

PROGRESSIVE

# Theodore Roosevelt

ELECTORAL VOTE 88, POPULAR VOTE 27.4%

REPUBLICAN

# William H. Taft

ELECTORAL VOTE 8, POPULAR VOTE 23.2%

SOCIALIST

# Eugene V. Debs

ELECTORAL VOTE 0, POPULAR VOTE 6.0%

PROHIBITION

# Eugene W. Chafin

ELECTORAL VOTE 0, POPULAR VOTE 1.47%

AUGUST HECKSCHER
is director emeritus of the Twentieth Century
Fund and has recently published a biography of
Woodrow Wilson. Other books of his include
*The Public Happiness* (1961); *When LaGuardia
Was Mayor* (1978); and *Open Spaces:
The Life of American Cities* (1977).

The campaign of 1912 was to be the stage for a great debate between the two towering political figures of the time—Theodore Roosevelt and Woodrow Wilson. It was to be the stage where the form and spirit of progressivism were defined. Not least, it was to be the arena where many of the techniques of modern political campaigning revealed themselves. All this came about through such mysterious and unanticipated events as make the study of American politics endlessly absorbing.

Four years earlier the Roosevelt-Wilson confrontation was as remote a possibility as might have been readily conceived. After two terms in the White House Roosevelt in 1908 renounced the opportunity to run again, making William Howard Taft, his hand-picked candidate and close friend, his successor. Wilson was still president of Princeton University. That Wilson would become a spectacularly successful governor of New Jersey, and that Roosevelt would come to a bitter break with Taft, defied prophecy.

By the spring of 1912 Wilson had emerged as an intriguing national figure, but by no means an obvious choice of the national nominating convention. At Baltimore his chief rival, Champ Clark, gained a majority of the votes; then in frenzied scenes Wilson climbed, ballot by suspenseful ballot, until on the forty-sixth roll call he gained the two-thirds majority required for the nomination. The Republicans' choice of Taft a week earlier had played a major role in making it seem expedient to Democratic strategists that they name their most dynamic and liberal candidate. The choice of Taft had also stimulated Roosevelt to enter the race as the nominee of the soon-to-be-formed Progressive party.

The Democratic convention had been turbulent, with popular opinion making itself felt at every turn. Pro-Wilson crowds in the galleries played almost as important a role—and made almost as much noise—as delegates on the floor. As with the nomination of Wendell Willkie a generation later, telegrams from an aroused and sympathetic public arrived by the thousands, the overwhelming majority in favor of the apparent underdog and outsider. The direct impact of the populace, embodied in the new presidential primaries, carried over into the convention, and played a part in Wilson's nomination.

The Chicago convention, which met in August to found the Progressive party and to anoint Roosevelt as its candidate, also provided wild scenes but with a different and unique character. It took its tone in part from the Roosevelt saga—the tradition of big-game hunting and of the Rough Riders—and in part from religious fervor. Roosevelt may have ached to battle like a Bull Moose, but most of his followers were more inclined to sing "Onward Christian Soldiers." The candidate bridged the gap (at least temporarily) by making his address to the convention a "Confession of Faith." A stirring appeal to the progressive spirit, it

Woodrow Wilson was elected governor of New Jersey in 1910. A political scientist and lawyer, he was the first nonclerical president of Princeton University (1902–1910).

FOR GOVERNOR

WOODROW WILSON

struck the characteristically Rooseveltian note of heroic and self-sacrificing leadership.

In the following three-cornered campaign (the nomination of Eugene V. Debs by the Socialist party was not at the time considered politically important) the Republican candidate quickly faded from view. Taft had disliked being President; he referred to his administration as "humdrum" and in private letters wondered why anyone should want to vote for him. His wife was ailing; Archie Butt, his trusted confidante, had recently died; and the break with Roosevelt both saddened and embittered him. An unreconstructed conservative, Taft found himself out of tune with the people's mood. He did not campaign actively, and the immense advantage of being an incumbent he was unable to make count, being both inept politically and

generally unpopular. He delivered an acceptance address and then withdrew from active campaigning. The field was left to Roosevelt and Wilson, as the fates no doubt had intended all along that it should be.

The debate between these two charismatic figures was slow in finding its central theme. Before starting on the campaign trail, Roosevelt had to get his new party organized. Wilson had a number of political chores to put out of the way. The problem of a campaign manager was particularly sensitive. The temperamental and ailing William F. McCombs had been his manager at Baltimore, yet seemed a poor choice for the larger challenge. Fearful of being charged with ingratitude, Wilson reluctantly stood by McCombs. The candidate also had scores to settle with the New York and New Jersey bosses, and a party to heal after the disruptions of Baltimore. Lingering at Sea Girt, the official residence of New Jersey governors, Wilson received delegations, delivered his acceptance address (in those days it was still the custom to await formal notification by messengers that might as well have come on horseback), and cleared his mind with regard to campaign issues.

In his primary campaigns Wilson had talked frequently about the trusts, but his policy in regard to them remained vague. In general he favored a legalistic approach, defining abuses and holding individuals responsible for misconduct. This seemed a pale remedy in comparison to the outright policing of big business long advocated by Roosevelt. A meeting with the noted liberal lawyer, Louis D. Brandeis, late in September at Sea Girt, changed all this. Brandeis expounded to Wilson the concept of a regulated market, one that would ensure competition even among large organizations. From Wilson's point of view this had the immense advantage of eliminating the necessity for a powerful governmental commission—of big government set up as a counterweight to big business. To establish by political intervention the conditions of a free market, and then to let businesses compete within that market, seemed to him the solution in accord with all his political predispositions. At Buffalo three days later, in an effective speech which opened his campaign, Wilson showed how much he had profited from the meeting with Brandeis.

This revised approach to the trusts issue formed the basis of Wilson's New Freedom; as Roosevelt's approach formed the basis of the New Nationalism. Between these two neatly packaged slogans, encompassing two opposed and meaningful concepts, the lines of the great argument were drawn. As that argument was spun out in campaign addresses, the vision of the two candidates went well beyond the issue of the trusts. The New Nationalism was set in relation to Roosevelt's whole approach to government, with its vigorous, unembarrassed use of power to achieve social as well as economic justice. The New Freedom became related to Wilson's ideal of a social order where the emphasis was upon those in the midst of the battle, men on the make, struggling toward the light; and where the aim of politics was to give them a fair field and mitigation of the worst of industrial ills.

In setting forth their disparate messages each candidate had his own style. Roosevelt's was abrupt, staccato, often shrill. He was not an orator in any traditional sense—Wilson he derided for his "empty locution,"

Representatives of the Democratic National Committee officially informed Wilson that the convention had nominated him for President. This notification ceremony took place at Wilson's Sea Girt, New Jersey, home on August 7, 1912.

*Postcard circa 1911–1912. Strife in Republican ranks broke into open warfare in 1910. Beginning in August, Roosevelt publicized his differences with President Taft. Some Republican clubs urged that Roosevelt receive the 1912 Republican nomination.*

he cared little about wooing his audiences, rather taking them by assault and startling them into recognition. He admitted to a "certain lack of sequitur that I do not seem able to get rid of." Yet his phrases, often cliches, stuck in the mind and seemed to be the essence of the man. "I try to put the whole truth in one sentence," he explained; a-gain: "find the phrases the newspapers will quote, and you can get your message across."

In this way Roosevelt was getting very close to the "sound bite" of today's television; with him, one recent scholar asserts, "we stand at the edge of the advertised politics of the late twentieth century."

Wilson's way of imparting his message was very different. From youth he had trained himself in the art of public speaking. He, too, despised oratory—the bombast of the spellbinder or the harangue from the stump. He cultivated the style of the great parliamentarians, conversational in tone, free of gestures, and addressed directly, it appeared, to each individual in his audience. His words—spoken extemporaneously (his speeches, he told reporters, "come right out of my mind as it is working at the time")—flowed seamlessly from a bottomless reserve, moving from the simplest discourse to highly colored, imaginative flights.

In the campaign of 1912 he dealt in simple terms with the more technical aspects of the tariff or the trusts: "My dream of politics, all my life," he said, "has been that it is the common business, that it is something we owe it to each other to understand." But this did not preclude passages of striking eloquence. Of William Pitt he had written when still a student at Princeton that his "imagination was powerful enough to invest

all plans of national policy with a poetic charm." The later Wilson was not devoid of this gift.

To reach the public they hoped to persuade the candidates were put to tests that even Roosevelt, the Bull Moose, was not always up to. After the summer of preparation the two criss-crossed the country by train, making three or four major speeches a day, often an hour or more in length, in conditions that seemed designed to defeat all attempts at rational discussion. They spoke in ball parks, on race tracks, at country fairs; in opera houses, in huge convention halls, sometimes before audiences as large as thirty thousand—all this without any means of amplifying the human voice.

Once back on the train, they found that a schedule of frequent stops brought more calls for speeches. Particularly disliking these rear platform appearances, Wilson demurred good humoredly. "This is the kind of platform that I don't like to stand on," he advised one waiting crowd. "It moves around and shifts its ground too often. I like a platform that stays put." Then he would embark

*1908 poster. An artist's blend of Roosevelt and Taft likenesses. By 1912, clear lines were drawn, forever distinguishing the two candidates.*

on an argument, and as often as not be cut short when the train whistled and started off.

Roosevelt's simplified appeal and bombastic speaking style seemed to get across better in such conditions. But Roosevelt was troubled by the kind of audiences he was drawing and by some of the manifestations of their enthusiasm. He had declared himself ready to stand at Armageddon and to battle for the Lord; but he was at bottom the self-disciplined patrician who mistrusted emotionalism and extremists of any kind. He had spoken of the "lunatic fringe" that surrounds efforts at reform; he had taken from Bunyan the epithet "muckraker" for those who saw more political corruption than he was prepared to take account of. Later he would look back upon the Progressive party as a home for the "cranks" of his day. The fevered demonstrations that greeted him, the hymn-singing, the display of bandanas, cowboy hats, banners, and cam-

paign buttons was disconcerting to one who, for all his flamboyance, was trying to speak seriously to the people.

In Roosevelt's advocacy of the New Nationalism there was more than a touch of Alexander Hamilton. Wilson, by contrast, wore the mantle of Jeffersonianism. The New Freedom was constructed on belief in the common man, and the candidate himself, in his patient, low-keyed approach to campaigning, in his emphasis upon lucid argument and rational appeals, bore something of the earlier Democrat's stamp. But Wilson's message, like that of his adversary, was almost drowned out by the fervor of the mass audiences. He had difficulty in making himself heard; he was in competition with brass bands and unruly demonstrators; he suffered from faulty acoustics in the halls where he spoke.

In an early speech, arguing in favor of the common man's ascendancy, Wilson let slip the assertion that "the history of liberty is a history of the limitation of governmental power, not the increase of it." Roosevelt saw this as proof that Wilson was not the progressive he pretended to be; in speech after speech he denounced what he considered an academic reversion to *laissez-faire*. Having found his issue, Roosevelt pounded upon it mercilessly. Repetition became a technique that later presidential campaigners would also use to their advantage. Yet if his charge was misleading and based upon a sentence taken out of contest, it was not a fair sample of the campaign as a whole, which was singularly free from personal attacks or unfair innuendoes.

Toward his rival Wilson adopted an attitude of jaunty defiance. The Bull Moose party was made up of "the irregular Republicans, the variegated Republicans," he said in one campaign speech; Roosevelt would, if elected, be a lonely man, but perhaps that did not matter since "he finds himself rather good company." Roosevelt was not moved by the extreme personal animosity he later felt toward Wilson. He was an able man, he wrote privately at the time, who would probably serve creditably if elected; indeed Roosevelt expressed some doubt as to whether he should be running against him. It was as if he had a certain fascination with this new type of adversary. "It was Wilson, Wilson, Wilson all the time in the private car," recalled one of Roosevelt's press aides.

By mid-October both candidates were feeling the strain of the long debate. Roosevelt's voice, never robust, was beginning to fail; Wilson referred to his own "impaired voice"—impaired, he told one crowd, "in your service." Both men needed a rest, and on October 14 the event occurred that dramatically changed the course of the campaign. Outside his hotel in Milwaukee, on his way to deliver a speech at the municipal auditorium, Roosevelt was shot by a fanatic; he narrowly escaped death, the bullet being deflected by his eyeglass case and the bulky manuscript of his speech. Roosevelt spent the next ten days in the hospital; Wilson, in Princeton, waited out his opponent's recovery.

Roosevelt's bravura performance immediately after the shooting underscored his innate bravery and the almost mythic quality of his leadership. He asked that his assailant be treated without violence; then he proceeded to the auditorium where he spoke to a hushed audience. "Friends," he began, "I shall have to ask you to be as quiet as possible. . . . I have been shot . . . the bullet is in me now [showing the location of the wound] so that I cannot make a very long speech. . . . I can tell you with absolute truthfulness," he continued, "that I am very much uninterested in whether I am shot or not." His speech lasted more than an hour, mixing familiar themes with exalted appeals for heroism.

It was questioned whether the shooting might not create a large sympathy vote for Roosevelt. But by then Wilson was clearly leading in the three-cornered race, and it was only left to close down the campaign with the customary ritual of mass rallies in the East, especially at the Madison Square Garden in New York. On the climactic occasion Wilson was cheered for seventy minutes, more than twenty minutes longer than Roosevelt had been on his dramatic reappearance the previous night. Clearly moved, Wilson said afterwards he forgot what he had planned to say, but he managed well enough to please the crowd, and victory was in the air.

The results, when they became known, showed Wilson to have a sweeping electoral victory—435 votes with only 88 for Roosevelt and 8 (Vermont and Utah) for the hapless Taft. But the popular vote told a different story. Wilson failed to get a majority, polling fewer votes than Roosevelt and Taft together. For reasons still obscure, after a campaign devoted mostly to invocations of Marx and praise of socialism, Debs polled nearly a million votes. Roosevelt retired to lick his wounds, and Wilson toiled for another four years before a remarkable personal victory gave him the popular majority that had eluded him in 1912.

1912 Progressive party cotton bandanna with legend
"WE WANT OUR TEDDY BACK/BORN IN 1912."
The Progressive party was nicknamed the Bull Moose
party after one of Roosevelt's favorite sayings
"I am as strong as a bull moose."

Novelty postcards with springs for tails. These were
sold during the 1912 campaign. A symbol of
Roosevelt's Progressive party was the bull moose.

Campaign ribbons from each of
the three major parties in 1912.

1912 celluloid buttons. Roosevelt
chose Hiram Johnson, a progressive Republican
senator from California, as his running mate.

ROOSEVELT

PROGRESSIVE
CONVENTION

LINCOLN, NEBR.
September 3, 1912

*Silk ribbon with Roosevelt photograph. On August 5, 1912, the Progressive party met in a national convention in Chicago and nominated Roosevelt. Throughout the next month, state conventions ratified the choice.*

*Selection of Roosevelt celluloid buttons with "Hat in the Ring" imagery. Many pins, postcards, and buttons celebrated this statement made when he declared his third-party candidacy.*

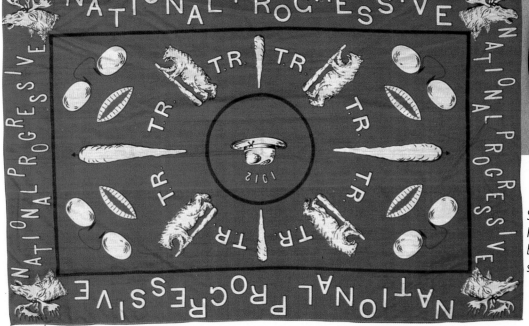

*Silk bandanna with symbols reflecting Roosevelt's extraordinary charisma— bull moose, bear, big stick, toothy smile, spectacles, hat in the ring.*

Roosevelt and Johnson

VOTE THE FULL ROOSEVELT

BULL MOOSE TICKET

THE ONLY REAL ROOSEVELT TICKET IN LANCASTER COUNTY

THE WINNER

AMERICA DEMANDS HIM

ROOSEVELT THE AMERICAN

"For there is neither East nor West,
Border nor Breed nor Birth,
When two strong men stand face to face
Though they come from the ends of the earth."
—Kipling

*Items from the
1912 Progressive (Bull
Moose) campaign.
Above left: Roosevelt
campaign buttons.
Above right: Poster of
Roosevelt and Johnson with
stirring Kipling quotation.
Right: Paper certificate given
for a $10 party contribution.*

PROGRESSIVE PARTY

"PASS PROSPERITY AROUND"

FOUNDERS' CERTIFICATE
1912 CAMPAIGN

ISSUED TO

THEODORE ROOSEVELT

HIRAM W. JOHNSON

THIS IS A RECEIPT FOR TEN DOLLARS CONTRIBUTED TO THE
CAMPAIGN FUND OF THE PROGRESSIVE PARTY. IT IS NOT
TRANSFERABLE, AND IS GENUINE ONLY WHEN COUNTERSIGNED

NATIONAL TREASURER

Group of celluloid buttons issued by the 1912 Progressive party. Roosevelt's followers used "Onward Christian Soldiers" as their campaign song and acted as crusaders in a national religious revival.

THE TEDDY SIDEWISE GLANCE MAKES THE POLITICAL BOSSES DANCE TO DO THIS LITTLE STUNT, MAKE HIS EYES LOOK STRAIGHT IN FRONT THEN YOU VOTE AND I'LL VOTE AND WITH OTHER VOTES GALORE WE'LL LAND THE BULL MOOSE PRESIDENT WITHIN THE WHITE HOUSE DOOR

PATENTS JUNE, 1908.

Lithographed tin game. The directions read: "The Teddy sidewise glance makes the political bosses dance. To do this little stunt, make his eyes look straight in front. Then you vote and I'll vote and with other votes galore we'll land the bull moose President within the White House door."

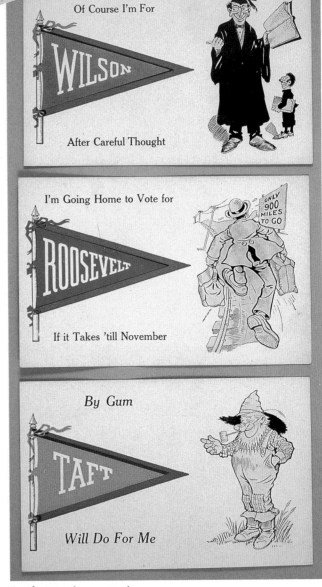

Above: Cotton pennant with a portrait of Wilson.
Right: Sized cotton banner with a portrait of Taft encircled by an oak wreath.

Set of pennant theme postcards.

Wilson postcard using rowboat motif for "Wood-Row" wordplay. Roosevelt struggles to catch up to a relaxed Wilson in the race to the White House. Taft flails behind.

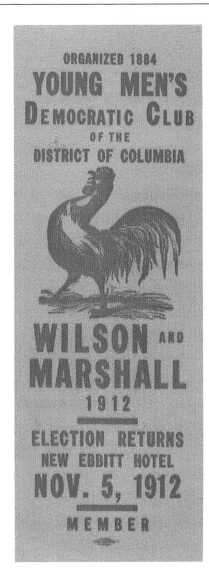

Woodrow Wilson items.
Wilson, as President,
supported women's suffrage.
Left: Menu card for inaugural
evening dinner given by
Wilson's 1879 Princeton
classmates. The tiger is
Princeton's symbol.

★

**1916**

48 STATES
IN THE UNION

*DEMOCRAT*

## Woodrow Wilson

ELECTORAL VOTE 277, POPULAR VOTE 49.4%

REPUBLICAN

## Charles E. Hughes

ELECTORAL VOTE 254, POPULAR VOTE 46.2%

SOCIALIST

## A.L. Benson

ELECTORAL VOTE 0, POPULAR VOTE 3.2%

PROHIBITION

## J. Frank Hanly

ELECTORAL VOTE 0, POPULAR VOTE 1.2%

AUGUST HECKSCHER
is director emeritus of the Twentieth Century
Fund and has recently published a biography of
Woodrow Wilson. Other books of his include
*The Public Happiness* (1961); *When LaGuardia
Was Mayor* (1978); and *Open Spaces:
The Life of American Cities* (1977).

By the spring of 1916 it was clear, at least on the Democratic side, *who* was to run. Woodrow Wilson had had doubts about a second term; after the death of his wife in August 1914, he passed through a period of depression when it hardly seemed to him worthwhile to carry on. But his marriage to Edith Bolling Galt sixteen months later removed all uncertainty from his mind. A tour of the Midwest on behalf of his defense program, undertaken in the early winter of 1916, confirmed his skill as a campaigner, and by spring he was prepared to head off any competition that might arise. When the Democratic convention gathered at St. Louis on June 14, it was Wilson's show, orchestrated by himself and his chief aides.

With the Republicans the situation was very different. No available candidate seemed capable of unifying the party's divergent factions. Theodore Roosevelt was an obvious, if controversial, choice. Already aging, his aura of progressivism tarnished as his militarism increased, he could promise an exciting battle but not the unity essential to victory. Assuring the party chieftains that he would not campaign for the nomination, he nevertheless did so, and he arrived at the convention in fighting form.

Who could be brought in to oppose him? Elihu Root, ex-secretary of state, was too old and too conservative even for the Republican bosses. The name of Charles Evans Hughes beckoned tantalizingly. Twice elected governor of New York State, he had led a reform program as dramatic as Wilson's in New Jersey. He was a man of brilliance, of unimpeachable integrity, immensely dignified in public, and in private said to be humorous and companionable. He alone seemed capable of healing the breach of 1912.

But Hughes was a justice of the Supreme Court. Appointed in 1910, he was finding a happy refuge from the politics he disliked and was fully enjoying the bench's intellectual and collegial life. As leader of the Court's liberal minority, he was, moreover, playing an important national role. He had no intention of giving it up. As pressures mounted through 1916 his mood grew from one of indifference to irritation. No major party had ever looked to the Supreme Court for its candidate; many good reasons—as the justice well knew—could be adduced for not doing so. Hughes maintained an unbroken public silence, and when he received the nomination on the third ballot at Chicago, the convention delegates did not know whether he would accept; or whether, if he did, Roosevelt would run against him.

A message to the convention, following a one-sentence letter of resignation, to Wilson (who found it unnecessarily terse), answered the first question. Roosevelt's course was more problematical. The Progressive party met and named him their candidate; he turned them down and promised to support Hughes. Embittered, he wrote privately that small parties "are a natural prey of cranks with a moral twist" (as if he had not led the Progressives four years previously!),

*Celluloid button. At the outbreak of World War I (1914), Roosevelt favored the Allies and criticized Wilson's neutrality policy.*

and gave himself to the sole cause of defeating the hated incumbent.

Hughes was determined to make Americanism his battle cry. So, as a matter of fact, were the Democrats. The scenario of the Democratic convention was carefully prepared to celebrate the American flag, to recapture the cause of patriotism from the Republicans, and to name Wilson in a blaze of nationalist fervor. On the eve of the convention, Flag Day was declared a holiday in Washington. The President (carrying a flag, of course) walked at the head of a five-hour march. He also made a rather dreadful speech, saying that "disloyalty" was active in the United States and that "it must be crushed."

Events at the convention changed the tune. To their confusion the party chiefs saw the delegates take matters into their own hands and reveal the cause of peace to be their overarching concern. The keynote speaker, ex-Governor Martin H. Glynn of Ohio, was heard in relative silence as he rehearsed accomplishments of the Wilson administration and expounded—as he had been instructed to do—the theme of Americanism. But when he spoke of the Pres-

ident's having preserved peace despite massive provocations, pandemonium broke loose. The next day the chairman of the convention, Senator Ollie James of Kentucky, took up the argument and in memorable sentences set the assemblage on fire. The Democratic party had found itself; it had also found its campaign slogan. "He kept us out of War" was to be emblazoned on banners at every Democratic rally; the words were to become the staple of impassioned Democratic orators.

In the White House, following the convention over the telegraph wire, Wilson pondered these events. In due course he would himself make powerful use of the peace sentiment revealed at St. Louis.

The contest ahead did not give promise of being relevant or enlightening. "It is a year," wrote Walter Lippmann in the *New Republic*, "in which the harlot words which serve any cause are to walk the street." Peace and Prosperity, Defense without Militarism, American Rights, American Honor—catchwords like these satisfied "almost everyone's fervent desire to proclaim his adhesion to ideas which almost nobody can dispute." The irrepressible Mr. Dooley declared that what was coming was not an election; it was "a contest in unpopularity." The two candidates were as far apart as the North and South poles, he said—and as similar.

Yet matters did not unfold in quite the expected way. Hughes managed to provide drama by his capacity to be more dull, querulous, and legalistic than even his opponents had anticipated. What had happened to a man so greatly admired, so intellectually acute and politically experienced, was the mystery of the campaign. His efforts

One of a poster series satirizing topical issues. On an expedition to Brazil in 1914, Roosevelt explored and mapped the "River of Doubt," now named Rio Teodoro in his honor.

to make certain that no one liked Wilson caused him to be the less likable himself. For a broad critique of the administration, for which he might have been thought ideally qualified, Hughes substituted a lawyer's pettifogging attacks.

Beside his understandable need to straddle, and his all-too recent reemergence onto the political scene, Hughes was handicapped by a basic misconception about the nature of campaigning and of the American political system. In his opening address at Carnegie Hall he described his ideal as "America the efficient." (Theodore Roosevelt sat in a box that night, keeping his own thoughts to himself.) A sympathetic reporter who traveled with Hughes on the first western tour wrote that the emphasis of the speeches was on "efficiency, economy and a budget system, the businesslike administration of government, the expert, the overthrow of the spoils system, a scientific tariff."

Toward the close of the campaign the Republican candidate issued a statement revealing what, from the start, had been his fatal misconception. His idea of the presidency, he declared, differed absolutely from Mr. Wilson's. "I look upon the President as the administrative head of the government. He looks upon the President as primarily the political leader and lawmaker of the nation." No wonder, seeing the office in this light, Hughes appeared pinched and chill; while his opponent was expanding with a natural eloquence upon large popular issues.

Both men spoke extemporaneously, to the confusion of the press but to the benefit of their immediate hearers. Hughes was "a vigorous stump speaker," Charles Eliot, the Harvard president, described him "but with-

Postcard of Hughes and his wife on a cross-country tour. This stop was at Spokane, Washington, on the Northern Pacific Yellowstone Park Line.

out charm." Wilson had not studied in vain from youth how to reach and move men by the spoken word. His speeches through the 1916 campaign often appear unstudied, but they ranged over the big questions and for the most part transcended the catchwords of the time.

The sound of the two candidates voices can be heard in almost any two parallel quotations that might be picked. Here is Hughes declaring his concern for international issues—precise, careful in phrasing, and deadly dull:

> If at the close of the present war the nations are ready to undertake practical measures in the common interest in order to secure international justice, we cannot fail to recognize our international duty.

Here is Wilson on the same subject— vague, but with a cadence touching the imagination:

> In the days to come men will no longer wonder how America is going to work out her destiny, for she will have proclaimed to them that her destiny is not divided from the destiny of the world, that her purpose is justice and love of mankind.

As in all campaigns, but with more need for it in this than in most, efforts were made to humanize the candidates. Hughes, whom Roosevelt had called "the bearded iceberg," was taken in hand, with results that must have made the candidate cringe. His physique was described in glowing terms. He was "tall and splendidly set, with a full powerful face and a massive forehead," according to the Roosevelt-dominated *Outlook*; he had "a splendid chest and back, great arms and legs"—and all this was crowned by "a well-trimmed beard which adds dignity and strength." His conduct was described as the opposite of austere and cold. On the first western tour almost his first act was to leap from his railroad car onto the concrete roof of the players' house at the Chicago ball park, shaking hands with both teams and chatting with Ty Cobb.

The public was informed that, at a typical campaign stop on the westward trek, the candidate gazed sympathetically forth across a sea of flags "upon the big, husky fellows . . . the cowboys and the girls, upon the little folks on big horses." Mrs. Hughes, one of the first candidate's wives to accompany her husband, represented "the power and the glory of American home life." Together they "coddled" Indian babies—"and the babies cried, and the crowds laughed and cheered."

Wilson, also, had his image problem. He was thought to be cold; at the same time gossip condemned him as a womanizer. These twofold charges were countered by articles solicited by the President's friends. One, in the *New York Times*, was written by the brother of the President's deceased wife, Stockton Axson, who told admiringly of a simple and ardently affectionate home life. Vetted by Colonel House so as to eliminate its more sentimental passages, the piece was effective as campaign literature. In addition, the noted journalist Ida Tarbell was granted a presidential interview which enabled her to paint for *Collier's* a sympathetic portrait of the private man.

Hughes's way of running for President was, first, to shake off the residues of judicial preoccupations. "He assembled stacks of magazines," his biographer tells us, "newspapers, reports, and the *Congressional Record* and crammed for his campaigning ordeal." Wilson's way was, of necessity, to continue to run the country. The spring and summer of 1916 were crowded with

events, both domestic and foreign. The British were interfering with U.S. shipping in ways reminiscent of 1812, provoking on the part of the President an hostility hardly less than that which he felt toward the Germans. The punitive expedition into Mexico, led by General Pershing against Pancho Villa, had barely been concluded. But the most absorbing event and the one having the most direct impact on the campaign, was a threatened railroad strike.

A strike in that railway age would have been catastrophic for the nation's economy. Through July and early August the labor leaders and the railway presidents dragged out bitter and fruitless discussions; then on August 17, Wilson summoned the parties to the White House. After listening to irreconcilable claims, he took it upon himself to propose terms of settlement, the *sine qua non* of which was the establishment in the railway industry of the eight-hour day. On the basis of this proposal the strike was called off. The so-called Adamson Law, embodying the eight-hour day, was quickly passed.

Paper blotter for Hughes "Who Will Blot Out THE PAST FOUR YEARS." Hughes's campaign items were nonthematic in an attempt to reunite the conservative and progressive factions of the Republican party.

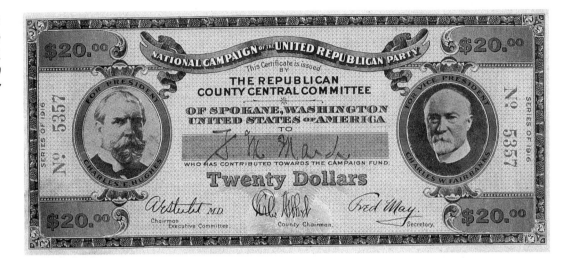

The coup caused consternation among both Republicans and Democrats. Hughes now had an issue, and he pounded at it remorselessly. Wilson had a cause. From his summer residence at Shadow Lawn, New Jersey, he announced in a fighting campaign speech that the eight-hour day was sanctioned by "the judgment of society" and urged that it be extended to all industry. The more conservative of Wilson supporters were appalled. At the campaign headquarters in New York contributions dropped off almost completely. A loan of $30,000 was necessary in order to keep the campaign going.

While Hughes stumped the country, Wilson lingered at Shadow Lawn, dealing with national problems and making more or less regular political addresses. He was not eager to get out on the campaign trail. "I think it is a certain impropriety for the President to campaign," Wilson told the newspapermen. He was responsible for the record; he was not the one to praise it. Indeed there was no method of campaigning by an incumbent, he said, that did not "more or less offend good taste." By Octo-

ber—prodded by a disturbing Republican victory in Maine—he overcame these scruples. From then until election day Wilson was energetically upon the hustings.

The object of campaigning was, for each side, to get as many as possible of the four million votes that had gone to the Progressives in 1912, plus a due share of the nearly four hundred thousand unexpected votes that had swung to the Socialist column. In the spring of 1916 Wilson had quietly put in place the foundations of a second New Freedom, emphasizing social justice and appropriating one plank after another of the earlier Progressive platform. Hughes could legitimately claim to be among progressives (with a small "p"); he was in favor —the Adamson law excepted—of virtually every advanced measure of social legislation. "I would not be here if I did not think of the Republican party as a liberal party," he stated frequently.

He came across to the voters, nevertheless, as a died-in-the-wool conservative. In the famous California incident, he showed to what extent he was tied to the right wing of his party. Entering the state when a primary contest for the Senate was in progress, he allowed himself to be shepherded about by the supporters of the Old Guard candidate; he spoke under their auspices, and completely neglected the Progressive leader, Governor Hiram Johnson, who had promised his support. It is not quite true, as legend has it, that Hughes "snubbed" Johnson by deliberately failing to greet him at a hotel where their paths crossed, yet he certainly gave the Progressive wing reason to feel offended.

Meanwhile Roosevelt, campaigning flamboyantly amid publicity normally reserved for a candidate, sought to bring his former supporters back into the Republican fold. The trouble was, he hated Wilson more than he cared for Hughes. Also, his increasing militancy scared the German vote. (Hughes was counting on this vote to swing the balance in industrial centers such as Milwaukee and Chicago, and until the very last days of the campaign he appeared to bend before it.) Roosevelt never did bridge the chasm separating him from former President Taft and from the latter's conservative followers. One encounter found a cold "William" shaking hands with a distant "Theodore." Republicans held for a day to the belief that the two men had at least slapped each other on the back. Even in this they were disappointed.

Gradually Wilson brought in a harvest of former Progressives. Walter Lippmann, Lincoln Steffens, Jane Addams, and John Dewey were among those who endorsed him. He was always strong with college students and had the support of outstanding literary figures.

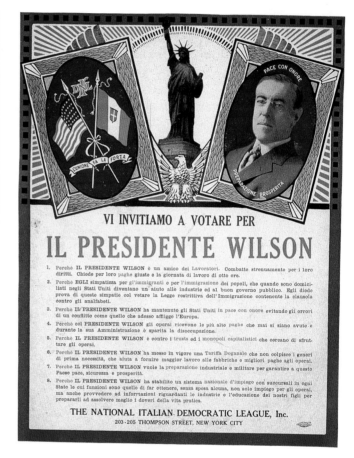

The opposing character of the two candidates showed itself in the financing of their respective contests. "The great mass of businessmen and bankers," writes Professor Arthur Link, "closed ranks and poured money into the Republican campaign." Precise figures are not known, but one careful investigation puts the amount at approximately $15 million—enormous for those days—with as much as $3 million going into New York State alone. The sum of $90,000 was said to have been spent on advertising in the foreign press. When Wilson came to New York City at the climax of his campaign, he was infuriated by the costly full-page advertisements

*1916 poster appealing to the ethnic Italian voter. Among Wilson's pledges is his support for Italian immigration and a European peace with honor.*

in the *New York Times* paid for by the Republican National Committee.

By contrast the Democrats limped along financially. Following the dearth caused by Wilson's advocacy of the eight-hour day, things picked up, largely because of contributions from old friends and supporters. Of these, Wilson's classmate, Cleveland H. Dodge, gave the most—$79,000 in honor of the Princeton class of '79. Thomas D. Jones, another generous contributor, had been a member of the pro-Wilson group on Princeton's board of trustees. The young Bernard Baruch gave $20,000. Wilson himself gave $2,500, and hundreds of small gifts were recorded, down to one penny donated anonymously. Up to October 26, 1916, the total Democratic war chest was reported as being $1,006,283 (at the end it reached $1.6 million)—plus, it must be presumed, the aforesaid one cent.

Wilson did not approve the slogan, "He kept us out of War," knowing too well how close he had brought the country to war with Mexico, and how precariously peace with Germany was being maintained. The disapproval did not prevent him from playing remorselessly upon the issue. If he did not claim that he was responsible for peace, he was more than ready to suggest that the Republicans would bring the country into war. As for the Democratic regulars, they cast off all restraints. A poster released toward the end of the campaign—the equivalent of a modern television commercial—showed a wartime scene of carnage with a mother and her children watching from the sidelines. "He has protected me and mine" was the inscription.

Hughes never fully grasped the full measure of the peace sentiment. His own program for defense and foreign policy was sufficiently vague to scare many people; besides, Roosevelt was beating something that sounded very much like a war drum. "While earnest," Hughes said of his co-campaigner, he proved to be "not altogether helpful."

To Hughes's credit, he was loath to make political capital out of inflammable incidents occurring during the campaign. The tense war situation provided plenty of fodder. In August the German U53, one of a new class of underwater giants, surfaced in the harbor of Newport, Rhode Island. The captain went calmly ashore, and in the next two days sank six Allied vessels. These bizarre and fearful actions were recognized as not being in violation of international law, and the Republicans withheld criticism of the President, confined as he was to summoning the German ambassador and delivering him a stiff lecture. Near the close of the campaign the British merchantman *Marina* was sunk with a loss of six American crewmen; again Hughes showed admirable restraint.

In the immemorial way of campaigns, foolish things were said and fantastic predictions of victory were made by both sides as the October days ran out. Hughes saw the issue of "Americanism" as giving him the edge; he promised "an American administration" with "exclusively American policies." Declaring that victory was "in sight," Wilson proclaimed that "certain gentlemen" would be deprived of the opportunity to drag America into war.

Lack of modern methods of polling intensified the impression of "ignorant armies" clashing by night. To be sure, there were always the betting odds to be consulted—omens issuing from the depth of Wall Street. These gave a steady lead to Hughes, ten to seven. Polls of various sorts, taken more or less at random, were telegraphed to the newspapers. On October 22 the *New York Times* reported that the Paris Millinery company in Kansas City favored Hughes 108 to 21; the Kansas Building favored Wilson 93 to to 19. A poll of Columbia University showed Hughes in the lead by two votes, 352 to 350. The *Literary Digest* had already embarked upon the path that would lead to the debacle of 1936. In 1916, instead of asking its subscribers for their preference, the *Digest* sought opinions as to the drift of sentiment in their localities.

The results in any case would perhaps have baffled the most scientific of today's pollsters. It was an exceedingly close election, but it was a not inaccurate reflection of the personal qualities and the campaign tactics of the two candidates.

Both candidates went to bed reasonably sure that Hughes had won. But California the next day reported a narrow Democratic victory and gave Wilson the election by 277 to 254 votes in the electoral college. His popular majority was small, but it represented a striking personal victory. He had polled almost three million more votes than in 1912. In almost every contest he had run ahead of the local Democratic candidates. Hughes carried most of the Northeast and the Midwest; Wilson the South and the West. Labor's vote was less united for the Democrats than had been anticipated, many workers in protected industries putting job security above the shorter working day. It had been the lawyer against the visionary—and the lawyer could do everything except touch the ultimate chord of popular feeling.

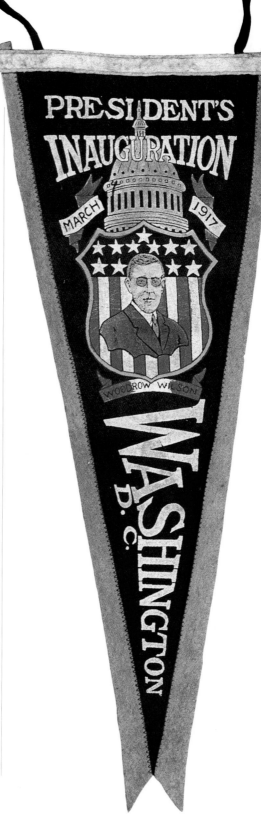

*Felt pennant commemorating Wilson's second inauguration, 1917.*

Tiffany & Co. bronze bust of Wilson.

*Wooden nautical wall plaque, circa 1917–1918.*

*Advertisement envelope for Long Branch, New Jersey. Thirteen gummed commemorative stamps were included in this promotional item.*

# Souvenir Wilson Notification Day

## Facts About The
# SUMMER CAPITAL CITY

A RESORT combining beauties of Ocean, Lakes, River and landscape scenery. Parks, Casino, Bluff-walk, Ocean Boulevard, Drives, Golf Links and Tennis Courts.
    Property values exceeding $16,000,000.
    Commission form of Government.
    5,000 acres of seashore property. Four miles of beach front 100 miles of attractive drives. Lowest tax rate of any New Jersey resort. Healthiest climate in America.
    Summer homes of General Grant, General Garfield, President Arthur, President McKinley, Vice President Hobart and President Wilson.
    Illustrated booklet on application.
        **MARSHALL WOOLLEY,** Mayor
Director of Department of Public Affairs, Long Branch, N. J.

SUMMER CAPITAL OF U. S. A.
LONG BRANCH, N. J.

# Long Branch, New Jersey--Sept. 2, 1916
This envelope contains 13 Summer White House Stamps.  Shadow Lawn was built 13 years ago.  13 is President
Wilson's Lucky Number.

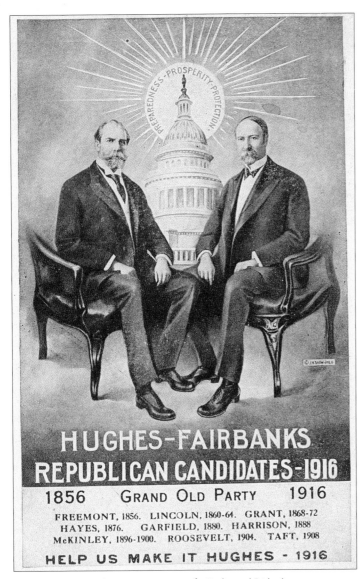

Sepiatoned celluloid button for
Hughes and Fairbanks.

Republican poster with the general campaign
slogan "PREPAREDNESS, PROTECTION, PROSPERITY."

Monochrome campaign poster for Hughes and Fairbanks.

Lithographed tin
pinback for Hughes.

★

Monochromatic Republican campaign portrait poster.

Silk woven ribbon. There are few examples of 1916 ribbons with Hughes's portrait.

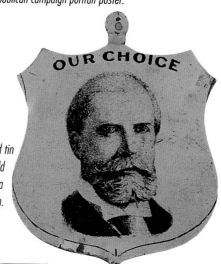

Lithographed tin lapel item held in place with a straight pin.

Massachusetts Republican campaign portrait poster.

Celluloid coin bank featuring Wilson and Marshall, measuring only 3½" in length.

Title page of the 1916 SOCIALIST HAND BOOK. Candidates Allen Benson and George Kirkpatrick received 3.2 percent of the popular vote.

Felt pennants of Wilson and his second wife, Edith, circa 1916. On September 25, 1919, while campaigning for the League of Nations, Wilson suffered a stroke. Until the end of his term, Mrs. Wilson controlled access to the President.

Figural caricature Toby mug. Wilson is flying an airplane. One of a set of similar items featuring Allied leaders.

# SOCIALIST HAND BOOK

FOR PRESIDENT

ALLEN L. BENSON

FOR VICE-PRESIDENT

GEORGE R KIRKPATRICK

## THE WORKERS' CANDIDATES

Not Backed by Wall Street or the War Trust

Price 10c.   50 Copies $3.25 Prepaid

PUBLISHED BY

THE SOCIALIST PARTY
803 W. Madison St.
CHICAGO

*Right: Several celluloid buttons from the 1916 campaign. Far right: Selection of 1916 delegate convention badges. Below: "WIN WITH WILSON" was the President's slogan.*

*Colorful pro-League of Nations sheet music.*

*Wilson-Pershing celluloid button.*

Between 1910 and 1920, a great
variety of ephemera appeared for
suffragette demonstrations and parades.
The item at right is a lithographed tin
window hanger in the form of a bluebird.

The campaign for giving
women the vote had a long
and hectic history
throughout the nineteenth
century. By 1914, eleven
states had amended their
constitutions to include
provisions for women's
suffrage. Suffragette
leaders began a campaign
for the adoption of a
national constitutional
amendment, which Wilson
supported. In June 1919,
Congress approved the
amendment and in August
1920, enough states
ratified what became the
Nineteenth Amendment to
the Constitution.

A variety of colorful items advocating women's suffrage appeared between 1910 and 1920, including sheet music, posters, buttons, china, pennants, sashes, and pamphlets.

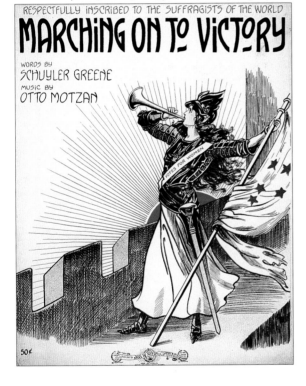

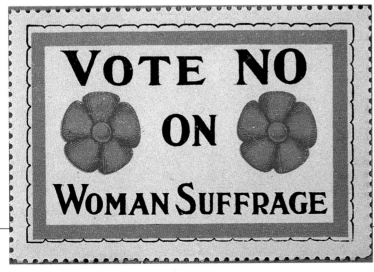

Gum-backed sticker opposing giving women the vote.

## 1920
### 48 STATES
### IN THE UNION

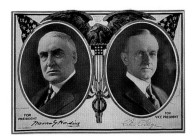

### *REPUBLICAN*
# Warren G. Harding
ELECTORAL VOTE 404, POPULAR VOTE 60.4%

### DEMOCRAT
# James M. Cox
ELECTORAL VOTE 127, POPULAR VOTE 34.2%

### SOCIALIST
# Eugene V. Debs
ELECTORAL VOTE 0, POPULAR VOTE 3.4%

### FARMER-LABOR
# P.P. Christensen
ELECTORAL VOTE 0, POPULAR VOTE 1.0%

DONALD R. McCOY
is University Distinguished Professor of
History at the University of Kansas. He is
the author of many works, including *Calvin
Coolidge: The Quiet President* (1967); *Coming of
Age: The United States During the 1920's and
1930's* (1973); *Landon of Kansas* (1966);
and *The Presidency of Harry S. Truman* (1984).

The presidential election of 1920 was not, as it has often been described, a turning-point at which America's voters repudiated pre-World War I progressivism and the League of Nations. Progressivism had died during the war, and there had been little interest in resurrecting it after 1918; in 1919 and 1920 the Senate had rejected the Treaty of Versailles with its provisions for the League. Moreover, new issues arose with great force during the 1920 election campaign. Among these were the high cost of living, high taxes and federal spending, labor-management antagonisms, immigration, and concerns relating to women and veterans. Perhaps the overall issue was President Woodrow Wilson, who was widely blamed for having failed to meet these issues and identified as the League's uncompromising champion. He was also seen by ethnic groups as having been severe with Germany and German-Americans and having refused to support Irish aspirations for independence and Italian territorial claims.

General Leonard Wood, Senator Hiram Johnson of California, and Illinois Governor Frank Lowden, scenting a sure Republican victory in November, waged expensive campaigns for the nomination. They were joined by a squad of dark-horse candidates, the most promising of whom was Senator Warren G. Harding of Ohio. The Democratic candidates for presidential nomination were more subdued, largely because of the possibility that Woodrow Wilson would seek reelection. Only Attorney General A. Mitchell Palmer conducted a high-paced campaign for nomination, although less visible efforts were made on behalf of Wilson's son-in-law, Treasury Secretary William Gibbs McAdoo, and Ohio Governor James M. Cox. There were also favorite-son contenders.

The Democratic and Republican conventions in 1920 had much in common. Not only were there numerous candidates for their nominations, but both conventions were unusually long and produced remarkably detailed platforms. An irony was that both platforms avoided one important issue, the prohibition of commerce in alcoholic beverages. The platforms were in principle often much the same. The great exception was on the most publicized issue of 1920, the League of Nations, which the Democrats wanted America to join; the Republicans vowed that they were for some international association to maintain peace, but not if it would impair the nation's freedom of action. The conventions also resembled each other in that they nominated none of the front-runners. Instead the Republicans and the Democrats chose, respectively, Senator Harding and Governor Cox, both Ohio newspaper publishers. The conventions quickly selected their vice presidential nominees, the Republicans Governor Calvin Coolidge of Massachusetts and the Democrats Assistant Secretary of the Navy Franklin D. Roosevelt.

There was also an abundance of third-party presidential nominees in 1920, representing the American, Farmer-Labor, Prohibition, Socialist, and Socialist-Labor parties.

Only the Socialist nominee, Eugene V. Debs, who had earlier run for President four times, was well known. His campaign was distinguished by his residence in the Atlanta federal penitentiary as a result of his conviction for violation of the Espionage Act. Debs was restricted in his campaigning to one five-hundred-word public statement weekly. This was enough to attract 919,799 votes for the Socialist party. The other minor party nominees together polled only 534,534 votes.

The Democratic and Republican presidential campaigns of 1920 are often interpreted as having been rather traditional. In many ways they were. Yet the Democrats gave their vice presidential nominee an unusually large campaign role. The Republicans pioneered in offering the first coordinated public relations packaging of a presidential nominee and his campaign.

The campaign organization of the two major parties differed greatly. The Democratic organization had been very effective during Wilson's winning campaigns in 1912 and 1916. Moreover, the Democrats had succeeded under National Committee Chairman Homer Cummings in extinguishing their 1916 campaign deficit. But Wilson's call for Cummings's reappointment encountered opposition on the Democratic National Committee, and Governor Cox felt forced to drop Cummings. Cox's astute personal campaign manager, Edmond Moore, was unacceptable to Wilson, largely because he opposed using the League of Nations as the prime campaign issue. George White, Moore's deputy, became the compromise choice to run the Democratic campaign. He proved to be a poor choice because of his limited experience in and talent for campaign management and fundraising.

By October 24 the Democrats had collected $695,000—only one quarter of the amount that had flowed into the Republican coffers. Indeed Democratic leaders had raised that much only because of their emergency efforts. These included publicizing a $500 contribution from Woodrow Wilson as part of a "Match the President" solicitation campaign. The Democrats employed many other traditional methods, including distributing campaign buttons, posters, press releases, and leaflets and making special appeals to women, foreign-born voters, and labor unions. Although Chairman White recruited 3,500 people to speak on behalf of Cox, much of this activity fell short because of inept organization, insufficient funds, and indifference among many voters to whom the Democrats appealed.

Consequently, the chief burden fell upon Cox and Roosevelt. The best use of funds probably was the financing of the nominees's far-flung tours. This included spending thirty thousand dollars to rent Cox's railroad train, including a print shop to facilitate the distribution of reading material en route. Cox and Roosevelt excited much public interest, but their mobility made coordination between them and Democratic national headquarters awkward. What the Democrats lacked in cash, they hoped to make up by enlisting campaign workers from the ranks of government employees and labor union members. These foot soldiers were, however, often less willing to serve than they had been in the past. One could hardly blame them, for the betting odds against Cox's election rose from two-to-one in July to as high as ten-to-one by November.

COX OR HARDING

"UNDER WHICH FLAG?"

REPRODUCED FROM "THE WORLD"
THE LEADING COX ORGAN

FROM "HARVEY'S WEEKLY"
SUPPORTER OF HARDING

*Poster suggesting Cox and the League of Nations are un-American. Although Cox strongly favored the League, he wavered on what amendments he might be willing to accept.*

The organization of the Republican campaign was far more effective. The Republicans retained their national committee chairman, Will Hays, who was a veteran political manager. Known as "Telephone Bill" for his effective use of that instrument, he was a diligent apostle of Republican unity. Hays was in charge of Republican finances, publicity, and organization, although he relied substantially on others in packaging the campaign, especially the advertising genius, Albert Lasker, and the talented publicist, Judson Welliver. Harding decided campaign strategy and issues, ably assisted by his nomination campaign manager, Harry Daugherty, and Hays and his forces. All this benefited from the fact that Hays had begun planning for the 1920 campaign a year before. The successes of the wartime Red Cross and government loan drives had not been lost on him. He established various national, state, and local campaign committees to solicit funds and generate publicity as well as to obtain information and advice. Every conceivable group of voters was appealed to for support.

Hays was unstinting in raising and spending money. The highest estimate of Republican campaign expenditures in 1920 was $8,100,739, compared to a high of $2,237,770 for the Democrats. With their funds the Republicans produced fifteen million campaign buttons, five million posters, fifteen million lithographs, three biographies of Harding, and a 496-page campaign textbook. They also financed the efforts of thousands of party speakers and other workers, including 2,000 women; issued pamphlets on 150 subjects as well as campaign movies and phonograph records; and regularly distributed press releases, advertising copy, and cartoons to newspapers and magazines. The Republicans spent $159,265 on billboards alone.

Cox-Roosevelt postcard. Democratic ephemera of all types is scarce for the 1920 and 1924 campaigns. Any item showing both Cox and running mate, Franklin D. Roosevelt, is highly valued.

The strategies employed in 1920 by the major party nominees were fairly simple. Harding presented himself as a dignified, amiable, unpretentious, and practical conciliator. He would not be a world-beater, nor would he rock the ship of state. Harding thought that most Americans would vote either their hates or their pocketbooks in 1920, and he was prepared to cater to both interests. Recognizing concern that he might be impetuous, he took pains to assure people that, as he wrote to one journalist, "nobody is going to make me lose my temper and indulge in impulsive utterances." The Ohio senator sought to be friendly to everyone, from business tycoons to working people. He especially courted the progressive Republicans who had left or who had had doubts about the party since 1912. Harding called himself a "rational progressive," and

he often complimented the late Theodore Roosevelt, calling him, for example, "the flag's bravest defender." Among those many individuals whom Harding wooed were Senator Hiram Johnson, a leading progressive opponent of the League of Nations and a man whom many blamed for the Republican loss of the 1916 presidential election because of a perceived snub, and former President William Howard Taft, a prominent conservative champion of the League. Harding was remarkably successful both in avoiding impetuosity and in courting people of various and often antagonistic backgrounds.

Cox's strategy was even simpler. He often emphasized high-minded over practical concerns, especially urging American membership in the League as mankind's best hope for enduring peace. Cox and the Democrats made much of Harding's appeals to people on both sides of the League issue. (Navy Secretary Josephus Daniels wittily described Harding's position by paraphrasing Theodore Roosevelt: "We stand at Armageddon and we straddle for the Lord.") An earlier part of Cox's strategy was to point with pride to his own and President Wilson's records in office. It soon became clear, though, that Cox's gubernatorial record was generally deemed irrelevant to the concerns of 1920 and that most voters did not admire Wilson. Cox campaigned assertively, which may have preserved much of his Democratic voting base. His Wilsonian moralizing and occasionally outrageous statements repelled many voters, however.

Cox and Harding set the tone for their campaigns during the ceremonies attendant upon the formal recognition, in their hometowns, of their nominations. On July 22 Harding gave his acceptance speech before two thousand people in Marion's Chautauqua Auditorium (thirty thousand others milled about outside). He was keenly aware, he said, of the awesome responsibilities of the presidency and of his own limitations, but faith in God and America would see him through. The effect, according to the journalist Mark Sullivan, was "exalted and moving," carried out in an "atmosphere usually associated with churches." On August 7 Cox, on foot, led a parade to Dayton's fairgrounds. There, in an aggressive acceptance address, he told 100,000 people that "this is no time for wabbling." Cox attacked the Republican platform as "so artfully phrased as to make almost any deduction possible." No one could say that about his declaration regarding his prime campaign issue: "I am in favor of going into the League."

Cox began his tour of the country on September 2. He campaigned in the Midwest and the West until October 3, after which he turned his attention to other parts of the nation. The Democratic presidential nominee spoke in thirty-six states, traveled 22,000 miles, and delivered 394 speeches as well as innumerable informal remarks. This was in addition to a great deal of handshaking, talking to reporters, conferring with Democratic leaders, and tending to other campaign business along the way. On one day in Indiana alone, Cox was active from early morning until 1:30 A.M. the next day, speaking twenty-six times. His was a strenuous experience, but it paid off in terms of the number of people, some two million, who turned out to see and hear him. Franklin Roosevelt campaigned almost as vigorously. He traveled 18,000 miles and delivered as many as ten formal speeches daily in addition to engaging in other campaign activities. Unfortunately for Cox and Roosevelt, most of the nation's newspapers warmly endorsed Harding and Coolidge and gave the Democratic nominees relatively little news space.

Harding's and Coolidge's campaigns were as different from each other's as they were from those of Cox and Roosevelt. Coolidge made only an eight-day tour of the South, some speeches in New England, and one each in New York City and Philadelphia. Harding began early and concentrated, from July 31 to September 25, on his famous "front-porch" effort at his home before delegation after delegation of supporters. Some 600,000 people came to hear him, representing, among many others, farm folk, veterans, Indians, black Baptists, Knights of Pythias, and even the "Harding and Coolidge Theatrical League, 40,000

Strong." In addition to hearing the Republican presidential nominee, they were entertained, by bands, choruses, and show business celebrities, including Al Jolson who serenaded the nominee and a crowd with "Mr. Harding, You're the Man for Us." Platoons of visiting politicians also required Harding's special attention. At least as important were the reporters who came to Marion. Once or twice a day, Harding would meet with them, light up a smoke or chew some tobacco, swap stories, and answer questions frankly and amiably. It was, all agreed, a virtuoso performance. When the front-porch campaign grew stale as time passed, Harding hit the road in September. The Republican nominee traveled on and off for five weeks, appearing in ten states and closing in Columbus, Ohio. Throughout, he maintained his image as a dignified, genial, and concerned conciliator.

Harding and Cox had special worries during their campaigns. The Ohio senator's wife, Florence, had been divorced before marrying Harding soon afterward; this was offset by the fact that Governor Cox had also been divorced. Possible leaks about Harding's extramarital adventures were taken care of by giving his girlfriend a campaign job in Chicago and sending a former mistress and her husband on a tour of the world. Early in Cox's campaign, he made some telling blows by accusing the Republicans of trying to buy the election. The amount he talked about in their "corruption fund" kept escalating, though, until he absurdly charged that it contained thirty million dollars. This issue boomeranged on Cox in several ways. It was taken by many as mudslinging, reduced financial contribu-

tions to his own as well as Harding's campaign, and raised questions as to how Cox, a millionaire, had amassed his wealth. The governor had other worries, especially the widespread Republican charges that he was variously Woodrow Wilson's puppet or a tool of New York's venal Tammany Hall or of provincial southern interests. Cox also had to deal with accusations that Wilson and the Democrats had fostered autocratic and unconstitutional government.

Harding's biggest concern was the rumor that he had black blood, a tale widely circulated by October. When Wilson's secretary, Joseph Tumulty, heard this story, he told the President, "we've got 'em beat." Wilson refused to have anything to do with the rumor, however, and Cox and Roosevelt repudiated the use of such information. This did not stop others, with the result that there was a proliferation of racist materials, including a cartoon of the White House with the legend "Uncle Tom's Cabin?" Moreover, Cox and the Democrats assailed Harding for his espousal of equal rights for black Americans. The Democratic nominee reinforced this with his comment that God intended America to be for white people. Apparently, though, the racial issue changed few votes on election day.

Cox proved a good speaker, but he too often erred by making personal attacks, a temptation Harding resisted. One example was the governor's remark that "Harding has always stood for the forces of reaction. He venerates the past." Not only did this seem abusive, but it played into Harding's hands at a time when many Americans yearned for what he championed as "Normalcy." This did not stop Cox, though, who likened Harding to "Happy Hooligan," labeled his nomination "a reactionary plot," and called Republican Senator Henry Cabot Lodge the "archconspirator of the ages." Cox outdid himself when, on election eve, he declared that "every traitor in America will vote tomorrow for Warren G. Harding." The governor had no monopoly on poorly considered remarks. Franklin Roosevelt claimed that as assistant secretary of the navy he had written Haiti's constitution and had helped run "a couple of little republics." He denied saying this, but he only further embarrassed himself for there were too many witnesses to his statement. In these ways the Democratic campaign gained a reputation for recklessness.

Also significant was that Cox's consistency on the League of Nations eventually crumbled. Harding had insisted that American membership in any world organization had to give the United States the freedom to act in its own defense and to decline participation in international military action. Neither the people nor the Senate, he asserted, would accept American membership on any other basis. Cox conceded the widespread support for Harding's position when late in October he stated that he would accept any compromise that would clear the way for America to join the League.

Whatever the reasons, Cox did not stand a chance. All the polls and most political analysts had agreed on this from the beginning of the campaign. The *New York Times* summed things up well after the election: "it was not [Cox] who was defeated; it was a composite figure of many illusions, legends, errors, dissatisfactions, grudges. . . ." These Harding and the Republicans had effectively exploited whether it was the

"I WANT YOU TO KNOW THAT I BELIEVE IN EQUALITY BEFORE THE LAW. THAT IS ONE OF THE GUARANTEES OF THE AMERICAN CONSTITUTION. YOU CAN NOT GIVE ONE RIGHT TO A WHITE MAN AND DENY THE SAME RIGHT TO A BLACK MAN." — (Senator Harding, at Oklahoma City, October 9, 1920).
Issued by Walter L. Brown, 2512 East 33d St., Cleveland, Ohio.

*Harding postcard aligning him with black politicians of Ohio. Harding promised no new crusades but simply a return to "normalcy."*

high cost of living, deepening recession, Cox's occasional rashness, anger at Wilson from the largest ethnic groups, or even slow delivery of the mail.

On election day, November 2, the voters showed their agreement with Warren Harding's campaign slogan, "Let's be done with wiggle and wobble." They cast their ballots overwhelmingly for him. Carrying 37 of the 48 states, Harding polled 16,143,407 votes to 9,130,328 for Cox; the electoral college vote would be 404 to 127. The Republicans expanded their majority in the House of Representatives to 170 seats and in the Senate to 22. One had to agree with Joseph Tumulty in assessing the election results: "It wasn't a landslide; it was an earthquake."

Republican
Campaign
Text-Book
1920

Issued by the

Republican National
Committee

Cover of a campaign book issued by the
Republican National Committee.

Harding and Coolidge
souvenir desk inkwell.

Above: Sepiatoned poster with photographs and biographies of Harding and Coolidge.
Below: Republican celluloid buttons. The button at left is the only known campaign memorabilia to
show Harding smiling. The center button includes Pennsylvania senatorial candidate Boies Penrose.

*Right: Republican window decal. Note the law and order slogan and the appeal to anti-League voters without actually opposing the League. Below: Ribbon. Politicians scrambled to attract the newly enfranchised female voters. In 1920, women overwhelmingly voted for Harding.*

*Poster with a sketch of Harding.*

Sepiatoned poster. The Capitol building is more prominent than the candidates. Grover Cleveland and Woodrow Wilson flank Jefferson.

Cover of a campaign book issued by the Democratic National Committee.

Poster for Cox and Roosevelt. Paper political items dominated this campaign.

In the Limelight

Important Men and Buildings

Democratic National Convention

San Francisco    :-:    1920

Left: Poster issued by the St. Francis Hotel publicizing the 1920 Democratic National Convention and the city of San Francisco.
Below: Nominees did not address national conventions until 1932. They were notified of their selection by a delegation which usually went to their home.

A rare pocket watch with printed portraits of Cox and Roosevelt on the face.

Of all political celluloid buttons, Cox and Roosevelt items are the most valuable. Eight designs are known.

Cox opposed the Prohibition Amendment which was adopted in 1919. The Franklin D. Roosevelt for Vice President button above is a most unusual item.

Democratic window decal with an ambiguous slogan.

PEACE WITH HONOR

OUR CHOICE

COX FOR PRESIDENT

ROOSEVELT FOR VICE PRESIDENT

Broadside.
The Democratic party
stressed continuity
with Wilson's policies
and supported American
membership in the
League of Nations.

A 78 rpm campaign phonograph recording of
Harding speeches. The earliest recording of a President's
voice was of President Benjamin Harrison in 1889.

Anti-Cox postcard showing Cox as Wilson's mascot.

Selection of celluloid
buttons supporting
Socialist candidate Eugene
V. Debs in his several
presidential campaigns.
The bust below depicts
Debs in prison garb. Debs,
pardoned by Harding in
1921, is the only
presidential candidate
nominated while in prison.

Felt inaugural pennant, 1921.

A variety of sheet music from the 1920 campaign.

Ribbon from Harding's 1923 western tour. He died in San Francisco on August 2, 1923.

## 1924
### 48 STATES
### IN THE UNION

*REPUBLICAN*
# Calvin Coolidge
ELECTORAL VOTE 382, POPULAR VOTE 54.0%

DEMOCRAT
# John W. Davis
ELECTORAL VOTE 136, POPULAR VOTE 28.8%

PROGRESSIVE
# Robert M. La Follette
ELECTORAL VOTE 13, POPULAR VOTE 16.6%

DAVID BURNER

has published several books on twentieth-century
American politics, most recently *John F. Kennedy
and a New Generation* (1988). His *Making Peace
with the '60s* is scheduled for publication by
Harvard University Press in 1994. He teaches at
the State University of New York at Stony Brook.

In 1924 three parties contended for the presidency: the Republicans, the Democrats, and the Progressives (Robert La Follette's temporary organization of mavericks on the left). Roughly described, there were two clashes: a cultural and ethnic encounter at the Democratic convention, and an inadequately articulated argument in the presidential campaign proper over economics and class and power. Both arguments by 1924 already had a long American past; both have had a history since. Each in that year took a form particular to the times and circumstances.

The style of campaigning itself, meanwhile, was adapting to the young media of radio, newsreels, and newspaper photography, and a shift in the popular understanding of how a presidential contender was supposed to act. What today would be called handlers, notably the advisers of the Republican nominee Calvin Coolidge, were learning modern techniques of packaging (as it is now labeled). But these had not yet become so cynically, so nearly boastfully separate from issues as is now the case. The presidential politics of the time, at any rate, had their most spectacular moments in an old-time and unstaged brawl that was the Democratic convention.

In New York City's old Madison Square Garden on East 24th Street, late in June assembled a collection of Democratic delegates whose squabbles traveled across the nation by way of the infant medium of radio. It was the first convention to have its proceedings hurled across the United States by airwaves. Revealing how deep were the country's ethnic and regional hostilities, radio was creating the instant national community that has been an American experience ever since.

The combatants have been variously described: inland and small town against big eastern city, old stock against immigrant, Protestant against Roman Catholic, fundamentalist against evolutionist, dry against wet. Divisions were more complicated than that, but popular perceptions shaped the election. The nation's Protestant hegemony, so a number of Americans feared, was losing ground to Catholic immigration. Rural and small-town virtues were crumbling to the vices of the cities, while urban political machines corrupted the nation's simple democracy. Cities had filled with immigrants of alien culture and manners, of alien religions, of genetic stock different from that of the old British and northern European breeds. To nervous inlanders the sensual rites of these new immigrants, their festivals, their dependence on urban political bosses, and of course their taste for drink appeared to be exactly concordant with the disorder and the vice that Americans had traditionally associated with the cities.

Democrats harboring such fears and resentments might have looked to William Jennings Bryan. But Bryan, now retired from direct political competition if not from speechmaking, was passing on his con-

*Automobile license accessory. Political license attachments were used for the first time during the 1924 campaign.*

stituency to William Gibbs McAdoo of California. The other faction within the Democracy was gathering meanwhile to Governor Alfred E. Smith of New York, a Catholic, Irishman, and Italian, an opponent of Prohibition, up from the streets and the machine politics of New York City.

The mentalities that clashed in New York, again, were not new; nor did they have in 1924 a last hurrah. The sense that a community must protect itself against the disintegrating intrusions of outsiders is perennial. It is because the established ethnicities (or rather the composite ethnicity) varies from moment to moment, each dreaded new arrival becoming in time part of the stable establishment, that the argument of 1924 today appears obsolete. Folk Catholicism in a later day would come to endorse superpatriotic Americanism, and one day the descendants of Haitian or Salvadorean immigrants to the United States will rush to defend the established culture against some new tide of immigrants.

McAdoo delegates, in their defense of what they conceived to be the old republic, saw themselves in a city of sin; streetwise city Catholics and urban sophisticates saw a visitation of bumpkins. A columnist described the fan that Bryan had brought with him as the kind that the local furniture store gives out at county fairs. When he spoke, Tammany New Yorkers booed in the galleries. The big fight over the platform was over whether to condemn the Klan by name. The platform committee rejected explicit condemnation; and so did the delegates, though narrowly. The meaning of the actual vote is obscured by the consideration many delegates must have had in mind—politicos proposed it to them—that censur-

ing the organization would simply be bad politics. It should be remembered of Bryan that, while he was among those to argue on political grounds against the inclusion of a Klan plank, he later endorsed the denunciation of the KKK by the party's nominee, John W. Davis. And of the McAdoo faction's hostility to the decadent city some complicating testimony came from McAdoo himself.

It occurred upon McAdoo's arrival at New York—where, in fact, he had lived for thirty years—to attend the convention. He excoriated "this imperial city . . . this city of privilege." It was "the seat of that invisible power represented by the allied forces of finance and industry which, reaching into the remotest corners of the land, touches the lives of the people everywhere," a place "unscrupulous, mercenary, and sordid." The comments of the progressive McAdoo, who also proposed tariff repeal, lower freight rates for farmers, and protection of natural resources, can be a reminder of a still earlier time when rural radicalism had perceived the urban East as the home of wealth, privilege, and power. Sin, to the thinking of hinterland Protestant Americans, need not be merely a matter of pleasure, drink, painted women, bishops in silken vestments; it could also be found in selfishness and luxury at the expense of the poor. Patriots did not believe, as chauvinists and flag fetishists have believed since, that American virtues are embedded in capitalism and economic power. They were as likely to locate virtue in simplicity, hard work, moderation of material needs and possessions, and plain neighborly democracy. Bryan and McAdoo Democrats of that stripe were at once traditionalist and radical, looking to fundamental economic reform that could restore what they thought of as the clear honest democracy of their nation's past.

For ballot after ballot, as the nation listened over the radio, the count did not yield either Smith or McAdoo the two-thirds of the delegates necessary for nomination. Davis, a West Virginian but a Wall Street lawyer essentially though moderately identifiable with the urban forces, was a persistent third choice. Also appearing were the respected Senator Thomas Walsh of Montana, a Catholic prohibitionist chosen chairman of the convention as a unifying presence, and Oscar W. Underwood of Alabama. Underwood was something of a phenomenon as a politician from the deep South: born in Massachusetts, son of a colonel in the Union army, foe of prohibition and the Klan. After the 82nd ballot, the convention adopted a resolution supported by Smith to release pledged delegates from their commitment. Still there was no breakthrough. On ballots 101 and 102, both Underwood and Davis were ahead of the rapidly declining McAdoo and Smith. On the next round, Davis was nominated by acclamation. On the 101st ballot, Underwood and Walsh together received far more than Smith; and the total for the three was far larger than the highest Smith had ever gotten. Walsh, despite his religion, got some McAdoo votes. All this suggests that the objection to Smith had been not to his religion alone or to his opposition to Prohibition alone but to the whole of what he represented as an American cultural phenomenon.

The convention had nominated an urbanite by adoption, a member of the legal and financial establishment, a very tentative supporter of Prohibition if a supporter at all. Perhaps to balance the urban finance law-

Sticker for the Democratic candidates, John Davis and Charles Bryan. The 1924 Democratic campaign had less of a variety of objects than any campaign since the Civil War.

yer with a hinterland radical, the convention chose as vice presidential candidate Governor Charles W. Bryan of Nebraska, brother of the famous orator whose mantle had passed to McAdoo.

Of the presidential nomination in the Republican convention, no large story is to be told. In Cleveland, the Republicans made the desirable choice for a party already possessing the White House: they nominated their President, Calvin Coolidge of Vermont and Massachusetts. Coolidge had succeeded to the presidency upon the death of the vague and misled Warren G. Harding. His reputation and manner were that of a New Englander of starchy integrity, so much so that instead of having his future threatened by Harding administration scandals, his distance from them enhanced his chilly appeal. (Scholarship has since discovered a private Coolidge who was talkative, eccentric, and a prankster.) Charles G. Dawes, unpopular with organized labor but capable of strengthening his party's needed ties to the Midwest, was vice presidential nominee.

1924 Progressive party poster. The platform called for government ownership of railroads, abolition of the injunction in labor disputes, and freedom for farmers and labor to organize and bargain collectively.

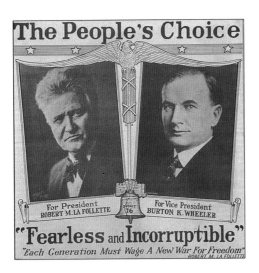

In a sober and morally resolute convention also in Cleveland the Progressives brought together farm and labor groups, Socialists and autonomous radicals. The convention predictably nominated the great Republican progressive Robert M. La Follette of Wisconsin, choosing the progressive Democrat Burton R. Wheeler of Montana to run with him.

The issues in the actual presidential contest must be sharply distinguished from the cultural and ethnic collisions in the Democratic convention. Within the McAdoo camp had been a degree of social and economic radicalism, or more accurately a traditionalism demanding restorative reform. The Democratic platform, reading as though produced by another convention and party than the organized squabble in New York City, was more combatively reformist on economic issues than Davis. The Progressive platform, of course, was the embodiment of belligerence. The debate in the platforms and in the speeches of the candidates had suggestions of present-day arguments over economic and social issues. Yet,

like the cultural and ethnic rhetoric among the convention Democrats, the vocabulary for addressing economic problems was particular and fixed in time.

What gives tone not only to the Progressive platform but to the Democratic is the stress on privilege. The attack on special interests, of course, is fundamental to popular politics: often it is merely a matter of defining the privileged group to be denounced. The distinction in tone between the politics of 1924 and that of more recent times is the suggestion then, especially in the Progressive statement, that the object was no more than the restoration of a simple, honest, old-fashioned democracy. The politicians of 1924 were unburdened with any need to confront the contradiction between racial justice and the white majoritarian democracy, or with the demands that mass education must meet in a high-technology society, or with the intensive involvement that the country later had in global affairs. They could therefore speak as though reform might consist of no more than the mere reassertion of American democracy, the shrugging off of a few unnatural monopolies.

"The democratic party"—its platform did not capitalize the names of parties— "believes in equal rights to all and special privilege to none. The republican party holds that special privileges are essential to national prosperity." That party "is concerned chiefly with material things; the democratic party is concerned chiefly with human rights."

In what is the most direct application of its contention that the Democrats were the party of equality and the enemy of privilege, the platform denounced a Republican scheme that would lighten the tax on the wealthy. It advocated a graduated income tax, "so adjusted as to lay the burdens of government upon the taxpayers in proportion to the benefits they enjoy and their ability to pay." But the plank argued for a lowering of all taxes.

The platform, in keeping with the traditions of the party, attacked the Fordney-McCumber protective tariff. The Democrats promised to lower railroad and water rates, to aid the cooperative marketing movement in agriculture, and to establish an export marketing agency that would help stabilize farm prices. A call for the protection of states' rights, which the Democratic statement claimed that the Republican administration had bureaucratically invaded, was in the spirit of this party of localism and the South. The platform spoke of the country's obligation to assume moral leadership in the world, commended the League of Nations, and urged that the country hold a popular referendum on American entry with whatever reservations the Senate might adopt. In a mildly social Democratic plank, the party statement endorsed collective bargaining, spending on public works in time of heavy unemployment, and federal cooperation with the states in the protection of children and the safeguarding of women in employment; and it reminded the public of the Democratic votes in Congress for the child labor amendment then being presented for ratification.

Of the three competitive parties, it was that farthest to the left in intention, committed by its name to progressivism, that spoke most clearly the language of tradition and return. "For a generation," declared the Progressive platform, "the people have struggled patiently" to get free of monopoly.

"The equality of opportunity proclaimed by the Declaration of Independence and asserted and defended by Jefferson and Lincoln as the heritage of every American citizen has been displaced by special privilege for the few, wrested from the government of the many." The party, the statement concluded in another use of restorationist language, was "applying to the needs of today the fundamental principles of American democracy, opposing equally the dictatorship of plutocracy and the dictatorship of the proletariat."

On the tariff, taxation, railroad shipping rates, farm policy, and child labor, the Progressives were essentially in agreement with the Democratic party. A few proposals put them clearly to the left of the Democrats. The platform pledged public ownership of railroads. It endorsed abolition of injunctions against labor unions. And in its advocacy of democratic empowerment it proposed extending the use of the referendum.

William Z. Foster of the Communist party dismissed the Progressive nominee as a reactionary wishing to break monopolies and return to a time of small business. Foster was exactly right in what La Follette and the Progressives were after (or nearly right: the Progressives wanted some degree of nationalization). What Foster and other Marxists could never accept was that in envisioning a nation of wage-earners and productive small-property holders joined in unions, farm cooperatives, and other such ventures, a workers' commonwealth spreading wealth and power downward rather than gathering it either into Bolshevik collectives or into business monopolies, American radicals were in fact radicals. They were addressing the problem of power as directly as Marxists have addressed it, and in an American idiom.

The Republican platform was the mildest of the three, for its task was to recommend to the public the party already in the White House. It too spoke for credits to farmers, for farmers' cooperatives, for a constitutional amendment dealing with child labor. The platform of the historic party of emancipation was the only one of the three to refer to race relations, looking to an effective antilynching law and talking of an investigation into the causes of black misfortune. And on one particular the Republican statement was especially at odds with the platforms of the rival parties: it endorsed a protective tariff.

So far, not much distinction was discernible between the techniques of 1924 and those of an earlier time. The Democrats in New York doubtless did not have the luxury of inventing clever strategies: they were too busy fighting and making up, meanwhile struggling with the touchy Klan issue, while radio allowed the nation to listen in on their civil war. The three platforms were essentially frank statements of ideologies and issues. It was in the contest following the conventions that something like modern packaging with the use of new media could take place.

The most successfully designed of the three candidates was Coolidge. It happened that his silence in public was genuine. But it was also a crafted reticence, and it had advanced media to put it on display.

A set of radio addresses, labeled nonpartisan, carried to about five hundred stations a speaking style that seemed the enunciation of silence. As President, Coolidge was also a good subject for photography and newsreels that, again, could be presented as though nonpartisan: a President, after all, is going to be in the news. Still in historic memory is a photo of Coolidge pitching hay, an activity that like the words of the other parties spoke of a traditional simple Americanness.

The style was perfect for the party and the day. The neat, retiring economy of self-presentation must have emphasized, it can be speculated, Coolidge's purity at a time of scandal. It implied an efficiency befitting to the candidate of the party of successful business. And it subjected to no risky commitments a President who at the moment needed to commit himself to nothing more than things as they were. The Republican vice presidential nominee Dawes was more aggressive, taking after La Follette as a radical.

Surely the least effective packaging was that of Davis. The Democrats had little to work with: a party torn by the forces revealed at the convention, an ideology that could neither win radicals nor isolationists from La Follette nor business conservatives from Coolidge, a candidate who appears to have belonged to that small body of public figures having no taste for the politicking thrust upon them. Davis did his best. Lacking the effective access to the radio and the visual media that Coolidge enjoyed, he stumped for twelve thousand miles, and his speeches were thoughtful and graceful. A Labor Day address is distinguishable for its evocation of the dignity of work, and for a character at once of conservatism and of social democracy. Davis did not engage in red-baiting of La Follette. And in an act that put him far above numbers of other politicians of his time, he attacked the Klan by name, as did La Follette. In the absence of anything better with which to seduce the public, reason and dignity would have to do. But Davis's brand of reserve could not compete with the visible and audible reticence of a candidate who had a very public executive mansion to be reticent in.

The Progressive candidate was the fiery partisan, determined to put ideas and controversy into the campaign. His style was of the kind that is now commonly called populist. But he did not succeed in drawing the public or the other campaigners into a fundamental discussion of the place of power and wealth in American society.

In the election La Follette won about 17 percent of the popular vote and something under a quarter of the votes in the ten major cities. Notable was his considerable following among urban working people and people of immigrant background, many of them of ethnicities sympathetic to his opposition to American entry into the World War. While his normal affiliation was with the Republican party, his more notable inroads were into the Democratic electorate. Except for Wisconsin, which went to La Follette, Coolidge carried the Midwest. He also won the West and the Northeast, in addition to the border states save for Oklahoma. He garnered 54 percent of the popular vote. As the Democrat, Davis won the former Confederacy, in addition picking up Oklahoma. He took just under 29 percent of the popular vote nationally. Coolidge's electoral college vote was well over twice that of his two combined major rivals.

After a campaign year marked by war within the Democratic party, after a victory granted to a candidate who did not even have to speak while his most leftist visible

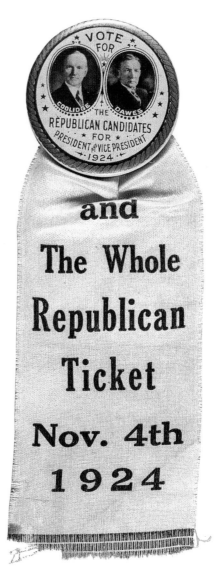

*Celluloid button with an attached ribbon for Coolidge and Dawes. More than two hundred varieties of buttons were issued during the campaign.*

rival argued and bellowed in vain, at a moment when business was honored above all else and the Republicans were the party of business, the Republicans must have looked to a long and comfortable future in possession of the executive mansion. In New York State, meanwhile, a young Democrat of the prominent Roosevelt clan, recovering from polio, was working on a political career that before long would take him via the total mastery of the radio to the White House.

Cover of a campaign book issued
by the Democratic National Committee.

Progressive party poster. The Progressive candidates were promoted on
pennants, fobs, brass pins, and on at least thirty varieties of buttons.

Celluloid pocket mirror. Political mirrors have been fairly
common campaign items since the 1920s.

Matched trio of celluloid buttons. La Follette received
almost five million votes, 16.6 percent of the total.

Monochrome postcard. "Keep Cool" with Coolidge became the
most memorable Republican slogan of the 1924 campaign.

Paper fan. Like items from the 1920 campaign, material
with portraits of both 1924 Democratic candidates is rare.

Matching pair of campaign window stickers.

134

A 78 rpm phonograph recording of Coolidge.

Celluloid buttons for the 1924 campaign. TEAPOT DOME refers to a major scandal of the Harding administration which involved the secret lease of federal oil reserve lands to private interests.

Three-part paper fold-out with a state seal beneath each candidate.

## The Candidates and the Klan

A vote for Coolidge is a vote for the Klan.

A vote for Davis is a vote for the Klan.

A vote for La Follette is a vote **against** the Klan, **against** invisible government, **against** mob rule;

And FOR **Law and Order**, **Representative government** and **Democracy**.

*During the 1920s, the Ku Klux Klan played a major role in national politics. La Follette is drawing his sword labeled "JUSTICE TO ALL" against the Klan figure.*

*Poster with drawn portraits of Coolidge and Dawes.*

CALVIN COOLIDGE
FOR PRESIDENT

CHARLES G. DAWES
FOR VICE-PRESIDENT

*Pair of small celluloid buttons. Notice the union label on right.*

JOHN W. DAVIS
FOR PRESIDENT

CHARLES W. BRYAN
FOR VICE PRESIDENT

COOLIDGE AND DAWES

*Button with suspended celluloid Republican elephant.*

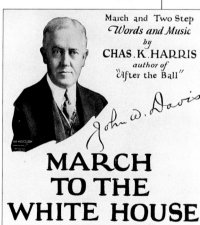

March and Two Step
*Words and Music*
*by*
CHAS. K. HARRIS
*author of*
*"After the Ball"*

John W. Davis

## MARCH TO THE WHITE HOUSE

Compliments of the
*Democratic National Committee*

Published by
CHAS. K. HARRIS

*Sheet music issued by the Democratic National Committee.*

Cardboard figural teapot door hanger.

*Graphic anti-Republican cigar box. "CROOKS,"*
*a cigar brand, is appropriately used with the imagery.*

*Paper lapel*
*ribbon for Davis.*

Democracy Offers *YOU*

"It is the supreme need of the hour to bring back to the people confidence in their government."
—JOHN W. DAVIS

For President
JOHN W. DAVIS

For Vice-President
CHARLES W. BRYAN

Davis and Bryan campaign items. Charles W. Bryan was the loquacious governor of Nebraska and younger brother of William Jennings Bryan.

1924 Democratic convention items.
Above: Convention floor staff admission ticket.
Far right: Delegate's badge. The convention was held in New York City, hence a metal montage of the city at the top.

Delegate badge with celluloid Coolidge button insert. Coolidge had been born in Vermont.

Automobile license attachment.

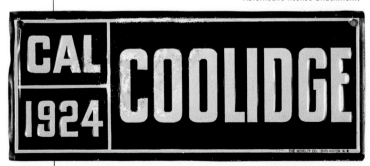

Painted aluminum thimble.

Assortment of campaign items. Right: Sheet music for Coolidge, including a picture of the dour Coolidge trying to smile.

Broadside promoting inauguration ball.

Advertisement cardboard fan with Coolidge and Davis. The advertiser offered Five dollars in merchandise to everyone who guessed the correct 1924 electoral vote. La Follette was not among the choices.

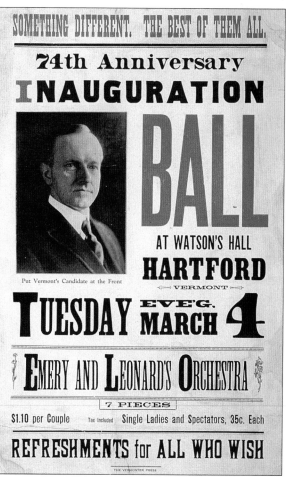

★

1928

48 STATES
IN THE UNION

HOOVER    FOR ALL OF U.S.    CURTIS

*REPUBLICAN*

## Herbert C. Hoover

ELECTORAL VOTE 444, POPULAR VOTE 58.2%

DEMOCRAT

## Alfred E. Smith

ELECTORAL VOTE 87, POPULAR VOTE 40.9%

## HENRY F. GRAFF

is professor emeritus of history at Columbia University. His books include *The Tuesday Cabinet* (1970), a study of Lyndon Johnson's policies in Vietnam; and *The Presidents: A Reference History* (1984). He is co-author with Jacques Barzun of *The Modern Researcher* (5th ed., 1992), the classic work on research and writing. Columbia has given him its Great Teacher Award.

The 1920s, now immortalized as the jazz decade, as the time of Lucky Lindy, Babe Ruth, Clara Bow, and Sacco and Vanzetti, was a watershed in American history. Little noticed—even as Robert Goddard's experiments in jet propulsion in New Mexico were also scarcely noted—the nation in that ten-year period was undergoing a vast change in its texture. The census of 1920 had revealed that for the first time more than half of the population was living in cities—defined as communities containing more than 2,500 people. And while there were still 20 million horses on the land, the gasoline age was giving the word horsepower new meaning. Names like Ford and Rockefeller had become household words. And accompanying the automobile as a force in the urbanizing of the country was the movie, first silent and then (as the thirties were beginning) talking.

The movie industry, through its giant cinema palaces, made the downtowns of the burgeoning cities the new Meccas of American culture. And the pictures they put on their screens became the vehicles for creating and then selling "the American Way of Life," a fantasy of small-town or rural existence, *sans* crime, people of color (except as menials), or significant economic hardship. All that was good could be found in that pristine world; all that was bad stemmed from the cities: crime, prostitution, slums, and the manipulations of high finance. Worst of all the cities was New York—a Baghdad on the Hudson. It was the bane as well as the envy of millions of Americans. Deep down they knew that it was the nation's imperial city, its influence reaching everywhere, the place to be for success in journalism, acting, singing, and the arts generally—not to speak of big banking and the world of fashion. New York's embrace of the endless stream of immigrants that flowed through the mighty ocean port at the foot of the Hudson also made the city the prime conduit for diluting white, Anglo-Saxon, and Protestant culture. Significantly, the city was the chief bastion of the Roman Catholic Church in the United States; its cardinal-archbishop stood second only to the pope in power and importance in its councils.

In the 1920s the dominant figure in Democratic politics was the voice and hero of New Yorkers, the governor of the state, Alfred Emanuel Smith. Smith, born on New York City's Lower East Side, a son of Irish immigrants, knew from his first day the stench and agony of urban poverty—although his own block was not yet a slum. His relief from the blistering heat of the summer was not a romp in the woods or a dip in a mountain lake but an occasional swim in the East River, which already in the 1880s was being polluted by the effluents of human and industrial wastes. Such local prestige as young Smith enjoyed came mostly from his service every morning as an altar boy at St. James's Church. His mother, especially, worked hard to mold Al into a good man, making him endlessly attentive

*Stereoscopic card of Herbert Hoover.*

to his bearing and dress—an attentiveness that would never leave him. Whatever Mrs. Smith's intuition, this was a curious characteristic built into the lives of many successful minority politicians, from Smith's time to David Dinkins's.

The elder Smiths inculcated substance, too, in Al. He grew up deeply committed to the idea of opportunity for all. He took the main chance where he found it and used his achievements to help others as well as to rise on the political ladder—for an Irish-American one of the few avenues of escape from a life of powerlessness and torpor. Starting out as a subpoena-server, in which role he spent eight years, Smith became acquainted with the men who conducted the affairs of his assembly district, and with the ways of politics. Elected to the assembly in 1904 and enhancing his office with hard work and the blarney that was part of his people's heritage, Smith, who had had to leave school at the age of fourteen, shortly was acknowledged to be the best informed member of New York's legislature. Eventually he became speaker of the assembly, thanks to the support of the leader of Tammany Hall, the Democratic political machine in Manhattan. By 1918, Smith's principled labors as a

representative of his district and as a reformer had earned him a statewide reputation, and he was elected governor. Defeated for reelection in 1920, he was returned in 1922, 1924, and 1926, standing for progressive laws even in that age of conservatism.

Smith and his wife, Catherine (who, like him had grown up in the shadow of the Fulton Street Fish Market), were living symbols of the melting-pot come alive, of the force of hard work and ambition, and of the rising urban political strength not yet registered in national politics. But could this pair reach even higher? Could they become President and First Lady? In a word, could Roman Catholics reared in the Big City be permitted to preside in the White House, historically a place reserved for Protestants sprung from village America?

A symbol of that other America in which Presidents historically had been recruited was Herbert Clark Hoover of California. Born in a cabin in the tiny town of West Branch, Iowa, he was orphaned at ten and sent to live with an uncle and aunt in Oregon. There he learned to fish and climb trees. Graduated from Stanford University as a geology major, he soon found his career taking him to exotic corners of the globe. A significant by-product was the opportunity to invest in the valuable metal ore resources he was helping to exploit as a mining engineer.

Having become wealthy at an early age, Hoover, drawing on the inspiration of his Quaker origins, yearned for a second career in public service. The door opened when the United States entered World War I in 1917. As the nation moved for the first time to large-scale governmental controls, the management of the production and distribution of the food supply became a necessity. Appointed by President Wilson to be food administrator, Hoover demonstrated remarkable ability as an organizer. Making the nation food-conscious as never before by establishing "meatless" and "wheatless" days, and by manipulating the market prices for grains and hogs, the "Great Engineer," as Hoover came to be known, performed the prodigy of trebling the amount of food the United States was able to ship to the Allies as compared with the pre-war period.

Hoover's labors in feeding the Allied peoples made him an international hero, and gave him a further reputation as the "Great Humanitarian." Franklin Roosevelt, later to be Hoover's arch-opponent, said at the time that Hoover is "a wonder" and that the nation ought to make him President. For certain, if successful wars must inevitably produce future Presidents, Hoover was an authentic hero on his way to the top no less than triumphant generals. Supreme Court Justice Louis D. Brandeis—surely no admirer of Hoover's conservatism when the Great Depression broke upon the nation—declared that Hoover was "the biggest figure injected into Washington life by the war." This rural-born man of affairs who could move nations with his skill as an administrator, who wrote learnedly on the subject of metallurgy as well as on the no less alluring subject of fishing, was destined to do battle for the presidency with Al Smith. Neither Smith nor Hoover knew anything of the world of the other.

The Republican campaign to retain control of the White House began on a wet day in August 1927, in the Black Hills of South Dakota where the Calvin Coolidges

*Stereoscopic card of Al Smith.*

were vacationing. In a local high school, the President without forewarning called the press into a meeting room and unceremoniously began to hand out slips of paper bearing this statement: "I do not choose to run for President in nineteen twenty-eight." Coolidge, usually sleeping twelve hours a day, had fallen into deep depression following the death of a son who had contracted blood poisoning after raising a blister on his foot while playing tennis on a White House court. The President would write in his autobiography that with the loss of his boy "went the glory of the Presidency." It is likely, also, that Coolidge had a sense of economic problems arising in the country which he was ill-equipped to deal with.

Upon Coolidge's announcement, Hoover was immediately the leading candidate for the Republican nomination. He had been in the running for the vice presidential slot in 1924, but lost out to Charles Dawes, a banker chiefly remembered for creating a plan to wrest war reparations from Germany—a lively issue of the day. Hoover, nevertheless, remained a darling of Republican politicians, seeing in him a progressive who had been untouched by the party scandals of the ill-starred Harding presidency. As Secretary

*Felt armband for Smith.*

of Commerce his influence under both Harding and Coolidge was pervasive, extending well beyond the range of his own formal responsibilities. As one commentator put it, "There is more Hoover in this administration than there is Coolidge."

Hoover had been constantly in the news. His most dramatic work was the management of the relief effort required by the catastrophic Mississippi flood of 1927. Hoover's labors reinforced grandly his old reputation for disaster-succoring that had brought him to the fore in the first place. Now he was a revered figure—and in the bargain, a doer with an awareness of the power of government to marshal resources in the interest of the people.

The Republican convention opened on June 12, 1928, in the Civic Auditorium of Kansas City, capital of the state most ardently in support of Prohibition. The power of Prohibition cannot be overstated. Passed during the moral uplift of World War I, the Eighteenth Amendment was the culmination of three-quarters of a century of crusading against demon rum. Aimed at strengthening the American fiber and protecting children especially from the conse-

quences of drinking fathers, the movement became an instrument for disciplining the wayward of an industrial, urbanizing society. In the minds of the prohibitionists, those requiring this discipline included whisky-drinking Irish and Poles and wine-drinking Italians—many of them newcomers to America, immigrants who gave strength to the multi-ethnic America now emerging. Hoover endorsed Prohibition, not enthusiastically but with enough zeal to assure himself the support of the so-called "drys."

Agricultural forces were also pressing their case, arguing that the much-discussed McNary-Haugen Bill must be passed. But prices were improving and the strength of the farm protest was gradually dissipating. Attentive to the discontent, however, Hoover was acceptable to the farmers.

On the first ballot at the convention, Hoover won 837 out of 1089 votes, and he was in. He toyed at first with the idea of asking the respected veteran Progressive Senator George W. Norris of Nebraska to be his running mate. In the end, though, he selected Senator Charles Curtis of Kansas, who boasted of being part Indian. Known as "Egg Charlie" because he constantly criticized the pricing of eggs, he was useful in the campaign as an experienced politician— even though his flamboyant style was muted by a severe case of laryngitis that lasted for weeks.

On the Democratic side the task was unique in the party's annals. The challenge was to make Al Smith—the leading contender to be the party's standard-bearer— acceptable in non-urban America. The undertaking had begun in 1924 when Smith's name was placed in nomination at the Democratic convention by Franklin Delano Roosevelt, whose qualifications as a dry, aristocratic Protestant were impeccable. Labeling Smith "the Happy Warrior," FDR made his fellow-New Yorker sound like a "regular guy" to all who might have doubts. To confront the issue of his Catholicism, Smith, through his friend Judge Joseph Proskauer wrote an article in the May 1927 issue of the *Atlantic Monthly* entitled "Catholic and Patriot." It argued persuasively that there was no incompatibility between the two, in spite of pervasive insistence that there was. The response to the piece, which was widely reprinted, gave the Smith camp the impression, soon revealed to be illusory, that the religious issue had been largely disposed of.

The Smith forces also took on the formidable trial of assuring the public that Katie Smith, the governor's wife, was not vulgar and coarse despite her upbringing on the Lower East Side. Women, only recently enfranchised, were beginning to vote in large numbers, and their good opinion mattered for the first time. Still, millions of women—and men—had shaped their expectations of a First Lady by idealizing White House women of earlier days like Dolley

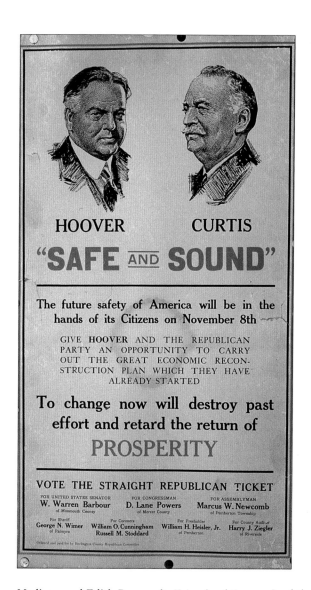

Madison and Edith Roosevelt. Friends of the Smiths, among them Eleanor Roosevelt and Frances Perkins, felt forced to speak publicly of Mrs. Smith's gracious manner in order to counter rumors to the contrary.

The able chief of the publicity bureau of the Democratic National Committee, Belle Moskowitz, was determined to make Smith President. She worked valiantly to bring

*Broadside. Hoover and Curtis 1932 reelection item praising their first-term economic policies.*

Enameled metal 1928 Hoover pin.

women into the nominating process, and ultimately the national committee had women in equal number to men. Mrs. Moskowitz appointed Mrs. Roosevelt chairman of the women's pre-convention activities, thus giving the prestige of a famous name to the commitment that both sexes must share in the Democrats' bid for the White House. Mrs. Moskowitz had also probed Smith's grass-roots strength by soliciting assessments of a Smith candidacy from hundreds of members of county committees. The results were encouraging.

So, in a buoyant mood, the Smith forces arrived for the convention at Sam Houston Hall in Houston on June 26, 1928. Selecting that Texas city was partly in concession to southerners, including especially Jesse Jones, an oil magnate whose fortune was useful to a party now out of office since 1921 and with only modest prospects for success in 1928.

The keynote address was delivered by Claude G. Bowers, the popular historian-journalist, who hammered away at the involvement of prominent Republicans in the oil scandals that had held the headlines only a few years earlier. Franklin Roosevelt, fully back in politics, and shortly to succeed Smith as governor of New York, was Smith's floor leader. When the moment came to place before the convention the name of "the next President of the United States," FDR stepped forward as he had in 1924 at Madison Square Garden in New York and read with his inescapably aristocratic and mellifluous tones the splendid nominating speech drafted by Judge Proskauer.

When the balloting began, Smith and his family and Mrs. Moskowitz and hers sat in the governor's mansion in Albany listening on the radio, still a new medium of communication, not yet an instrument for political discourse. As the roll call proceeded, the little gathering, with mounting delight, could sense the result: Smith would get the necessary two-thirds vote on the first ballot, an outcome assured when Ohio switched its support to him. Out of a total of 1,097 votes, he received 849. Despite the alarm of the anti-Catholic, anticity, antiwet cohorts, Smith would carry the standard of the party of Thomas Jefferson, Andrew Jackson, and Woodrow Wilson—although, as one historian has written, "street-corner evangelists predicted that God would intervene to avert the catastrophe."

Following FDR's speech, there was the traditional march and hoopla in the convention hall for the nominee, but, significantly, one delegation from the South refused to take part in it and, in the end, four southern delegations would not vote for Smith, rendering it impossible to make the nomination unanimous. The cleavage in the party was clear. Not only the Catholic issue but also the wet-dry issue cost Smith dearly within his party's ranks. While the party platform supported Prohibition, Smith sent a telegram stating his support for "fundamental changes in the present provisions of national prohibition"—thus apparently placing the Democrats on both sides of the question.

For vice president, the party selected Senator Joseph T. Robinson of Arkansas, a dry, a Protestant, and a southerner, completing the familiar combination of a New York governor and a border-stater that had characterized Democratic-party presidential tickets since the Civil War.

Hoover began his campaign at Stanford University in Palo Alto, California, where he made his acceptance speech on August 11, his fifty-fourth birthday. In the address, and in many thereafter, the candidate emphasized the roaring prosperity of the country and his fervent belief that before long poverty would be banished from the land. And above all, he spoke out for "rugged individualism," expressing horror at the thought of "state socialism," words that had lively resonance at that moment when, across the world in the land of Bolshevism, Lenin's mantle had fallen on Joseph Stalin. Money for the Hoover canvass quickly poured into the party's coffers, with Wall Streeters especially eager to assure the election of the third Republican in a row.

In the East where support for Prohibition was weak, the party's voices emphasized and took credit for the good times the Republican claimed to have produced. In the depressed farm regions they harped on Prohibition and Tammany. To hold the allegiance of black voters to the party of Lincoln, they pointed to the antilynching plank in the Republican platform. And Hoover's

notably "color-blind" relief work in the Mississippi flood disaster strengthened the bond with black voters.

Smith, on the other hand, had nothing to offer blacks, eager as he was to avoid offending the solid white South that he counted on to support him as it had supported Democratic presidential candidates since Reconstruction. He was, moreover, notably unfriendly to female suffrage and to women in politics—despite his dependence on Belle Moskowitz. His style and self-presentation also handicapped him with middle-class women. His brown derby, his ever-present cigar, his rasping voice, and his New York accent, accompanied by some idiosyncratic pronunciations—"rad-dio," for example—made him seem to many people an unpolished man, unworthy to sit in the chair of Washington and Lincoln. While his reputation as a devout and humble family man won him some female backing, it could not outweigh the negative impression he gave, particularly among women of above-average means.

Despite the hurdles they confronted, the Democrats (led by the New York financiers John J. Raskob and Herbert H. Lehman) raised almost five-and-a-half million dollars, the largest sum the party had ever collected for a presidential campaign. Still, even this swollen war chest was not enough to fight successfully the whispering campaign against Smith. It took many forms and it was everywhere.

The principal rumor was that if the governor became President, he would bring the pope to the United States and set him up in residence. A picture of Smith at the recently opened Holland Tunnel, which connected New York to New Jersey under the Hudson River, was accompanied by the explanation that the tunnel was soon to be extended under the Atlantic right into the Vatican basement! Periodically, also, concocted reports circulated that Smith had appeared in public highly drunk.

Patently, the very characteristics that favored Smith in the industrial areas—his big-city brashness, a career based on his mastery of machine politics, his Catholic piety—seemed anathema in the other America. Smith was unable to counter the Republican insistence that prosperity must not be damped down by this alien-seeming New Yorker, and that a Tammany wet was not qualified to help agriculture out of its doldrums.

Possibly the most organized force committed to defeating Smith was the Methodist Episcopal Church in the South, under the unwavering leadership of Bishop James Cannon, Jr. Cannon was bent, not on electing Hoover so much as crushing Smith, on the conviction that America must never have a Catholic in the White House. In the vanguard against Smith also were the Anti-Saloon League, the Women's Christian Temperance Union, the Ku Klux Klan, and various other crusading organizations.

Smith put on an energetic campaign, crisscrossing the country and attracting large crowds, drawn, however, more by curiosity than by conviction. But the new medium of radio was now in 30 percent of American households; and while it did not supersede personal campaigning, it acquired a new salience in the election. Smith proved more appealing in person than on the air. Awkward and unaccommodating before a microphone, he came over as strange—even foreign—to small town America. Though far less rousing before a crowd, Hoover was more effective on the airwaves.

Smith did not seem to know how to broaden his support. Sometimes he and his followers were so eager to be themselves that southern Democrats thought the candidate had nothing less than contempt for the South. Also, some legitimate concerns of Protestant America over whether Catholics had dual loyalty and whether the leaders of the American church were able to give unqualified support to some civil liberties should have been systematically and fully addressed. Smith, instead, remained a provincial man. When a reporter asked him, for instance, what plans he had to meet the needs of states west of the Mississippi, his response in a sad effort to be amusing was, "What are the states west of the Mississippi?"

Hoover valiantly denounced the bigotry that sullied the campaign. And to his credit he refrained from even pointing out publicly the uncommon political activity of priests and nuns in drumming up votes for their favorite.

In the end, Hoover was the winner. In August when he visited his birthplace, where the cabin in which he was born still stood, he had reaffirmed the expectation that the best of leaders arise from humble, frontier origins. A decade that had seen the appearance for the masses of automobiles, refrigerators, radios, and "talkies," seemed to require a link to the assured, to the proven past.

Hoover received 21,411,991 popular votes to Smith's 15,000,185. In the electoral college the result was even more overwhelming: for Hoover, 444 votes; for Smith, 87. For the first time since the Civil War, states of the Old Confederacy—Virginia, North Carolina, Tennessee, Florida, and Texas—went Republican. The support was widespread: the industrialized portions of the South identified with Hoover's outlook on business and free enterprise, and went for him; the religious devout, including moonshiners, went for a continuation of Prohibition; blacks once again registered their gratitude to the party of emancipation, as well as for Hoover's sympathy with their plight as a people. But the determinative element was the anti-Catholicism, which had become rampant by election day, although it is said that the vote of middle-class women clinched the decision against Smith.

Smith, as expected, was strong in the cities with substantial Irish-American enclaves. Indeed, Smith succeeded in capturing every city over 400,000 people in size, except Cincinnati—a portent of the mighty urban sweeps that the Democrats would soon enjoy under Franklin Roosevelt and Harry Truman. Moreover, Smith found support in some of the areas where farmers were in economic straits.

Most disturbing was the note of "we-against-them" that had characterized the voting for both candidates. Many Republicans concluded that the possibility of a Catholic in the White House was now doomed for good, while Democratic politicians concluded that they must never again make the mistake of naming a Catholic for President. Both sides could see that the turnout of 70 percent of the eligible voters—a figure that has not been reached again—showed how stirred, as well as divided, the electorate had become. Neither side could imagine the economic disaster which shortly engulfed Hoover and the nation, and when it did Al Smith would say somberly that in 1932 the Democrats could elect even "the one-eyed O'Leary."

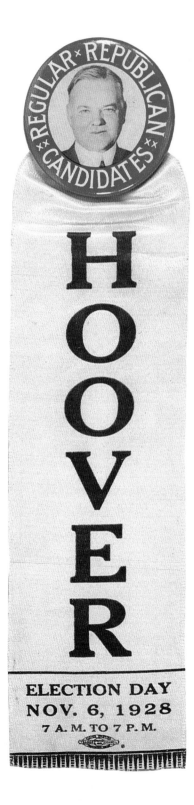

*Celluloid Hoover button attached to a 1928 election day silk ribbon.*

Cardboard hanging sign with Smith
looming over the American landscape.

Campaign pinback brooches.

OUR NEXT PRESIDENT

AL SMITH

Cardboard Smith campaign poster. The 1928
campaign saw a colorful and creative array
of material perhaps because Smith's nomination
became a referendum on religion, geography,
and on the Prohibition issue.

Rings with portrait
inserts of Hoover and Smith.

COLLECTION OF JONATHAN H. MANN

The 1928 campaign inspired several hundred varieties of buttons, many automobile license attachments, cigars, pencils, textiles, and a seemingly endless amount of paper items.
Right: Oilcloth banner.
Below: Cardboard Hoover campaign poster.

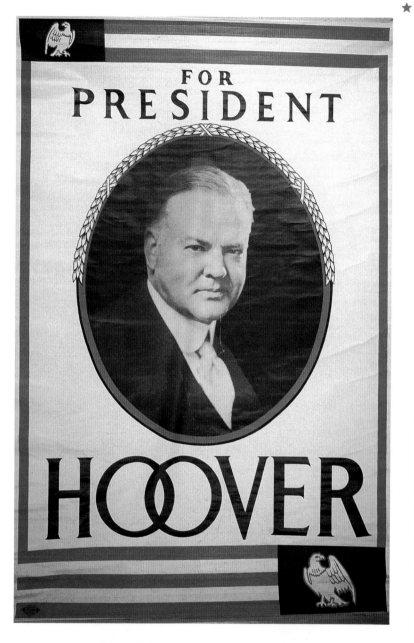

Selection of Hoover buttons. Mass-produced lithographed buttons were introduced in the 1920s. Artistic quality was inferior to the more expensive celluloids (pictured right).

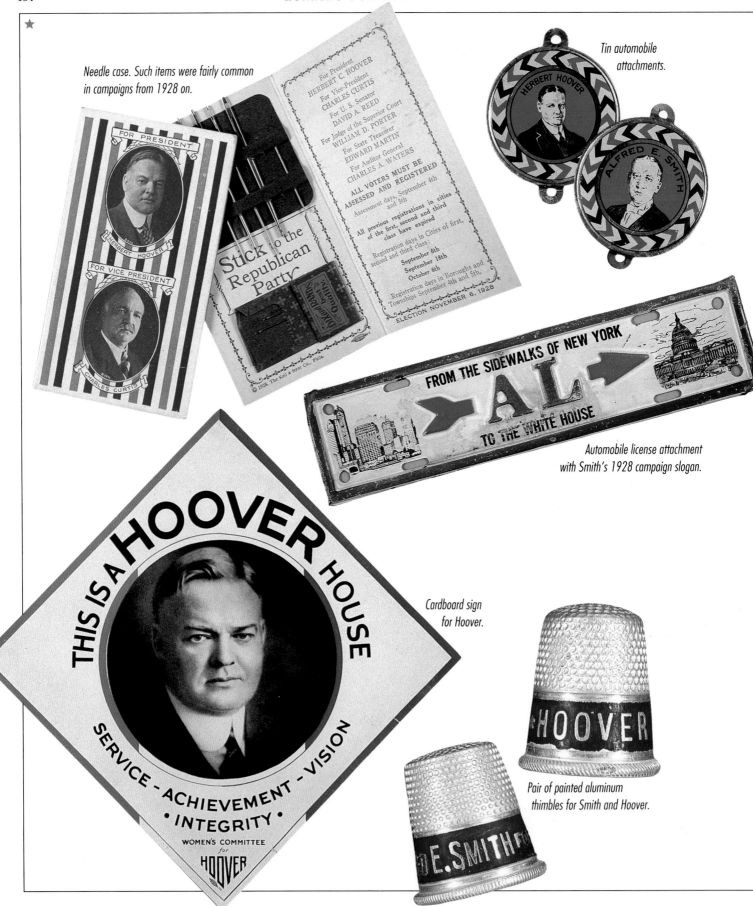

Needle case. Such items were fairly common in campaigns from 1928 on.

Tin automobile attachments.

Automobile license attachment with Smith's 1928 campaign slogan.

Cardboard sign for Hoover.

Pair of painted aluminum thimbles for Smith and Hoover.

VOTE FOR HERBERT HOOVER and CHARLES CURTIS for the Prosperity of your Country and the Happiness and your home....

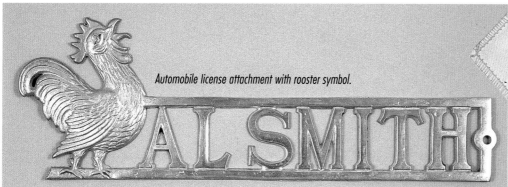

Automobile license attachment with rooster symbol.

Asbestos potholder.

Bring Back PROSPERITY

WITH A REPUBLICAN VOTE

KICK IN—WITH A VOTE FOR HOOVER AND CURTIS

COPYRIGHT 1932 CHARACTER DISPLAY CO.

FOR PRESIDENT

VOTE FOR

HERBERT HOOVER    CHARLES CURTIS

Matchbook for Hoover and Curtis.

Prohibition was an issue throughout Hoover's administration. These two 1932 stickers delineate the Democratic and Republican positions.

Kick out DEPRESSION

with a DEMOCRATIC VOTE

PUT A—KICK IN YOUR BEER WITH A KICK LIKE THIS

Copyright 1932 Character Display Co. Chicago, Ill.

Toby mugs of Smith and Hoover.

WHO? WHO? HOOVER

© COPYRIGHT 1928, BY WOMEN'S BRANCH HOOVER FOR PRESIDENT ENGINEERS' NATIONAL COMMITTEE 17 BATTERY PLACE, NEW YORK CITY

Hoover window sticker.

Above: Poster showing famous sports heroes who endorsed Smith.
Below: Selection of Smith buttons.

Smith wearing his characteristic derby hat.

Sheet music including Irving Berlin's, "BETTER TIMES WITH AL,"
and "SIDEWALKS of NEW YORK," Smith's campaign song.

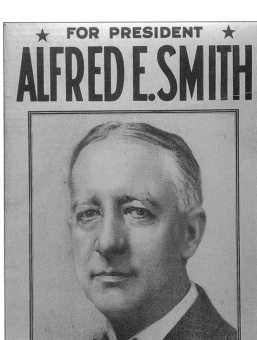

Monochrome poster
for Smith.

Celluloid buttons for
Smith and Hoover.

1929 inaugural program with an aerial view of Washington on cover.

Lithographed tin button. Tin buttons are easily scratched and seldom found in mint condition.

COLLECTION OF JONATHAN H. MANN

Wooden plaque of Hoover.

COLLECTION OF JONATHAN H. MANN

Hoover buttons, both celluloid and tin. The "Christian" reference is an anti-Catholic attack on Smith.

48 STATES
IN THE UNION

*DEMOCRAT*

# Franklin D. Roosevelt

ELECTORAL VOTE 472, POPULAR VOTE 57.4%

REPUBLICAN

# Herbert C. Hoover

ELECTORAL VOTE 59, POPULAR VOTE 39.7%

SOCIALIST

# Norman Thomas

ELECTORAL VOTE 0, POPULAR VOTE 2.2%

**FRANK FREIDEL**
was Warren Professor of American History,
Emeritus, Harvard University, and Bullitt
Professor of American History, Emeritus,
University of Washington. Among his books are
four volumes on *Franklin D. Roosevelt*
(1952-1973); *FDR and the South* (1965); and a
full one-volume biography, *Franklin D.
Roosevelt: A Rendezvous with Destiny* (1990).
Freidel served as president of the
Organization of American Historians.

Franklin D. Roosevelt, concluding his acceptance address to the Democratic convention, stated "I pledge you, I pledge myself, to a new deal for the American people."

The election of 1932, which swept Franklin Roosevelt into the White House, was an emphatic protest against the Great Depression. Few of the voters could have been aware that it was also the fanfare for one of the most fruitful eras of reform and modernization in American history. Roosevelt, the Democratic challenger, established himself as an exceptionally adroit and innovative campaigner. He astutely offered few specifics of his blueprint for a New Deal, uniting diverse supporters with pledges of action. President Herbert Hoover, earlier hailed as a great engineer and humanitarian, had become the symbol of the old order. Hoover was the issue in 1932, Roosevelt pointed out to his advisers. For his part, Hoover was orthodox in campaigning, as he warned the nation of disasters ahead if it were to abandon the prudent course he had set.

Four years earlier, Hoover, the exponent of prosperity through self-reliance, or "rugged individualism," won by an overwhelming margin, but he had become the scapegoat for the deepening depression. He was sensitive and reserved, no favorite of either the Congress or the reporters, one of whom observed that Hoover was ungenerous to a fault. A joke went the rounds of the Senate in May 1932 that Hoover had been kidnapped. The ransom note read, "If we do not receive $500,000 within two hours, we'll bring him back."

Hoover had been bolder than any previous President in combatting a depression, but his measures—a crop purchase program and the Reconstruction Finance Corporation (which made emergency loans, mostly to large banks and corporations)—were too limited to stimulate effective recovery. In June 1932, as the conventions were about to meet, Hoover urged an uncooperative Congress to vote a manufacturers' excise tax, comparable to present-day value-added taxes.

In November 1928, newspapers suggested that Roosevelt, elected governor of New York despite the Hoover landslide, was the prime candidate for the 1932 Democratic nomination. It seemed at the time an empty honor, but the depression transformed the nomination into a coveted prize. Roosevelt had come a long way since 1921 when polio deprived him of the use of his legs, apparently ruling him out of high office. Previously he had been Wilson's assistant secretary of the navy and Democratic vice presidential candidate in 1920. In the 1920s, out of competition, he was a premature "elder statesman" seeking to mend the rift in the Democratic party between the "wet" Catholic wing (centered in eastern cities) and the "dry" Protestant Democrats in the South and West. His wife, Eleanor, became a skilled political surrogate, and his alter ego Louis McHenry Howe developed an expanding correspondence and publicity schemes to build support. In 1938, Emil Ludwig, a biographer, asked Roosevelt when he had first thought of the presidency. "I, never!" parried Roosevelt, "but Louis Howe never forgot."

When he ran for governor, Roosevelt successfully created the illusion that he was lame, not a paraplegic. With braces on his legs, with a cane in one hand, and with the other grasping the arm of a son or aide, he could move slowly to a rostrum. Newspapers published no embarrassing photographs; that would have been considered unsporting, and Roosevelt, fit and dynamic, was obviously in excellent health. Al Smith, the 1928 Democratic candidate who had persuaded Roosevelt to run for governor, gave the definitive response to doubters: "You don't have to be an acrobat to be governor." Or, as Smith later discovered, for Roosevelt to be a contender for the presidency.

As governor, Roosevelt long denied he was eyeing the White House, but after he won reelection in 1930 by a wide margin, he was in all but name a candidate. Howe's letter-writing and fund-raising operation became known as the "Friends of Roosevelt." James A. Farley, the indefatigable chairman of the New York Democratic Committee, was a "political drummer," selling support for Roosevelt throughout the nation. Roosevelt, in response to the depression crisis demonstrated his qualities as an innovator by establishing a state relief agency, model for the subsequent New Deal program, and advocated large-scale action to restore the economy.

In the spring of 1932, with Roosevelt the front-runner by a wide margin, Al Smith announced his candidacy and drew strong support from conservative Democrats. Many of them hoped, after using Smith to stop Roosevelt, to nominate Newton D. Baker (who had been Wilson's secretary of war). The most persistent criticism of Roosevelt

was that he had failed to take action against Mayor James Walker and corrupt members of the Tammany machine in New York City. To do so might have cost Roosevelt the nomination. Reformers denounced him as a straddler, amiable but superficial. Walter Lippmann made the most telling attack: "Franklin D. Roosevelt is no crusader. . . . He is a pleasant man who, without any important qualifications for the office, would very much like to be President." President Hoover and his counsellors thought Roosevelt the weakest of the Democratic candidates and hoped for his nomination.

When the Republican convention met in Chicago in mid-June 1932, Hoover's managers maintained tight control over the dispirited delegates. The platform endorsed Hoover's economic measures, and the keynoter proclaimed that without "that stalwart American," the depression would have been much worse. In nominating him, Representative Joseph L. Scott declared that Hoover "has taught us to strain our individual selves to the limit rather than cowardly to lie down under a paternal government." There was some slight stirring against the dull, conservative vice president, Charles Curtis, notable only for his Indian ancestors, but the delegates contentedly gave Hoover the daunting task of seeking reelection. The Democratic convention, meeting in Chicago, later in June, was more tense and uncertain, than the campaign that followed. Roosevelt had more than a majority of the delegates but sixty-six less than the two-thirds required for nomination. Conservative Democrats in alliance with urban bosses might, under the banner of Smith, stop Roosevelt, then consolidate the convention behind a compromise candidate, probably Baker. Smith, who wanted the nomination for himself, was not disposed to be a stalking horse for any other candidate, and he launched his attack against Roosevelt. As the convention assembled, the Smith mimeograph machines poured out copies of a Heywood Brown column vilifying "Feather Duster" Roosevelt, the "cork-screw candidate."

Roosevelt's candidacy was touch and go. The struggle began when Roosevelt supporters opened a drive to eliminate the venerable two-thirds rule. Opposition was so clamorous that Roosevelt decided not to push the challenge. Next came a nasty clash over the election of a Roosevelt adherent, Senator Thomas J. Walsh, to serve as permanent chairman of the convention. Opponents accused Roosevelt of bad faith, since earlier he had promised with a weasel word to "commend" Jouett Shouse, a conservative who could have been expected to rule against Roosevelt at critical junctures.

The crucial test of strength came with the balloting for the nomination. For hours in the steaming convention hall extravagant nominating speeches and lengthy demonstrations went on and on while the managers of the candidates tried unsuccessfully to negotiate deals to switch delegates. The galleries were packed with vociferous Smith supporters. It was 4:28 on the morning of July 1 when the first balloting began. Farley held a few votes back, and Roosevelt received 666, only 104 short of the nomination. At 9:15 A.M., after two more ballots, he was still 88 short. As the convention recessed until evening, opponents predicted Roosevelt would crack on the next ballot.

Throughout the day, still going with-

out sleep, managers engaged in deal-making. Many of those involved even peripherally claimed later that they had been responsible for the dramatic outcome. The key figure was Speaker John Nance Garner of Texas, whose views were closer to Roosevelt's than those of the opposition. He had no interest in a stalemate. Farley conferred with Garner's manager, Sam Rayburn, who phoned Garner. "Hell," said Garner, "I'll do anything to see the Democrats win one more national election." He agreed

*Poster for Roosevelt's 1930 New York State gubernatorial reelection campaign.*

VOTE FOR HOOVER

DON'T CHANGE NOW

*Poster for Hoover's reelection. Paper items were the dominant ephemera of the 1932 presidential campaign.*

to release the Texas delegation and to placate them by accepting nomination for the vice presidency. The publisher, William Randolph Hearst, opposed to the internationalist Baker, backed the switch of the California delegates for Garner. When the convention reconvened, the shift of Garner votes to Roosevelt brought his nomination on the fourth ballot. Smith refused to release his delegates to make the nomination unanimous, but the struggle led to no disruption in the Democratic party.

Tradition, dating back to the days of stagecoaches, prescribed that some weeks later a delegation would make a formal call upon the nominee and that he would re-spond with an acceptance address. Roosevelt, demonstrating the dynamism that his wife's Uncle Teddy had made famous, broke with tradition and announced he would accept the nomination before the convention. Much as he disliked flying, Roosevelt had arranged weeks in advance for an airliner to bring him from Albany to Chicago. Against strong headwinds the plane bumped along for nine hours en route, but Roosevelt emerged grinning into a crush that knocked off his glasses.

Radio enabled the nation to follow his flight and to hear his acceptance address. It was a broad array of progressive promises, as attractive to many Republicans as it was to Democrats—drastic government economy, crop limitations to raise farm prices, regulation of securities markets, refinancing of mortgages, and relief for the needy. In his peroration he declared, "I pledge you, I pledge myself, to a new deal for the American people." The term "new deal" was commonplace. But the next day a political cartoon by Rollin Kirby depicted a farmer gazing up at an airplane emblazoned "New Deal." FDR's use of the term had caught the popular fancy.

Roosevelt, although serious obstacles faced him, acted as though he were certain of victory. Powerful party leaders had been aligned against him; much of the better informed electorate agreed with Lippmann that Roosevelt was charming but weak, as seen in his failure to cope with Tammany. A few intellectuals found the Socialist candidate, Norman Thomas, more attractive. Campaign funds were also a problem in that depression year; the Democrats had difficulty in raising $1,500,000, although Roosevelt's goal was only a quarter of that of 1928.

President Hoover was disheartened despite reassurances from advisers that Americans, fundamentally conservative, would bury Roosevelt as they had William Jennings Bryan. He steered his campaign along traditional lines trying without much success to appear informal in photographs—riding on horseback and fishing for trout at his previously off-limits hideaway in Virginia. His acceptance address of mid-August warned against experimentation (which Roosevelt had advocated in the spring) and praised his own prudent measures. The nation must turn a deaf ear to demagogues and slogans. The speech was more graceful and forceful than had been expected. One listener wired, "Rivaled Lincoln at Gettysburg."

At about the same time, an upturn of stock and commodity prices in a "baby bull market," provided an interlude of optimism for Hoover, who decided, in keeping with the dignity of his office, to defer major campaign speeches until October. Republicans began to refer to the depression in the past tense, but few if any economic gains trickled down to the millions in economic peril.

Hoover's unpopularity increased. In August, Milo Reno in Iowa proclaimed a farm strike: "Stay at Home—Sell Nothing." More damaging was the reaction when Hoover directed the army to remove from Washington eleven thousand World War I veterans seeking early payment of a service bonus. Before newsreel cameras, General Douglas MacArthur turned the eviction into a drama. Tanks and soldiers wearing gas masks and fixed bayonets drove the Bonus marchers out of their makeshift hovels. Across the nation irate veterans stood at traffic lights selling "Hoover whistles" which made a raspberry noise, and shanty towns on dumps and along railroad tracks bore the name "Hooverville."

Meanwhile Roosevelt was making detailed preparations for an extensive campaign. Late on the night of his acceptance speech in Chicago, he was outlining speech topics and even contents to Raymond Moley, the head of his "Brains Trust." Unlike Hoover, the last President entirely to write his own speeches, Roosevelt long since had assembled a team that was both expert on issues and skilled at speechwriting. He labored with them painstakingly, reassessing and revising, and always himself writing the perorations—"snappers" he called them.

Farley, who with Roosevelt's nomination had become chairman of the Democratic National Committee, extended nationally the techniques he had used in building the Democratic party in upstate New York. He sent bundles of campaign literature and posters to county and precinct workers, and gave them recognition through letters, each bearing his signature in distinctive green ink.

The effective participation of women in the campaign, Farley estimated, increased the Democratic vote as much as 10 to 20 percent. Mary ("Molly") Dewson, who had been effective in New York, established a strong national division of the Democratic party. Women campaigners, Farley noted, "took their jobs in deadly earnest" and were "more faithful . . . in distributing literature . . . and other little irksome tasks."

Both the Democrats and Republicans issued pamphlets, and of course, traditional campaign buttons and insignia, including covers to put on the spare tires carried on the running boards or rear of automobiles.

*Oilcloth spare-tire covers. Spare tires were mounted on the rear or side of an automobile and highly visible.*

The largest expenditures were upon campaign tours and radio time. The Republicans, raising about a half-million dollars more than the Democrats, spent more heavily on national broadcasts, purchasing seventy hours for $437,000. There was no cost at all for one of the most influential of the media, the newsreels in which candidates, rallies, and parades appeared before movie-going millions.

Both Democratic and Republican campaigns focused upon the other's candidate for President. While Roosevelt strategy was to emphasize Hoover's failure to remedy the depression, the Republicans from the outset portrayed Roosevelt as a weak nonentity with a leaning toward socialism. Newspapers helped spread the image. The *New York Post* suspected that he lacked "both conscience and intelligence," and the *New York Times* deemed him indefinite and irresolute.

Roosevelt erased doubts of his decisiveness and character by settling the unfinished business with Mayor Walker of New York City. In August he summoned Walker to Albany to answer charges of corruption. Day after day for long hours Roosevelt interrogated Walker in an acute, relentless fashion until suddenly on September 1 Walker resigned. Tammanyites were resentful, but, when they tried to punish Roosevelt's lieutenant governor, Smith joined Roosevelt to block Tammany. The two rivals were reconciled, at least temporarily, and Smith helped win eastern voters to the ticket. Nationally, Roosevelt began to appear strong and masterful.

While campaigning was the favorite sport of Roosevelt—smiling, outgoing, and energetic—to Hoover (who disliked crowds) it was a distasteful task and he appeared fatigued, grim, and dull. In September, after the Democrats won state offices in Maine, Hoover reluctantly agreed to a lengthy tour as far as California. Roosevelt, in contrast, against the recommendation of Farley and Howe, insisted upon entraining on a wide sweep of the West. He followed it with a tour of the South, safely Democratic, where, presumably looking beyond the election he could build support among voters and politicians for future programs.

Roosevelt particularly enjoyed campaigning by train. Cheerful, chatty, and appearing in fine health, he did much to counter rumors that he was too crippled to serve as President. Nor did he always try to hide his condition. At Seattle, he visited crippled children at a hospital and remarked to them, "It's a little difficult for me to stand on my feet too." But on the rear platform of the Pullman car Pioneer, on the arm of his six-foot-three son James, polio seemed irrelevant. "This is my little boy, Jimmy," he would begin, eliciting a laugh. Between stops as the six-car train rolled along slowly he would renew ties with local politicians or work on speeches.

Each of Roosevelt's major campaign speeches dealt with a specific issue in an interesting but not always enlightening way as he moved to left or right to occupy the middle ground. His farm address at Topeka, Kansas, could be seen as favoring several different agricultural recovery programs and was so general that it did not alarm the East. On the tariff he so equivocated that Hoover compared him to a chameleon on plaid, and warned that if Roosevelt were elected, "grass will grow in the streets of a hundred cities." On electric power, he was specific, favoring regulation and some government production of power to act as a yardstick for the measurement of private rates.

Overall, Roosevelt was vigorous in his attack upon the Hoover administration. Late in the campaign he denounced the Republican leadership as the four "Horsemen of Destruction, Delay, Deceit, Despair." The Republicans controlled the Congress, the presidency, and, he ad libbed, the Supreme Court. Hoover denounced the remark on the Supreme Court as atrocious. "Does he expect the Supreme Court to be subservient to him and his party?"

Hoover's nine omnibus speeches were variations on the theme that without the Republicans the depression would have been worse. There was little that fall to en-

courage him or his audiences. Shortly before he spoke in Des Moines, Iowa, Reno and the farm strikers paraded through the streets with signs, "In Hoover we trusted; now we are busted." Republicans assembling to hear the President yelled, "Give 'em hell, Hoover." But the President's delivery was, *Time* taunted, singsong monotony broken by an occasional tremulous note. As election day approached, Hoover became more strident in sounding an alarm. At Madison Square Garden he scoffed at the "new deal" as a "new shuffle" of cards and warned, "This campaign is a contest between two philosophies of government."

Roosevelt, who had stumped seventeen thousand miles, a record at that time, was far in the lead, and concluded his campaign by summing up his impressions of the countless people he had seen. They had not all agreed with him, he said, but they had all been kind and tolerant. Out of their unity he hoped to fabricate the strongest strand to lift the nation out of the depression.

The election results were as decisive as the straw polls had indicated. Roosevelt received 22,800,000 votes to 15,750,000 for Hoover (57.4 percent to 39.7 percent), and carried 42 states with 472 electoral votes, compared with 6 states and 59 electoral votes for Hoover.

What Roosevelt had offered the voters seemed reminiscent of earlier progressivism, but he had avoided divisions within his party and had won the support of numerous progressive Republicans, onetime adherents of Theodore Roosevelt and Robert M. La Follette. He had received a firm national mandate for change. He was to make full use of it.

The Republican campaign stressed that only a Republican administration could bring back prosperity.

Above: Celluloid button for Hoover and Curtis.
Left: Paper poster for Pennsylvania Republican rally.

Pocket mirror for Roosevelt with a colorful birthstone motif.

Cigar box with Roosevelt paper label.

British-made etched glass crystal goblet commemorating Roosevelt's first inauguration and the repeal of Prohibition. This is perhaps the finest modern glass item with a political theme.

Far left: Ceramic pitcher manufactured by the Stangl Co. with caricature of Roosevelt. Left: Toby mug with a smiling Roosevelt.

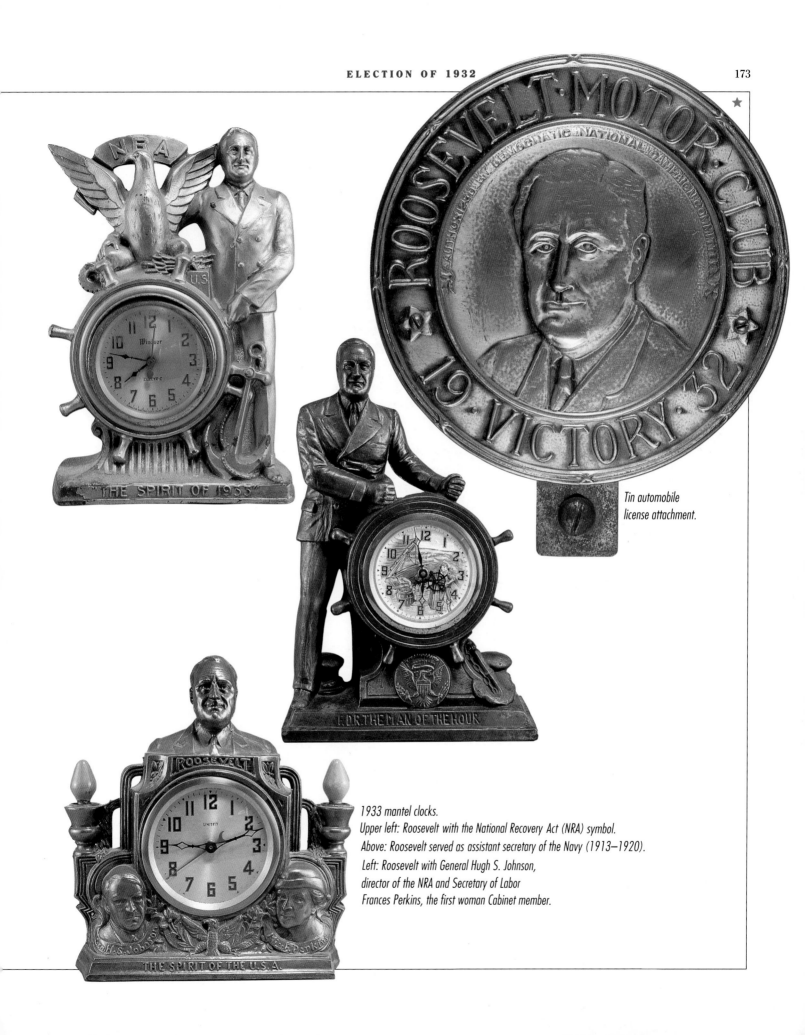

Tin automobile
license attachment.

1933 mantel clocks.
Upper left: Roosevelt with the National Recovery Act (NRA) symbol.
Above: Roosevelt served as assistant secretary of the Navy (1913–1920).
Left: Roosevelt with General Hugh S. Johnson,
director of the NRA and Secretary of Labor
Frances Perkins, the first woman Cabinet member.

Tin automobile license attachment. The Democratic party favored repeal of the Prohibition Amendment. This occurred with the ratification of the Twenty-First Amendment (December 1933).

Oilcloth spare-tire cover for Hoover.

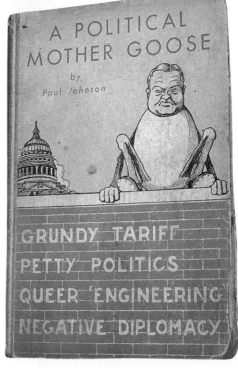

A 1932 satirical campaign book.

Poster for the 1932 Socialist candidates.
They received 2.2 percent of the popular vote.

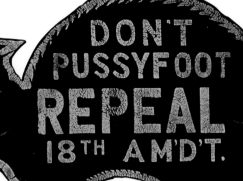

Both sides of the Prohibition issue were expressed on a variety of novelties. The tin tray below shows the three little pigs enjoying beer while an Andrew J. Volstead caricature of the big bad wolf threatens them. Congressman Volstead drafted the Prohibition Amendment (1919).

ROOSEVELT AND REPEAL

The Creed of Jefferson, "Man over money, human rights over property rights, equal and exact justice to the rich and poor, with special privilege to none." This is the creed of American Democracy.

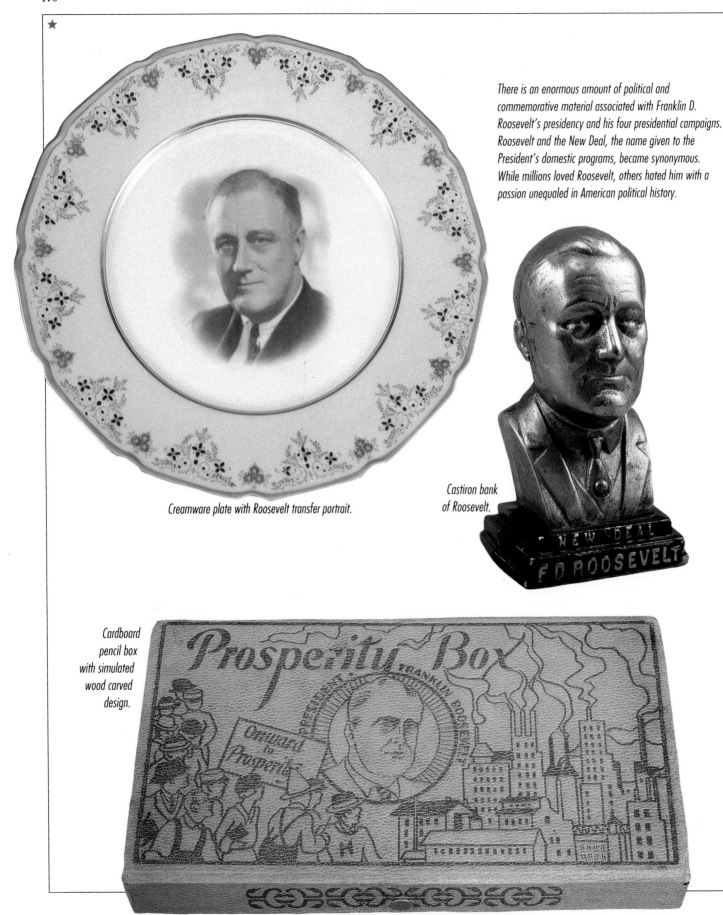

There is an enormous amount of political and commemorative material associated with Franklin D. Roosevelt's presidency and his four presidential campaigns. Roosevelt and the New Deal, the name given to the President's domestic programs, became synonymous. While millions loved Roosevelt, others hated him with a passion unequaled in American political history.

Creamware plate with Roosevelt transfer portrait.

Castiron bank of Roosevelt.

Cardboard pencil box with simulated wood carved design.

*Mirror with Roosevelt portrait.*

*Pressed-cardboard hanger, possibly intended as a lamp-chain pull.*

*The peak period for political neckties was from the 1930s through the 1960s.*

In 1933, the District of Columbia began issuing
a limited number of license plates for each presidential inauguration.

Sheet music.
Top: Photograph is of comedian
Eddie Cantor, the "ME" in the title.
Bottom: An excellent example
of Art Deco design.

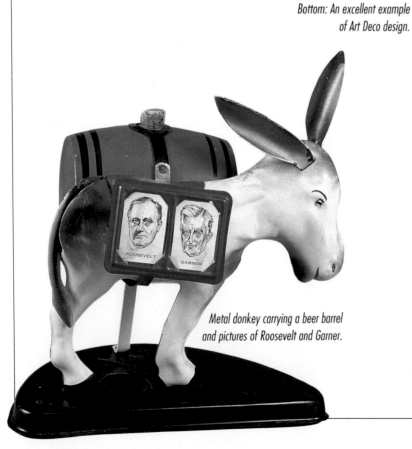

Metal donkey carrying a beer barrel
and pictures of Roosevelt and Garner.

Roosevelt's birthday received national attention during his presidency. Parties were held throughout the country raising money to aid crippled children. This charity event was the forerunner of the March of Dimes. Poster is by Howard Chandler Christy.

Sheet music. Marching with the slogan, "We Do Our Part," many NRA parades were held in American cities to encourage participation in the program, circa 1934.

48 STATES
IN THE UNION

*DEMOCRAT*
## Franklin D. Roosevelt

ELECTORAL VOTE 523, POPULAR VOTE 60.8%

REPUBLICAN
## Alfred M. Landon

ELECTORAL VOTE 8, POPULAR VOTE 36.5%

UNION
## William Lemke

ELECTORAL VOTE 0, POPULAR VOTE 1.9%

ALAN BRINKLEY
is professor of history at Columbia University.
He is the author of *Voice of Protest: Huey Long,
Father Coughlin, and the Great Depression*
(1982) and the forthcoming *The Transformation
of New Deal Liberalism, 1937–1946.*

*Celluloid button of Roosevelt with a 1936 campaign slogan.*

So decisive was Franklin Roosevelt's victory in the presidential election of 1936 that the campaign preceding it has been largely forgotten. Accounts of the contest generally note the highly-charged, class-based rhetoric of several of Roosevelt's most dramatic speeches; or they describe the haplessness of Alf Landon, the governor of Kansas and the Republican candidate for President, who tried ineffectually for a time to present himself as a more responsible New Dealer than the President. Beyond that, the campaign has generally disappeared in the shadows of the historic Democratic landslide in November that gave Franklin Roosevelt 60.8 percent of the popular vote and 523 of 531 electoral votes.

But the campaign of 1936 was, in fact, one of the most important of the twentieth century. It solidified what has become known as the New Deal coalition and helped ensure the national dominance of the Democratic party for more than a generation to come. It validated the domestic policy initiatives of the New Deal; never again, for example, would a major candidate run for President by attacking Social Security (as the Republicans unwisely did in 1936). And it marked a significant crossroads in the art and craft of campaigning; for in that year one can detect, even if in nascent form, many of the techniques and tactics that in the postwar era would transform the electoral process.

Both major parties, and several organizations outside the two-party system, tried to be innovative in 1936 in an effort to ad-

just the campaign process to their rapidly changing society. They made extensive use of radio, which played a much more important role than it had in 1932. They incorporated advertising and public relations professionals into their campaign organizations more centrally than ever before; already, journalists and others were referring to campaign aides as "handlers." They made tentative use of scientific public opinion polls, available for the first time in 1936. They relied almost as much on campaign organizations outside the formal party structures as they did on the parties themselves, evidence of the continuing erosion of the institutional power of the major parties. And they courted the support of extra-party interest groups and attempted to mobilize previously ignored or excluded blocs of voters.

Commercial radio had been a part of American life for more than a decade before the 1936 campaign, and part of American politics since at least the early 1930s. But never before had political leaders been so aware of its potential effectiveness. That was in part because of the success of dissident leaders of the early and mid-1930s—Huey Long, Father Charles Coughlin, Francis Townsend, Gerald L. K. Smith, and others—in using the radio to build substantial national movements. Several of them also made radio the central vehicle of the new Union Party in 1936, which mounted a feeble challenge to the President through its colorless presidential candidate, William Lemke. But the growing interest in radio was in greater

*Tin automobile attachment with the Kansas sunflower design. The sunflower motif, representing Landon's home state, featured prominently in his campaign items.*

measure a result of President Roosevelt's extraordinarily effective use of the medium throughout his first term. His popular "fireside chats" thrust him into the homes of millions of Americans and had created a strong, if artificial, sense of intimacy between the President and the voters. They had also done much to reassure the public in trying times and to persuade the electorate of the wisdom of New Deal programs. By 1936, leaders of both parties recognized that radio was now the most potent political medium available to them.

Until relatively late in 1936, Roosevelt continued his fireside chats, which were ostensibly nonpolitical and for which the networks had always provided free air time, but which he now was making vehicles of his reelection campaign. By the end of the summer, however, the practice had become con-

troversial. The Republicans demanded equal time, and some station owners began refusing the President free access to the air. At that point, the Roosevelt campaign became somewhat more conventional, but no less oriented toward radio. The President delivered a series of highly-publicized addresses: his acceptance speech at the Democratic convention in Philadelphia in June; an important foreign policy address at Chatauqua, New York, in August; an appearance before the New York State Democratic Convention in September; a dramatic speech to close his campaign at Madison Square Garden in New York in late October; and others—all delivered before large and enthusiastic crowds, but all targeted primarily to the radio audience.

Governor Landon, too, tried to use radio, but with limited success. Franklin Roosevelt was one of the most magnetic radio speakers of his time. Landon had a flat, dull, twangy voice, ill-suited to the airwaves. He had not used radio much before 1936, and he never felt very comfortable with it. The country, he once said, needs "less radio talks, less charm, less experiments, and a lot more common sense." But he quickly realized that as a relative political unknown, he could not compete with the best-known man in America without using the airwaves. The party hired a voice coach to help him, but there was no discernible impact. His monotonous, listless, and all-too-frequent speeches—culminating in a dreary election-eve radio address from the governor's mansion in Topeka—bored his audiences and heartened the Democrats. "If that is the best that Landon can do," Harold Ickes remarked at one point after hearing the Republican candidate over the radio, "the Democratic campaign committee ought to spend all the money it can raise to send him out to make speeches."

Both parties tried to use radio in other ways as well. Since 1933, New Deal agencies had frequently broadcast political messages disguised as conventional programming. The Agricultural Adjustment Administration, for example, produced a series of "newscasts" in which government spokesmen recited the accomplishments of the agency in ostensibly objective terms. Network and station executives, fearful of increased federal regulation of the airwaves through the new Federal Communications Commission, had tamely provided free air time even for some of the most egregiously partisan broadcasts.

By 1936, the Republican National Committee had responded by creating a radio division of its own. Thomas Sabin, head of the division, and Henry Fletcher, the party's national chairman (until Landon replaced him later in the year with John Hamilton), hired a professional radio writer early in the election year to create a series of dramatic skits ridiculing the New Deal. In one, "Liberty at the Crossroads," actors portraying young farmers named John and Mary decide not to marry because federal taxes were so high that they could not support a family. Both NBC and CBS refused to air the programs, and the Republicans had to scramble to find independent stations willing to broadcast them, with limited success. The Roosevelt administration's control of the regulatory mechanisms it had created gave it an enormous advantage in access to the air.

Another technological innovation that helped shape the 1936 campaign, although much less decisively than radio, was public

*Felt sunflower with celluloid anti-Landon button.*

opinion polling. Genuinely scientific polling was new to America in the 1930s and still not well developed. Neither campaign was yet entirely comfortable making basic decisions on the results of such surveys. But the Democrats, at least, had begun to incorporate polling into their party organization. Emil Hurja, a pioneer in modern survey techniques, worked for the Democratic National Committee and produced a series of polls in 1935 that demonstrated some of the strengths and weaknesses of the President's programs. There is reason to suspect, although no decisive evidence to prove, that the results of such polls helped shape the policy initiatives of the so-called "Second New Deal" that year. Hurja continued polling through the 1936 campaign, and his were the only surveys accurately to predict the magnitude of Roosevelt's victory. When James Farley made his bold but ultimately correct prediction that the President would carry every state but Maine and Vermont, he was responding to data Hurja had gathered. George Gallup's American Institute of Public Opinion, *Fortune* magazine, Archibald Crossley, and others were also engaged in scientific polling; beginning in 1935, Gallup was publishing opinion surveys on a wide range

Paper game, published in Redbook magazine, which undoubtedly appeared prior to the death of Huey Long in September 1935. (Long is shown at lower left.) A satirical comment on the AAA (Agricultural Adjustment Act) appears in upper left.

of public issues, the results of which affected the calculations of both major parties.

The most celebrated poll of the 1936 campaign, however, was the least scientific and least accurate: the hitherto respected *Literary Digest* poll, which had accurately predicted the results of the 1932 contest. The *Literary Digest* invited its readers to send in ballots expressing their preferences, and the result was a prediction of a Landon landslide; the flaw, of course, was in the nature of the sample—the relatively elite (and relatively Republican) readership of the mag-

azine itself. The failure of the *Literary Digest* poll did as much as anything else to legitimize the new, scientific techniques of Hurja, Gallup, and others.

As the rise of polling suggests, the 1936 contest also represented an important step toward the professionalization of campaigns, a step toward replacing traditional party leaders with advertising and public relations experts as the directors of strategy and tactics. The Republican party, in particular, recruited leading figures from the advertising industry to craft not just its radio efforts, but its enormous distribution of slick campaign literature and, more important, the activities of Governor Landon and vice presidential candidate Frank Knox. The Democrats relied more heavily on party leaders and elected officials, partly because they had more of them and partly because that was the inclination of James Farley, chairman of the Democratic National Committee and a product of Democratic machine politics. But the Roosevelt campaign, too, recruited advertisers, journalists, professional writers, and others to help craft the President's image and public statements. The President's most notable addresses of 1936—his acceptance speech at the Democratic National Convention and his closing address at Madison Square Garden—were collaborative efforts, written not just by New Deal officials such as Thomas Corcoran and Samuel Rosenman, but also by Stanley High, whom the Democrats had hired from NBC.

For both parties, but particularly for the Democrats, 1936 was a watershed year in the movement of campaign activities outside the structure of the party and into organizations representing particular constituencies and interest groups. Most notable, perhaps, was the growing role of organized labor in Democratic politics. The trade union movement had grown dramatically since 1932, in large part because of New Deal legislation (the National Industrial Recovery Act of 1933 and the National Labor Relations, or Wagner, Act of 1935) guaranteeing workers the right to organize and bargain collectively. That labor legislation was one of the principal targets of conservative Republicans, and labor leaders threw themselves energetically into the Roosevelt campaign in part to defend their gains. The labor movement's Non-Partisan League, organized by John L. Lewis and Sidney Hillman, was the principal political arm of the trade union movement; and despite its misleading name, it poured money and organizational talent into the Roosevelt campaign. Among other things, it helped sponsor a nightly radio program that ran for six weeks on CBS beginning late in September, with speeches by leaders of labor, business, religion, blacks, and women attacking the Republicans and praising the humanitarianism of the New Deal.

The Roosevelt campaign also spearheaded the formation of another organization outside the structure of the Democratic party: the Good Neighbor League. The brainchild of Roosevelt's longtime political adviser Louis Howe (who died in April 1936), it presented itself as an organization to bring to American politics the same spirit of idealism that the Good Neighbor Policy had tried to bring to United States relations with Latin America. Its real purpose was to provide an institutional home (and a fundraising vehicle) for people who admired Roosevelt but felt uncomfortable with the Democratic party, particularly middle-class Protestants uneasy with the prominence of immigrants and Catholics within the Democratic leadership. Lillian Wald, a prominent social worker, and George Foster Peabody, a noted philanthropist, were the national chairmen. But Stanley High, a Roosevelt speechwriter, was its actual director. Other nonparty organizations—among them, the Committee of One, the Progressive National Committee, the Roosevelt Agricultural Committee, the Progressive Republican Committee for Franklin D. Roosevelt—were also active on the President's behalf.

The Republicans relied less heavily on extra-party organizations, and at times found them more embarrassing than helpful. The activities of the Liberty League are a case in point. Created by a group of conservative eastern businessmen led by the Du Pont family, the League spent over $500,000 in its efforts to defeat Roosevelt. But its starkly reactionary message alienated many of the moderate voters the Landon campaign was trying to attract and undercut the efforts of Republican leaders to dissociate the party from its most conservative wing.

In all, nonparty organizations supporting Roosevelt spent over $760,000 during the 1936 campaign, compared to slightly under $5.2 million spent by the Democratic National Committee itself. Extra-party organizations supporting the Republicans spent just under $654,000, while the party's national committee spent almost $8.9 million. Obviously the bulk of the fundraising fell to the parties themselves; but the increasing importance of independent campaign organizations was a sign of the gradual weakening of the national party structures and their inability to contain all the contending interests participating in the campaign. That process would accelerate dramatically in the postwar era, to the point that party organizations themselves ultimately played almost no role at all in the presidential campaign.

The most striking, and perhaps the most important, innovation of the 1936 campaign was the effort of both parties, but especially of the Democrats, to mobilize black voters. Never before had the major parties targeted black voters so openly and courted them so assiduously, in large part because never before had so many blacks lived outside the South, in places where they were able to vote without interference from Jim Crow laws. Those efforts contributed to a historic and enduring shift of the black electorate to the Democratic party.

The attempt to lure black voters did not affect the platforms of either major party in 1936. The Republicans incorporated a vague statement of support for "equal opportunity for our colored citizens," the weakest such statement in its history, some black leaders complained. The Democrats said nothing at all about race. But the Democratic party, far more than the Republican, made a series of important symbolic gestures toward black voters. Ten black delegates and twenty-two alternates were seated at the national convention; in the past, the party had permitted

*Paper handbook distributed to local Democratic leaders in 1936.*

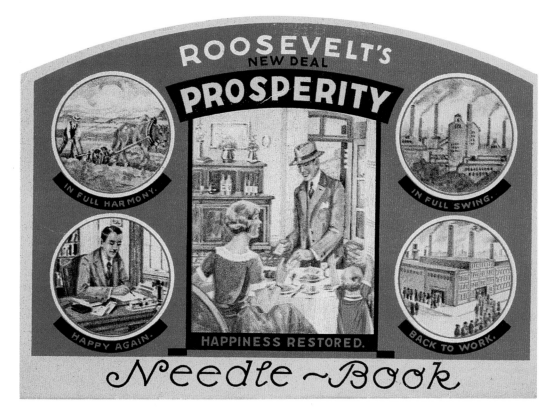

ROOSEVELT'S
NEW DEAL
PROSPERITY

IN FULL HARMONY.

IN FULL SWING.

HAPPY AGAIN.

HAPPINESS RESTORED.

BACK TO WORK.

Needle~Book

*Throughout the 1936 campaign, the Democrats stressed the New Deal economic achievements.*

blacks to serve only as alternates, and as recently as 1928 had forced them to sit at the back of the hall in an area screened off with chicken wire. Black reporters were accredited to sit in the press box at the convention for the first time. And a black minister delivered the invocation at one of the sessions of the convention, also for the first time (prompting an indignant walkout by Senator "Cotton" Ed Smith of South Carolina, who sputtered "This mongrel meeting ain't no place for a white man").

Both parties advertised extensively in the black press during the fall campaign, sought endorsements from black leaders, created "colored divisions" to mobilize African-American voters, and staged mass meetings in black communities. But in all these activities, the Democrats were far more successful than the Republicans. The editors and publishers of the most impor-

tant black newspapers and the most prominent black political and cultural leaders generally supported Roosevelt. And many more black voters flocked to Democratic or pro-Roosevelt political organizations than to those supporting Landon. A Roosevelt rally in New York's Madison Square Garden organized by the National Colored Committee of the Good Neighbor League drew 16,000 people, "the biggest Negro rally ever held," its organizer claimed.

The Landon campaign failed to exploit its one clear advantage in appealing to black voters: its willingness to support federal anti-lynching legislation, something Roosevelt felt unable to back for fear of alienating crucial white southern support. Instead, it relied largely on appeals to tradition, reminders that theirs was the party of Lincoln and Emancipation. "The history of the Republican party and that of our colored citi-

# Half a Million Life Insurance

Twenty-two life insurance companies, less than two years ago, underwrote $500,000 life insurance for Franklin D. Roosevelt. No physical tests are more searching than life insurance examinations on which money is risked. They found that

**Franklin D. Roosevelt is sound, healthy and physically fit.**

Three eminent doctors, Dr. Samuel W. Lambert, outstanding diagnostician; the late Russell A. Hibbs, chief surgeon of the New York Orthopedic Dispensary and Hospital, and Dr. Foster Kennedy, nerve specialist, examined Franklin D. Roosevelt last year at the request of *Liberty Magazine*. They reported:

**Franklin D. Roosevelt's health and powers of endurance are such as to allow him to meet any demand of private and public life.**

Twelve years ago Franklin D. Roosevelt suffered an attack of infantile paralysis. Today he is fully recovered except that his legs are partially disabled. For four years, as Governor of New York, he has worked tirelessly, early and late, for the people of his state. In this presidential campaign he has made a strenuous cross-country tour that would exhaust the ordinary person. Franklin D. Roosevelt's magnificent and victorious fight against the handicap of a dread disease is another proof—perhaps the most dramatic—of his grit, his courage, his strength of character.

### Stop the Whispering Campaign
### Elect a Strong Leader — FRANKLIN D. ROOSEVELT

Issued by the Democratic National Campaign Committee
Hotel Biltmore—New York City

*This 1932 leaflet was one of the very few campaign items ever to mention Roosevelt's health.*

zens are so interwoven," Landon claimed, "that it is impossible to think of freedom and the remarkable progress of colored Americans without recalling the origin of our party."

The Democrats, on the other hand, reminded black voters of all the material benefits they had received, or might soon receive, from New Deal relief agencies. Alfred Edgar Smith, a black who served as "racial" adviser to the Works Progress Administration,

produced a flood of campaign literature publicizing the participation of black workers in WPA projects. He even produced a sixteen-minute film, *We Work Again*, celebrating the WPA's contributions to black Americans. The WPA, the film proclaimed, "changed the haggard, hopeless faces of the bread lines into faces filled with hope and happiness, for now we work again!" The WPA and other relief agencies also targeted funds to strategic black communities in northern cities as the election approached, an example of the political tools that the expansion of the federal government was making available to incumbent Presidents. But the effort to mobilize black voters for Roosevelt extended well beyond the administration and the campaign. Black churches, the black press, CIO unions with significant black membership, the NAACP, and others all exhorted blacks to vote Democratic.

The result of these efforts, and of the New Deal relief and welfare policies of the previous four years, was that Roosevelt received an overwhelming majority of the black vote in 1936, almost exactly reversing the results of four years before. For example, Hoover had received 67 percent of the black votes in Detroit in 1932; in 1936, 66 percent of those same black votes went to Roosevelt. A similar pattern was evident in large black communities throughout the Northeast and Midwest.

Ultimately, of course, the results of the 1936 campaign contest depended less on any particular campaign technique than on the effectiveness of the strategies of the two major candidates. Landon began the campaign hoping to present himself as a moderate, a representative of the long tradition of Republican progressivism. He would not repudiate the New Deal entirely; he would, rather, offer a more "responsible" alternative program of reform. But Landon was never able fully to overcome the power of the party's eastern conservative leadership, who continued to denounce all aspects of the New Deal even as Landon was trying to accept some aspects of the Roosevelt program. Toward the end of the campaign, out of desperation or frustration or, more likely, both, Landon grew more strident and more reactionary, issuing warnings of socialism and dictatorship nearly indistinguishable from those Herbert Hoover had been offering over the previous four years. Roosevelt, for his part, chose to ignore Landon almost entirely (except for some occasional ridicule) and to focus instead on Herbert Hoover and the Republican right. Using some of the most boldly class-based rhetoric of any presidential candidate in American history, he attacked the Republicans as the agents of "economic royalists" and the "malefactors of great wealth." In his final campaign address in Madison Square Garden, he said:

> Never before in all our history have these forces been so united against one candidate as they stand today. They are unanimous in their hate for me—and I welcome their hatred. I should like to have it said of my first Administration that in it the forces of selfishness and lust for power met their match. I should like to have it said of my second Administration that in it these forces met their master.

But perhaps more effective was the Roosevelt campaign's success in persuading Americans who were still suffering from the worst depression in their history that the economy was once again thriving. In Pittsburgh in early September to open his campaign, Roosevelt spoke in the same ball park where he had campaigned four years earlier. He told them:

> At that time I could see mile after mile of this greatest mill and factory area in the world, a dead panorama of silent black structures and smokeless stacks. I saw idleness and hunger instead of the whirl of machinery. Today . . . I saw mines operating. I found bustle and life, and hiss of steam, the ring of steel on steel—the roaring song of industry.

Roosevelt was exaggerating considerably both the health of the economy and the success of the New Deal. But there was enough truth to his claims to make them plausible. The nation's economy was in considerably better shape than it had been in 1932, when many feared capitalism itself was on the verge of total collapse; and it was becoming possible to believe that full recovery was on the near horizon. That perception—the perception that the nation was on the mend and that a dynamic, ebullient, compassionate President was responsible for the improvement—made Landon's task in 1936 virtually hopeless. Not for the first time, and not for the last, Americans "voted their pocketbooks" in 1936. Most Americans accepted Roosevelt's claims that his policies were most likely to help them weather the hard times and lead them to better times. So on election night, Alf Landon waited forlornly in Kansas for what he knew was inevitable defeat. And Franklin Roosevelt, surrounded by family, friends, and political associates, sat at his dining room table in Hyde Park, New York, celebrating the most overwhelming victory in the history of American presidential elections.

*1932 cotton sailcloth banner for Roosevelt and Garner.*

Graphic poster in the WPA art style distributed by the New York State American Labor party.
Herbert Lehman was governor of New York and running for reelection.

Roosevelt tin automobile attachments.
Left: Rebus item [rose+velt].

*Landon campaign items, including a castiron elephant,
"LAND ON ROOSEVELT." Landon polled nearly
a million more votes than Hoover had in 1932.*

Glass teacup with the slogan "ELECT LANDON—SAVE AMERICA."

Landon button criticizing the federal
defecit increase under the New Deal.

The NEW DEAL
is spending $15,000.00
Every Minute, Night and Day

TURN THIS OVER AND SEE
WHO PAYS THE BILL

VOTE FOR

LANDON AND KNOX
AND END THIS EXTRAVAGANCE

L. S. BONIME, NEW YORK        156

Reverse side of a Landon-Knox mirror.

Membership card of a Landon-Knox club. Such clubs
were encouraged by the Republican National Committee.

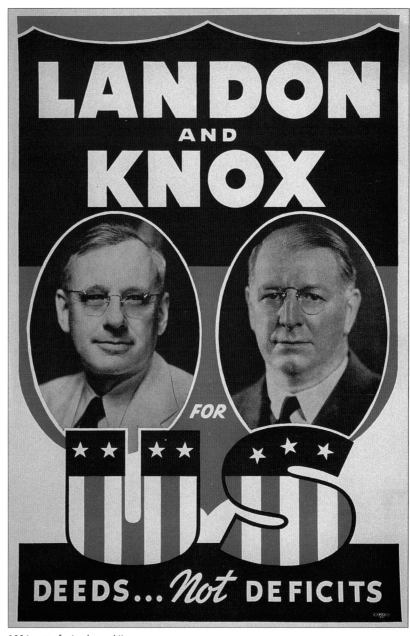

1936 poster for Landon and Knox.

*Glass sign, hand-painted by a member of the United Mine Workers Union, Clarksville, Pennsylvania.*

*Tin automobile attachments from the 1936 campaign.*

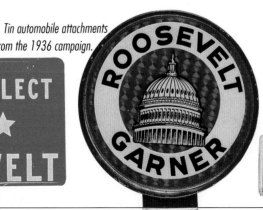

Sheet music from the 1936 campaign. The "OUR
LANDON" item was autographed by Landon.

Poster for a fundraising birthday ball
for the infantile paralysis charity, 1936.

*Assortment of automobile license plate attachments. The Uncle Sam with Roosevelt example is made from pressboard.*

Poster for the Socialist candidates
Norman Thomas and George Nelson.
Thomas ran for President six times.

**He Picked 'im.**

Labor newspaper cartoon
showing Landon being
controlled by the Hearst
interests. William Randolph
Hearst had supported
Roosevelt in 1932 but broke
with his policies by 1934.

Assortment of Roosevelt buttons issued by various
associations. The "YOUNG DEMOCRATS OF KANSAS for
ROOSEVELT" button mimics Landon's sunflower motif.

Felt novelties with inserts of
Landon and Roosevelt plastic buttons.

48 STATES
IN THE UNION

OUR FIRST THIRD TERM PRESIDENT

FRANKLIN D. ROOSEVELT

*DEMOCRAT*

## Franklin D. Roosevelt

ELECTORAL VOTE 449, POPULAR VOTE 54.8%

REPUBLICAN

## Wendell Willkie

ELECTORAL VOTE 82, POPULAR VOTE 44.8%

JUSTUS D. DOENECKE
is a professor of history at New College of the
University of South Florida. Among his
publications are *Not to the Swift: The Old
Isolationists in the Cold War* (1979); *The
Presidencies of James A. Garfield and Chester A.
Arthur* (1981); and *From Isolation to War,
1931–1941* (2nd ed., with John E. Wilz, 1991).
He has edited *In Danger Undaunted: The
Anti-Interventionist Movement of 1940–1941
as Revealed in the Papers of the America
First Committee* (1990).

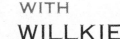

NO FOREIGN WAR
WITH
WILLKIE

"We shall go into our campaign as into a crusade," said a forty-eight-year-old rumple-haired public utilities executive as he addressed a shirt-sleeved audience that possibly numbered two hundred thousand. The date: August 17, 1940. The place: a town in central Indiana called Elwood. The occasion: the acceptance speech of the Republican nominee for President of the United States. The speaker: Wendell Lewis Willkie, a man who had been a Democrat all but four years of his life.

Willkie was the last presidential nominee to defer to an old tradition: accepting the nomination in a speech delivered well after the convention and in another place. The Republican candidate spoke in the town's Callaway Park, formerly a meadow through which he had often driven his neighbor's cow, and in his remarks he described the type of crusade he had in mind. He endorsed much of the foreign policy of his opponent, President Franklin D. Roosevelt, including aid to the foes of Hitler. He also backed major parts of the New Deal, such as federal assistance to farmers, wages-and-hours legislation, old-age pensions, and unemployment insurance. Yet, quick to go on the attack, Willkie accused FDR of risking war by dabbling "in inflammatory statements and manufactured panics." By ignoring the tenet that "only the strong can be free and only the productive can be strong," Roosevelt was leading the nation to "economic dislocation and dictatorship."

The Republican nominee entered the campaign with several advantages. He was blessed with a warm personality, characterized by sincerity, optimism, and that intangible something known as "the common touch." Here was a candidate who held press conferences while sitting on a lawn with reporters and who established his headquarters on the second floor of a two-story frame building in Indiana's Rushville. His bulky frame, raspy voice, and Hoosier drawl conveyed a "countrified" demeanor that held particular appeal to a middle-class seeking renewed links to an older, less complicated America. Far less aloof than his major rivals for the presidential nomination of the Grand Old Party (Ohio Senator Robert A. Taft and New York City prosecutor Thomas Dewey), the gregarious Willkie was the Republican who could match the magnetism of Roosevelt himself.

There were other assets. The blunt-talking Willkie was one of the nation's first "media candidates," the beneficiary of a massive publicity buildup fostered and promoted by Henry R. Luce's Time-Life empire and by much of the eastern press. The fact that he never served in Congress was in itself an advantage, for he had avoided stands on controversial issues that could only have made him enemies.

At first Willkie expressed gratitude that the Democrats had again nominated Roosevelt, saying he would be glad to debate "the champ" himself. "Boy, I think my wor-

*The 1940 campaign inspired an exceptional volume and variety of ephemera, like this Willkie stick of chewing gum.*

*Buttons for and against the candidates' wives. Eleanor Roosevelt, because of her activism and visibility, became an issue in the campaign of 1940.*

ries are over," he commented to reporters. And the fact that FDR was again the candidate did not immediately weaken Willkie. In mid-July 47 percent of those polled by George Gallup's American Institute of Public Opinion claimed to favor Willkie, while 10 percent were still undecided.

The GOP candidate, however, was taking no chances. Recognizing that he had long been a political unknown, he centered his campaign on maximum personal exposure to the voters. Seeking to gain rapport with an electorate who knew him only through press articles stressing his "hard-headed business sense," he undertook the most vigorous race since William Jennings Bryan ran in 1896. His twelve-car railroad train virtually became his headquarters.

During September Willkie journeyed through eighteen western and Pacific states. For the rest of the campaign, he worked the East and industrial Midwest, hoping to make inroads upon the Democratic electorate. By the end of his travels, he had covered over thirty thousand miles, seen twelve million Americans, and had spoken some 550 times to some two-and-a-half-million people. Occasionally he gave addresses ten times a day.

He was engaging, Willkie stressed, in no mere political campaign; his was a crusade "to preserve the American way of life."

This crusade had three main themes: preserving democracy (which he defined as cooperation, fair play, and self-reliance), supporting an adequate defense, and restoring full productivity. Yet much of Willkie's campaign was standard GOP fare. The Roosevelt administration, he charged, was marked by expanding bureaucracy, mounting national debt, distrust of business, and doles to farmers and the unemployed. At Coffeyville, Kansas, Willkie claimed that reelecting Roosevelt would place the nation "under a American totalitarian government before the long third term is finished." At Peoria, he called the President "the great appeaser": "Of all the men I know, Franklin D. Roosevelt is least qualified to lead this nation through this period of crisis."

The third-term issue was frequently exploited. Factory workers in DeKalb, Illinois, transported a coffin labeled "Third Term" to a lonely burial ground. In Cleveland, elephants paraded down Euclid Avenue, their blankets inscribed with anti-Third Term comments of prominent Americans. The Republicans proclaimed October 23 National No-Third Term Day and planned over a thousand rallies for the occasion.

As for the President, Roosevelt initially played a waiting game. It was best, thought FDR, to let Willkie campaign alone for weeks at a time, so that the Hoosier's popularity could peak well before the election. The world crisis, he had said when accepting the nomination on July 19, would not permit him to engage in ordinary electioneering. He ignored Willkie's challenge to debate issues face-to-face.

But FDR certainly made the most of "non-political" appearances. One day he would be photographed hailing the destroyer-bases deal as "probably the most important thing that has come for American defense since the Louisiana Purchase." Another day he would appear in newsreels signing the Selective Service bill and declaring, "We must and will marshal our great potential strength to fend off war from our shores." Cameras remained on him as he "inspected" one defense installation after another, always surrounded by guns, planes, and tanks. On the very morning of Willkie's Elwood speech, Roosevelt reviewed army war games that, in his words, involved "the largest gathering of American troops since the close of the Civil War." That evening he conferred at Ogdensburg, New York, with Canada's Prime Minister William Lyon Mackenzie King.

Of course, in a presidential race, there is no such thing as a non-political address. Visiting the Chattanooga area, FDR pointed with pride to dams erected by the Tennessee Valley Authority. The dedication of three new schools in his hometown of Hyde Park, New York, included praise for New Deal public works projects. Addressing the annual convention of the Teamsters Union on September 11, he promised to broaden Social Security, unemployment insurance, and old-age pensions. At the University of Pennsylvania bicentennial held on September 20, he warned against "selfish seekers for power and riches and glory." Speaking on Columbus Day, he endorsed hemispheric defense, which he said included "the right to the peaceful use of the Atlantic and Pacific Oceans."

Roosevelt also used his political lieutenants to good advantage. Vice presidential candidate Henry A. Wallace, then secretary

of agriculture, roamed the prairie states, denouncing Republican farm policy and its international "appeasement" posture as well. To respond directly to the Elwood speech, Roosevelt chose his acerbic Secretary of the Interior Harold Ickes, who called Willkie a "simple, barefoot Wall Street lawyer" and the "rich man's Roosevelt."

Even before FDR had cast off pretense and entered the race, the Willkie campaign was in trouble. Although in August the polls had looked most promising for Willkie, by mid-September they indicated defeat. On September 20, a Gallup canvass showed Roosevelt pulling ahead of Willkie in electoral votes by 453 to 78; the President was the choice of 56 percent of the electorate, Willkie only 38 percent. By the end of the month, when Willkie returned from his western tour, his campaign had hit rock bottom.

Willkie's portable campaign headquarters was badly organized, and he often ignored local and state party leaders. He refused to discuss matters of patronage, the "bread-and-butter" of precinct workers. He gave autonomy to the Associated Willkie Clubs, whose four thousand units often disdained cooperation with the regulars. Congressman Joe Martin, Jr., of Massachusetts, the GOP national chairman, later wrote that Willkie "treated some of the regular Republicans shabbily"; two-thirds of his time, the Massachusetts congressman said, was taken up with making peace among quarreling party factions.

Displacing the usual old-time politicos in the candidate's entourage were a battery of non-party speechwriters and public relations experts, types soon to be fixtures in

Wooden Willkie stogy box.

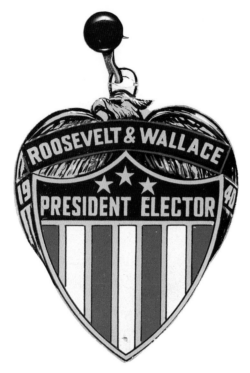

Rare cardboard lapel badge issued to the 449 electors won by Roosevelt in the 1940 election.

subsequent presidential races. Although it is a great exaggeration to say that Time, Incorporated, "invented" Willkie, the Republican standard-bearer was the hand-picked protégé of Henry R. Luce, publisher of *Time* and *Life,* the most popular news magazines in the western world. Madison Avenue played a major role in defining Willkie's "image." Russell Davenport, the managing editor of Luce's *Fortune,* was informally crowned the candidate's "number one braintruster." Willkie was the first "media-made" candidate, something at this point more helpful in gaining nominations than in winning elections.

In comparison to Willkie's penchant for "non-political amateurs," FDR's national chairman, Bronx boss Ed Flynn, was a seasoned pro, as was FDR himself. From the start of the campaign, Flynn insisted upon personal control of all patronage. He centralized the Democratic effort under the direction of the national committee and met frequently with members of Congress.

Willkie's passion to speak out on all issues created further problems. Running mate Charles McNary, a progressive Republican from Oregon and minority leader in the Senate, had given Willkie advice the Hoosier was quick to ignore: "Don't forget, young man, in politics you'll never be in trouble by not saying too much." Willkie endorsed Selective Service, though the majority of congressional Republicans voted against it. Many Republican senators favored a measure that would authorize the government to commandeer any industrial plant that refused to cooperate with the defense program. Willkie, however, called it an effort "to Sovietize or socialize" American businessmen. When FDR first announced that the United States was swapping fifty overage destroyers for ninety-nine-year leases of British bases in the hemisphere, Willkie merely criticized the President for not securing congressional approval or permitting public discussion beforehand. Then he suddenly became belligerent, saying, "If he [Roosevelt] is reelected, he may trade away the Philippines without consulting Congress." Under pressure from isolationist Senator Arthur H. Vandenberg, Willkie called the agreement "the most arbitrary and dictatorial action ever taken by a President."

Early in the campaign, while talking to fifteen thousand blacks in a Chicago baseball park, his voice gave out, a problem that plagued him throughout the race. However, he still spoke whenever he encountered a group of ten, and he bellowed as if they were all deaf. One throat doctor, finding him obstinate, left the campaign train in disgust.

Willkie committed blunders that more seasoned campaigners would have avoided. At Cicero, Illinois, he blurted out "To hell with

Chicago." Women were antagonized by his pledge that, when he removed Frances Perkins as secretary of labor, her replacement "will not be a woman." At one point he engaged in outright falsehood. At Joliet, Illinois, Willkie claimed that "Roosevelt telephoned Hitler and Mussolini and urged them to sell Czechoslovakia down the river at Munich." (His press secretary said he had "misspoken," and Willkie corrected his statement before an audience of nine thousand in Peoria.)

Toward the campaign's end, Willkie's attacks on Roosevelt grew increasingly bitter. He said in Chicago, "If his [Roosevelt's] promise to keep our boys out of foreign wars is not better than his promise to balance the budget, they're almost on the transports." The charge was often repeated. Before the *Herald Tribune* forum, he predicted that "if the present Administration is restored to power for a third term, our democratic system will not outlast another four years!" The political commentator Richard Rovere found Willkie as much in opposition to positions he himself had held a few months earlier as he was to FDR.

For two months Democratic stalwarts begged Roosevelt to start campaigning in earnest. Often they were less worried about FDR's chances, which many saw as relatively secure, than about the possibility that the President's "coattails" might not carry along state and local candidates. By mid-October, Roosevelt feared that the final polls might show Willkie gaining heavily. Willkie's "warmonger" accusations appeared to be cutting into Democratic support.

On October 23, Roosevelt jumped into the campaign. His five formal campaign speeches skillfully employed his greatest weapon, the radio, for he projected to an unseen audience far better than the rasping Willkie ever could. FDR told sixteen thousand cheering citizens in Philadelphia's Convention Hall, "I am an old campaigner and I love a good fight." The Republican leaders, he continued, had been "willing to let the workers starve if they could not get a job." Five days later, in New York's Madison Square Garden, he was so concerned with impressing upon his audience that he opposed intervention that he even defended the rigidly isolationist Neutrality Act of 1935. That night he caught the imagination of voters by his rhythmic attack on three GOP congressmen who had voted against "cash-and-carry" legislation in 1939. The phrase "Martin, Barton, and Fish" might have been deliberately imitative of Eugene Field's "Wynken, Blynken, and Nod," but it was successful enough to be used constantly thereafter. (Bruce Barton was an advertising executive and congressman running for senator from New York, Hamilton Fish an isolationist congressman from FDR's home district.) In Boston on October 30, Roosevelt responded to Willkie's charge earlier the same day that a Democratic victory would mean war in six months.

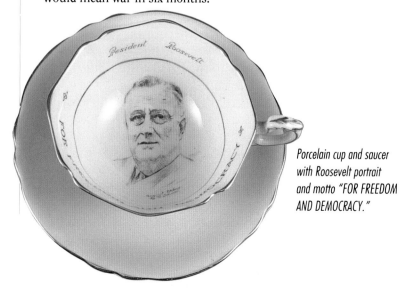

Porcelain cup and saucer with Roosevelt portrait and motto "FOR FREEDOM AND DEMOCRACY."

*1942 calendar with the patriotic slogan "REMEMBER PEARL HARBOR."*

REMEMBER

★ ★
★ ★
★ ★
★ ★
★ ★

★ ★ ★ ★ ★ ★ ★ ★

PEARL HARBOR

| 1942 **JANUARY** 1942 | | | | | | |
|---|---|---|---|---|---|---|
| SUN | MON | TUE | WED | THU | FRI | SAT |
| | | | | | 1 | 2 | 3 |
| 4 | 5 | 6 | 7 | 8 | 9 | 10 |
| 11 | 12 | 13 | 14 | 15 | 16 | 17 |
| 18 | 19 | 20 | 21 | 22 | 23 | 24 |
| 25 | 26 | 27 | 28 | 29 | 30 | 31 |

And while I am talking to you mothers and fathers, I give you one more assurance. I have said this before, but I shall say it again and again and again: Your boys are not going to be sent into any foreign wars.

In Brooklyn, the President exploited a remark, made by a leading GOP lawyer in Philadelphia, that he was only backed by "paupers, those who earn less than $1,200 and aren't worth that." Playing the comment for all it was worth, Roosevelt called such paupers "the common men and women who have helped build this country, who have made it great, and who would defend it with their lives if need arose." He also noted that the GOP was not above advertising in the Communist *Daily Worker*. In a particularly eloquent address delivered in Cleveland, he called for further social reform: "Is the book of democracy now to be closed and placed away upon the dusty shelves of time?"

Willkie experienced far more harassment than FDR. Quipped *Time* of the Republican candidate:

> He had heard more boos, catcalls, razzberries in more States than any other man since Herbert Hoover; he had argued with more hecklers than anyone but John Barrymore; he had more assorted vegetables thrown at him than anyone since old Mississippi showboat days.

Michigan in particular appeared violent. A woman in Detroit threw a metal wastebasket at the Willkie cavalcade, injuring a spectator. Just outside Grand Rapids, a stone crashed through a window of his train. Faced with a tomato in Missoula, Montana, he said, "That's the only kind of argument I get from the other side." Only once did he lose his temper, when an egg in Pontiac splattered the dress of Mrs. Willkie.

There was much mudslinging on both sides. The Colored Division of the Democratic National Committee released a scurrilous mimeographed pamphlet linking Willkie's German ancestry to Hitler's hatred of blacks, claiming that Willkie liked to say "I am a white man," and describing his floor manager at the convention, Harold Stassen, as "the Governor of the 'German' state of Minnesota." (The Democratic leadership immediately disowned the circular, which had been written by a subordinate without permission. Flynn did, however, accept responsibility for a leaflet saying that neither Willkie nor his father had ever protested the ban on black residents in Elwood.)

Both Wallace and New York Governor Herbert Lehman implied that Willkie was Hitler's choice for the presidency, and early in October Roosevelt cited a *New York Times* dispatch from Rome reporting that the Axis hoped for FDR's defeat.

The Democrats too were targets of prejudice and slander. Said one billboard in Philadelphia: SAVE YOUR CHURCH! DICTATORS HATE RELIGION! VOTE STRAIGHT REPUBLICAN TICKET! Leaflets asserted that the Roosevelt family had made millions off the presidency. Willkie denounced the President for employing "the tactics of Lenin, the strategy of Hitler and the preaching of Trotsky." When the President's son Elliott (who had received a waiver for bad eyesight) was appointed a captain in the procurement division of the Army Air Corps, Willkie referred publicly to "overnight captains." Republicans organized "I Want to Be a Captain, Too" clubs, while the American Music Company published the words and music for a song of that title.

In the election on November 5, Roosevelt polled 27.3 million votes, almost 5 million more than Willkie. He captured 449 electoral votes to Willkie's 82. Though the Hoosier drew more votes than any previous GOP candidate, he only captured ten states: Colorado, Indiana, Michigan, Nebraska, Iowa, Kansas, North Dakota, South Dakota, Maine, and Vermont. The Republicans had vastly outnumbered their rivals in press endorsements and had outspent them as well, but these factors mattered little. In general the press gave Willkie more praise but FDR more coverage.

The international situation was the strongest factor in Roosevelt's victory, with the fall of France in June playing a particularly prominent role. Also aiding Roosevelt was an economic upturn based heavily on defense orders, important to a public continuing to vote on class lines. Even a last-minute endorsement by labor leader John L. Lewis failed to help Willkie; labor—including Lewis's own United Mine Workers—stayed with the Democrats. Compared with haunting memories of the recent depression, anxieties over a third term proved minor indeed. Certainly the issue was no problem to Carson Robinson's Buckaroos, who serenaded FDR in Hyde Park with a special rendition of Irving Berlin's "God Bless America":

> God Bless Our President,
>   Our native son
> Stand beside him, and guide him,
> And the fight for the right will be won;
> For a third term, Or a fourth term,
> Put your shoulder to the wheel;
> God Bless Our President,
>   That's how we feel.

It is still debated whether Willkie should have taken the advice of party "pros," who wanted even stronger attacks on FDR's foreign policies. As it was, he polled a record number of Republican votes, and in the process activated nearly six million new voters. It remains doubtful whether any party regular could have done so well. He ran ahead of the Senate and House Republican candidates, though their rhetoric was often far more strident. Roosevelt himself considered Willkie the most formidable opponent the Republicans could nominate, and he was undoubtedly right.

Left: Poster for Willkie. Right: Willkie celluloid button.

Poster for Willkie. A businessman is first in the marching line followed by farmers, labor, mothers, and youth.

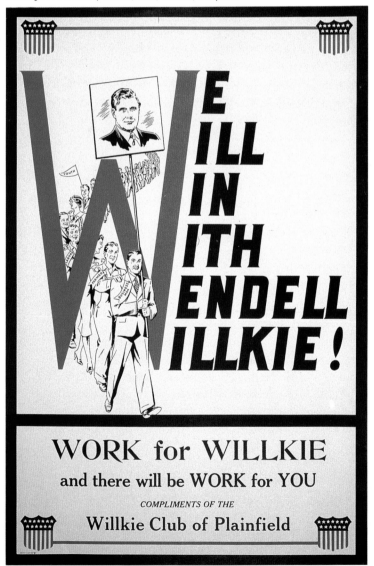

The outcry against a third term was shown in the vast array of anti-Roosevelt buttons issued during the 1940 campaign.

NO THIRD TERM!

DEMOCRATS FOR WILLKIE

HOWARD SCOTT

*Gummed window sticker opposing a third term.*

A Third Term?

Yes!                                    No!

| | | |
|---|---|---|
|  | **EARL BROWDER** Communist Candidate for President of the U.S. "The tradition against a third term in the presidency must be set aside." | **GEORGE WASHINGTON** Declined a third term and thereby set the precedent of a two term limit for President. |  |

**BOSS EDWARD J. KELLY** *Mayor of Chicago*

"I suppose I was one of the very first to go on record for a third term."

**THOMAS JEFFERSON**

"Should a President consent to be a candidate for a third election, I trust he would be rejected on this demonstration of ambitious views."

**BOSS FRANK HAGUE** Mayor of Jersey City, N.J. and Vice-Chairman, Democratic National Committee. "Absolutely 100% for a third term for Mr. Roosevelt."

**ANDREW JACKSON**

"It would seem advisable to limit the service of the Chief Magistrate to a single term of either four or six years."

**HAROLD L. ICKES** Secretary of the Interior. "But, after all, what is a 'sacred tradition' among friends?"

**WOODROW WILSON**

"It is intolerable that any President should be permitted to determine who should succeed him—himself or another."

# THERE CANNOT BE A FOURTH TERM IF THERE IS NO THIRD TERM

*Republican National Committee*

*Broadside issued by the Republican National Committee.*

*Two clever novelty pins. The key is a rebus item [will+key].*

I'd give my Shirt for WILLKIE

WILLKIE McNARY

KEY TO PROSPERITY

THE WINNER AND NEXT PRESIDENT

WENDELL L. WILLKIE "THE HOPE OF OUR COUNTRY"

Copyrighted 1936 · Erickson, Des Moines

## RE-ELECT ROOSEVELT

*Tin automobile license attachments for Roosevelt.*

*Paper leaflet for Chicago rally for Roosevelt and Wallace.*

## LA GUARDIA *Speaks!*

★ A GREAT INDEPENDENT ★          ★ A REAL AMERICAN ★

FIORELLO H. La GUARDIA, MAYOR OF NEW YORK CITY

*for* **ROOSEVELT** *and* **WALLACE**

FRANKLIN D. ROOSEVELT          HENRY A. WALLACE

AT A

### GIGANTIC MASS MEETING
#### AND PATRIOTIC RALLY

ENTERTAINMENT!                          MUSIC!

Sponsored by ILLINOIS COMMITTEE of INDEPENDENT VOTERS
CHARLOTTE CARR—Co-Chairmen—WILLIAM F. CLARKE
Sixth Floor—HOTEL CHICAGOAN—Phone ANDover 4000

### CHICAGO STADIUM      1800 WEST MADISON STREET
7:00 Tuesday Evening   **OCTOBER 29**

— EVERYBODY WELCOME! —

## FREE — Admission — FREE

---

## LET'S FOLLOW THRU

FRANKLIN D. ROOSEVELT          HENRY A. WALLACE
For President                          For Vice President

## THE CHOICE BEFORE US

In the past seven years, the NEW DEAL has traced a Design for Democracy—a Democracy destined to make America one country where every citizen, regardless of race or color, may enjoy the fullest rights of citizenship without molestation or embarrassment. A country where every person may be free to develop a full, rich life, secure in his right to seek an education, enjoy religious freedom and earn a decent living.

The choice before us is whether to vote the Republican ticket, realizing that for a quarter of a century the Republican Party has failed the Negro—whether to support the Democratic Party with a seven-year record of offering the Negro opportunities for advancement.

The Democratic Party is proud of its seven-year record of magnificent achievement . . . a record of building . . . a record of fighting against fire and flood . . . a record of fighting against poverty and disease . . . a record of youth and courage fighting its way towards a sound and solid prosperity.

Mr. Colored Citizen:—Look at this record and be proud. Put your hopes in men who have given you, and will continue to give you what you need most in this emergency—*a sound leadership in Government and Jobs commensurate with your training and ability.*

The NEW DEAL is marching on to make America . . . the "Land of the Future."

•

## Help Finish the Job

•

## Vote Straight Democratic Ticket

PREPARED AND ISSUED BY COLORED DIVISION—
DEMOCRATIC NATIONAL CAMPAIGN COMMITTEE

*Pamphlet urging blacks to support Roosevelt. Because of New Deal economic policies, black voters en masse switched to the Democratic party in 1936 and 1940.*

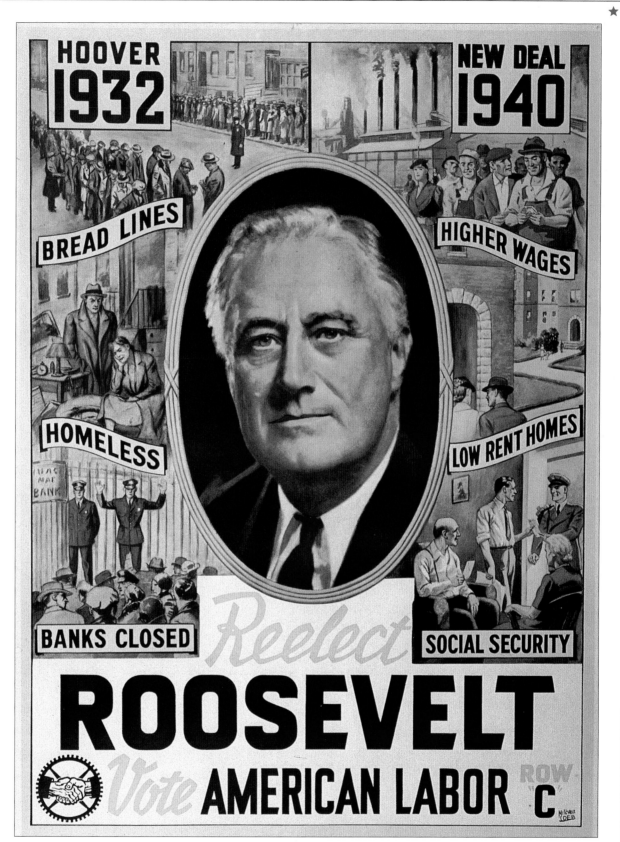

*Poster issued by the New York State American Labor party.*

Tin automobile license plate attachment.

WE WANT WILLKIE

FOR PRESIDENT

Satin wall banner for Willkie.

Selection of Willkie buttons. Shocked by the defection of blacks to Roosevelt, Willkie supporters attempted to win back their votes by using an endorsement from boxing champion Joe Louis (above center).

Glass paperweight with Willkie insert. Willkie is smoking a cigarette.

Silk bandannas for Willkie and Roosevelt using statements made by each candidate. The Willkie item contains a challenge to the President to "debate the fundamental issues of this campaign."

Tin face powder compacts shown both open and closed.

1940 Communist party contributor's paper certificate.

Inaugural program, 1941.

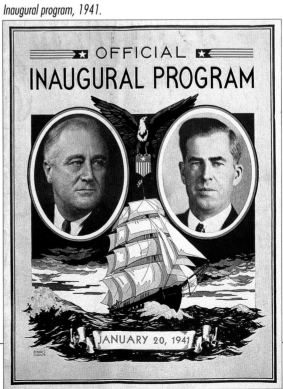

★

1944

48 STATES
IN THE UNION

*DEMOCRAT*

# Franklin D. Roosevelt

ELECTORAL VOTE 432, POPULAR VOTE 53.5%

REPUBLICAN

# Thomas E. Dewey

ELECTORAL VOTE 99, POPULAR VOTE 46.0%

**STEVEN FRASER**
is vice president and executive editor of Basic
Books in New York. He is the author of *Labor Will
Rule: Sidney Hillman and the Rise of American
Labor* (1990) and the co-editor of *The Rise and
Fall of the New Deal Order, 1930–1980* (1990).

For only the second time in American history a presidential election was to take place while the country was at war. Eighty years earlier, in 1864, the nation was at war with itself; in 1944 its enemies were abroad. But no less than Abraham Lincoln, Franklin Delano Roosevelt campaigned under the protective mantle of the Commander-in-Chief, a sacred aura his opponent would have somehow to dissipate to have any serious chance of victory.

Thomas E. Dewey, the governor of New York, secured the Republican nomination easily, perhaps too easily. Wendell Willkie, the party's titular leader as its nominee in 1940, thoroughly estranged himself from much of the Republican leadership as well as from its rank and file and suffered a crushing defeat in the Wisconsin primary. Deliberately cautious and coy, Dewey had hardly campaigned, at least publicly. This turned out to be the worst sort of tactical preparation for the presidential contest ahead where, unless he came out full of fire and fight, he risked being ignored entirely. Still, with the country at war, Dewey's people most feared being thought divisive. The governor thus tried his best to seem composed, judicious, even aloof, a mien his advisers considered "presidential"—but which a great many others, including the press, found boring and bland.

This studied dullness persisted through the June nominating convention in Chicago where the delegates reacted to the stupefying heat (105 degrees in the hall) and the soporific convention proceedings by adjourning a day early—one wag likened the convention to a cross between an oven and morgue—having selected Dewey practically without opposition. They chose as his running mate the undistinguished but mediagenic governor of Ohio, John Bricker—according to William Allen White, "an honest Harding"—whose principal virtue, besides his sheer good looks, was the solace he offered midwestern Republicans that the party had not been captured by the eastern Wall Street establishment. Born in a log house south of Columbus (from which he walked four miles to school each day) and having worked his way through college, Bricker was warmhearted and charming where Dewey was not. And if he was none too bright—his mind was compared to stellar space, a huge void filled with a few wandering cliches—and prone to an oratory "of the John Wintergreen variety," it was precisely these qualities which were reassuring to heartland Republicans who never entirely trusted their slick and sophisticated brethren from the Atlantic gold coast.

In the weeks ahead Dewey paid the price for this excessive "presidential" prudence. Like some malodorous albatross, he carried around with him a reputation for being rigid, humorless, fastidious, icy, slick, bland, stuffy, and prim, suffocated by an exaggerated sense of his own dignity. In the public eye he became the "Boy Orator of the Platitude," the bridegroom atop the wedding cake, a candidate who when asked by a reporter to smile replied, "I thought I was," a man afflicted with "intellectual halitosis," so self-important he could "strut while sitting down"; in a word, an insufferably pompous pretender to the throne. In image and style one could hardly imagine a starker, more damning contrast to FDR, the patrician democrat whose wit, spontaneity, self-confidence and mastery of "conversational oratory" had charmed a whole political generation.

Yet Dewey was not innately so stiff and machinelike, so overly careful and prepped. During his term as New York City's racket-busting district attorney, and in his campaigns for governor in 1938 and 1942, a scrappier, more combative and dynamic Dewey excited the press and electrified the populace. All of that, however, was purposely repressed in favor of a presidential coolness which froze the campaign just as it was about to get underway.

Dewey's campaign managers faced a real dilemma: to deflate the majesty enveloping an enormously popular three-term sitting President in wartime, their candidate would need to project a maturity far beyond his forty-two years and limited political experience; at the same time, Dewey needed to capitalize on his obvious youthfulness and energy, and thereby remind the electorate of the President's increasingly noticeable frailty. But it was difficult to appear both vigorous and bland at the same time and so an impression of Dewey as a youthful doer never managed to come alive. Dewey the man remained stillborn; one not unfriendly account compared his brain to a photoelectric cell, not exactly the sort of energetic image Deweyites were looking for. The editors of *Look* urged the campaign to add "a dash of humanity" to counter Dewey's "precision-tool image," but nothing seemed to relieve the air of lifelessness that surrounded the candidate.

All the more reason, then, to emphasize that his opponent was himself nearly dead. Sophisticated in the tactics and techniques of mass media electioneering, Dewey's campaign managers did all they could to dramatize how truly sickly FDR had become. And indeed Roosevelt looked haggard and emaciated, his body seemingly ravaged. He endured excruciating pain whenever he attempted to stand while delivering a public address. When he presented his first nationwide campaign broadcast from the Bremerton Navy Yard near Seattle, he experienced such pain from an angina attack that he had to grip the lectern for support. His evident difficulty in turning the pages of his speech gave it a faltering tone that shocked listeners accustomed to his composure, confidence, and cheerfulness. Polls following the speech registered a precipitous drop in Roosevelt's standing. All this fed widespread anxiety that FDR might not be able to survive a fourth term.

Accordingly, Dewey's early speeches repeatedly characterized the administration as a group of "tired, old men." Campaign photographs of Dewey invariably showed him hard at work or hard at play. Meanwhile, a picture of FDR showing him gaunt, exhausted, and glassy-eyed as he delivered his acceptance speech was widely reproduced in Republican party pamphlets and in newspapers sympathetic to the governor. Campaign manager Herbert Brownell huddled with the archconservative Colonel McCormick of the *Chicago Tribune* to further an already active whispering campaign about the President's health—that he had suffered a heart attack, a stroke, or both; that he was confined to a Miami sanatorium; that he had suffered a breakdown while visiting Bernard Baruch at his South Carolina plantation. Pictures of Roosevelt at two-year intervals, beginning in 1932, were carefully selected to display in the harshest way how much he had aged and were juxtaposed against shots of Dewey on the golf course.

In other respects as well, the Dewey campaign, however strategically misdirected, was meticulously plotted. Thus the governor was a strong believer in the efficacy of scientific polling, having hired the Psychological Corporation of New York for his 1942 gubernatorial race. He and his managers coordinated the governor's itinerary with the Gallup poll, avoiding those states the Gallup surveys declared safely Republican and scheduling special trips to undecided areas like New York, Massachusetts, Missouri, and Maryland. Especially in the latter stages of the election, the campaign responded to every fluctuation in the polls. When Gallup showed slippage in Missouri, Dewey hurried off to deliver a speech in St. Louis.

A special train, mobilized for Dewey's first campaign swing in early September, catered to the media. On board were seventy-five print and radio reporters, photographers, and researchers. There were special cars for speechwriters, for press conferences held once a day, for the various media, for local potentates. Journalists were fed well and supplied with typewriters. The train was wired for sound so that reporters could hear the candidate's speeches without venturing outside.

*Plaster figurines depicting the wartime "Big Three"—Stalin, Roosevelt, and Churchill.*

Dewey's appearances remained overly formal through the first phase as he resisted most pleas for him to press the flesh and kiss babies. His speeches were rigorously scoured, not only for their political ramifications, but for their publicity potential and news value. Dewey then rehearsed their delivery, penciling in pauses, stops, and emphases. Slowly he loosened up and as the train moved west he found himself in torchlight parades adorned by Indian war bonnets and ten gallon Stetson hats. In Los Angeles, 93,000 gathered at the Coliseum for a Cecil B. DeMille extravaganza with elephants doing handstands and a parade of luminaries including Cary Grant and Ginger Rogers. But Dewey was determined to remain dignified and high-minded. Amidst all this Hollywood hoopla he delivered a deadly oration about Social Security and unemployment insurance.

As a consequence, his advisers watched gloomily as his Hooper rating for the share of the radio audience plummeted from 20.5, after his first speech in Philadelphia, to 14.5 a few weeks later in Seattle. This fall-off in radio listeners was especially worrisome because wartime shortages of cars and gasoline meant more people derived their political information via the radio than by traveling to traditional campaign rallies. Moreover, there had been a tenfold increase in the size of the radio audience between 1936 and 1942, from 6.3 million to 61.3 million. (After the election a survey sample indicated that 30 percent of the voters were influenced by radio as compared to 23 percent by the press.)

The Dewey campaign made heavy use of radio, both nationally and through statewide hook-ups at prime-time evening slots. The Republican National Committee spent $2 million on radio advertising alone. As compared to speeches before rallies, radio speeches were short—no more than twenty minutes—and were presented in punchy, clipped sentences. Dewey made almost as many radio speeches as he delivered less formal rear-platform or streetcorner orations.

But however sensitive the campaign was to the lures of modern technology and the "science" of public relations, it still did the traditional things. Thus, a campaign biography, *Thomas E. Dewey: An American of This Century*, originally prepared for Dewey's 1938 run for governor, was updated and reissued. Even the candidate considered it "too sugary" and critics compared it "very favorably with some of Albert Payson Terhune's hymns to the collie." Although wartime shortages of metals and plastics impoverished the "material culture" of the '44 election, there were still buttons and lapel devices, posters, pennants, banners, ribbons, and stickers—Brownell saturated New York, a doubtful state, with a thousand color posters and five million buttons, among the most popular of which were "Dewey the Racket-Buster/New Deal Buster" and "No Fourth Term."

The Democratic party produced its own inventory of buttons and banners intended to milk patriotic sentiments "Support Your Commander-in-Chief"—and to counter Republican propaganda about FDR's alleged dictatorial ambitions—"Three Good Terms Deserve Another"—and one button that combined both objectives—"Go 4th to Win the War." One grey, metallic lapel badge took the shape of a small, scottie dog—a replica of the President's pet, Fala—above which was inscribed the slogan, "Fala Me to the Polls." Behind that odd little piece of campaign paraphernalia, however, lies the story of how a once polite, if sedate and even boring, electoral contest was transformed into what Roosevelt would describe as the "meanest" of his long career in public life.

Ed Flynn, Democratic party boss in the Bronx, thought Roosevelt so sick he ought not to run. Although the President's health was indeed parlous, he was unlikely to step down with the war still far from over, and on July 11 he removed any lingering doubts by announcing his candidacy. Little suspense attended the Democratic convention, which gathered in Chicago in late July, except who the delegates would select as Roosevelt's running mate. A bloody backroom battle resulted in the dumping of Vice President Henry Wallace, spokesman for the country's liberal-labor coalition, in favor of Harry S. Truman, a moderate senator from the border state of Missouri—"the Missouri Compromise of 1944"—acceptable to all the party's contending factions. It was a decision that would soon come to haunt the campaign.

At first, Democratic strategy seemed self-evident. The President's physical frailty on the one hand and his exalted stature as

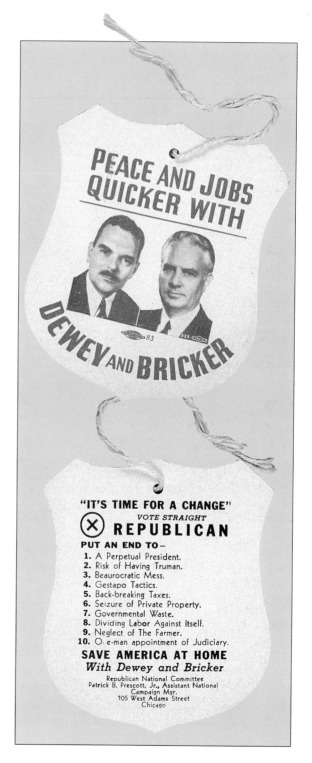

*Paper coat tag for Dewey and Bricker.*

*Missouri Democratic party poster. A paucity of campaign items were issued in 1944 because of World War II.*

For nearly two months the President became an absentee candidate, remaining aloof and making precious few partisan appearances except those that could easily be linked to the war. Thus, his nationwide broadcast from the Bremerton Navy Yard was delivered from the deck of a destroyer with its great guns clearly etched in the background. While the President maintained his olympian distance, speaking sparely and only on semi-ceremonial occasions, Truman raced around the country delivering speeches everywhere, even polishing his radio style under the tutelage of media counsellor, J. Leonard Reinsch. Meanwhile, the country was saturated with buttons and banners featuring the Roosevelt visage beneath the "V" for victory symbol.

But the strategy began to backfire. Roosevelt's passivity only fed rumors he was seriously ill and unable to campaign, much less to endure the rigors of a fourth term. Close advisers, including Harry Hopkins and Sam Rosenman, worried about Roosevelt's apparent indifference. Public opinion polls, about which the Democrats were no less sensitive than the Republicans, seemed to confirm their anxieties. Roosevelt relied on Hadley Cantril who ran the Office of Public Opinion Research at Princeton. Cantril's sophisticated election district sampling and secret ballots suggested a serious problem of voter apathy—in part a testimony to the essential dullness of the campaign so far—and an equally worrisome trend showing upper-income voters somewhat more and lower-income voters (especially Irish, Italian, and German Catholics) somewhat less pro-Roosevelt than everyone had assumed. Poor and working-class voters es-

Commander-in-Chief on the other suggested that the wisest course was to campaign little if at all, implying that with the country at war the President would not be distracted by petty political squabbles; and those who were thereby betrayed a lack of patriotic fervor. Not surprisingly, then, FDR's campaign managers did all they could to exploit the inherent advantages of their candidate's prestige as the nation's defender, a status recently enhanced by the successful D-Day landings in France.

pecially seemed far more concerned with domestic than with foreign affairs. Cantril advised the Democrats to inject a greater sense of national crisis into the campaign. A *Fortune* poll during the third week in September showed a decline in FDR's lead over Dewey from 9 percent to 5 percent. And still the President did nothing.

Everything changed on the evening of September 25 in Washington at the Hotel Statler, where Roosevelt delivered what Sam Rosenman considered the greatest campaign speech of his illustrious career. Speaking before a friendly gathering of Teamster Union officials, and simultaneously over the radio to the nation at large, FDR miraculously recovered all the charm, wit, and vigor of past campaigns and in the process turned a scottie dog into the most celebrated pet in presidential history. Sometime earlier an obscure Republican congressman from Michigan, Harold Knutson, had publicly insinuated that after a presidential excursion to Alaska, FDR had committed an extravagant abuse of the public treasury by sending a naval destroyer all the way back to the Aleutian Islands just to fetch the family dog, Fala, who had been inadvertently left behind. Amusingly indignant, feigning a righteous wrath, the President sprang to the defense of his pet:

> The Republican leaders have not been content to make personal attacks upon me—or my wife—or my sons—they now include my little dog, Fala. Unlike the members of my family, Fala resents this. When he learned that the Republican fiction writers had concocted a story that I left him behind on the Aleutian Island and had sent a destroyer back to find him—at a cost to

the taxpayer of two or three or twenty million dollars—his Scotch soul was furious. He has not been the same dog since. I am accustomed to hearing falsehoods about myself, but I think I have a right to object to libelous statements about my dog.

Once the laughter and cheers subsided Roosevelt continued the gentle mocking of his opponent, in the process undermining the premises upon which Republican strategy up to that point had been based. In a few lines

*New York State Republican party poster. The campaign item shortage was especially evident on the Republican side.*

the President managed to defuse damaging rumors about his advanced age and to reignite smoldering popular anxieties about the Great Depression. "Well, here we are together again," he told his by now gleeful listeners, "after four years—and what years they have been! I am actually four years older—which seems to annoy some people. In fact, millions of us are more than eleven years older than when we started in to clean up the mess that was dumped in our laps in 1933." Caustically, he warned Republicans attempting to blame him for the depression: "Never speak of rope in the house of a man who has been hanged."

The effect of the speech was electric. Masterfully delivered, craftily combining deadpan innocence and biting ridicule, it convinced its listeners, including the large contingent of reporters in attendance, that the old Roosevelt was back, fully armed and ready to do battle in the remaining weeks before election day.

If the Washington speech reinvigorated a seemingly exhausted President, it positively inflamed an otherwise placid Dewey. Speedily, Republican fundraisers collected $27,000 to expand their radio network from 164 to 288 stations in preparation for Dewey's rebuttal. In Oklahoma City's packed Municipal Auditorium the candidate lashed back, accusing FDR of "mudslinging, ridicule, and wisecracks," of "plumbing the depths of demagoguery," of making "reckless charges of fraud and falsehood" which Dewey reluctantly felt compelled to answer. "He has made his charges. He has asked for it. Here it is." Roosevelt had never managed to solve the depression, Dewey claimed, and his woeful ineptitude in preparing for the war had cost the country countless lives. In a word, the President's record was "desperately bad."

The audience roared in delight. Somnolent party apparatchiks exulted, describing Dewey's new oratorial pyrotechnics as "an earthquake." The New York *World-Telegram*, a Republican paper, shouted its approval in banner headlines: "FDR Asked For It." Suddenly the campaign's coffers swelled. In keeping with the new combative tone, advisers urged that the final rounds of the campaign "demand body punches and head-rocking." Phase Two of the 1944 election was underway, as different as it could possibly be from the studied civility of Phase One.

In the interests of "body punches and head-rocking," the Dewey campaign made a potent addition to the symbolic vernacular of presidential electioneering. While continuing to rake the administration for its bungling, chaos, and incompetence, Republican spokesmen—both candidates, party officials and publicists, sympathetic newspapers and magazines—hammered away at what they alarmingly alleged was a lethal link between President Roosevelt and the Communist party of the United States. The Red bogeyman introduced an element of diabolism into the dramaturgy of presidential politics.

What provided the Dewey people with this ammunition was the vital role played by the newly established Political Action Committee of the CIO in the President's campaign. The CIO's PAC was the single most important innovation of the 1944 election. Yet in style and tactics PAC was a throwback, deploying twentieth-century technology on behalf of the nineteenth century's forms of mass political mobilization. Martial in tone, drawing upon all the instincts of ritualistic solidarity, deeply partisan, information-rich, and abundantly dramatic, PAC was designed to remedy the Democratic party's most threatening vulnerability: namely, a creeping voter apathy, especially among the working class and poorer parts of the population that had reached truly frightening proportions during the 1942 off-year elections.

Organized in fourteen regional centers, PAC attacked the problem with a vengeance, organizing massive voter registration drives in war plants and such critical cities as Detroit, Chicago, San Francisco, St. Louis, and Los Angeles. In Detroit, for example, a thousand PAC canvassers blanketed the city; during a single day in St. Louis PAC workers managed to enroll thirty-six thousand new voters. PAC distributed eighty-five million pieces of literature and instructed its canvassers that: "Canvassing is like love. There is no substitute for love. There is no substitute for doorbell ringing." Telephone banks were installed to call voters on election day while other PAC workers were ready to fill in as babysitters or to provide car pools to the polls. At national headquarters in New York, 135 full-time staffers, not to mention a host of volunteers, issued a stream of weekly bulletins tailored for labor newspapers, Negro publications, and other sympathetic audiences. PAC pamphlets were illustrated there under the guidance of noted artist, Ben Shahn. Together with a sister organization, the National Citizens Political Action Committee, created by the CIO to extend its political reach into the liberal middle-class, PAC staged "prestige advertising" through parades, rallies, and radio extravaganzas that featured such Hollywood stars as Humphrey Bogart and Edward G. Robinson. All in all, the editors of *Time* concluded, it was "far

Anti-Roosevelt button with the Republican slogan.

and away the slickest piece of political propaganda in a generation."

Sidney Hillman, an immigrant Jewish refugee and onetime Socialist, who had fled Russia following the defeat of the 1905 revolution, was chairman of PAC. Hillman was president of the Amalgamated Clothing Workers Union, a founder of the CIO, and a confidant of the President's. As an immigrant, a Jew, and an ex-radical, Hillman became grist for a Republican propaganda mill looking to churn out "body punches." The immediate pretext was provided when Arthur Krock, a senior *New York Times* Washington correspondent of known conservative inclinations, published a rumor that during the Democratic convention FDR had instructed party chieftains regarding the choice of his vice presidential running mate to "Clear it with Sidney."

"Clear it with Sidney" instantly became the Republicans' slogan of choice as they worked assiduously to spread the toxic logic it seemed to unleash: If Sidney Hillman possessed this much power, then so did the CIO; and since the CIO was known to harbor an

active Communist party faction, then so too did the Communists. Hardly shy about finishing the equation, Deweyites everywhere drew the obvious conclusion: President Roosevelt and the Democratic party had become the captives, wittingly or not, of a Red virus intent on worming its way into the heart of the republic.

Thus Republican pollsters in search of issues to emphasize urged their employers "to castigate the Hillman group as extremists and radicals." Party propagandists ran variations on this theme, a favorite slogan being: "Sidney Hillman and Earl Browder's Communists have registered. Have you?" Dewey himself picked up the refrain, first in his Oklahoma City rebuttal where he included Earl Browder along with Hillman in a list of unsavory characters who considered Roosevelt "indispensable." In a Boston address late in the contest he grew more strident: "This is that same Earl Browder who was convicted as a draft dodger. . . convicted again as a perjurer and pardoned by Franklin Roosevelt in time to organize the campaign for his fourth term."

Dewey's running mate, John Bricker, was even less restrained as he warned New England Catholics that "insidious and ominous are the forces of communism linked with irreligion that are worming their way into national life." Bricker treated Connecticut voters to the most unvarnished formulation of this diabolic menace: "First the New Deal took over the Democratic Party

and destroyed its very foundation. Now the Communistic forces have taken over the New Deal and will destroy the very foundations of the republic." Nationally syndicated columnist Westbrook Pegler lashed out at a CIO-CP alliance built upon "naturalized but unassimilated European parasites." Dewey radio ads promised to clear everything with Congress and the American people. William Randolph Hearst ordered his editors "to play up Hillman and his PAC on every occasion. It is really a political bribery committee." Hearst papers sponsored a "Sidney Limerick Contest" which featured such winning verses as:

> Clear it with Sidney, You Yanks
> Then offer Joe Stalin your thanks
> You'll bow to Sid's Rule
> No Matter How Cruel
> For that's a directive of Frank's.

It was a remarkable outpouring of vitriol; a practically unprecedented attempt to tar a sitting President with the brush of subversion. Naturally, it elicited a response. PAC propaganda, in both its visual and written forms, went out of its way to emphasize the organization's essential "Americanism" and patriotism. "'I am an American.' You are proud when you say that. We are all proud when we say that. We have a right to be proud. It is good to be an American. We love America." Hillman accused the Republican party of "red-baiting and Jew-baiting." Roosevelt chastised Dewey and Bricker: "When any political candidate stands up and says, solemnly, that there is a danger that the Government of the United States—your Government—could be sold out to the Communists—then I say that candidate reveals a shocking lack of trust in America."

Privately, FDR confided his "unvarnished contempt" for Dewey. Publicly, however, he concentrated instead on perpetuating the image of renewed vigor and self-confidence he had displayed at the Teamster dinner. But he carefully husbanded his resources. With the exception of a single radio talk from the White House, he made no major campaign speeches for nearly four weeks following the Teamster address. Then he dramatically stepped up the pace with a speech on foreign policy at the Waldorf-Astoria on October 21, followed in quick succession by appearances at mass rallies in Shibe Park in Philadelphia, Soldiers Field in Chicago, and Fenway Park in Boston. It was his remarkable procession through the boroughs of New York City, however, on the day preceding his Waldorf speech, which made the most lasting impression. Beginning at Ebbets Field, riding in an open car for four hours through a bitter cold wind and driving rain (stopping just once to change his clothes in a Brooklyn garage), Roosevelt seemed exhilarated rather than exhausted by the ordeal. Thousands stood in the downpour to welcome the President, mute witnesses to his astonishing vitality.

By the end of October, FDR's reelection seemed certain. Still the Democrats were taking nothing for granted. Paul Porter, the Democratic National Committee's campaign publicity director, still worried about voter apathy, asked the well-known screenwriter, Norman Corwin, to put together an election-eve radio show to air on all four national networks and designed to generate a "sense of urgency" about getting to the polls. Corwin crafted a masterpiece. It consisted of short personal statements by a wide spectrum of Americans: a soldier and sailor returning from action; a TVA farmer; several union members; a World War vet who had sold apples during the Depression; an industrialist; a small businessman; a prominent Republican for Roosevelt; an old man voting in his fourteenth election; a young girl voting for the first time who would introduce the President. Very short statements by famous personalities followed, accompanied by choral and orchestral music intended to sound like a locomotive—"The Roosevelt Special":

CHORUS: All Aboard for Tomorrow.
LUCILLE BALL: This is Lucille Ball. I'm on the Train.
CHORUS: Vote.
TALLULAH:: This is Tallulah Bankhead. So am I.
CHORUS: Vote.
DEWEY: John, not Tom, Philosopher.

Even lady luck made an appearance. The Republicans had purchased time for a coast-to-coast program of their own to immediately follow Corwin's production. But the Democratic broadcast ended unexpectedly early and was followed by several minutes of soporific organ music. At the time, this was considered a brilliant, Machiavellian media maneuver designed to deflate the anticipated excitement for the Republican rebuttal to follow. Listening to this ponderous organ recital at home in Hyde Park, Fala fell asleep on the President's lap, causing FDR to allegedly remark, "They've even put my dog to sleep." Actually, Corwin's broadcast ended early quite by accident when the comedian, Jimmy Durante, was forced to withdraw at the very last moment. Even fate, it seemed, had decreed it a Democratic year and the last laugh was on Dewey. Roosevelt won 54 percent of the popular vote and swept the electoral college by 432 to 99.

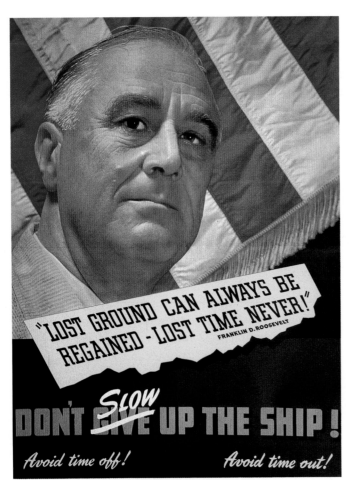

"LOST GROUND CAN ALWAYS BE REGAINED - LOST TIME NEVER!"
FRANKLIN D. ROOSEVELT

DON'T ~~GIVE~~ Slow UP THE SHIP!

Avoid time off!      Avoid time out!

REGISTER AND VOTE DEMOCRATIC

ROOSEVELT      TRUMAN

FOR LASTING PEACE ★ SECURITY FOR ALL

Above: Poster for Roosevelt, using rooster symbol.
Left: War poster showing an aged Roosevelt.

ROOSEVELT-TRUMAN DEMOCRATIC ASSN.

Selection of Roosevelt-Truman buttons. Fewer than one hundred varieties of buttons appeared during the 1944 campaign.

ROOSEVELT
TRUMAN

OUR LEADER
FRANKLIN D. ROOSEVELT

*James Montgomery Flagg poster.*

*Masonite automobile license attachment.*

*Paper leaflet criticizing Dewey's New York State gubernatorial policies.*

*Toby mug of Roosevelt.*

## To Assure VICTORY and SECURITY
## Elect ...

**FRANKLIN D. ROOSEVELT          HARRY S. TRUMAN**

The November 1944 election will be the most critical in the history of our Nation. The men and women we elect will decide our future. The war—the peace to follow—the kind of world we are to live in will be in their hands. FRANKLIN D. ROOSEVELT was chosen by an overwhelming majority of the people to lead us out of the depths of the Hoover depression. Under Roosevelt's dynamic and humane leadership our country has emerged as a nation able to meet the needs of its people with restored faith and confidence in the American way of life.

Under the Democratic administration of Franklin D. Roosevelt we have seen America achieve a production miracle which has made our American fighting machine the best equipped, best trained, best fed, and most powerfully armed of any nation in the world.

At this time of war crisis when experienced leadership is vital, it is imperative that we continue President Roosevelt in office, and that we elect public officials who can, and will, co-operate with him.

**Let Our President Finish the Job . . . . VOTE Tuesday, November 7**

*Selection of Roosevelt-Truman items, including lithographed tin buttons and paper handbill.*

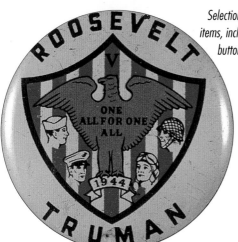

*Three-dimensional plastic sign. Light shines through from the back.*

# THIS AMAZING, VIVID PICTURE IS THAT OF OUR NEXT PRESIDENT

INSTRUCTIONS: Hold card in both hands, look at DOT on nose, try not to blink, count slowly to forty, then look steadily for 10 seconds up at the sky or a blank wall and there will appear his VIVID IMAGE.

FOR THE SECURITY OF THE NATION, FOR THE PRESERVATION OF THE UNION AND FOR LASTING PEACE AT HOME AND ABROAD, OUR COUNTRY NEEDS

**THOMAS E. DEWEY**

VOTE ⊠ REPUBLICAN
TUESDAY, NOVEMBER 7, 1944

Copyright 1944 by E. A. Dalziel

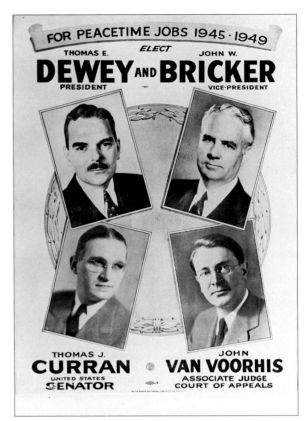

FOR PEACETIME JOBS 1945·1949
ELECT
THOMAS E. **DEWEY** AND **BRICKER** JOHN W.
PRESIDENT                    VICE-PRESIDENT

THOMAS J. **CURRAN**          JOHN **VAN VOORHIS**
UNITED STATES                 ASSOCIATE JUDGE
SENATOR                       COURT OF APPEALS

*Above: New York State Republican poster.*
*Left: Novelty optical illusion cardboard item for Dewey.*

*Plaster doll of Dewey holding the New York Times, which endorsed him in 1944.*

MOTHERS · DEWEY BRICKER · SISTERS · WIVES · SWEETHEARTS

*Lithographed tin button implying criticism of Roosevelt's wartime leadership.*

*Cloth shopping bag for Dewey.*

DEWEY
DEWEY

Lithographed tin buttons.

Pressboard delegate badge to the
1944 Republican National
Convention.

Sheet music
for Dewey.

John L. Lewis, head of the United Mine
Workers union, supported Dewey and headed
the United Labor Committee.

**1948**
48 STATES
IN THE UNION

TRUMAN
and
BARKLEY

*DEMOCRAT*

# Harry S. Truman

ELECTORAL VOTE 303, POPULAR VOTE 49.5%

REPUBLICAN

# Thomas E. Dewey

ELECTORAL VOTE 189, POPULAR VOTE 45%

STATES' RIGHTS

# J. Strom Thurmond

ELECTORAL VOTE 39, POPULAR VOTE 2.4%

PROGRESSIVE

# Henry A. Wallace

ELECTORAL VOTE 0, POPULAR VOTE 2.4%

IRWIN ROSS

is the author of articles on politics, public
policy issues, labor, and business, which have
appeared in many magazines, but chiefly in
*Fortune* and *Reader's Digest*. He served as roving
editor for *Reader's Digest*. Mr. Ross is the author
of *Strategy for Liberals: The Politics of the
Mixed Economy* (1949); *The Image Merchants:
The Fabulous World of Public Relations* (1959);
and *The Loneliest Campaign: The Truman
Victory of 1948* (1968).

P erhaps the most vivid memory of the 1948 presidential election for anyone who lived through it is of a triumphant President Harry Truman holding aloft the front page of the *Chicago Tribune* with the banner headline DEWEY DEFEATS TRUMAN. It was the *Tribune*'s first edition, of course, which went to press long before the final returns next morning upended all forecasts. But the 1948 election was notable not only for one of the most startling upsets in American presidential politics but for a sophistication of campaign management and tactics that, oddly, was not apparent at the time.

What was apparent was in many ways a dull campaign in which a beleaguered incumbent went barnstorming around the country, hurling invective at the opposition party and especially at the national Congress which it controlled, while the challenger, Governor Thomas E. Dewey of New York, took so elevated a high road that at times he seemed not to be participating in the same campaign. To be sure, there were many lively moments along the way, mostly contributed by Truman, but the campaign basically seemed dull because it never possessed any of the qualities of a horse race.

From the outset, it was clear to almost all observers that Dewey was destined to win. Truman was neither a dynamic leader nor a brilliant speaker; in his first year or two he presided over the country without providing any clear sense of direction, except in foreign policy; at times he seemed incompetent, and sometimes downright silly. So certain were Democratic leaders that Truman was doomed to defeat that many, in the spring of 1948, sought to dump him and nominate General Dwight D. Eisenhower—whose party affiliation was not known. But the general would not play. Truman was finally nominated at the Democratic convention in July pretty much *faute de mieux*.

Early in August the Gallup poll showed Truman trailing Dewey 37 percent to 48 percent; some days later the Roper poll gave Truman a mere 31.5 percent of the vote. Not only did later polls always place Dewey in the lead but Truman had also suffered two defections that seemed insurmountable. Former Vice President Henry Wallace led a left-wing exodus that created the Progressive party, with himself as its presidential nominee, while a large group of rebellious southern segregationists created the States' Rights party, which nominated Governor J. Strom Thurmond of South Carolina for President. The Dixiecrats were expected to take several states in the South, whereas Wallace was thought to be sufficiently popular in the Northeast, California, and sections of the Midwest to throw a handful of states to Dewey.

Not only was the outlook dismal, but the Truman campaign seemed both improvised and disorganized. Yet there was both method and long-range strategy behind the President's effort, though few if any outsiders realized it. Campaign planning had

*Neckties for three of the 1948 candidates.*

ties at that early stage. He asserted that there would be no southern breakaway—the one major error in the forecast. He correctly anticipated that the Wallace defection would cost Truman several states, but argued that the President could still win:

> If the Democrats carry the solid South and also those Western states carried in 1944, they will have 216 of the required 266 electoral votes. And if the Democratic party is powerful enough to capture the West, it will almost certainly pick up enough of the doubtful Middle Western and Eastern states to get 50 more votes. . . . We could lose New York, Pennsylvania, Illinois, New Jersey, Ohio, Massachusetts—all the "big" states and still win.

To achieve all that, Clifford argued that Truman had to adopt an unabashedly liberal line on economic issues, appealing to all the elements of the old Roosevelt coalition of labor, the farmers, Negroes in the North, middle-class liberals, as well as the South, whose voters were then predominantly white. (In the end, Truman did take the bulk of the South, despite the loss of four states.) Clifford thought the farmers were safe for Truman, but stressed the importance of heavy labor-union participation. There was no danger of labor going Republican, but it could stay home as it did in 1946, causing the Democrats to lose the Congress.

Clifford also urged that the President start his reelection effort with his state of the union message in January, an event that offered him an unparalleled opportunity to broadcast his themes to the nation above the heads of a hostile Congress. He should announce his maximum program, for there was no chance of getting anything passed and hence no need for moderation or

actually begun in the summer of 1947. The key strategy document was the now famous Clifford memorandum, presented to the President in November by Clark Clifford, the White House counsel. For many years Clifford got sole credit for this prescient paper, but he tells us in his memoirs, published in 1991, that it was based on a memorandum prepared by James Rowe, who had formerly served as an assistant to Roosevelt. Truman thought so highly of the Clifford paper that he kept it in a desk drawer throughout the campaign.

It was indeed a remarkable piece of forecasting and analysis. Clifford stated flatly that Dewey would be the Republican candidate and that Wallace would run on a third-party ticket, neither of which were certain-

attempts at compromise. The speech was scheduled for January 7, 1948, and for maximum impact Truman agreed to deliver it in person, which was by no means routine in those years. There was no TV coverage but it was carried by radio. And it was hard-hitting. Truman called for an aggressive anti-inflation program (a rapidly rising price level had been a major issue throughout 1947), a generous federal housing program, increases in the minimum wage, unemployment compensation and Social Security benefits, wideranging civil rights legislation, a program of national medical insurance, more dams and reclamation projects, and continual price supports, of course, for the farmer. By the time he finished, Truman had articulated a full-blown welfare state, which was not completed until the Johnson administration—apart from national health insurance.

After the program was announced, the White House never let up. Week after week, Truman sent messages to the Congress, each urging the adoption of specific items on his agenda. The civil rights message—so important to retaining the loyalty of black voters—came in February. For his pains, Truman was met with indifference and ridicule, but it was his goal to dramatize congressional inaction. Week after week, he was accumulating ammunition for his campaign assaults on the "do-nothing" Eightieth Congress.

A further step in this strategy came in the early hours of July 15 when Truman ended his acceptance speech before the Democratic convention by announcing that he was calling the Eightieth Congress back into session on July 26 in order to enact various pressing items of domestic legislation, some of which had been favored in the Republican platform adopted three weeks

before. "If there is any reality behind the Republican party platform," said Truman, "we ought to get more action from a short session of the Eightieth Congress. They can do this job in fifteen days, if they want to do it. They will still have time to go out and run for office." It was a transparent, not to say preposterous, political ploy, but it focused renewed attention on Truman's domestic program, and it put the Republicans on the spot. Truman again journeyed to the Hill to deliver his proposals, and he was again scorned.

Meantime, Dewey and his advisers devised a campaign that assumed victory and was designed to avoid any mishaps or intemperate responses as well as any specific commitments that might embarrass him after he took office. This was not a nonsensical approach (although it did not excuse the dullness of his speeches), given the unanimity of expert opinion that he was certain to win, a conviction that was reinforced every fortnight or so when another set of opinion polls came out.

Campaign techniques, style and rhetoric flowed naturally from the candidates' divergent strategies. This was the last of the pretelevision campaigns; though the conventions were televised, so few homes had sets that politicians could be indifferent to the camera eye. It was also the last of the major whistle-stop campaigns, though some use of campaign trains occurred in 1952 and occasionally later. In 1948, however, there were only two ways of reaching the electorate directly—radio speeches and public rallies. Newspaper accounts of what the candidates said were fairly comprehensive—and there were of course far more newspapers—but national radio news broadcasts were limited to fifteen minutes and provided no opportunity for "sound bites," a term that was decades away from being invented.

Both Truman and Dewey campaigned extensively by rail, criss-crossing the country and living on their trains with a large entourage of staff and press. The standard format provided several short back-platform appearances each day, culminating in a large rally for several thousand in a hall. The Republicans were also able to afford a campaign train for their vice-presidential candidate, Governor Earl Warren, but the Democratic candidate, Senator Alben Barkley, had to content himself with a chartered plane, as did Henry Wallace. No presidential candidate ever devoted himself more energetically to whistle-stop campaigning than Harry Truman. He sometimes spoke a dozen times a day. On the first full day of his September tour, he addressed his first crowd at 5:45 A.M. in Rock Island, Illinois, and made his final appeal at 8:10 P.M. in Polo, Missouri, confiding to the audience that "I didn't think I was going to be able to do it but the railroad finally consented to stop."

Truman was effective as a back-platform campaigner because he had finally mastered the art of ad-libbing. For three years, he had been the despair of his advisers, for he was incapable of reading a text with pace or emphasis, not to speak of dramatic flourish or passion. In a word, he droned. Finally, in April 1948, he was prevailed upon by his handlers to try an experiment. After a prepared speech before the American Society of Newspaper Editors in Washington, he launched into an extemporaneous talk about American relations with the Soviet Union. He was informal, relaxed, and sur-

prisingly lively—in sync with the audience as he usually was when speaking to a small group in the White House. He was not quite speaking off the top of his head, for he had notes prepared by his staff that outlined the topics to be covered.

So well received were these off-the-cuff remarks and a few similar exercises in Washington that Truman continued his improvisations on his so-called "non-political" tour in June. The excuse for the trip was Truman's acceptance of an invitation to deliver a commencement address at the University of California in Berkeley. Truman could have flown, of course, but instead he aped Roosevelt's wartime precedent of an "inspection tour." It was an elaborate operation, involving a sixteen-car train and a journey to eighteen states. The opposition was understandably outraged, but, as always, helpless to prevent a President from managing the news by creating an event.

The June trip was really the start of Truman's public campaign. Advance work for the trip was poor and there were many snafus, but Truman became quite accomplished at the back-platform ad-lib and he was wowing the crowds. By September, his performance followed a standard pattern, aided by an outline from which he took off. He generally began with an appropriate local reference, never forgot a plug for a local Democratic candidate, and concentrated on a single main subject that involved the immediate economic interests of his listeners—jobs, inflation, the housing crunch, the shortage of grain storage bins in the farm belt, dams and reclamation projects in the West and so on.

Truman would contrast the Democrats and Republicans in the starkest populist terms—the party of the people against the party of the rich. No old-fashioned socialist orator could have put more of a class spin on Truman's rhetoric. In his first major speech of the September tour, at the National Plowing Contest in Dexter, Iowa, he denounced "Wall Street reactionaries" and "gluttons of privilege" as well as the Republican Congress, which he charged had "stuck a pitchfork" in the farmer's back. Truman was relentless:

> I wonder how many times you have to be hit on the head before you find out who's hitting you. . . . These Republican gluttons of privilege are cold men. They are cunning men. . . . What they have taken away from you thus far would only be an appetizer for the economic tapeworm of big business.

Truman's extravagant assaults never provoked Dewey to an angry retort, even when late in the campaign the President linked the threat of fascism to a Republican victory. In a speech in Chicago on October 25, Truman first inveighed against "the powerful reactionary forces which are silently undermining our democratic institutions." He warned that "when a few men get control of the economy of a nation, they find a 'front man' to run the country for them." Thus, in Germany, "they put money and influence behind Adolf Hitler. We know the rest of the story." Similarly in Italy. "PRESIDENT LIKENS DEWEY TO HITLER AS FASCISTS' TOOL," reported the *New York Times* the next day.

But Dewey would not take the bait. The last thing he wanted was a slanging match with Harry. Dewey made occasional slighting references to the failings of the

Cardboard sign. Reference is to Lyndon Johnson's narrow and controversial victory in the 1948 Texas Democratic senatorial primary.

Democratic administration, and he sometimes defended the Eightieth Congress, but never in ringing terms. He had obviously made the shrewd political decision not to let his opponent set the campaign agenda. The result was that there was no long distance debate of the issues, no thrust and counterthrust to enliven the headlines.

Dewey's entire campaign had an air of relaxation. While Truman had been campaigning since June, Dewey only began his first train tour on September 19, two days after Truman set out from Washington. Nor did Dewey exert himself as much. He made half as many back-platform appearances as Truman and, unlike Truman, always delivered the same set speech, apart from local references and perhaps a paragraph or two from his main speech scheduled for that evening. At times he seemed to be exerting himself more on behalf of candidates for House and Senate, many of whom were thought to be in trouble, than in his own cause. He had no desire as President to confront a Democratic Congress.

From the outset, Dewey's tour of the country struck a tone of moral high-mindedness from which he rarely deviated. His first major speech of the September tour, in

Celluloid button for
Dewey and Warren.

Dexter, Iowa, was characteristically entitled "The Challenge of Tomorrow." In his rich, mellifluous baritone, he told the nation that

> Tonight we enter upon a campaign to unite America. On January 20, we will enter upon a new era. We propose to install in Washington an administration which has faith in the American people, a warm understanding of their needs and the competence to meet them. We will rediscover the essential unity of our people and the spiritual strength which makes our country great. We will begin to move forward again shoulder to shoulder toward an even greater America and a better life for every American, in a nation working effectively for the peace of the world.

At times Dewey put a bit more bite into his message—as when he continually promised that come January 20 Washington would witness "the biggest unraveling, unsnarling, untangling operation in our nation's history"—but he never failed to give the impression that he was engaged not in a political campaign but in a stately coronation march. His composure desert-

ed him only once, in a famous incident in Beaucoup, Illinois. As Dewey started to speak from the rear of the train, it rolled backward into the crowd. No one was hurt but Dewey exploded, "That's the first lunatic I've had for an engineer! He probably ought to be shot at sunrise, but I guess we can let him off because no one was hurt." The Democrats kept recalling Dewey's crack to the end of the campaign, charging that he was hostile to working folk.

The words of both candidates were available to millions of their countrymen via radio, but Dewey's oratory could be more readily tuned in, for the Republicans had more money available to buy time. Throughout the campaign, the Democrats were strapped for funds. The networks were often so concerned about the party's poverty that they demanded payment in advance. On occasion the national committee could not get the money in enough time to channel it through a bank account and the committee chairman, Senator J. Howard Mc-Grath, would hasten to the studio with $25,000 or $30,000 in cash. It would be just enough to pay for the stipulated time and Truman was sometimes cut off the air when he ran over.

Perhaps more important to campaign managers than radio exposure was corralling the populace to see and hear the candidates. This was still the era of the large campaign rally, in auditoriums, open-air stadiums and even the street. In New York City, for example, no self-respecting campaign could come to an end without a rally in Madison Square Garden. In 1948, the Garden was populated not only by the Democrats and Republicans but by the Progressives, who attracted 19,000 to Truman's

16,000. With television not a factor, there was no fear, as in recent campaigns, of organized heckling that would make a shambles of a show that was being produced largely for an unseen audience. Crowds were important not only in the halls but in the streets, along the line of the motorcade. This was also still an era of relative innocence, before the ever-present fear of assassination, and so the routes of motorcades were widely publicized, with the candidates on display. Not only did these processions help stimulate voter enthusiasm, or so it was thought, but the size of the crowds was taken as an indication of a campaign's relative success.

Throughout the campaign, Truman attracted large throngs, with more and more people emerging in the final days. In mid-October, 100,000 people in Akron, Ohio, watched his motorcade, 50,000 came out in Dayton. Huge throngs showed up in the small cities of Indiana—25,000 in Kokomo, 20,000 in Hammond, 12,000 in Logansport. In Chicago, in the final weeks of the campaign, 50,000 people paraded through the downtown streets to the Chicago Stadium and an estimated 500,000 watched on the sidelines. In Boston the street crowds were estimated at 250,000. All this was duly chronicled in the papers, but its significance was discounted. Journalists tended to attribute Truman's drawing power to curiosity, little more. Meantime, from mid-October Dewey was pulling fewer people into the streets, a fact that was again noted but not regarded as significant.

The final polls showed a decline in Dewey's support, but still a substantial lead. Gallup gave Dewey 49.5 percent of the vote

Kentucky Democratic party poster. There is an abundant variety of paper items from the 1948 campaign.

to 44.5 percent for Truman; Crossley produced almost the same numbers—49.9 percent to 44.8 percent. The experts were thus confirmed in their views. What they did not realize was that the pollsters had stopped interviewing much too soon. The Gallup poll published on the eve of the election was derived from two national samples taken in mid-October. Thus Gallup, like Crossley and Roper (who had stopped polling in September), could not pick up last-minute switches as well as the late decisions of previously undecided voters; the net effect of both favored Truman and helped him get 2,000,000 more votes than Dewey—49.5 percent as against 45 percent for Dewey and 2.4 percent each for Thurmond and Wallace—and a top-heavy majority—303 to 189 with 39 for Thurmond—in the electoral college. Clearly those crowds in late October were voting with their feet before they got into the polling booth.

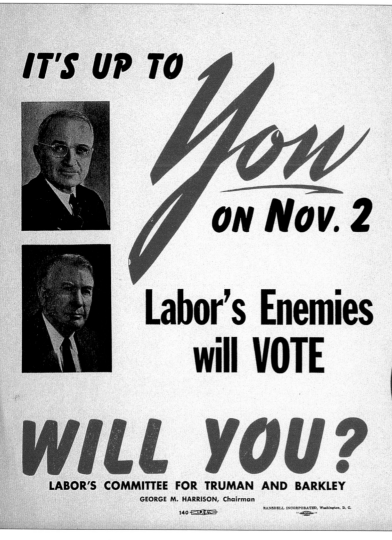

Selection of items from the 1948 campaign. The end of wartime shortages led to a revival in ephemera—buttons, ribbons, pennants, pencils, and all types of novelties.

Selection of paper items. A wealth of political paper exists from this campaign.

Henry Wallace, Truman's secretary of commerce, broke with the President over his Cold War policies. In December 1947, he announced he would run for President on a third-party ticket. Above: Large celluloid button with Roosevelt's shadow shown behind Wallace. Right: Cardboard poster for Wallace and Taylor.

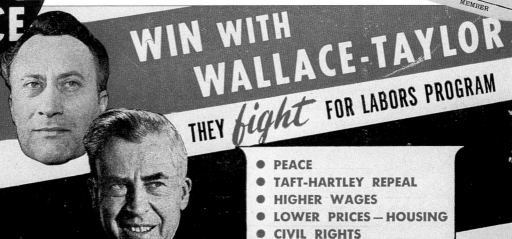

*Your right to VOTE cost many American Lives . . .*

VOTE NOV. 2

LABOR'S COMMITTEE FOR

# TRUMAN and BARKLEY

GEORGE M. HARRISON, CHAIRMAN 1621 K ST., N. W., WASHINGTON, D. C.

*Paper poster for Truman.*

FORWARD WITH PRESIDENT TRUMAN "NO RETREAT"

*Truman advocated an expansion of Roosevelt's depression-born policies in a period of unprecedented prosperity.*

# VOTE DEMOCRATIC
## NOVEMBER 2, 1948

PRESIDENT
ARRY S. TRUMAN

GOVERNOR
FORREST SMITH

VICE-PRESIDENT
ALBEN W. BARKLEY

LIEUTENANT-GOVERNOR
JAMES T. BLAIR, JR.

SECRETARY OF STATE
WALTER H. TOBERMAN

STATE AUDITOR
WILL H. HOLMES

STATE TREASURER
M. E. MORRIS

ATTORNEY GENERAL
J. E. TAYLOR

## ELECT EXPERIENCED DEMOCRATS
## FOR GOOD GOVERNMENT

*Poster for Truman and Barkley with Missouri state Democratic candidates.*

WITH TRUMAN for CIVIL RIGHTS

*Lithographed tin button for Truman. The President's civil rights program was the most controversial feature of his Fair Deal.*

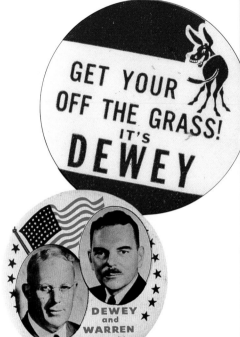

Republican campaign buttons featured caricatures of jackasses to help form slogans.

Celluloid button for Dewey and Warren.

# DEWEY GETS THINGS DONE!

## LOOK WHAT DEWEY DID!

**Personal Income Tax cut 40%**

One of Governor Dewey's most phenomenal contributions to good government has been his sound fiscal policy. He has been able to cut taxes, build up surpluses, and at the same time render state services that make New York government the most progressive in history. Personal income tax was cut 40% and business income taxes were cut 25%.

**Surplus built up of $673,000,000**

A $673,000,000 surplus was built up in four years and put aside for post-war construction and tax stabilization reserves. State aid to local governments has been increased by almost two-thirds under Governor Dewey.

**Taxpayers' savings $800,000,000**

Under Governor Dewey, taxpayers saved this sum through reduction of regular state taxes, mostly since the war.

**$400,000,000 Veterans' Bonus Paid**

And by ten-year financing—instead of the usual forty years—taxpayers will save $140,000,000 on interest.

**Housing for 160,000 persons**

The Dewey program now under way—38 public housing projects—will provide homes for almost 160,000 persons otherwise doomed to unsafe, unsanitary places. Veteran housing is in addition to this. New York leads the nation in slum clearance and public housing for families of low income.

**State debt reduced 27% in 4 years**

In four years under Governor Dewey, New York State has reduced its debt by $136,-000,000 or 27%. Dewey believes in pay-as-you-go.

**140,000 new small businesses established**

A special campaign to aid small business resulted in an increase of 130,000 in the number of business firms in the state since V-J Day. Governor Dewey set up a program of individual assistance to small businessmen and to men and women starting a business of their own.

# VOTE DEWEY-WARREN

Cardboard poster praising Dewey's achievements as governor.

# WIN WITH DEWEY AND WARREN

Tin automobile license attachment.

Painted metal figurine of Dewey.

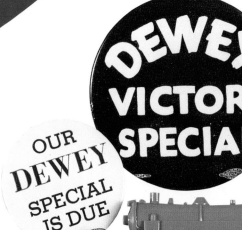

These buttons refer to Dewey's September-October train tour. The lower button is attached to a plastic train-shaped whistle.

Brochure for Dewey and Warren. While 65 percent of the nation's newspapers endorsed Dewey, only 15 percent favored Truman.

Celluloid button for Truman.

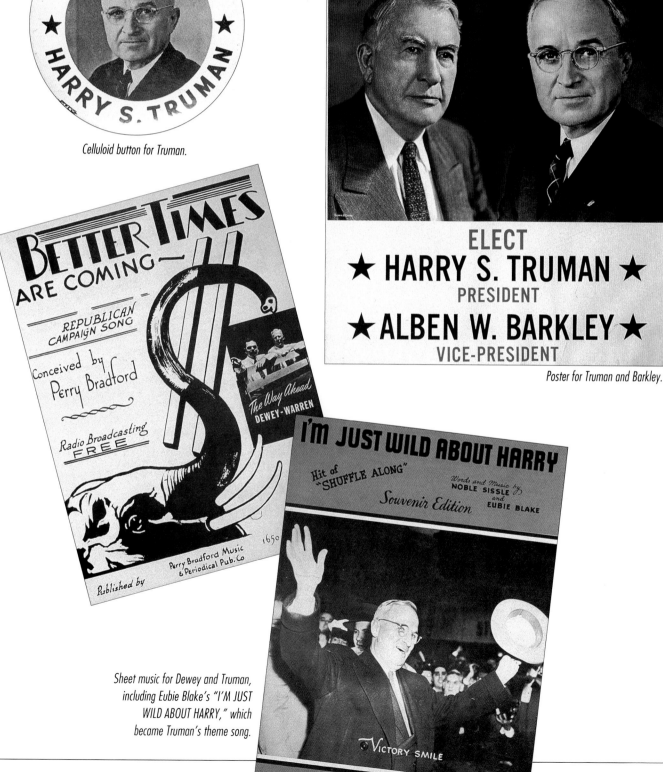

Poster for Truman and Barkley.

Sheet music for Dewey and Truman,
including Eubie Blake's "I'M JUST
WILD ABOUT HARRY," which
became Truman's theme song.

# Chicago Daily Tribune

THE WORLD'S GREATEST NEWSPAPER

AN AMERICAN PAPER FOR AMERICANS

## HOME ★★

VOL. CVII — NO. 264

WEDNESDAY, NOVEMBER 3, 1948

. . FOUR CENTS—PAY NO MORE

# DEWEY DEFEATS TRUMAN

## *G.O.P. Sweep Indicated in State; Boyle Leads in City*

### REPUBLICAN TICKET AHEAD OF 1944 VOTE

#### Town Balloting Gives Trend

### *Tops Coghlan in Hot Race for Attorney*

### RECORD CITY VOTE SEEN IN LATE TALLIES

#### Suburban Ballot Near 375,000

### BULLETINS ON ELECTIONS

### *Early Count Gives G.O.P. Senate Edge*

### PUTS G.O.P. BACK IN THE WHITE HOUSE

#### Sizable Electoral Margin Seen

### THE WEATHER

Wednesday, Nov. 3, 1948

CHICAGO AND VICINITY: Partly cloudy, not much change by tomorrow; high 68, low 44; precedent wind 10 to 15 miles per hour. Thursday fair and warmer.

FOR SEPTEMBER, 1948
DAILY 985,000

in Excess of
THE CHICAGO TRIBUNE

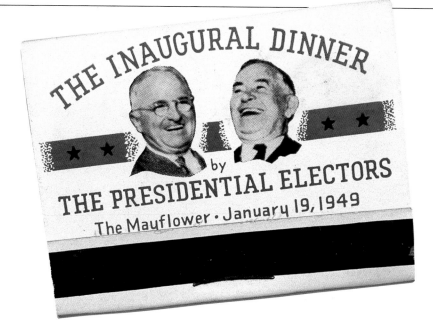

THE INAUGURAL DINNER

by

THE PRESIDENTIAL ELECTORS

The Mayflower · January 19, 1949

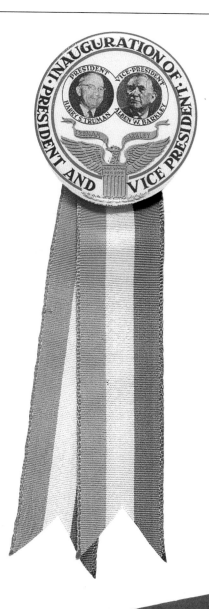

*Opposite: Perhaps the most famous newspaper headline in American history, Chicago Daily Tribune, November 3, 1948.*

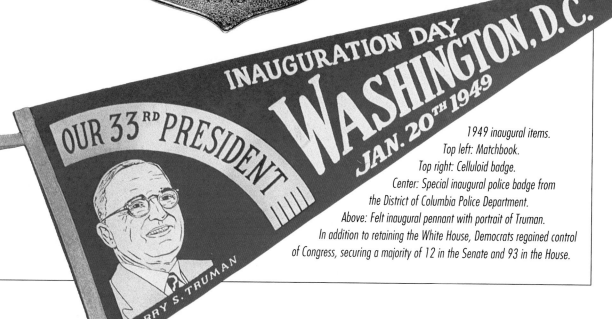

1949 inaugural items.
Top left: Matchbook.
Top right: Celluloid badge.
Center: Special inaugural police badge from the District of Columbia Police Department.
Above: Felt inaugural pennant with portrait of Truman.
In addition to retaining the White House, Democrats regained control of Congress, securing a majority of 12 in the Senate and 93 in the House.

★

**1952**

48 STATES
IN THE UNION

*REPUBLICAN*

# Dwight D. Eisenhower

ELECTORAL VOTE 442, POPULAR VOTE 55.1%

DEMOCRAT

# Adlai E. Stevenson

ELECTORAL VOTE 89, POPULAR VOTE 44.4%

ALONZO L. HAMBY
is professor of history at Ohio University. He is the
author of *Beyond the New Deal: Harry S. Truman
and American Liberalism* (1973); *The Imperial
Years: The United States since 1939* (1976); and
*Liberalism and Its Challengers* (1985; 2nd ed.,
1992). He has edited *The New Deal: Analysis and
Interpretation* (1969; 2nd ed., 1981) and
*Harry S. Truman and the Fair Deal* (1974). A
fellow at the Woodrow Wilson International
Center for Scholars in 1991–92, he is currently
working on a biography of Harry S. Truman.

In terms of technique, the presidential campaign of 1952 might appear to stand midway between the traditional party battles of the early twentieth century and the independent, television-oriented struggles of today. New methods of communication and persuasion, however, may convey an illusion of change far greater than the substance. The 1952 contest displayed characteristics of American political campaigning that date from the inception of mass political parties in the early nineteenth century. In truth, John Quincy Adams and Andrew Jackson are not bad similes for Adlai E. Stevenson and Dwight D. Eisenhower.

Adlai Stevenson, although the candidate of an incumbent party, had not been part of its national administration, either in the executive or legislative branches. Governor of Illinois since 1949, he had been altogether detached from Harry S. Truman and the doings of Washington Democrats. Yet in carrying the standard of the national Democratic party, he inescapably also carried the banner of the Truman administration. The situation was awkward both for him and the outgoing President.

Truman represented both the virtues and vices of the Democratic party as it had developed by 1952. He had identified himself strongly with a liberal ideal that included American international leadership in opposition to Communist totalitarianism abroad, a generous extension of the social welfare state at home, and a stronger commitment to racial equality than had been undertaken by any Democrat before him. He also was intensely partisan, closely identified with and supportive of local political machines often rooted in corruption and underworld connections, untroubled by a sense of the complexity of political issues, and absolutely convinced that his administration embodied the public interest. Consistent with his ordinary family background, he wholeheartedly identified with the "common people."

Stevenson, while not in disagreement with the main lines of Truman's policies, was a vastly different man. Of patrician stock, he had attended the best schools, traveled widely, and belonged to the American social elite. Robert Donovan superbly describes him: "A man of good taste, he was intelligent, polished, sophisticated, literate, and at times eloquent. He was also wealthy, divorced, stylish, cosmopolitan—a twentieth century man to the core and, because of, or in spite of it, fragile and self-doubting." On matters of social policy, he was a bit to the right of Truman, on foreign policy, more hopeful that diplomacy could manage the Cold War between the United States and the Soviet Union. Where Truman had a visceral appeal to the working class, Stevenson excited an important and growing Democratic constituency that had never achieved a strong sense of identification with Truman—the liberal-minded, affluent, educated middle classes.

Neither man could unite the Democrats in a common effort nor would they

*Postcard showing that Truman had supported Eisenhower for the presidency until he became the Republican candidate.*

work well in tandem. After his nomination, Stevenson replaced Truman's appointee as chairman of the Democratic National Committee, and in a symbolic demonstration of his need to distance himself from the administration ran his campaign from Springfield, Illinois. In an inadvertent, but nonetheless telling, usage he adopted the Republican sound bite "mess in Washington." The incident left Truman angry and bitter.

Stevenson's vice presidential candidate, Senator John Sparkman of Alabama, underscored another source of disarray among the Democrats. A decent, liberal-minded man with enlightened views (for that time) on race relations, he was forced by his constituency to be a stronger supporter of segregation than he would have preferred. His nomina-

tion was primarily a sop to the southern wing of the party and was taken as an affront by increasingly militant black leaders.

Eisenhower was a near-perfect candidate for the Republicans. In 1952, he was the greatest American hero, combining the strength and authority of a successful supreme commander with a warmth and democratic sensibility that made him more attractive to the ordinary American than the other imposing World War II general, Douglas MacArthur. Eisenhower's impressive political skills as much as his ability had propelled him to the top during World War II and later had made him the consensus choice as military leader of NATO. Previously so disengaged from politics that he was not a registered member of either party, he had been sought as a presidential candidate by both. He could appeal to the growing numbers of independent voters and present himself as a candidate above party, waging a "crusade" to restore the nation to an era of peace, prosperity, and public virtue.

The way in which he had obtained the Republican nomination forecast his fall campaign. He had allowed Republican emissaries to place his name in early primaries, had run strongly as an absentee candidate, then had resigned his NATO post to return home and campaign openly. Asserting that the Taft regulars were attempting to stack the convention and thwart the will of the people, his forces intimidated the party organization into awarding them key disputed seats. Eisenhower had launched himself, not as a partisan figure, but as the leader of a popular crusade.

Partisanship fell to his vice presidential candidate, Senator Richard M. Nixon of California. Far more controversial than any of the other major candidates, Nixon was a dynamic young conservative from an important state. A visceral anti-Communist, he could be presented as the man who got Alger Hiss but who operated with a greater sense of responsibility than the McCarthyite wing of the party. A tough, slashing campaigner, he seemed ideally suited for a role often assigned to vice presidential aspirants. From the beginning, he had the job of hatchet man, leaving to Eisenhower the role of leader of all the people.

An American presidential campaign had always been an exercise in the arts of communicating issue positions and personal images. By the mid-twentieth century, it had become generally accepted that the candidates themselves would travel widely, speak extensively, and show themselves to as many people as possible. Harry Truman's exhausting 31,000-mile 1948 drive, done almost entirely by rail, had set a new standard for a peacetime incumbent. The maturing of passenger air traffic now made even more extensive itineraries possible. Eisenhower traveled 33,000 miles, approximately 22,000 of them by air, and made 228 speeches; Nixon 42,000 miles and 375 speeches. Stevenson logged 32,500 miles and 203 speeches; Sparkman, although leaving the smallest footprints, made more than 450 speeches. President Truman, unable to resist the lure of the campaign trail and determined to defend his administration, undertook a tour that exceeded his mileage in 1948.

Inevitably, however, most voters formed their impressions through less direct means. In the past, this had meant print, usually with an overt, hard-edged partisan slant. Newspapers and magazines still ap-

peared dominant. Even small cities tended to have at least a couple of papers. The great triad of news magazines—*Time, Newsweek,* and *U.S. News & World Report*—were growing and prospering. *Life* and *Look*, both emphasizing photojournalism, reached homes across the country. So did such venerable publications as *Collier's* and *The Saturday Evening Post* (if closer to the end of the line than most people understood).

As a group, the print media long had favored the Republican party. Approximately three-quarters of those newspapers making editorial endorsements backed Eisenhower—about the same percentage that had supported Dewey in 1948. By and large, voters discounted the often obvious partisan predilections of the press and rarely let newspaper editorials determine their presidential choices.

By 1952, however, film and the electronic media offered both the impression of direct contact with the candidates and new means of persuasion more powerful than print. Franklin Roosevelt had used radio to

Anti-Truman celluloid button. More than a thousand button varieties were issued for the 1952 and 1956 campaigns.

*Comic book biographies of Eisenhower and Stevenson.*

establish an intimate bond with the voters. Movie newsreels displayed him as a jaunty, optimistic leader from whom the people could take heart. Radio and newsreels remained important, but by 1952 they were already beginning to be displaced by the most potentially powerful medium of all, television.

Television was still very much in its infancy. In July 1952, 108 stations were on the air, almost all in large cities, thereby depriving much of rural, small-town America of real access to the medium. Live coast-to-coast transmission was possible only along the route of a transcontinental cable available only to CBS and NBC. Stations that

could not hook into it had to make do with films, kinescopes, and local programming. Network news coverage was primitive, scarcely less superficial than newsreels.

Still, perhaps as many as nineteen million sets in homes across the country provided television for a majority of the electorate. For some politicians, moreover, the amateur character of most news coverage presented an opportunity. No TV journalistic establishment had yet arisen to filter coverage of events in ways that inevitably added its own perspectives. Politicians who could use the medium had a free hand.

The emergence of television coincided with and fostered an important development—the movement of professional advertising into presidential campaigns. Here and there in the past, paid advertising consultants and agencies had worked in local elections. John F. Kennedy's first campaign for Congress in 1946, for example, had employed an agency; Whittaker & Baxter, a "political consulting" firm that was in effect an ad shop for politicians, had been a force in California politics for twenty years. Yet professional advertisers had never played a role in presidential campaigns.

The Republicans changed this for once and for all by retaining the old-line firm of Batten, Barton, Durstine & Osborn (BBDO) for overall management of their campaign message and by using Rosser Reeves, a top creative executive at the Ted Bates Agency, to produce short "spot" commercials. The Democrats reacted with horror. A Stevenson spokesman deplored the "high-powered hucksters of Madison Avenue" and asserted that Republican admen were trying to merchandise an inferior political ticket "in precisely the way they sell soap, ammoniated toothpaste, hair tonic or bubble gum." Stevenson himself declared: "This isn't Ivory Soap versus Palmolive."

Actually, the Democrats also used some advertising professionals, but they lacked the funds to launch a big media campaign and in any case would have found it impossible to attract the best talent. Madison Avenue in those days was overwhelmingly Republican. The attack on the hucksters was an understandable attempt by the Stevenson campaign to turn a disadvantage to its favor. But, aside from bringing a certain professionalism and expertise to the exercise, the advertisers did nothing that politicians had not attempted to do for years. They were simply better at it.

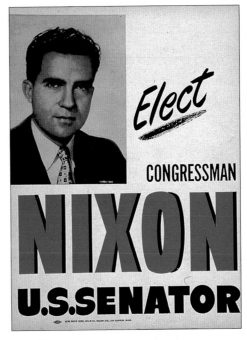

Poster from Nixon's 1950 California senatorial campaign.

In the age of print, mass politics in America, contrary to today's popular understanding, had been organized around the one-line slogan. Candidates, it is true, once made longer speeches; today they are more likely to issue long position papers. However, neither speeches then nor position papers now are long remembered unless they contain a pithy phrase that epitomizes a major campaign issue, expresses the positive appeals of a candidate, or limns the negative characteristics of one's opponent. Styles of communication change, but mass politics always has required the simplification of issues to a relatively low common denominator (slogans then, sound bites now); it also has entailed the reduction of personalities to simple images. Both sides played the game; the Republicans, perhaps because they had more promising material with which to work, did it best.

*Compact with telephone dial design. "I LIKE IKE" became one of the most successful slogans in American political history.*

The selling of personality had begun when George Washington's admirers designated him "Father of His Country." In the mid-twentieth century, the task required a bit more effort. BBDO urged Eisenhower to avoid long, stiff, formal speeches in favor of quasi-extemporaneous talks from notes; for a thirty-minute TV slot, the speech itself should run no more than twenty minutes. The rest of the time would be taken with shots of Eisenhower (accompanied by Mamie as a none-too-subtle reminder that Stevenson was divorced), moving among adoring followers. The idea was to maximize Eisenhower's natural warmth and the adulation of the crowds.

The crusher Republican slogan was "I like Ike." It captured perfectly the Republican candidate's popular appeal and deemphasized his military background—a fit beginning for a campaign aimed at an electorate that throughout its history had distrusted military posturers. (If Douglas MacArthur had been the Republican candidate, it is impossible to believe that the party could have used "I like Mac.") Yet the military ingredient, properly handled, was significant. Eisenhower made the maximum effective use of it in late October, when he uttered the most memorable sound bite of the campaign: "I shall go to Korea." The statement underscored the fact that in one corner stood the leader of the greatest military effort in American history, in the other, a man with no real military experience. Stevenson had no credible response; he and his advisers had already decided that a similar promise from him would not be taken seriously.

For all his talent, Stevenson had no effective answer for Eisenhower's unique personal appeal. Most voters probably considered him an improvement over Truman, and he might well have defeated Taft. But, unlike Eisenhower, he was charismatic to only a narrow slice of the electorate and was open to attack as an "egghead," i.e., an ineffectual intellectual out of touch with the real world of everyday Americans. Balding and paunchy, he appeared so good a physical match for the term that it stuck to him irretrievably. One doubts that it produced many votes against him, but no one could believe the term helpful.

The most memorable attempt to humanize Stevenson came after a photographer caught him seated on a platform with a conspicuous hole in the sole of one shoe; the photo quickly brought forth hole-in-the-shoe lapel pins. The image was twenty years out of date and unconvincing. As Nixon's Checkers speech would demonstrate, the "common man" was no longer an unemployed worker walking the streets in worn-out footwear.

The most effective use of television and one of the most memorable incidents of personality packaging, Richard Nixon's Checkers speech was nonetheless technically one of the least slick and in no way a product of advertising. The charge that Nixon had dishonestly accepted funds from businessmen had to be answered because it would otherwise neutralize the Republican use of the corruption issue. For Nixon, the talk was a desperate effort to save his political career. What neither he nor anyone else realized was the extent to which he had become the focus of a national soap opera; nor could he have been fully aware of his chances of achieving a valuable identification with the "common man" in the age of postwar affluence.

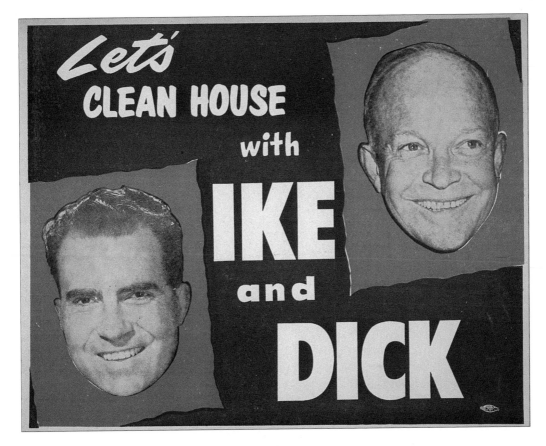

*Poster for Eisenhower and Nixon.*

Fifty-eight million people watched the speech, the largest audience in the history of television until the first Kennedy-Nixon debate of 1960. Nixon pushed all the expected partisan buttons—Stevenson had his own supplementary fund; Sparkman had put his wife on the Senate payroll; the Nixon fund had been used to further the struggle against communism. But Nixon also had to refute charges that he had dipped into the cash for personal expenses. Viewers saw an earnest young man, his attractive wife briefly appearing on screen, explaining the difficulties of raising two small children and maintaining a middle-class standard of living on a senatorial sal-

ary. They scrimped to meet mortgage payments, drove a used Oldsmobile, and Pat (unlike the wives of some corrupt administration officials) had no mink coat, just "a respectable Republican cloth coat." The only gift they had taken was for the children, the little dog Checkers.

Partisan Democrats, even well-off Republicans might find the speech nauseatingly maudlin, but it resonated with a lot of upwardly mobile Americans who had made their way into the middle-class after World War II and were struggling to stay there. General Lucius D. Clay thought it ridiculous—until he encountered his elevator operator in tears. More than a million people like that elevator operator wired support, although Nixon had run out of time before he could give them the address of the Republican National Committee.

The GOP slogans demonstrated that the party had seized the initiative in attack politics. As one leader expressed it, the campaign formula was K-l, C-2—Korea, Communism, Corruption. The solution to the Cold War was "liberation of captive nations," not containment—a maxim underscored by Nixon's reference to Secretary of State Dean Acheson's "cowardly College of Communist containment." The sound bite that wrapped up in a few words all the nation's domestic frustrations was "the mess in Washington," which of course could be cleaned up only by the Republicans.

Such rhetoric was just old-fashioned politics, some of it pretty dirty. The admen on the whole played fairer with the issues,

although of course playing them for partisan advantage. Rosser Reeves turned out some forty spot commercials of less than a minute each in which Eisenhower produced quick answers to questions asked by "ordinary Americans" who had been selected from the tourists at Radio City Music Hall. (Reeves later described them as "people from different sections of the country—real people, in their own clothes, with wonderful native accents.")

Each person read a packaged question which was followed by an answer the candidate already had filmed. The questions involved such issues as war, peace, taxes, inflation, and corruption. Their content had been determined by another relatively new informational technique, the public opinion survey, designed and carried out in this case by the Gallup organization. Twenty-eight spots eventually were run extensively in key states. A representative example: Black man

*Inaugural license plate, 1953.*

in plaid shirt and sportscoat: "General, the Democrats are telling me, I've never had it so good." Eisenhower: "Can that be true when America is billions in debt, when prices have doubled, when taxes break our backs, and we are still fighting in Korea? It's tragic and it's time for a change."

The real world was of course more complicated, but the spot did fairly state the basic Democratic slogan and delivered an answer to it that was hardly outrageous by past standards of American political rhetoric. Neither it nor the other Eisenhower spots were particularly clever; rather they amounted to the simple application of a hard sell. Spoken by a politician from a podium or expressed in print as part of a campaign pamphlet, Eisenhower's responses would have attracted little attention. The commercials got their impact from the image that only television could convey of an ordinary citizen attempting to make sense of his political world and being directly answered by a presidential candidate.

The Democrats' best slogan might have been a winner at most times: "You never had it so good." But in 1952, the American people, although economically well-off and materially more comfortable than at any time in their history, suffered from a sense of malaise that left incumbents vulnerable. The national unease stemmed from diverse sources—recent reverses in the Cold War (especially the fall of China and Soviet development of an atomic bomb), the stalemated shooting war in Korea, an inflation that had raged in the immediate post-World War II years and that seemed to have been reignited by Korea, numerous examples of petty but highly publicized corruption in Washington. These issues along with all the

grievances that had accumulated during twenty years of Democratic control of the presidency gave the Republicans limp "It's Time for a Change" more credibility than normally would have been the case.

The failure of Stevenson's hole-in-the-shoe image probably was as indicative as any single episode of the reason for the Democratic loss in 1952. Fear of depression was no longer a reason to vote for the Democrats. The Republicans spoke more convincingly to the anxieties of affluence and were better positioned to capitalize on the frustrations of foreign involvement. They also were better organized and far more effective in their use of the media. Above all, they had a candidate of insurmountable appeal. Adlai Stevenson, an extraordinary man who in other circumstances might have been an important President, had the misfortune to be placed in front of a political locomotive. On election day, Eisenhower defeated him by six-and-a-half-million votes.

One is tempted to emphasize the novel elements of his victory—television and the Madison Avenue men, especially—but Rosser Reeves thought Eisenhower would have won without such efforts. Television did indeed begin to have a special impact in 1952, but much of what appeared fresh was old wine in new bottles. Eisenhower benefited from foreign and domestic situations that had nothing to do with technique; his personal charisma, moreover, was in no way an artificial creation of television or Madison Avenue. His victory was probably about as foreordained as that of another Old Hero over an egghead opponent in 1828. The passions and appeals of mass politics in the end transcended even the technological revolution.

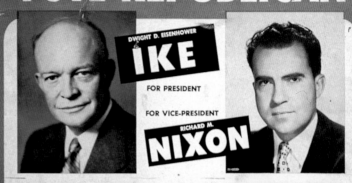

Felt pennant for Eisenhower.

The 1952 and 1956 campaigns
of Eisenhower and Stevenson produced
a substantial number and variety of
items limited only by the imagination of
designers and manufacturers.

Cotton bandanna
for Eisenhower.

This Is The Year To

# VOTE REPUBLICAN

DWIGHT D. EISENHOWER
**IKE**
FOR PRESIDENT

FOR VICE-PRESIDENT
RICHARD M.
**NIXON**

WALTER J.
**KOHLER**
FOR GOVERNOR

FOR U. S. SENATOR
JOSEPH R.
**McCARTHY**

**ELECT THE FULL SLATE**

THOMSON for ATTORNEY GENERAL

**SMITH**
FOR LIEUTENANT GOVERNOR

**ZIMMERMAN**
FOR SECRETARY OF STATE

**SMITH**
FOR STATE TREASURER

GARDNER R. WITHROW
for CONGRESS

BEN TREMAIN
for ASSEMBLYMAN

*Vote* Republican NOV. 4th

Wisconsin Republican poster which includes Senator
Joseph McCarthy, who was running for reelection.

Salesmen's fold-out offering a variety of Eisenhower posters.

Eisenhower celluloid button.

# JOHN J. SPARKMAN

John J. Sparkman of Alabama, candidate for Vice President, has fifteen years experience in the United States Congress. He has been a leader in the fight for legislation to improve housing, agriculture, small business, public education and the welfare of veterans. As a delegate to the United Nations and a member of the Senate Foreign Relations Committee he has gained first hand knowledge of foreign relations problems facing our country. He will bring to the executive department a wealth of knowledge and valuable experience.

# A MAN NAMED STEVENSON

At this most critical period in American History, unusual qualities of civilian leadership are demanded in our government. We are fortunate to have a candidate for the Office of President of the United States who is an experienced administrator, a respected statesman and a man of proven integrity. With confidence, the people of our nation can look to the able leadership of Adlai E. Stevenson to guide us through the challenging years ahead.

Above: Lithographed button for Stevenson-Sparkman.
Below: Lithographed tin button.

Above: Front and back covers of a Stevenson-Sparkman comic book.
Left: Checkered flag for Indiana Democratic candidates, inspired by the Indianapolis 500.
Below right: Plaster ashtray shows the Democratic donkey kicking the Republican elephant.

*Stevenson-Sparkman garter.*

NIX-ON-IKE

Lithographed button for Stevenson
designed by cartoonist Bill Mauldin.

Poster for Stevenson using the same graphics
as a 1940 Roosevelt poster.

Dime-store display card holding six pairs of Eisenhower sunglasses.

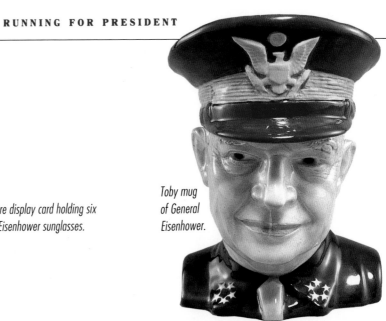

Toby mug of General Eisenhower.

Eisenhower T-shirt.

Canvas tote bag with "I LIKE IKE" slogan.

Sheet music for the Eisenhower-Nixon campaign. The same publisher set Lincoln's Gettysburg Address to music.

Celluloid button for Eisenhower.

During the 1952 campaign, novelty buttons could combine a personal photo with a favorite candidate's. These items are rare.

★

1956

48 STATES
IN THE UNION

*REPUBLICAN*

# Dwight D. Eisenhower

ELECTORAL VOTE 457, POPULAR VOTE 57.6%

DEMOCRAT

# Adlai E. Stevenson

ELECTORAL VOTE 73, POPULAR VOTE 42.1%

### GEORGE GALLUP, JR.

is co-chairman of The Gallup Organization, Inc. He is a lecturer and an author of numerous public opinion studies including *Forecast 2000* (1984); *The Great American Success Story* (1989); and *The People's Religion: American Faith in the 90s* (1989).

### ALEC M. GALLUP

is co-chairman of The Gallup Organization, Inc. A specialist in public opinion research, he is the author of numerous studies and articles including *Death Penalty Sentiment in the United States* (1989) and *Presidential Approval: A Sourcebook* (1990).

The 1956 presidential election contest, pitting Dwight Eisenhower against Adlai Stevenson, was the last of the traditional barnstorming whistle-stop campaigns. The race between Richard Nixon and John Kennedy in 1960 ushered in the modern era of "high tech" election campaigns, characterized by the packaging of candidates by media specialists, extensive private polling, and heavy television coverage of even the minutiae of presidential contests.

The 1956 campaign was one of the calmest in U.S. history. An air of inevitability hung over the race, a rematch between the 1952 presidential candidates. Few political observers gave Democratic challenger Adlai Stevenson much chance of wresting the White House from one of the most popular Presidents of all time, Dwight Eisenhower. Not only had Ike defeated his rival by the landslide margin of 55 percent to 45 percent in 1952 but he had shown far more potential vote-getting strength than Stevenson in every Gallup poll trial heat conducted in the intervening years.

Both presidential candidates were selected at their respective political conventions in 1956 with a minimum of fuss. Stevenson won renomination on the first ballot on August 16 at the Democratic National Convention in Chicago's International Amphitheater. Stevenson received 905.5 votes with only 686.5 needed to nominate, while Governor Averell Harriman of New York was a poor second with 210, despite active support by former President Harry Truman. Senator Estes Kefauver of Tennessee was nominated for vice president on the second ballot. On the first ballot Kefauver won 483.5 votes, while Senator John Kennedy of Massachusetts was second with 304. On the next ballot Kefauver received 755.5 to Kennedy's 589.

President Eisenhower and Vice President Richard Nixon were renominated by unanimous vote of the Republican National Convention at the Cow Palace in San Francisco, August 22. The vice presidential nomination followed the collapse of a "dump Nixon" drive by Harold E. Stassen, who ended by seconding Nixon's nomination.

Stevenson formally opened the Democratic presidential campaign in a nationally televised speech on September 13, in which he attacked Eisenhower as a part-time President who was no longer "master in his own house." He charged that future Republican leadership "will depend not on Mr. Eisenhower, but the Republican heir-apparent Mr. Nixon."

The Republican presidential campaign officially began on September 12 at a picnic supper for five hundred party leaders from every state in the union on President Eisenhower's farm in Gettysburg, Pennsylvania. President Eisenhower addressed two topics expected to be cutting issues in the campaign: his health and Vice President Richard Nixon's place on the ticket. He assured party leaders that he "felt fine" and about Nixon said, "There is no man in the history

*Lithographed tin button for Eisenhower.*

275

CIVIL RIGHTS FOR ALL AMERICANS

*Postcard of Eisenhower with black leaders. In May 1954 the Supreme Court's momentous decision, Brown v. Board of Education of Topeka, ordered the end of public school segregation.*

of America who has had such a careful preparation as has Vice President Nixon for carrying out the duties of the presidency, if that duty should ever fall on him."

Both presidential candidates appeared eager for the fray. Eisenhower's sturdy confidence, according to *Newsweek*, rested on his belief that he had done well in office, that the economy was in good shape, and that he had ended the Korean War. Stevenson, the same magazine noted, was also more upbeat than he had been four years earlier, and had improved his campaign technique and style. He was more at ease at meeting and greeting people, and was coming across as less aloof and unapproachable than previously. In 1952 Stevenson was slow in initiating his campaign, but in 1956 he jumped right into the race. In the previous election, his headquarters was located in Springfield, Illinois. This time it was in Washington. Despite the bleak trial heat percentages reported by Gallup and other polling organizations, Stevenson now seemed ready to plunge into the mad scramble of a presidential campaign. And the September* primaries, in which Democrats scor-

ed larger than expected victories in hard-to-win states, clearly boosted the hopes of the Stevenson camp.

U.S. presidential elections are usually decided on the basis of four factors: voter appraisal of the personal merits of the candidates; of their capacity to deal with key issues; basic party strength; and the effectiveness of the party organizations. Of the four considerations, the lead in the polls in the 1956 race went to the GOP on handling of issues and on candidates, while the Democrats had the edge in measurements of basic party strength and in grassroots party activity.

When Gallup poll interviewers asked voters midway in the campaign to name what they regarded as the top problems facing the nation, they put the threat of war and foreign policy far ahead of all others, followed by civil rights, the high cost of living, and farm problems. The same voters were then asked which party they felt could better handle the particular problem they had mentioned. The GOP came out ahead, by the healthy margin of 55 percent to 45 percent, an advantage not enjoyed by the Republicans in previous election campaigns.

Even more than in 1952, for many voters the contest came down to a choice between a *man* (Eisenhower) and a *party* (the Democrats). Voters talked about why they were voting for Eisenhower or why they believed the Democrats would better look out for their interests. Rarely did they express a glowing admiration for the Democratic candidate or a spirited defense of the Republican party.

*In 1956 some states did not have presidential primaries, but held primaries for state offices in September. In Maine, the general election for all offices, except President and vice president, was held in mid-September.

Eisenhower ran on his personal popularity and on a strong economy. He sought successfully to project the image of a President who was firmly in control. Stevenson throughout the campaign relentlessly held to the themes of ending the draft, halting the testing of H-bombs, Republican "graft and corruption," Nixon's "dishonesty and the danger of having him as vice president," and Eisenhower's health.

To determine the "why" behind the vote, the Gallup Poll in the summer and fall of 1956 sent teams of reporters from its Princeton headquarters, headed by John Fenton, to conduct in-depth interviews among key voter groups. These interviews, which were not included in the scientifically drawn national samples, provided insight into the factors behind the national horserace numbers. As fledgling pollsters and members of this team, the writers of this essay learned first-hand about the perplexities of the voting behavior and attitudes of the American people. This experience spurred our interest in politics, as did attending the party conventions in Chicago and San Francisco, with all the surrounding excitement, hoopla, and nonsense.

The Democratic convention in Chicago and the GOP convention at the Cow Palace became major media events. Television was making its grand entrance on the American political scene. At both conventions large numbers of reporters, pundits, radio and TV performers, technicians, and others swarmed about, in contrast to just four years earlier. A new era was dawning, and politicians were increasingly mindful of the new television age and the fact that the cameras were on at all times. Gone were the days of smoke-filled rooms.

In Gallup's in-depth interviews, the focus was on the Midwest farm belt, a key battleground in every election campaign up to that point. Despite talk of a potential farm revolt, we found Midwest farmers more confused than angry about the farm situation and viewing new agricultural measures as "just another scheme coming out of Washington."

Other groups that were canvassed included northern blacks (still solidly wedded to the party of FDR), young voters (closely divided between the GOP and Democratic tickets), and labor union members (still Democratic, but more Republican than ever before).

Another group whose opinions the Gallup Poll sought were intellectuals, or in the parlance of the day, "eggheads." The formation in 1956 of the Committee of Arts and Sciences for Eisenhower had stimulated interest in the political opinions of the country's intellectuals. The Gallup poll therefore inter-

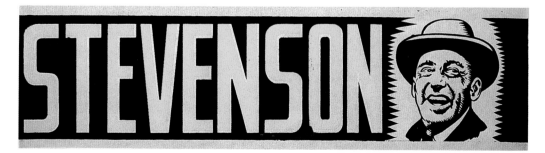

Automobile bumper sticker for Stevenson.

viewed a sample of notables in the fields of education, science, and arts. Despite the supposed attraction of Stevenson to intellectuals, they showed little inclination toward uniting behind him. Eisenhower actually had a majority of the vote among those interviewed.

In the 1956 campaign the roles of the parties were reversed—for the first time in a quarter century Republicans placed their record before the voters—while the *Democrats* went on the attack.

Eisenhower said he did not want to get dragged into a back alley fight; he wanted to stand by and run on his record. Ike described the campaign as "hard hitting but high level," and the 1956 campaign generally has been considered to be a clean campaign, relatively free of mudslinging. However, as is invariably the case, rhetoric escalated as the campaign wore on. While both sides seemed determined to avoid personal vilification, heated remarks were exchanged.

Stevenson's approach was to remind voters of the corruption by government officials during Eisenhower's term. In response to Stevenson's attacks on Eisenhower, Nixon replied: "The American people aren't going to settle for any warmed over Truman hash when they can have Eisenhower meat and potatoes."

As crises in the Middle East and Eastern Europe intensified so did attacks on Eisenhower and the GOP by the Stevenson camp. Critics charged that these crises threatened to draw the United States into war, and that the nation was in such a position because Eisenhower had misled the American people about the severity of the situation.

Stevenson's 1956 campaign style was more hard-hitting and down-to-earth than four years earlier. He was best, observers noted at the time, when he spoke off the cuff. When reading a speech the Democratic contender could be long-winded with a poor delivery.

Stevenson traveled more than his rival on the campaign trail, although the President's campaigning (with Nixon's urging) picked up considerably as the race progressed. Vice President Nixon "hit the hustings" in three well-staged trips that covered most of the nation in September and October.

Moving into November, Ike was on the road almost as much as was Stevenson, but crises in the Middle East and Eastern Europe kept him in the White House a great deal of the time. Eisenhower canceled his last planned trip—a swing through the South—and his final address from the White House conveyed the image of a national leader at a time of crisis rather than the candidate of the Republican party.

*Lithographed tin fold-over lapel tab for Stevenson and Kefauver.*

COLLECTION OF JONATHAN H. MANN

Twin international crises in the final days of the campaign—the Soviet revolt in Hungary and the Anglo-French invasion of Suez—dramatically changed what had been, according to surveys, a remarkably flat race. Eisenhower's already impressive survey margins suddenly swelled. The American people, with memories of World War II and Korea still strong, wanted a leader who would keep the nation at peace in what were clearly times of international tension. And, if war occurred, they wanted a strong leader with the experience to get the job done. Eisenhower appeared to offer both qualities to voters—a man who wanted peace, but who would be strong in the event of war.

The President's popularity showed a sharp upsurge in the final week of the 1956 campaign—a week in which uprisings shook Europe and war broke out in the Middle East. President Eisenhower and Vice President Nixon were reelected on November 6 in a landslide. The GOP nominees carried 41 states with 457 electoral votes, while the Democratic ticket won only 7 states and 73 electoral votes. Eisenhower took 57.6 percent of the popular vote as against 42.1 percent for Stevenson.

Yet despite the resounding Eisenhower-Nixon victory, Democrats retained control of both houses of Congress with majorities of 49 to 47 in the Senate and 233 to 200 in the House of Representatives, with one vacancy and one seat in doubt. During the presidential campaign Eisenhower had made fervent pleas for the election of a Republican Congress. The public listened respectfully and then elected a Democratic Congress. John Fenton (later editor of the Gallup poll) wrote about this man versus party theme in his book, *In Your Opinion:*

Even in the closing days of the campaign, the basic conflict for many voters between the Democratic party and the GOP candidate was unresolved. It was not until the early morning hours of the day after the election that the decision of the electorate became clear. Eisenhower was back in office, by a plurality of nearly 10 million voters. The Democrats would still control Congress for another two years—and by a slightly bigger margin. The President started his second term faced with an electorate which clearly liked him (his Gallup Poll popularity was at an all-time high of 79 percent in January, 1957), but just as clearly rejected his party.

One of the most interesting aspects of the 1956 election was women's vote, more decisive than ever before in determining the outcome of an election, according to pre- and post-election analysis by the Gallup Poll. Women voted overwhelmingly for the GOP ticket (fear of war was a major factor), while men were closely divided in their choices.

One of the major developments in recent election campaigns has been the increased use of scientific sampling techniques, first employed on a national basis in the mid-1930s by polling pioneers Archibald Crossley, George Gallup, and Elmo Roper.

The number of polling organizations has increased greatly since 1960. In 1956 only a few survey groups covered the race—perhaps most prominently, the Gallup Poll and the Roper Poll—and a few state polling organizations. Polls are now conducted with far greater frequency, and used to explore and track the attitudes, values, and motivations of voters much more extensively than in the past.

In addition, beginning in 1960, private, confidential polling has increasingly be-

*Prior to the 1956 Democratic convention, there was a move to have Senator Hubert Humphrey nominated for vice president.*

*The worn-shoe image originated with a September 2, 1952, photograph showing a tired Stevenson sitting cross-legged with a large hole in the sole of his shoe. This imagery was used both for and against Stevenson's candidacy.*

come the centerpiece of political campaigns, with private pollsters moving from the background to a position front and center among a candidate's closest election advisers. In 1960 pollster Louis Harris gained prominence as one of John Kennedy's key campaign strategists. Polls, both public and private, subsequently became a fixture of every presidential campaign.

Although polling techniques had gradually evolved in the two decades since 1935, the 1956 presidential election produced the first major advance in survey methodology since that time. Probability sampling procedures, developed by Michigan Survey Research Center researchers and others, were adopted in place of the less accurate "quota" sampling method used previously. Although

Gallup had experimented with this sampling technique in the 1952 election, this approach was employed exclusively in 1956.

Polling organizations in 1956 also applied a lesson learned the hard way from the 1948 contest between President Harry Truman and Thomas E. Dewey—the importance of polling right up to the eve of an election, in order to measure any last minute shifts in voter preferences. In 1948 survey organizations stopped polling too soon and missed the swing to Harry Truman in the final weeks of the campaign. This time Gallup, Roper, and others caught the final upsurge to Eisenhower. The last Gallup estimate of Eisenhower's vote was only 1.7 percentage points from the actual election vote.

Polling techniques have steadily improved. Evidence that progress has been made can be seen by comparing a survey organization's final pre-election estimates with the actual election returns, the "acid test" of technical proficiency. Take, for example, the record of the Gallup Poll (a credit to painstaking experimentation by George Gallup and his chief statistician, Paul Perry). The average deviation of final Gallup survey presidential findings from the actual results for the period 1936 through 1952 was 4.3 percentage points. From 1952 through 1968 it was 2.0 percentage points; from 1968 through 1988, it was 1.6 percentage points.

The campaign of 1956 provided the classic demonstration of the futility of the traditional whistle-stopping, barnstorming campaign. Between August and early October, intense campaigning by the presidential and vice presidential candidates of both parties produced virtually no movement in the polls. An August test race, conducted following both conventions, showed Eisenhower and Nixon with 52 percent to Stevenson and Kefauver's 41 percent. The next three tests were a carbon copy of these results, with an October survey showing the GOP ticket with 51 percent to 41 percent for the Democratic ticket. Only events (the international crises) caused the standings to change.

George Gallup, looking back on his polling experience, said in a 1957 speech titled, "There Must Be A Better Way":

> In all the twenty-one years of my polling experience, I have never known one instance when a speech made any difference in the national vote for or against a candidate. Even the whistle-stopping which enables a candidate to get out among the people—to wave at women hanging out of upstairs windows, to shake hands with strangers in front of the local drug store, to kiss babies, and to give the candidate of the opposition party unshirted Hell—all this seems to be just so much wasted effort. In fact, these tactics, which reduce political campaigning to the intellectual level of professional wrestling, seem to do a candidate more harm than good. Our people would prefer that their presidential candidates act like presidential candidates.

In searching for a "better way," Gallup proposed that there be an agreement to limit campaigning to perhaps six major speeches on the part of each candidate. The speeches would be limited to one-half hour, he suggested, and all television stations would be asked to allocate this time to each candidate. All channels would carry the speech. Gallup commented, "Certainly, in a democracy which depends upon an informed electorate, this is the least we can expect of our TV networks, and the least we can ask of our peo-

ple." When presented to the public in Gallup polls in the late 1950s, this idea met with substantial support as a way to replace the traditional barnstorming campaign.

TV debates were, of course, soon to become a fixture of presidential campaigns, starting with the famous 1960 debate between Vice President Richard Nixon and Senator John Kennedy. And in at least three of the last five presidential campaigns in which these post-nomination confrontations have taken place—in 1960, 1976, and 1980—debates appear to have played a decisive role in the outcome of the November elections.

The technology that has helped shape the campaigns of the last three decades could, in some ways, be considered a mixed blessing. On the one hand, television—a key feature of this technology—has brought presidential election campaigns into the living rooms of America and has made the political process in general more accessible to voters.

On the other hand, television has contributed to certain abuses of the electoral process—for example, the cynical image manipulation of candidates by media specialists, and the trivialization of campaigns by ten-second "sound bites." Such abuses, coupled with the use of private polls for promotional and publicity purposes rather than information gathering (for "support rather than illumination"), and massive and escalating campaign spending, have in the view of many contributed to a lower regard for politics and to the steady downturn in voter participation since the 1960s.

The 1956 presidential election campaign marked not only the last of the traditional campaigns, but perhaps in a certain sense a loss of innocence as well.

★

WELCOME

MR. PRESIDENT

Cotton sailcloth banner for Eisenhower.

Celluloid button of Mrs. Eisenhower and Mrs. Nixon.

MAMIE

PAT

Salt and pepper shaker figurines of President and Mrs. Eisenhower.

Eisenhower
umbrella.

1956 saw a plethora of campaign items including nylon stockings, hand lotion, cigarettes, bubble gum cigars, rulers, pens, key chains, shopping bags— and television commercials. There were more than fifty types of automobile bumper stickers.

Cardboard promotion for Stevenson and Kefauver.

Contributors' ticket books. Proceeds were to be used for television time for Stevenson.

Lithographed tin button for Stevenson and Kefauver suggesting the emergence of television in campaigns.

Stevenson umbrella.

Celluloid buttons for
Stevenson. Democratic
television commercials
presented Stevenson as
an intelligent, decent,
and thoughtful person.

Stevenson-Kefauver cigarette lighter.

Stevenson's talented speechwriters included Willard Wirtz, John Bartlow
Martin, John Hersey, John Kenneth Galbraith, and Arthur M. Schlesinger, jr.

Four-leaf clover button showing
Democratic areas of strength.

Eisenhower cufflinks.

I LIKE IKE

PEACE — PROSPERITY — PROGRESS

IKE'S WORKINGMAN'S CLUB

67

MILLION MEMBERS

ALL WORKING

MEMBERSHIPS INCREASING

DAILY

AMERICA'S RECORD EMPLOYMENT

RCA VICTOR
LM-2071
RED SEAL
A "NEW ORTHOPHONIC" HIGH FIDELITY RECORDING

THE PRESIDENT'S
FAVORITE MUSIC

Record album of
President Eisenhower's
"favorite music."

ONE DOLLAR (Tax Included)

*Official Program*
43rd INAUGURATION
*1957*

*1957 inaugural program with cover illustration by Norman Rockwell.*

★

1960

50 STATES
IN THE UNION

DEMOCRAT
# John F. Kennedy
ELECTORAL VOTE 303, POPULAR VOTE 49.9%

REPUBLICAN
# Richard M. Nixon
ELECTORAL VOTE 219, POPULAR VOTE 49.6%

GIL TROY

is the author of *See How They Ran:*
*The Changing Role of the Presidential Candidate*
(1991). He is professor of history at McGill University.

**WILL IT SPLIT?**

The presidential campaign of 1960 promised to revolutionize American politics. As President Dwight D. Eisenhower approached his seventieth birthday and the end of his second term, a new generation of leaders emerged. Born in the twentieth century, these urban sophisticates were freer of party commitments and more comfortable on television. They embraced a modern campaigning style.

One of these leaders, Vice President Richard M. Nixon, had spent eight years paying his dues—wooing party leaders, serving as Eisenhower's hatchet-man, representing the United States abroad. Most notably, during his July 1959 visit to Moscow, Nixon had clashed with the Soviet Premier Nikita Khrushchev. In this "Kitchen Debate," the vigorous young American defended capitalism's sparkling technologies and essential freedoms before the gruff pig-breeder-turned-Communist-party-boss. Nixon trusted that such triumphs solidified his image as a statesman and would prove once and for all that he was not "Tricky Dick."

Having dispatched a last-minute convention challenge from New York's Governor Nelson Rockefeller, Nixon entered the campaign confidently. The forty-seven-year-old Californian distanced himself from "old-fashioned" partisan politics. He would emphasize not the "man" over "the party," but "issues" over "personalities."

Still, Nixon had to tread carefully. The vice president had to champion the Eisenhower administration without being too defensive. He had to inject passion into the campaign without being unstatesmanlike. And he had to project confidence without stirring memories of Thomas Dewey's smug 1948 campaign. To prove, he recalled, "that a Republican campaign could be exciting and even inspiring," Nixon pledged in his acceptance speech to campaign in all fifty states.

The Democratic nominee had to work harder for his nomination. Estes Kefauver's early victories over Adlai Stevenson in 1956 made primaries the new springboards for popular candidacies. Harvard-educated, a World War II hero, scion of a legendary family, Senator John F. Kennedy treated the primary campaign as a dry run for the general election. Kennedy and his brother and campaign manager Robert constructed a soon-to-be-legendary machine. They built the campaign on a pile of experts. Harvard professors helped write the candidate's addresses; speech tutors improved his delivery; social psychologists assessed his crowds; and pollsters charted his popularity. "All I have to do is show up," Kennedy marveled, in a tribute to the "unsung heroes" of his campaign, the advance men who arranged each appearance down to the color of the bunting.

Victories in the Wisconsin and West Virginia primaries catapulted Kennedy to the nomination, as the flashy Massachusetts senator upstaged his solid but loquacious rival, Senator Hubert H. Humphrey of Minnesota. The race exhausted Kennedy and earned him wry invitations from Republicans to "drop in" on the Senate some time. But the primaries helped defuse the anti-Catholic prejudice that threatened Kennedy's efforts. Shrewdly and to Humphrey's frustration, Kennedy made the primaries a referendum, equating a vote for Kennedy with a vote for religious tolerance.

While campaigning, Kennedy learned about the country. In West Virginia, tanned and relaxed from a quick vacation in Montego Bay, Kennedy encountered Appalachian poverty. "Imagine," he said to an aide, "just imagine kids who never drink milk." Such discoveries sensitized Kennedy to the needs of the underprivileged, and proved that stumping could enlighten the candidate as well as the people.

Still, Kennedy entered the fall campaign as the underdog. Nixon played the experi-

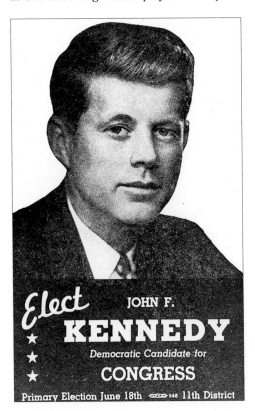

*Postcard from John Kennedy's Massachusetts Democratic congressional primary, June 18, 1946.*

enced statesman to Kennedy's upstart playboy—although they had been freshman congressmen together in 1947. Kennedy looked forward to facing Nixon, who had already revealed his unique capacity to inspire hatred among Democrats. Kennedy should project a sense of "calm, dignity and command of the situation," strategists advised, "avoiding artificiality" while generating "excitement." In the wake of Harry Truman's whistle-stop tour, "the press and professionals" demanded that all candidates travel and speak "more than is either desirable or necessary," Professor John Kenneth Galbraith of Harvard wrote. Kennedy had to be "a hot campaigner" without burning out.

Nixon also mounted an energetic campaign. The hard-working grocer's son was determined to outhustle the millionaire playboy. The two candidates would push themselves, Theodore White noted, "until the choice of an American President seemed to rest more on pure glands and physical vitality than on qualities of statesmanship, reason or eloquence." By the end, Nixon flew 65,000 miles, delivering more than 150 major speeches in 188 cities to over ten million people. His Democratic rival, speaking eight or ten times a day, traveled 44,000 miles, for a total of 229,000 since October 1959. Of the two vice presidential candidates, the Democrat Lyndon B. Johnson of Texas concentrated effectively on the South, while the Republican Henry Cabot Lodge, Jr., campaigned in more leisurely fashion in the North and West.

Although Kennedy and Nixon disagreed on many substantive issues, both preferred to address broader themes. Nixon promised continuing peace and prosperity. Kennedy positioned himself as the "real leader for the six-ties," the man who would get America moving again. "I think we can do better," the senator would declare. "I think this is a great country, but we can be a far greater country." These nostrums did not please everyone. Although the campaign would achieve mythic proportions in later years, many contemporaries mourned the callow candidates' jejune sloganeering. One bumper sticker announced: "Cheer up! You can't elect both of them."

Still, the Nixon campaign started strong, with a southern reception so frenzied that the venerable editor Ralph McGill declared it "the greatest thing in Atlanta since the premiere of *Gone With the Wind*." Three days later, Nixon bumped his knee on a car door. From August 29 through September 9, Nixon lay in the hospital, suffering from a knee infection. The inflamed knee and penicillin shots caused great pain, he later recalled, "but the mental suffering was infinitely worse."

To offset Nixon's name recognition, the Kennedy machine flooded the nation with campaign artifacts, including twenty-four million buttons, nineteen million lapel tabs, fourteen million brochures, ten million bumper stickers, and 297 banners. The most popular pin proved to be a tie clasp commemorating Kennedy's Pacific war heroics on PT 109. The total cost of $805,303.67 contributed to the Democrats' four million dollar deficit—25 percent more than the maximum each party was supposed to spend on the entire campaign.

Old-fashioned stumping and leafletting were upstaged by speculation about "The Great Debates" between the major party nominees. Although Nixon originally tried to avoid these unprecedented confrontations,

Poster from Kennedy's 1958 Massachusetts senatorial campaign.

he realized he had no choice. In its first decade, television had disappointed many Americans by its apparently chronic superficiality. Now, many were convinced, the four televised debates would make American politics meaningful, as it had been in the days of Lincoln and Douglas—forgetting, of course, that the famous debates took place during a senatorial election two years before the 1860 presidential contest.

The debates would "test" the people as well as the candidates, the journalist Marquis Childs claimed. Deprived of "Gunsmoke" and the "Untouchables," would "the mass audience . . . listen to a serious debate or will the ratings show a number of sets blacked out?" Before the two combatants had spoken a single word in Chicago on the night of

September 26, 1960, the people had passed the test. Seventy million people stopped what they were doing, turned on their television sets and watched their leaders clash.

It quickly became apparent, however, that great expectations would not be met. The two nominees circled around each other, fearful of offending the mass audience. Years later, many would contrast the appearance of the tanned, relaxed Massachusetts senator and the ailing, five-o'clock-shadowed vice president. But at the time, more than anything else, viewers were bored. "You need a diagram to follow what they're talking about," a North Carolina housewife complained. However, by showing at least equal command of the issues, Kennedy neutralized arguments about youth and inexperience.

As the debates wound on, and benumbed commentators muttered about their redundancy, Kennedy challenged Nixon to a fifth debate. Nixon balked. His campaign had more money for a final television blitz, and he had no desire for more debates. Nixon's hesitation allowed Democrats to condemn this attempt "to keep the voters in the dark." With this move, Kennedy solidified his

claim on the debates as his own, and of his victory in the debates as complete, when the debates truly were bipartisan events and were, at best, a draw.

At least thirty-one different studies measured public response to the debates. As the numbers proliferated, television executives and others rejoiced. For, as the *San Francisco Examiner* declared, "The more informed the electorate, the better for our country."

A more primitive and more integrated "living portrait" of the "whole" man emerged from the debates than from any other campaign forum, Theodore White wrote. The people now knew their candidates.

Nevertheless, the grand expectations had not been met. At best, the debates "supplement[ed]" but did not "supplant" what the *Baltimore Sun* called "the cruel grind and the inanities of conventional campaigning." "Who cares" which candidate showed "less tension" and created an "image of maturity," one voter asked. "Every good actor shows poise and appeal . . . but I have a higher regard for Abe Lincoln than I have for the actor who shot him."

In addition to the four debates, the candidates enjoyed unprecedented exposure on TV. The nightly news shows, specials, and talk shows featured the two candidates, their running mates and their families. NBC alone provided over one-and-a-half million dollars' worth of coverage. With the two national committees also purchasing three million dollars' worth of radio and television advertising time, the people learned about their nominees as never before.

Each candidate approached his advertising campaign gingerly. The Democrats were still reeling from what Frank Church of Idaho called the "barrage of bland ballyhoo"

*Postcard of Richard Nixon with Soviet Premier Nikita Khrushchev at the American National Exhibition in Moscow, July 24, 1959.*

**DICK NIXON — *The One Man to Deal With Khrushchev***

Republicans unleashed in the two Eisenhower campaigns. To demonstrate his virtue, Nixon exiled his admen to an office one block east of Madison Avenue. He refused all scripts for commercials, insisting "I'll just sit in front of the camera and talk." Although the Democrats also claimed that their advertising agency did not "provide campaign advice or slogans," but simply "purchase[d] time and space in the commercial media," they mounted a more sophisticated effort. Commercials showcased Senator Kennedy and his wife, Jackie, in formal and informal settings and featured celebrities—including the actress Myrna Loy and the childrearing expert Dr. Benjamin Spock. One Kennedy jingle sang:

> Do you want a man for President
> who's seasoned through and through,
> But not so doggone seasoned
> that he won't try something new,
> And a man who's old enough to know
> and young enough to do?
> It's up to you, it's up to you
> It's strictly up to you.

All this media exposure enhanced the candidates' stumping campaigns. "The turnouts for Senator Kennedy have suddenly become impressively huge," a reporter gasped as over six hundred thousand people hailed the Democratic motorcade in Ohio on September 27. As Kennedy drove by, teenagers shrieked. Women sighed mindlessly, "Oh, Jack I love you, Jack, I love yuh, Jack—Jack, Jack. I love you." Broadcasting these receptions triggered television's internal accelerator. Mirroring the reactions elsewhere, the crowds became even wilder. Kennedy is no longer a politician, one southern senator remarked, but a "thing," combining "the best qualities of Elvis Presley and Franklin D. Roosevelt."

Record album containing the four 1960 televised campaign debates between Kennedy and Nixon.

Kennedy did not "have all the neurotics by any means," Taylor Grant of Mutual Broadcasting noted; Nixon was also mobbed. Ironically, both candidates had begun the campaign noted for their reserve on the stump. Nixon's famous victory wave always seemed an awkward imitation of Eisenhower's. Kennedy and his Ivy League advisers disdained these "folk rites." "If I have to wave both hands above my head in order to be President, I won't have the job," Kennedy confessed. It was not Kennedy or Nixon so much as television itself that transformed politicians into rock stars.

Electronic exposure altered the nature of the political audience and of the message politicians broadcast. Until now, political communication had been most effective in mobilizing partisans. All of a sudden, the campaign was reaching undecided voters. No longer simply preaching to the converted,

*Celluloid button for Nixon. More than five hundred varieties of buttons exist from the 1960 campaign.*

candidates now aimed to convert the uncommitted. To achieve that, the candidates offered the fullest portrait a mass electorate had ever received. The people could "know more about" what candidates "think, their appearance, their verbal ability, their mannerisms and manners" than ever before, the *Atlanta Constitution* observed. And by moderating their message to reach more people, the candidates became more palatable. As one Minnesota farmer told the journalist Samuel Lubell after the debates, "Before I tuned in I was afraid neither man was fit to be president. But they both handled themselves well. The country will be secure with either man." According to Lubell, the stumping, the television programs, and especially the debates, "threaten to upset one of our more deeply-rooted political habits—the habit of not listening to the candidates."

As Kennedy kept his focus on the nine large states his pollster Louis Harris identified as keys to victory, Nixon found himself scrambling to reach all fifty states. From the start, Kennedy had relied on a regional strategy emphasizing the Northeast, while Nixon molded a national image. Nixon, therefore, was forced to campaign in marginal or se-

cure states while Kennedy concentrated on strategically important ones.

On Sunday, November 6, Nixon jetted into Anchorage, Alaska, fulfilling his fifty-state pledge. Nixon heralded his great achievement as he launched a finale that Theodore White labeled the "greatest electioneering effort ever made to move men's minds." Nixon delivered fifteen-minute addresses on TV nightly. His campaign spent half-a-million dollars on a nationwide election eve telethon that had celebrities like Ginger Rogers mingling with Nixon's allies and family.

Nixon's final push featured an endorsement from Dwight Eisenhower, but it came a little too late. Eisenhower was quiet throughout the campaign. Once, when asked what major ideas the vice president had contributed to the administration, the President hesitated. "If you give me a week I might think one up," he said. As Democratic commercials replayed that snippet, many said that the President's aloofness indicated his longstanding disdain for his vice president. In his memoirs Nixon would insist that Eisenhower's doctor begged the Republican National Committee to spare the President's health and limit his campaign appearances.

Kennedy's final push received an unexpected boost when the civil rights leader Martin Luther King, Jr., was arrested in Atlanta. Both Kennedy brothers sprang into action—independently. The candidate called Mrs. King, while Robert Kennedy called the Georgia judge responsible for jailing him. The Kennedy intervention helped swing thousands of black votes to the Democrats. "I've got all my votes and I've got a suitcase, and I'm going to take them up there and dump them in his [Kennedy's] lap," the jailed activist's father, "Daddy" King, rejoiced. A Protestant minister, King Senior confessed that "I had expected to vote against Senator Kennedy because of his religion."

The elder King was not the only American still harboring anti-Catholic prejudice. Over three hundred anti-Catholic tracts, some with circulations as high as five million, blanketed the country. The Catholic church is "Satan's superb organization on earth," they warned. Ironically, Nixon more than Kennedy tried to keep Catholicism out of the presidential campaign.

Early in the campaign, Nixon ordered "all of the people in my campaign not to discuss religion" and "not to allow anybody to participate in the campaign who does so on that ground." Although Nixon disapproved of pandering to prejudice, he also realized that exploitation of the religious issue would be unwise. In her study of campaign advertising, Kathleen Hall Jamieson argues that Kennedy and not Nixon benefited from the issue. Democrats broadcast Kennedy's pleas for religious toleration disproportionately in Catholic areas, less to mollify Protestants than to mobilize Catholics. The strategy worked. Some estimate that while 50 percent of Catholics voted for Adlai Stevenson in 1956, over 80 percent voted for Kennedy in 1960.

The election was one of the closest in the twentieth century. The result hung in the balance until Illinois went to Kennedy—thanks, many said, to hundreds of corpses who voted in Mayor Richard Daley's Chicago wards. (Had Kennedy lost Illinois, however, he would still have won in the electoral college.) Nixon bitterly concluded that images and tactics swayed the campaign. In his memoirs, Nixon claimed that Kennedy's campaign had "unlimited money" and was "led by the most ruthless group of political operators ever mobilized for a presidential campaign." Nixon "vowed that I would never again enter an election at a disadvantage by being vulnerable to them—or anyone—on the level of political tactics."

Americans feared that TV threatened their country's political soul. Richard Nixon's many faces proved that politicians did not know how to resolve the struggle. On the campaign trail, Nixon was at once scoundrel and saint, the prophet of calculation and virtuously oblivious. In his Checkers speech of 1952, and in a well-publicized 1955 speech, Nixon acknowledged that candidates could only achieve the intimacy and spontaneity TV demanded through careful preparation. "[T]here isn't any such thing as a nonpolitical speech by a politician," he told broadcasting executives. But by 1960, Nixon himself was the "nonpolitical" politician, eschewing personalities and victimized by the mysterious new medium. Only in retrospect did he "learn" to pay attention to appearances over issues. As techniques would become more sophisticated, and more ubiquitous, the confusion, and the doubts, would intensify.

But while many blamed modern technology, these problems were not new. Television and advertising accelerated and nationalized the campaign—but the dissatisfaction and dilemmas stemmed from the paradoxical political system the Founding Fathers created. Americans were still not sure if they wanted style or substance in a candidate, a dignified king or a candid prime minister. The disappointments of the 1960 campaign—as with its predecessors and successors—were part of the nation's historic failure to make peace with American democracy.

*Figurines of the President's children, Caroline and John Kennedy, Jr., circa 1964.*

Three posters for Kennedy. The broadside at right advertises a Harvard "COLOSSAL POLITICAL RALLY" with "5 MILITANTLY PARTISAN SPEECHES" including one by Arthur M. Schlesinger, jr.

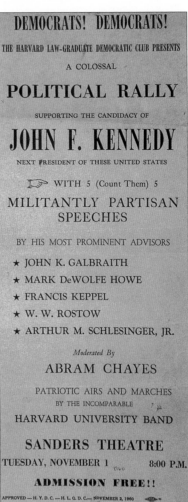

*Poster for Kennedy and Johnson.*

*Cardboard and silk lapel badge for Kennedy.*

*Three Kennedy celluloid buttons. Willian J. Vanden Heuvel unsuccessfully ran for Congress from New York City.*

*Paperweight with PT 109 design, given to Kennedy delegates at the 1960 Democratic convention.*

# KENNEDY-JOHNSON
## two great Democrats

DEMOCRATIC NATIONAL COMMITTEE, WASHINGTON 6, D. C.

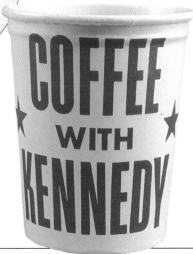

"A PROFILE IN COURAGE"

ELECT U. S. SENATOR
**JOHN F. KENNEDY**
VICE PRESIDENT

Celluloid button promoting
Kennedy for the 1956 vice
presidential nomination. In
1957, Kennedy received the
Pulitzer Prize for his book
Profiles in Courage, a study
of senators who risked
their careers for what they
regarded to be right.

Above: Poster for
Kennedy and Johnson.
Right: Invitation to the
Texas Welcome Dinner,
November 22, 1963,
in Austin. Kennedy
was killed in Dallas a
few hours earlier.

*In honor of*
*President John F. Kennedy*
*and*
*Vice President Lyndon B. Johnson*

*The State Democratic Executive Committee*
*requests the pleasure of your company*
*at the*
*Texas Welcome Dinner*
*on Friday evening the twenty-second of November*
*One thousand nine hundred and sixty-three*
*at half after seven o'clock*
*at the Municipal Auditorium*
*in the City of Austin*

*Contribution card enclosed*               *Mr. Eugene M. Locke, Chairman*
*Optional dress*                           *Mrs. Alfred Negley, Vice-Chairman*
                                           *Mr. Frank C. Erwin, Jr., Secretary*

YOUTH FOR KENNEDY

301

Kennedy's pledge to "get America moving again" inspired a variety of campaign items which used the theme of leadership. Others utilized Kennedy's "New Frontier" slogan. His World War II naval record was recalled on many PT 109 articles, especially lapel pins.

A TIME FOR GREATNESS

U. S. SENATOR JOHN F. KENNEDY FOR PRESIDENT

A NEW LEADER FOR THE 60's

KENNEDY FOR PRESIDENT

FACTS FOR NEW YORK VOTERS:

KENNEDY FOR PRESIDENT JOHNSON FOR VICE PRESIDENT

N. Y. Democratic State Campaign Committee Biltmore Hotel, N. Y. 17, N. Y.

302

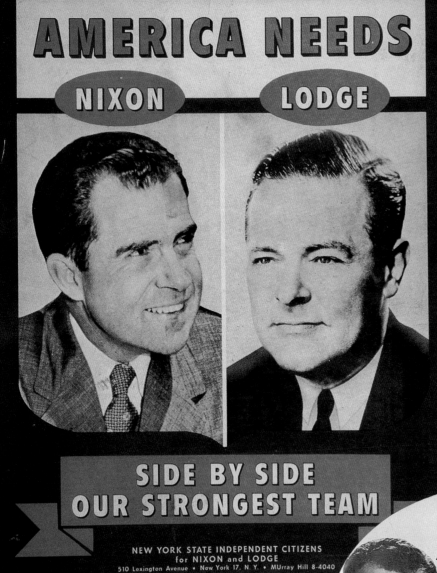

Cardboard poster for Nixon and Lodge.

Celluloid button
for the Republican candidates.

Mrs. Nixon's picture appeared on many
buttons with such slogans as "Pat
for First Lady" and "We Want Pat Too."

Nixon-Lodge paper sticker.

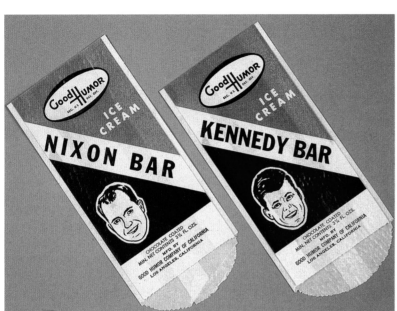

The 1960 election was a watershed for political ephemera of many varieties—the twilight of a tradition to be replaced by the emergence of television.

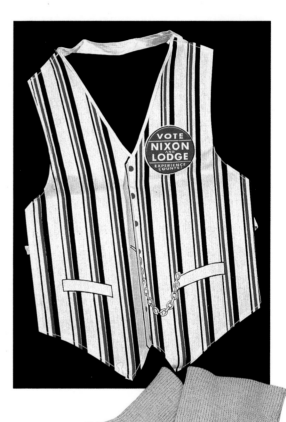

The 1960 presidential election saw an aged general succeeded by the youngest man ever elected President. To some, Kennedy's thousand-day presidency seems a romantic chapter in the often sordid history of American politics. He, his family, and advisers conveyed an exciting sense of elitism, a sense that the best people had been summoned forth from the country.

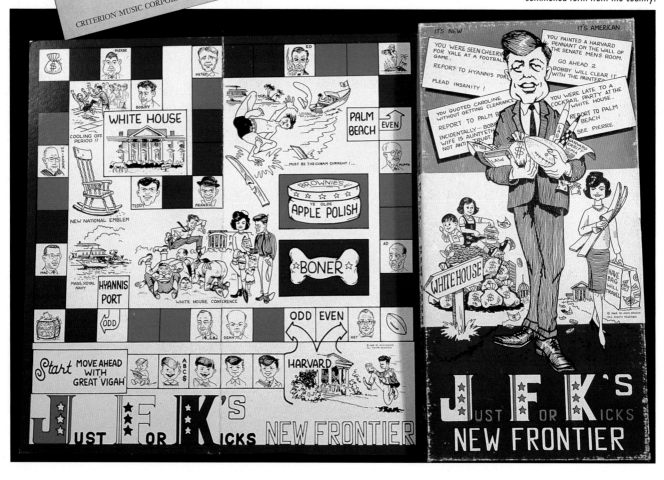

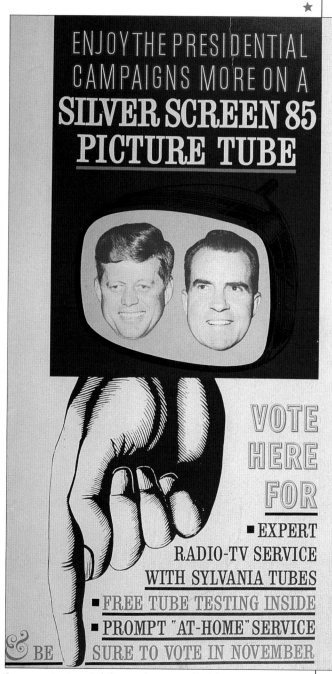

Paper campaign items including an advertisement for Sylvania television sets focusing on the 1960 presidential debates.

★

**1964**
50 STATES
IN THE UNION

JOHNSON    HUMPHREY

DEMOCRAT
## Lyndon B. Johnson
ELECTORAL VOTE 486, POPULAR VOTE 61.1%

REPUBLICAN
## Barry M. Goldwater
ELECTORAL VOTE 52, POPULAR VOTE 38.5%

ROBERT DALLEK
is a professor of history at the University
of California, Los Angeles. He is the author of
several books, including *Franklin D. Roosevelt
and American Foreign Policy, 1932–1945* (1979),
which won a Bancroft Prize, and *Lone Star
Rising: Lyndon Johnson and His Times,
1908–1960* (1991).

*Celluloid button of Lyndon Johnson with a shadowy image of Kennedy in the background.*

The election of 1964 pitted two of the more flamboyant characters of twentieth-century American politics against one another—Democratic President Lyndon B. Johnson and Arizona's Republican Senator Barry Goldwater. The campaign, as Goldwater intended, produced "a choice, not an echo" and some hard hitting Johnson tactics never used before in a presidential contest.

Goldwater was a character out of the American past—a conservative ideologue with an affinity for old-fashioned individualism and *laissez-faire* economics that seemed more appropriate to the age of McKinley than the post-New Deal era in American history. Early in the campaign one commentator suggested that a film on Goldwater's life would best be made by Nineteenth-Century Fox. Predictions that Goldwater's uncompromising stance as a conservative would produce a Democratic landslide made little impression on him. At the Republican convention in San Francisco, where conservative delegates shouted down moderate New York Governor Nelson Rockefeller speaking in support of a minority plank condemning the Communist party, the John Birch Society, and the Ku Klux Klan, Goldwater asserted that "extremism in defense of liberty is no vice. And . . . moderation in pursuit of justice is no virtue." An attractive man but with limited political understanding, Goldwater, in his best-selling 1960 book, *The Conscience of a Conservative*, described politics as not the art of the possible but "the art of achieving the maximum amount of freedom for individuals."

Goldwater's nomination was the result of a fluke. Conservative Republicans were a minority, but their organizing tactics and devotion to their cause gave them an edge over the party's more numerous moderates. Moreover, when the moderates backed Nelson Rockefeller, a man whose recent divorce and remarriage offended Republican voters, Goldwater became the Republican nominee. Goldwater mistakenly saw his candidacy as evidence that the nation was ready for a shift from liberal to conservative domestic and foreign policies.

During his campaign, Goldwater attacked big government and the welfare state at home and excessive restraint in combatting international communism abroad. He called for an end to federal farm subsidies and aid to education, the progressive income tax, and mandatory Social Security. He urged the sale of the Tennessee Valley Authority (TVA) to private interests, declared his opposition to federal pressure to desegregate schools, and described programs like Medicare and Medicaid and Johnson's War on Poverty as destructive to the work ethic and the moral fiber of the nation. He warned Americans that "there is no single field in which he [Johnson] is not going to move in and take over your lives."

Goldwater was no less uncompromising on foreign affairs. His 1962 book, *Why Not Victory?* had attacked the containment of communism as a prescription for defeat. He argued against coexistence and for an aggressive strategy of rolling back communist regimes like Castro's in Cuba. He denounced John Kennedy's nuclear test-ban treaty and all arms negotiations with the Russians, called for a buildup of America's nuclear arsenal, and seemed willing to drop the bomb if necessary in a showdown with the Soviets and the Chinese. He advocated the use of American power to assure a victory against communism in Vietnam. He wanted NATO commanders to have "authority over the tactical nuclear weapons appropriate to NATO's defenses."

Some moderate Republicans described Goldwater as "trigger happy" or likely to "shoot from the hip." In response to Republican campaign posters announcing that "in your heart you know he's right," Democrats attached bumper stickers to their cars, saying, "In your heart you know he might," and "You know in your heart he's right—far right." Placards attacking Goldwater as an extremist became commonplace: "VOTE FOR GOLD-WATER AND GO TO WAR; STAMP OUT PEACE—VOTE GOLDWATER; IN YOUR GUT YOU KNOW HE'S NUTS; WELCOME DOCTOR STRANGEWATER; GOLDWATER IN 1864."

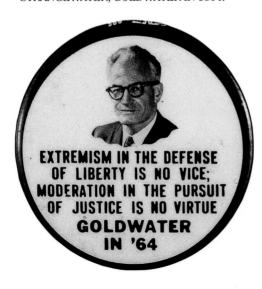

*Celluloid button for Barry Goldwater. The quotation is from Goldwater's speech accepting the Republican nomination, July 17, 1964. This passage formalized the conservative-liberal split within the party.*

The only issue in the campaign on which Goldwater seemed capable of scoring against the President was Johnson's reputation for backroom deals and sleazy politics. A prominent religious leader said that Lyndon Johnson was "a man whose public house is splendid in every appearance, but whose private lack of ethic must inevitably introduce termites at the very foundation." In 1963–64, an investigation of Robert G. (Bobby) Baker (Johnson's principal Senate aide in the 1950s) for influence peddling, and the arrest of Walter Jenkins (Johnson's longtime aide and White House chief of staff) on a morals charge gave Goldwater the chance to attack Johnson's character. His campaign publicists, in fact, prepared a television film "picturing America as a modern Sodom and Gomorrah. The film included shots of a girl in a topless bathing suit, pornographic magazine covers, strip-tease joints, blacks rioting in the streets, teenagers on a rampage, and even . . . Bobby Baker." Although polls showed Goldwater with an advantage over Johnson on the question of personal integrity, Goldwater refused to allow his campaign to use the film, saying it was racist.

There is little question that Goldwater could have scored points in the campaign if he had aggressively attacked Johnson's record as a vulgar, overbearing, manipulative, grandiose character who would do anything to win a political fight and gain center stage. "I understand you were born in a log cabin," a foreign visitor said to LBJ in a joke of the time. "No, No!" Johnson replied. "You have me confused with Abe Lincoln. I was born in a manger." Johnson's egotism and need to be top dog was legendary. On the night of the 1960 election, he told John Kennedy, his presidential running mate, "Jack, I see you are losing Ohio.

Well, I'm winning Texas, and we're doing all right in Pennsylvania." In the fall of 1964, when the Johnson-Hubert Humphrey campaign issued a button on which Humphrey's head appeared to be larger than Johnson's, LBJ had a tantrum. Campaign officials recalled the button and issued a new one displaying Johnson more prominently than his running mate. Johnson's nomination by only eighty-seven votes out of a million cast in the 1948 Texas Democratic primary for a U.S. Senate seat made him vulnerable to charges that his campaign had stuffed ballot boxes and stolen the election. Dubbed "Landslide Lyndon" by opponents after 1948, Johnson would have been hard-pressed to answer renewed accusations about his tainted victory. Moreover, a very visible fortune in radio and television properties also made Johnson vulnerable to attack as an elected official who had used his office to manipulate the Federal Communications Commission and enrich his family.

Yet even the sharpest attacks on Johnson's character could not have turned the election in Goldwater's favor. Johnson had assets which made him nearly impossible to beat. The successor to a popular assassinated President, whose legacy Johnson emphasized he was fulfilling, LBJ had the JFK mystique on his side. In addition, Johnson had the power of incumbency—the presidential office with its capacity to command the attention of the media and the public. In one week during the spring of 1964, for example, *Time* described the President as having made "nearly two dozen speeches, traveled 2,983 miles, held three press conferences, been on national television three times, appeared in person before nearly a quarter of a million people, and made his right hand bleed and puff up from handshaking." Johnson himself

emphasized that he was too busy as President to worry about the election and that the people's business came first. "We have a job to do here and we are going to try to do that first," Johnson said. "When, as, and if we can, we will make as many appearances as we think we can without neglecting the interests of the nation."

Then, there was Johnson's record since becoming President in November 1963. When nine Johnson aides met on August 9, 1964, to plot strategy for LBJ's campaign, they agreed to point up his significant domestic achievements, including the Kennedy civil rights and tax cut measures that promised to relieve racial tensions and spur the nation's economy. During the campaign, in which Johnson made more than two hundred speeches in forty-five days, he pointed out that Kennedy had left fifty-one major bills before the Congress and that he, Johnson, had persuaded the Senate to pass all of them and the House all but four or five. In addition, Johnson made much of the fact that he intended to build a Great Society, especially marked by

*New York State poster for Johnson-Humphrey. Note Robert Kennedy running for senator.*

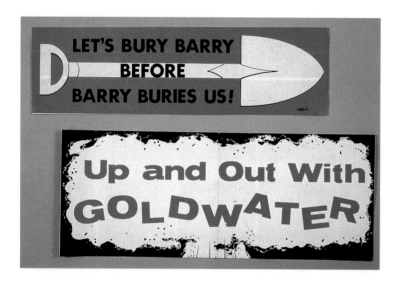

*Anti-Goldwater automobile bumper stickers. These items were standard fare at most Democratic campaign headquarters.*

educational opportunities allowing all Americans to realize their full potential.

One of Johnson's great assets in '64, as in earlier campaigns, was his phenomenal energy and capacity for work. The journalist Theodore White captured some of this when he described "a day of twenty-two hours' exertion," in which Johnson worked an eight-hour day in the White House and then spent fourteen hours traveling and speaking in Boston, Pittsburgh, Evansville, Indiana, and Albuquerque. After four and a half hours of sleep, he flew to southern California, where he "actually spoke for some five and a half hours of personalized campaign oratory."

There was no more dramatic moment in the campaign than Johnson's speech in New Orleans when he dramatized his break with southern parochialism on civil rights and his emergence as a leader committed to the well-being of all the nation's citizens. "Whatever your views are," Johnson said, "we have a Constitution, and we have a Bill of Rights, and we have the law of the land

[the 1964 Civil Rights Act], and two-thirds of the Democrats in the Senate voted for it and three-fourths of the Republicans. I signed it, and I am going to enforce it . . . and I think that any man that is worthy of the high office of president is going to do the same." Johnson then recounted a story Sam Rayburn told him about Texas Senator Joseph W. Bailey, who said, "What a great future the South could have if we could just meet our economic problems, if we could just take a look at the resources of the South and develop them." Bailey added that he would love to give one more "Democratic" speech in Mississippi. "The poor old state, they haven't heard a Democratic speech in thirty years. All they ever hear at election time is 'nigra, nigra, nigra.'"

The Johnson campaign hoped to persuade voters not only to vote for Johnson but also to vote against Goldwater. The Johnson message was that Goldwater was "an extremist reactionary rather than just . . . a conservative with a conscience." To win over Republican moderates, Johnson told them: "I'm not sure whether there is a real Republican candidate this time."

Johnson's comment was relatively benign alongside of a secret "Anti-Campaign" issuing "black propaganda." Organized by what journalists Rowland Evans and Robert Novak described as "a dozen brainy Washington-based Democrats, some in and some out of the government," it kept no records of its meetings, which took place in "a small conference room on the second floor of the West Wing of the White House." Johnson kept close tabs on the "Anti-Campaign," or Team D or the "Five O'Clock Club," as they liked to call themselves, vetoing and approving plans as the "Club" hatched them. The objective was what they called "negative advance," keeping track of Goldwater's campaign schedule, obtaining advance copies of his speeches, and arranging for local Johnson supporters to refute or contradict Goldwater's assertions. "Full of tricks," journalist Theodore H. White wrote, "the club was also responsible for some of the best of the slogans, counterdemonstrations and hostile placards that greeted Goldwater wherever he went."

The "negative" campaigning found its most successful expression in three television ads prepared by the advertising firm of Doyle Dane Bernbach. The objective was to make Goldwater appear as a radical unfit to deal with either the country's domestic or foreign affairs. In an ad the Democrats ran repeatedly during the campaign, the fingers of two hands were shown tearing up a Social Security card. In a second, more controversial ad, which ran only once, a little girl licked an ice-cream cone while a woman's voice in the background explained about fallout from strontium-90 and pointed out that Goldwater was against Kennedy's test ban on nuclear explosions in the atmosphere.

The most controversial ad, which also ran only once, but made a memorable impression, showed a beautiful young girl plucking petals from a daisy while a voice-over counted down from ten to zero. As the scene of the girl in a field dissolved into a mushroom cloud, Johnson's voice said, "These are the stakes. To make a world in which all of God's children can live, or go into the dark. We must either love each other or we must die." Though Goldwater's name went unmentioned, the ad provoked an outcry which convinced Democrats to shelve it. After the ad ran, Johnson summoned Bill Moyers, an aide responsible for television advertising in the campaign, to the White

Poster for Goldwater rally done in nineteenth-century style. Richard Nixon was rally chairman.

House. Johnson dressed Moyers down for the ad, but, as Moyers remembered it, Johnson's "voice was chuckling all the time." After Moyers explained that he had ordered only one showing of the ad and began to leave, Johnson followed him to the elevator, where he asked: "You sure we ought to run it just once?" Moyers said, "Yes."

Few issues in the campaign worried Johnson as much as Vietnam. Disturbed by the instability in South Vietnam after a November 1963 coup toppling Ngo Dinh Diem and determined to prevent a Communist takeover there, Johnson struggled to find an

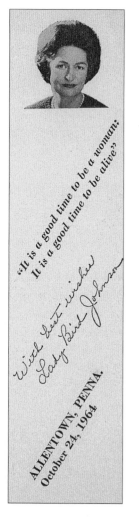

Mrs. Johnson actively campaigned in 1964. These souvenir items were distributed during her trips.

effective policy. Goldwater's hawkishness about communism in general and about Vietnam in particular drew Johnson in two directions at the same time. On one hand, he wished to establish himself as more moderate than Goldwater in dealing with the crisis in Southeast Asia. Consequently, he declared in speeches during the campaign that "I have not thought we were ready for American boys to do the fighting for Asian boys. What I have been trying to do, with the situation that I found, was to get the boys in Vietnam to do their own fighting with our advice and our equipment." In a later speech he stated more emphatically: "We are not going to send American boys away from home to do what Asian boys should be doing for themselves."

On the other hand, Johnson did not want Goldwater to make him appear weak on Vietnam and be in a position either during or after the campaign to charge that Johnson's cautious policies were "losing" Vietnam. Although Goldwater told Johnson in a secret meeting in July 1964 that he did "not believe it . . . in the best interest of the United States to make the Vietnam War or its conduct a political issue in this campaign," Johnson did not take him at his word. In August, after North Vietnamese torpedo boats attacked the U.S. destroyer *Maddox*, which was engaged in electronic spying in the Gulf of Tonkin off the North Vietnamese coast, the White House ordered a second destroyer, the *C. Turner Joy* to join the *Maddox* on patrol. When reports came into the

Pentagon three days later of North Vietnamese attacks on both ships, the administration decided to retaliate.

Although subsequent reports raised doubts as to whether the attacks had occurred, Johnson went ahead anyway with air strikes against torpedo boat bases and oil storage facilities. He then used the episode to win passage of a congressional resolution authorizing the President to take "all necessary measures to repel any armed attacks against the forces of the United States and to prevent further aggression." Johnson did not view the Tonkin Gulf resolution as a blank check for expansion of the war. Rather, he wanted to persuade Hanoi that the United States would not back away from a fight in Vietnam and the American people that he could be as tough as Goldwater about Communist expansion without being reckless. With unanimous approval in the House and only two dissenting votes in the Senate, the resolution provided a strong endorsement of Johnson's leadership. A national poll showed a 30 percent jump in Johnson's approval rating. Though the episode later raised questions about Johnson's credibility, it defused Vietnam as a potential issue in the campaign.

The outcome was never really in doubt. The question throughout the campaign was:

How much will Johnson win by? His aim was to win the biggest presidential victory in American history. He came close. He won 44 out of 50 states, two less than Franklin Roosevelt in 1936, and 61.1 percent of the popular vote, the largest to that point in U.S. history. The electorate also gave the Democrats a better than two-thirds margin in the Senate, 68 to 32, and a lopsided 295 to 140 advantage in the House.

Johnson's victory opened the way to the passage of more reform legislation than even FDR managed to achieve in his first term. But it also encouraged the illusion that Johnson had a mandate to do as he saw fit in Vietnam. His errors in judgment about what could be achieved in Vietnam went far to destroy his credibility with the public and deny him the chance to run for another term in 1968. In only three years' time the national unity achieved by Johnson in the 1964 election dissolved into riots in black ghettos and antiwar demonstrations that moved one European travel agent to urge customers to "See America while it lasts." The 1964 election was the last great electoral victory for American liberalism. The excesses and failures of Johnson's term ushered in an era of conservative control that has lasted for twenty-eight years.

Anti-Johnson automobile bumper sticker. Most anti-Johnson items were produced by independent conservative groups.

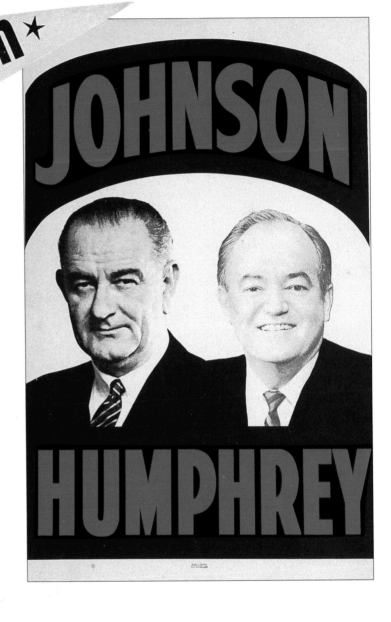

VOTE FOR
THE DEMOCRATIC TEAM

VICE PRESIDENT
**HUMPHREY**

PRESIDENT
**JOHNSON**

U. S. SENATOR
**KENNEDY**

GOVERNOR
**BELLOTTI**

LT. GOVERNOR
**COSTELLO**

ATTY. GEN.
**HENNIGAN**

SEC. OF STATE
**WHITE**

TREASURER
**CRANE**

AUDITOR
**BUCZKO**

TAKE THIS CARD TO THE POLLS WITH YOU

*Paper campaign material proliferated in 1964. The Massachusetts poster at left includes Senator Edward Kennedy, who sought reelection in 1964.*

"*LBJ for the USA*" became a campaign slogan. A thousand or so different buttons were issued. Many anti-Goldwater items, with an assortment of rhymes, parodied the Republican candidate.

HE SAYS NO TO CIVILIZATION AND SURVIVAL
HE VOTED AGAINST
NUCLEAR TEST BAN
CIVIL RIGHTS ACT
TAX REDUCTION
MEDICAL CARE FOR THE AGED
MINIMUM WAGE LEGISLATION

SAY NO TO THE NO-SAYER
**VOTE JOHNSON**

Anti-Goldwater
Ben Shahn print.

To move away from Johnson being labeled as a
southern candidate, numerous 1964 campaign items
stressed his Texas and western roots.

Miniature Mexican sombrero distributed by the
Latin American Democratic Club.

Miniature Conestoga wagon emphasizing Johnson's western heritage.

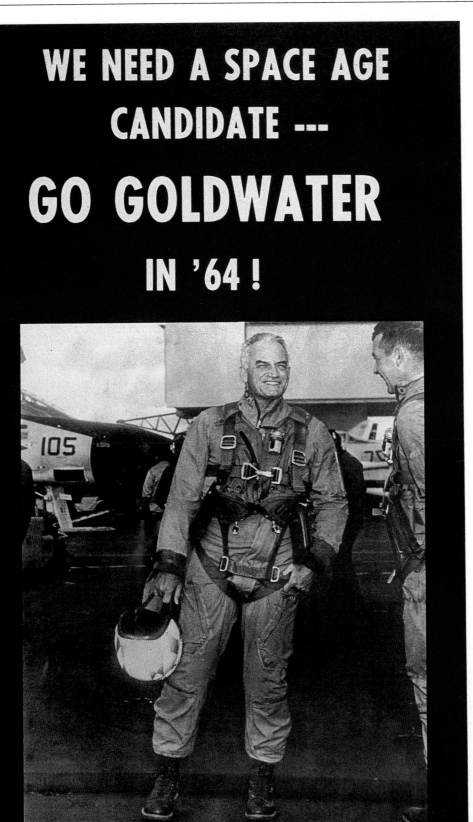

WE NEED A SPACE AGE CANDIDATE --- GO GOLDWATER IN '64 !

After distinguished service in World War II, Goldwater became chief of staff of the Arizona Air National Guard and a major general in the USAF Reserve. He later served as commanding officer of the 999th Combined Air Force Reserve Squadron, made up of members of Congress and congressional employees. He remained forever a friend of the military.

Throughout 1963 conservative groups sought to draft Goldwater. When he did receive the 1964 nomination, conservatives openly flaunted their views.

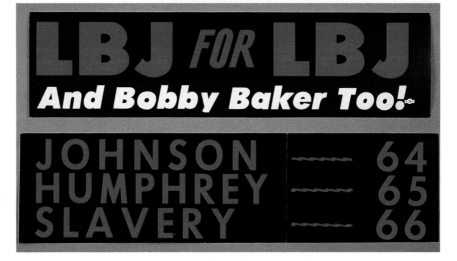

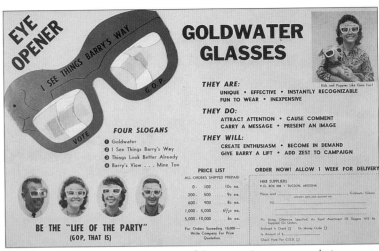

Advertisement for Goldwater paper glasses, one of the campaign's numerous novelty items.

Conservative greeting card parodying
Soviet leader Nikita Khruschev.

Campaign items playing on the literal meaning of the Republican candidate's name.

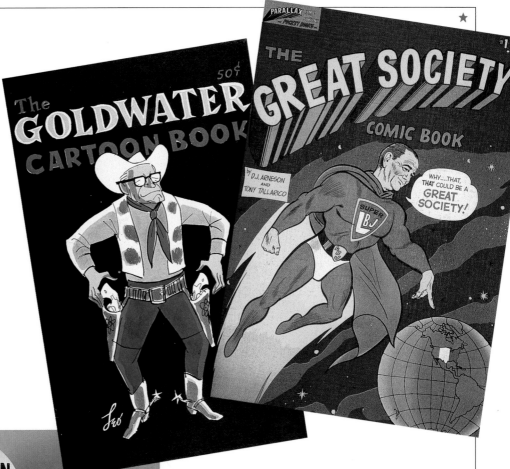

An assortment of campaign novelties.

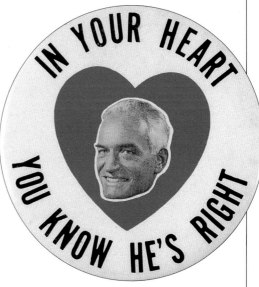

Celluloid button for Goldwater using a principal campaign slogan.

1968

50 STATES
IN THE UNION

*REPUBLICAN*

# Richard M. Nixon

ELECTORAL VOTE 301, POPULAR VOTE 43.4%

DEMOCRAT

# Hubert H. Humphrey

ELECTORAL VOTE 191, POPULAR VOTE 42.7%

AMERICAN INDEPENDENT

# George C. Wallace

ELECTORAL VOTE 46, POPULAR VOTE 13.5%

STEPHEN E. AMBROSE
is Boyd Professor of History and director of the
Eisenhower Center at the University of New
Orleans. He is the author of numerous books on
American history, including biographies of
Dwight Eisenhower and Richard Nixon.

# NIXON'S THE ONE!

Washington State Nixon For President—Gordon S. Clinton, Chairman

It was a tumultuous year, full of sharp surprises, shocking events, and fundamental changes in American society and politics. In January, victory in Vietnam seemed just around the corner; by November, the number of Americans killed in action was approaching twenty-five thousand and victory seemed farther away than ever. At home, the generation gap, the gender gap, and the racial gap grew deeper and wider. Political assassinations sickened the nation; riots swept the country. Perhaps most surprising of all, President Lyndon Johnson dropped out of politics and Richard Nixon rose from his political grave to win the presidential election.

America's young people, especially on the college campuses, rejected the authority of their elders and the rules of their society. Some burned their draft cards, a few burned American flags, a handful openly called for a Communist victory in Vietnam. Widespread drug use became accepted, even common, as did rock-and-roll music, dirty blue jeans, long hair, and the slogan, "Don't trust anyone over thirty." American women embraced feminism in ever-increasing numbers. American blacks, many of them, rejected non-violence and took to the streets to demand equal rights or to call for "Black Power." In response to these and other developments, there was a "backlash" by the white middle-class. The American people had not been so badly divided since the Civil War. As in 1861, in 1968 they split into two distinct groups: "doves" who opposed the war and embraced the social and political changes, and "hawks" who supported the war and traditional values.

The event that had the greatest impact on the presidential election came at the end of January on the other side of the world. The Communists in South Vietnam launched a country-wide offensive on the Vietnamese religious holiday of Tet. Although the offensive failed, it had a tremendous effect on the American people, who realized for the first time that they were not winning the war and that the Viet Cong were far more numerous and well-armed than anyone in power had ever indicated. The enemy inflicted heavy casualties on the American forces and stunned President Johnson. When his field commander, General William Westmoreland, asked for more than 200,000 reinforcements (at a time when he had more than 550,000 troops in country), Johnson knew that the American people would not support such an escalation and instead began, secretly, the long, slow process of withdrawal. His plan was to turn the war over to the South Vietnamese. The almost certain Republican nominee, Richard Nixon, who had been calling for escalation for the previous four years, agreed with him—although he did not say so. Tet thus marked a turning point in world history; for the first time since 1898 the United States was reducing rather than increasing its armed forces in Asia.

The impact of Tet on the public was as great as its impact on American leaders,

*Automobile bumper sticker with Richard Nixon's most popular 1968 campaign slogan.*

*Plastic hat with paper hatband issued for the Democratic convention. Senator Eugene McCarthy ran in the Democratic primaries as an anti-Vietnam War candidate.*

shown dramatically in the first presidential primary election, in March in New Hampshire. A little-known senator from Minnesota, Eugene McCarthy, challenged Johnson on an antiwar platform. He was given no chance, but he won 40 percent of the votes in the Democratic primary, which was interpreted as a defeat for Johnson and a rejection of his war policy. Four days after the primary Senator Robert Kennedy entered the contest for the Democratic nomination on an antiwar platform.

Two weeks later, on March 31, with the polls indicating that he was facing almost certain defeat in the upcoming Wisconsin primary, Johnson went on national television to make two surprise announcements. First, he was halting nearly all bombing of North Vietnam and offering to enter into peace negotiations with the Communists. His previous position had been to demand a complete Communist withdrawal from South Vietnam. (Negotiations began in Paris in May and immediately stalled over the issue of South Vietnamese participation; the United States insisted on it, Hanoi refused to consider it.) Second, "I shall not seek, and I will not accept, the nomination of my party for another term as your President." The Democratic nomination was suddenly wide open. The three leading candidates were McCarthy, Kennedy, and Vice President Hubert Humphrey, who was pledged to continue the war and who counted on the party regulars rather than the votes of the people in the primaries for the nomination.

On April 4, another shock. Civil rights leader Martin Luther King, Jr., was assassinated in Memphis. The murder led many young blacks to despair. A wave of riots swept the country. Parts of the nation's capital were in flames as buildings burned within blocks of the White House; Johnson brought fifty thousand troops into Washington, D.C., to enforce a curfew and protect government property. Two weeks later another form of violence jolted the public, as young white students at Columbia University seized administration buildings to protest both the war and black oppression. The Columbia radicals had many imitators. Campus violence erupted across the country.

The chief beneficiary of the backlash caused by the violence was Governor George Wallace of Alabama, who entered the race for the presidency as head of a third-party (the American Independent party) ticket. His running mate was Air Force General Curtis LeMay, whose policy toward the enemy in Vietnam was to "bomb 'em back to the Stone Age." Wallace's slogan was, "Send Them a Message." He said that there wasn't a dime's worth of difference between the Republicans and the Democrats and attacked "pointy headed" intellectuals. He was antigovernment, antiblack, antiviolence, and pro-war. The polls showed that he spoke for millions of angry Americans; they indicated that he was attracting more than 20 percent of the voters.

In the Democratic race, meanwhile, Kennedy was forging ahead. On June 5, he won a narrow victory over McCarthy in California that seemed to assure his nomination. But that night, at his victory celebration, he was assassinated by an Arab nationalist angry over his support of Israel. South Dakota Senator George McGovern, rather than Senator McCarthy, got the support of Kennedy's delegates, meaning that the doves in the party were split.

With the Democratic party in turmoil, the Republicans met in early August in Miami to nominate Nixon. He had been campaigning, more or less nonstop, since his 1962 loss to Pat Brown in the California gubernatorial race, and had easily turned back the candidacies of Governors Nelson Rockefeller of New York and Ronald Reagan of California. Nixon picked Maryland Governor Spiro Agnew as his running mate; Agnew had propelled himself into national prominence in April with a get-tough policy toward black riots in Baltimore; his selection was an obvious attempt to persuade Wallace supporters not to throw away their vote on a third party but to get behind Nixon, who recognized that one of the chief battles in the November election would be for the traditionally Democratic white southern vote.

Nixon's platform was a moderate version of Wallace's: no busing for racial balance in the schools, an all-out attack on permissiveness, crime, and the Supreme Court's liberal decisions, and a restoration of family values and patriotism. All this was a part of what he called his "southern strategy." His slogan was "Nixon's the One!"

On the number one issue, Nixon said he had a "plan to end the war and win the peace" but he gave no details (actually, his plan was the same as the policy Johnson had already—but still secretly, while denying it in public—initiated, the gradual withdrawal of American troops and the negotiation of a ceasefire). He had strong support from wealthy Americans, who put up enough money to give him the best financed campaign in American history to date. His campaign staff, headed by his law partner John Mitchell, was well-organized.

In an innovation that became a permanent feature of presidential campaigning, he relied almost exclusively on television.

The emphasis on television was the idea of Nixon's chief of staff, H. R. "Bob" Haldeman. In a devastating critique of Nixon's 1960 campaign, Haldeman said that Nixon had spent too much time on the road, too much time making speeches. He wanted the candidate to make, at most, one speech per day. Television news programs would have to use a minute or two of it. Haldeman pointed out that the "sound bite," as it later came to be called, would reach more people in a day than three months of barnstorming.

Another Nixon innovation was to use professional advertising men rather than professional politicians as his principal advisers. Most of them came from the J. Walter Thompson advertising firm in Los Angeles. Frank Shakespeare, a CBS executive, was also on the staff. Nixon ignored the Republican National Committee and the party; he almost never used the word "Republican," nor did he campaign for Republican candidates.

The Democrats met in Chicago at the end of August. Their convention was a disaster. The world watched aghast as the world's oldest political party tore itself

*Robert Kennedy Democratic convention hat. Senator Robert Kennedy was killed on June 4, 1968, two months prior to the convention.*

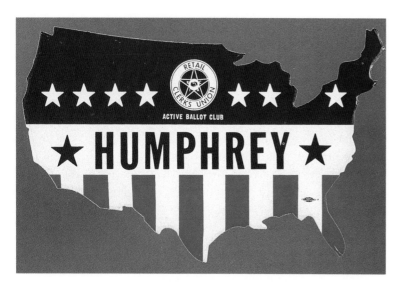

*Paper sticker for Humphrey.*

apart. Inside the convention hall the delegates, tightly controlled by Johnson, nominated Hubert Humphrey, who had not won a single primary, and Senator Edmund Muskie. Outside the hall the Chicago police, stirred up and encouraged by Mayor Richard Daley, went on a rampage against the youthful antiwar demonstrators, who for their part provoked the cops in every imaginable way.

The Democratic platform pledged to continue Johnson's policies in Vietnam. This left the doves without a candidate in the general election. This was dangerous not only to the Democratic party, where the doves were a majority, but to democracy in America, as it left the doves feeling helpless, disillusioned, and frustrated. The number-one political issue of 1968 was the war in Vietnam, but when the Democratic delegates turned back a "stop the bombing" resolution, the American people had no chance to vote on that number-one issue. This situation contributed heavily to the extreme bitterness of the presidential campaign. The only real winner from the Democratic convention was Richard Nixon, whose election now seemed assured—the polls indicated that he had a 43 percent to 31 percent lead over Humphrey (Wallace had 19 percent).

When Humphrey began campaigning, he was greeted by hecklers chanting "Dump the Hump." It was a mark of how much the doves detested the Vietnam War that they forgot how much they detested Nixon. All three candidates were subjected to merciless heckling and disruptive tactics in their campaign appearances. Shouting matches replaced political discourse. Humphrey tried to reason with his hecklers; Wallace ridiculed and threatened his hecklers; Nixon's campaign staff screened out longhairs from his rallies or roughed them up.

Nixon took the high road, promising an end to the draft as soon as he had ended the war, the appointment of conservative strict constructionists to the Supreme Court, a balanced budget, and revenue sharing with the states (the federal money would presumably be used to lower state property taxes). In sharp contrast to his 1960 campaign, he scarcely mentioned foreign policy and refused to reveal his plan to end the war. He also refused Humphrey's demand for a debate, which led Humphrey to call him "Richard the Chickenhearted." Agnew took the low road, accusing Humphrey of being "squishy soft on Communism and soft on law and order."

Slowly, Humphrey began to cut into Nixon's lead, helped by the leaders of organized labor who could not stand Nixon and who were fearful of Wallace. Humphrey's greatest asset was that he was the candidate of the majority party, and he used it wisely. In sharpest possible contrast to Nixon, Humphrey consistently linked himself with his party. He worked closely with the Democratic National Committee Chairman Larry O'Brien. He mentioned Franklin Roosevelt, Harry Truman, John Kennedy, and even Johnson at every opportunity. He worked hard for Democratic congressional candidates.

Humphrey also helped himself by apparently putting some distance between his position and Johnson's (and Nixon's) on the war: toward the end of September, Humphrey declared that "it would be my policy to move toward a systematic reduction in American forces. I think we can do it. I am determined to do it." Johnson was already doing it, but denying it; Nixon planned to do it once elected, but denied it. The doves began, finally, to gather at the Humphrey roost. They flocked to it after September 30, when Humphrey came out for a bombing halt, saying he would take a "risk for peace."

Nixon fought back. He said the risk was not Humphrey's but the lives of American boys in Vietnam. He abandoned his promise to not indulge in "personal charges" and asserted that Humphrey had "a personal attitude of indulgence and permissiveness toward the lawless." Muskie, he said, was "giving aid and comfort to those who are tearing down respect for law across the country." In October, the Republicans ran a television commercial that showed battle scenes in Vietnam, black rioters in a burning American city, and a frail, starving child interspersed with scenes of Humphrey laughing and promoting "the politics of joy."

Wallace, meanwhile, was slipping, as third-party candidates traditionally do as election day approaches. By mid-October, he was down to 18 percent. Nixon was at 40 percent, Humphrey at 35 percent and moving up. It appeared all but certain that if Johnson declared a complete bombing halt and the beginning of serious peace negotiations,

with President Nguyen Van Thieu's South Vietnamese government in Saigon participating, Humphrey would forge ahead.

Anticipating that Johnson would do exactly that, Nixon moved to scuttle the peace prospects. "We do not want to play politics with peace," he declared as he began to do so. He made contact with Thieu through Mrs. Anna Chan Chennault, the Chinese widow of World War II hero General Claire Chennault. She had extensive contacts with the Saigon government. John Mitchell persuaded her to tell Thieu that if he refused to go to the peace table before the election, he could expect better treatment from a Republican administration.

On his own, Nixon attempted to undercut Johnson. On October 26 he praised Johnson for resisting pressure to contrive a "fake peace." But he said he had heard rumors about a bombing halt and charged that if true (he said they were), "this spurt of activity is a cynical, last-minute attempt by President Johnson to salvage the candidacy of Mr. Humphrey." He then added he did not believe Johnson would do such a thing. But if the President did halt the

Auto license attachment for Wallace. George Wallace, former governor of Alabama, ran as a third-party candidate for President, endorsing segregation and conservative causes.

bombing, Nixon went on, it would constitute a "thinly disguised surrender."

Hanoi got into action. On October 27 the Communists agreed to respect the de-militarized zone separating North and South Vietnam, and to allow Saigon to sit at the negotiating table in return for a bombing halt. Johnson, meanwhile, was pressuring Thieu to accept a bombing halt in return for a place at the peace table, but Thieu refused. Desperate, Johnson decided to go ahead without Saigon. On October 31 he announced that he had ordered a bombing halt and that the expanded peace talks would get started on November 6, the day after the election.

A wave of relief swept across the nation. Polls conducted on November 1 showed a 55–28 approval for the bombing halt. Humphrey made it clear that "an enormous burden" had been lifted from his candidacy. Even as Humphrey passed him in the polls, Nixon let the euphoria build, counting on Thieu to sabotage the peace talks. On November 2, Humphrey went ahead of Nixon, 43 percent to 40 percent (Wallace was down to 13 percent). But that same day Thieu announced that his government "deeply regrets not being able to participate in the peace talks."

Now Nixon went into action. In his memoirs, he admitted that "I wanted to plant the impression . . . that [Johnson's] motives and his timing" were political. His aides charged that Johnson had instituted the bombing halt as a ploy in the election. In a television interview, Nixon said "many people . . . seem to share that view . . . because the pause came so late in the campaign." He added that one of his aides felt that the halt "was politi-

cally motivated and was timed to affect the election. I don't agree with him, but he is a man in his own right and has made this statement." Then he offered to help persuade Saigon to sit down at the negotiating table after he won the election.

On Monday, November 4, in a nation-wide telethon, Nixon pounded home the point that "the high hopes for peace of three days ago" had dwindled. He said he would not criticize Johnson's motives, "but when we consider the fact that hopes for peace . . . are quite discouraging because of the developments [since the bombing halt announcement] it is clear that if we are going to avoid what could be a diplomatic disaster, it is going to be necessary to get some new men and a united front in the United States." Then he said he had heard "a very disturbing report" that since the bombing halt went into effect, "the North Vietnamese are moving thousands of tons of supplies down the Ho Chi Minh Trail, and our bombers are not able to stop them."

He had heard no such report. He simply made that up. Humphrey, on his own telethon, made that point and added, "It does not help the negotiations to falsely accuse anyone at this particular time."

Agnew was not present for the Nixon telethon. He had become an embarrassment to the Republicans (a Democratic radio spot opened with a soft, steady "thump, thump." Then, above the thumping, a voice asked incredulously: "Spiro Agnew? A heartbeat away from the presidency?" The Democrats had used a somewhat similar negative advertisement against Barry Goldwater in 1964; a trend was being established). On the Democratic telethon, Muskie got equal billing with Humphrey, who declared, "My co-pilot,

most of the Northeast; Nixon won the Middle West six states to two (Minnesota and Michigan); Humphrey won Texas; Nixon got Florida, South Carolina and the border states; Wallace won Arkansas, Louisiana, Mississippi, Alabama, and Georgia.

Nixon was the first candidate since Zachary Taylor in 1848 to win the presidency while his party failed to carry either the House or Senate (the Democrats had a majority of 58-42 in the Senate, 243-192 in the House).

The campaign had been characterized by lies, deceit, and cynical contempt by the politicians, and by hostility, anger, disruptive tactics by the people. Campaigns are supposed to divide the people into "them" and "us," but within the confines of a recognition that they are all Americans, one people living together in one country.

In his victory speech on November 6, Nixon spoke to the problem the campaign had created for him. He said he had seen many placards during the campaign, some friendly, some not. "But the one that touched me the most was the one that I saw in Deshler, Ohio, at the end of a long day. . . . A teenager held up a sign, 'Bring Us Together.'

"And that will be the great objective of this administration at the outset, to bring the American people together."

The people very badly needed to be brought back together after the most divisive presidential campaign since 1860. Less clear was whether Nixon was the man who could do it. His campaign had capitalized on the polarization among the people. The tactic had worked. But now he had to govern, and his campaign had so badly divided the already badly divided nation that it was going to be at best difficult for him to do so..

Ed Muskie, is ready to take over at any time." Humphrey's praise of Muskie became so effusive that one reporter composed a make-believe lead for his election day story that read, "Vice President Hubert H. Humphrey pledged today that if elected, he will resign immediately and let Senator Edmund S. Muskie become President."

The election was one of the closest in American history. As the votes were counted first Nixon, then Humphrey had slight leads. Not until noon the following day was Nixon declared the winner. He had won 31,770,000 votes (43.4 percent) to Humphrey's 31,270,000 (42.7 percent). Wallace got 9,906,000 (13.5 percent). In the electoral college, however, Nixon had a solid victory, 301 votes to Humphrey's 191 and Wallace's 46. Nixon had carried all the Great Plains states and the Far West (except Washington state); Humphrey had carried

Poster for Humphrey and
Muskie issued by the AFL-CIO.

Celluloid button for Humphrey from
Minnesota, his home state.

Poster for Wallace.

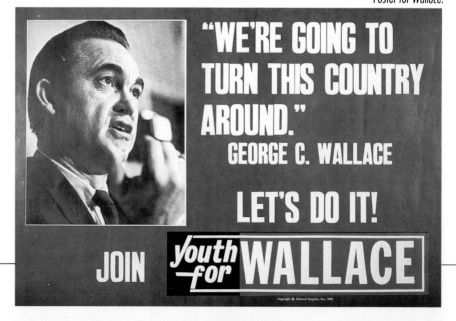

Official Nixon Material – Feeley & Wheeler Inc., 370 Lexington Ave., New York, N.Y. 10017

Poster for Nixon and Agnew.

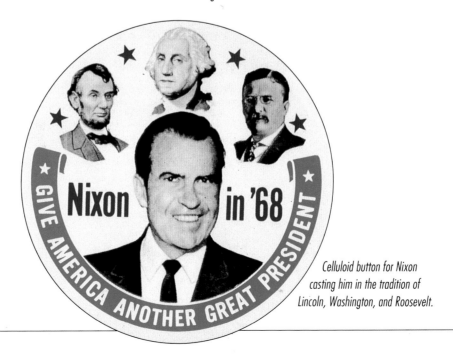

Celluloid button for Nixon
casting him in the tradition of
Lincoln, Washington, and Roosevelt.

...dreams CAN be rebuilt! NOW !

YOU MUST VOTE

HUMPHREY
For President

MUSKIE
For Vice President

For New Yorkers who value Human Dignity, the choice is clear.

VOTAR ES PODER
NOVEMBER 5

CONCERNED CITIZENS

NEW YORK STATE CITIZENS FOR HUMPHREY-MUSKIE
7 East 52nd Street          New York, N.Y. 10022

Poster for Humphrey and Muskie associating them with John and Robert Kennedy and Martin Luther King, Jr.

Poster issued by the International Ladies Garment Workers Union promoting a series of campaign radio programs.

Labor union sticker for Humphrey-Muskie.

Humphrey celluloid button with moving eyes.

## HUBERT HUMPHREY MARCH

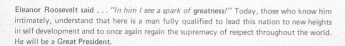

Eleanor Roosevelt said . . . *"In him I see a spark of greatness!"* Today, those who know him intimately, understand that here is a man fully qualified to lead this nation to new heights in self development and to once again regain the supremacy of respect throughout the world. He will be a Great President.

1968 was a year of trauma and tragedy in America. The limited amount and variety of Humphrey campaign items may be due to the lateness of the Democratic convention (August 26–29) and to the divisions within the party over the Vietnam War. The Republican campaign relied heavily on television, usually from studio sessions with a carefully screened audience.

A variety of Nixon campaign ephemera.

Opposite: The most widely circulated poster of
the 1968 campaign. Perhaps every American
college dormitory had one on a wall—either
to show support or to throw darts at.

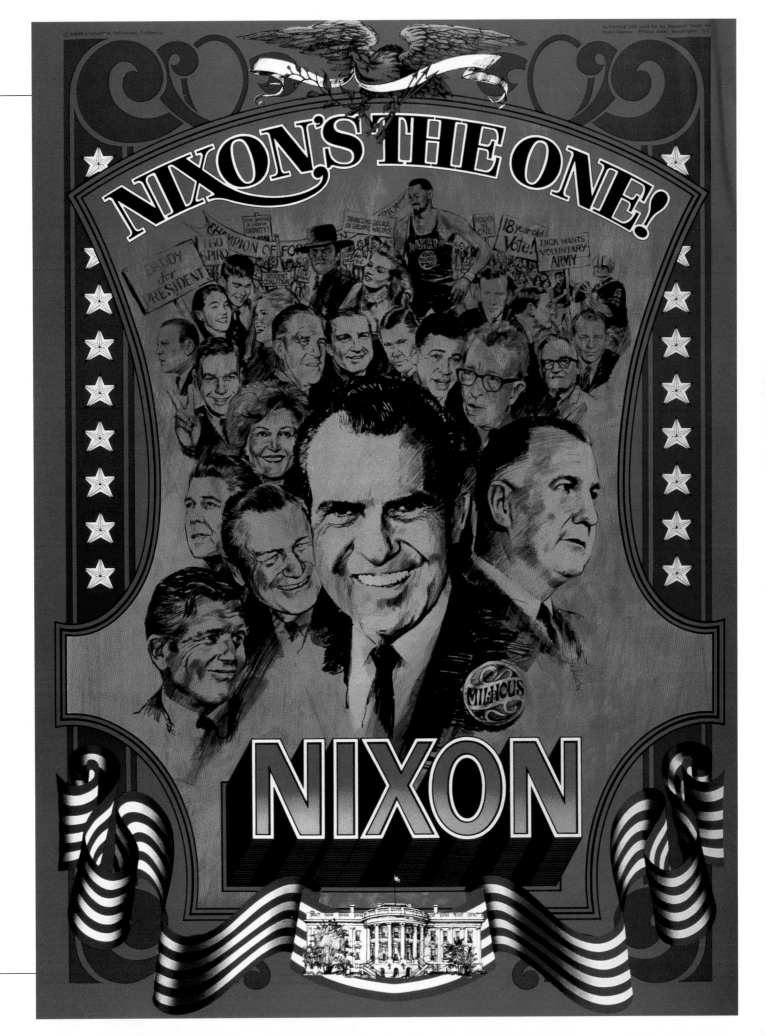

Eugene McCarthy became the hero of the "politics of protest," the hero of the new counterculture. Vietnam, the assassination of President Kennedy, the Mississippi Freedom Summer of 1964, police violence in the ghettos, and the murder of civil rights demonstrators contributed to the emergence of a protest movement—a dissenting generation.

Automobile license attachments for Wallace. Wallace found it difficult to outdo the determination of Nixon and Agnew to bring "law and order" to the country.

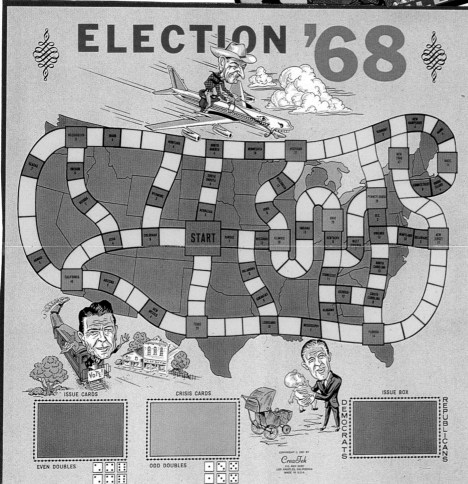

Lithographed tin button for Robert Kennedy.

Boxed game on
political strategy.

Celluloid button for
McCarthy reflecting
his opposition to
the Vietnam War.

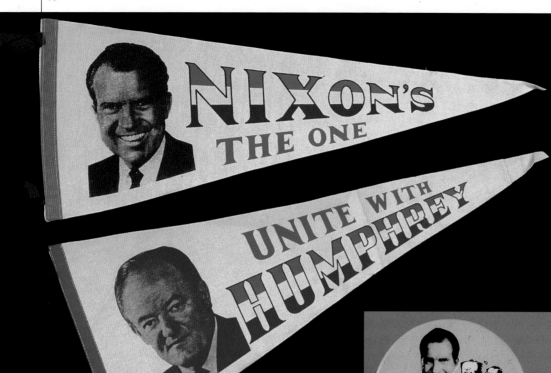

Campaign record for Nixon with excerpts from his acceptance speech, August 8, 1968.

Cartoon-type campaign buttons. Humphrey was the son of a South Dakota druggist.

Large plastic campaign buttons inspired by the Laugh-In television show.

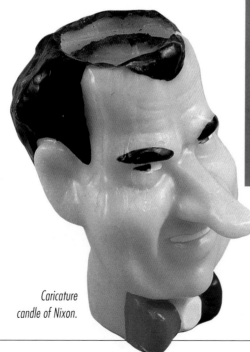

Caricature candle of Nixon.

Cardboard Halloween-related campaign item.

Cardboard hanger for Humphrey.

Campaign clothing items for Agnew and Humphrey.

Humphrey's detractors insisted that he was a Johnson puppet, especially on the Vietnam War issue.

**1972**

50 STATES
IN THE UNION

\*REPUBLICAN\*

# Richard M. Nixon

ELECTORAL VOTE 520, POPULAR VOTE 60.6%

DEMOCRAT

# George S. McGovern

ELECTORAL VOTE 17, POPULAR VOTE 37.5%

HERBERT S. PARMET
is Distinguished Professor of History at
Queensborough Community College and the
Graduate School of The City University of New
York. He is the author of many works of
history and biography, among them
*Richard Nixon and His America* (1990).

**P**icking the winner was the easiest thing about the Nixon-McGovern campaign of 1972. Less simple were other elements that helped to determine the course of American politics for years to come. Still to be resolved at the outset of George McGovern's candidacy was the future direction of the Democratic party, whether to take a progressive, social justice route by representing the formerly disfranchised or to accommodate the desires of the postindustrial middle-classes.

Was McGovern another idiosyncratic erratic interloper, reminiscent of Horace Greeley exactly one hundred years earlier, or was he a fiery prairie populist, with the ability of a William Jennings Bryan to animate a grass-roots reform movement? The nominations that summer of 1972, starting with the Democratic confirmation of McGovern's successful primary campaign, and then with the inevitable Republican renomination of President Nixon, revealed not so much that the party really was "over," as some analysts were then contending, than the fact that some rules were changing. Democrats, trying to regain the presidency by ousting an incumbent, coped with the consequences of their own success in writing reforms that promoted participatory democracy. Their achievements backfired. When the choice was left to the American people, the President, as humorist Art Buchwald put it, was still the suspect used-car salesman. McGovern, unfortunately, looked like the man who bought the car.

His moral fervor made it easy for Republicans to ridicule him as a fringe ideologue. Nixon agreed that the choice of McGovern was the most fortunate development for his own reelection prospects. He therefore endorsed a suggestion of the Republican national chairman that his surrogates use the word "McGovernite" rather than Democrat to avoid offending labor. McGovern should be depicted as "not the man we want to entrust world peace to." Pat Buchanan, his chief conservative speechwriter, suggested that the Democrat should be increasingly portrayed "as the pet radical of Eastern Liberalism, the darling of the *New York Times*, the hero of the Berkeley Hill Jet Set; Mr. Radical Chic." Anti-McGovern campaigning should emphasize the issues of "abortion, amnesty, pot, the removal of the personal tax exemption (a killer for large Catholic families); these should be targeted for speakers, and for pamphlets and for ads in Catholic and ethnic areas, Catholic and ethnic papers, Catholic and ethnic forums." For good measure, it would also be helpful to tie McGovern to "black radical schemes."

**T**he Democratic delegates who convened in Miami Beach that July reflected the changes of the past decade, the result of Vietnamese War dissension, racial and social upheavals. Reforms of the delegate selection process, put together by the McGovern-Fraser Commission, fulfilled the 1960s "New Politics" ideal, participatory democracy. The Democratic party, as speaker after speaker proclaimed, would be the party of "inclusion not exclusion," open not only to conventional politicians but also to the formerly underrepresented and unrecognized, women and minorities of every variety, even those with the most unorthodox lifestyles. It was, suggested the journalist Theodore H. White, a utopian view of "what America might be in the future."

The most important reform called for the bulk of delegates to be elected rather than, as in the past, appointed by political leaders. Eighty-two percent were chosen by the party's voters in primaries or caucuses. Only four years earlier, such "popular" delegates numbered just 43 percent of the total. Especially galling to the regulars was the exclusion of 225 of 255 Democratic congressmen, together with most of the country's prominent mayors. The absentees included the venerable and powerful Mayor Richard Daley of Chicago, which prompted an incredulous observer who was also at the center of the McGovern camp, to say, "I think we may have lost Illinois tonight."

McGovern's background appealed to activists who had opposed Johnson in 1968, especially those who had resisted Hubert Humphrey's nomination to the end. Despite a conservative South Dakota constituency, his voting record was 92 percent acceptable to the liberal Americans for Democratic Action. Perhaps of even greater significance was the strength of his antiwar credentials. He was also a man of personal military distinction. He held a Distinguished Flying Cross and was credited with thirty-five missions over Germany, Austria, and Italy during the great war against the Nazis.

Similar determination animated McGovern's fight for his party's nomination.

However great his subsequent failures, that achievement could not be ignored. The odds-on early favorite had been Senator Edmund Muskie of Maine. Of the four national candidates who ran on the major two-party tickets in 1968, he most clearly emerged with enhanced stature. The establishment of the Committee to Re-Elect the President and, it may be said, of the entire apparatus that emerged as the Watergate scandals, was in large part activated by fear that the Democrats would choose Muskie to oppose the President in 1972. He became the target of a series of pranks financed by the Committee (or CREEP, as it was known to its critics) and carried out by several operatives with ties to the White House.

One of the several tricksters wrote a bogus letter alleging that Jane Muskie, the senator's wife, had laughingly said that while Maine did not have blacks, "we have 'Cannocks' [sic]." William Loeb, the vitriolic right-wing publisher of New Hampshire's most influential newspaper, the *Manchester Union Leader*, ran the letter together with an editorial that contained the flat statement, "Sen. Muskie Insults Franco-Americans."

On February 26, little over a week before the key New Hampshire primary, Muskie stood on a flatbed truck before Loeb's newspaper office in downtown Manchester amid falling snow and emotionally defended his wife from the falsehood. Tears ran down his face along with melting snowflakes. The picture, of a crying senator, seen over and over again on television, shattered Muskie's standing. Especially damaging was the contrast with the video pictures Americans saw of their President, at just about the same time, looking triumphant and strong during his historic trip to China. Muskie nevertheless beat McGovern in New Hampshire by 46 to 37 percent. Still, it was a disappointing performance for one whose political base was in the adjacent state of Maine.

Coming out of that two-man contest, McGovern had a relatively clear field from then on. His main competition thereafter came from two Senate colleagues, Hubert H. Humphrey of Minnesota and Henry Jackson of Washington. Meanwhile, Alabama's Governor George C. Wallace was eliminated from contention midway, not by voters but by a potential assassin. He was shot and seriously wounded during a campaign rally at a shopping mall in Laurel, Maryland, just outside the District of Columbia.

Humphrey, who was by then the leading choice of the party's traditional New Dealers, fought McGovern all the way and especially in that California fight, seriously wounded the South Dakotan's chances. In a state heavily dependent on defense spending, Humphrey savaged McGovern's dovishness. He also exposed McGovern's inability to explain his thousand-dollar guaranteed family income plan, variations of which had been offered by Nixon himself and through several negative income tax schemes. When challenged on just how it would work, McGovern was vague, unable to say just how much it would cost those on different income levels. Worse, he gave the impression of having conceived just another giveaway program, and one that the candidate himself did not seem to fully understand.

All this came out during that campaign before the California primary. The entire experience tarnished the McGovern halo. First, there were the advance media expectations, which had virtually conceded him a landslide victory. His actual 5 percent mar-

*Fabric jacket patch with the Republican symbol.*

gin was immediately interpreted as evidence of weakness, not success. Still more embarrassing was the insistence of the front-runner, though a champion of the reformed methods of selecting delegates, on holding to California's winner-take-all rules, which gave him all of the state's convention votes. At the convention, McGovern did not hesitate to claim his bonanza. He promptly rejected a last minute Muskie offer to strike a compromise. Muskie warned that he was trying to avert the threat of "self-slaughter." Then, on the convention floor, the reformers prevailed. The final delegate vote tally gave McGovern 1,715.35, followed by Henry Jackson with 534, George Wallace's 385.7, and 151.95 holdouts for New York City's black congresswoman, Shirley Chisholm.

More important was that the number of Americans relying on television for most of their information had, by 1972, increased to nearly two-thirds of the population and, on that Wednesday evening, somewhere between seventeen and eighteen million sets were actually tuned in to the Democratic convention. Their impressions were less the routines of convention business, of delegates uttering their usual platitudes and te-

"I stake my hopes in 1972 in large part on the energy, the wisdom and the conscience of young Americans."

McGovern

WORK    It's Your
         Campaign

He's Your
Candidate    VOTE

CALL

ABSENTEE BALLOT PROBLEMS? CALL ABOVE NUMBER.

*Campaign pamphlet for George McGovern, an avowed anti-Vietnam War candidate.*

dious roll calls, than of the counterculture filling the hall, all the "enemies" the President had been warning about. Most startling for those at home was the lack of familiar political types, replaced to an unprecedented degree by women and blacks, the latter twice as numerous as four years earlier. Placards boosted such causes as gay liberation, black power, abortion rights, the rights of criminals to a legal defense, feminist causes, and civil rights. The event was, in effect, a "happening," a Woodstock at Miami Beach.

The next night, any chance to retrieve the situation was lost when debates within state delegations were allowed to drag interminably while, in homes throughout America, lights went out. When McGovern began his acceptance speech, it was 2:48 A.M.. on Friday morning. Only about one-fifth of the television audience was still awake. McGovern's highly effective performance with its call for withdrawal from Vietnam and exhortation to "come home, America" was largely lost, seen in prime time only in the outer reaches of Alaska and Guam. There were other lapses. Such regulars as the party's current national chairman, Larry O'Brien, and Pierre Salinger were brushed aside under pressure from reformers to ignore McGovern promises and give key posts to others.

The crucial travesty involved McGovern's vice presidential running mate, Senator Thomas Eagleton, who had been nominated before the acceptance speech. Word about his past began seeping out even while McGovern spoke. The Missouri senator finally admitted to a history of psychiatric problems. He had been hospitalized three times and had undergone two electro-shock therapy sessions. He also acknowledged taking occasional tranquilizers. All that, he assured McGovern in the aftermath of the publicity, was in the past.

The guessing was whether McGovern would stand by his man, as he had indicated in private. Contrary pressures came from his inner circle, influential segments of the press, and potential contributors. Then came McGovern's fatal remark when he said he was "1,000 percent for Tom Eagleton and I have no intention of dropping him from the ticket." In Hawaii, Eagleton vowed to stay on forever.

A few days later, after television appearances and more meetings, McGovern caved in and Eagleton withdrew. McGovern, who had been turned down by his first five choices before Eagleton's acceptance, went through the process all over again, this time in full view of the national media. He ended with Sargent Shriver, the Kennedy brother-in-law, Peace Corps director, and old-fashioned liberal Democrat. Post-Democratic convention surveys showed McGovern losing rather than gaining support.

The Nixon renomination machinery had only one hitch, but, as things went, that was hardly consequential. Not until April did the Republicans decide to also take their show to Miami Beach. The original commitment of some $400,000 from the International Telephone and Telegraph Company to select San Diego, and the Justice Department's subsequent dropping of an antitrust suit against ITT constituted a scandal with little lasting effect. Miami Beach, Republicans then claimed, was on a sandbar that simplified the problem of providing security against potential rioters.

The convention that followed after its August 21 opening was strictly a public relations gala. President Richard Nixon and Vice President Spiro Agnew were renominated by acclamation. Nixon, unlike McGovern, made his acceptance speech at prime time. And, also unlike at the earlier convention, all was well orchestrated; a carefully prepared script detailed the precise times for each step. Speakers were cued when to pause, when to accept cheers, even when one speech was to be interrupted in mid-sentence for a "spontaneous" demonstration. Nixon's nomination was set for 10:33, to be followed by an equally "spontaneous" release of balloons.

The Nielsen ratings of television audiences calculated that all this was seen by sixty million people. It was all, wrote Timothy Crouse in a lively account of the working press during the campaign, "a perfectly scripted TV Convention." Shortly after, opinion polls showed Nixon with a better than two-to-one advantage.

Two months before the start of the Republican convention, five "burglars," some with White House connections, were caught breaking in at the Washington headquarters of the Democratic National Committee on the night of June 17, 1972. Early accounts were hard to find, especially in the 93 percent of the newspapers that took an editorial stand in favor of the President's reelection.

For that fraction of the public that followed the unraveling of Watergate from its very beginnings, McGovern labored to exploit the issue. Polls showed that most Americans had neither heard about Watergate or, if they did, were attributing it to the President's reelection committee. The stories of White House improprieties were, in any event, hardly enough to stop most Americans from safeguarding the republic by keeping the Vietnam War and national security out of the hands of Senator George McGovern and his "radical" followers.

Richard Nixon, in effect, went on that fall to take a cue from the FDR campaign of 1940. Over a year-and-a-half earlier, CREEP had selected and briefed thirty-five surrogates so that the President could remain in the White House, monitor the war, track Henry Kissinger's peacemaking efforts with Saigon and Hanoi and simply look "presidential." The separation of CREEP from the Republican National Committee effectively divorced the President's personal reelection interests from the needs of the party.

On balance, the war clearly boosted his reelection strength. In May came the mining and bombing of Haiphong and military targets in North Vietnam. By August, Louis Harris polls showed the public skeptical that McGovern's terms for peacemaking were honorable. By 49 to 33 percent, Americans banked that Nixon rather than the antiwar senator could achieve an earlier and better disengagement.

McGovern, for his part, made three national speeches opposing the war, but, as the Democrat realized, more to encourage further financial contributions than because they were resonating with the American public. The impact of his message, noted White, "was that of a pin dropping."

McGovern's own media adviser, Charles Guggenheim, agreed that the election "may have been a case in which George McGovern's appearances on television hurt us more than they helped us." Both sides, in fact, showed concern about media overkill. Both

preferred to bombard the electorate with direct mail. Nixon's campaign was able to establish a vast network of computerized mail and telephone campaigning.

The Nixon administration, of course, had already done its utmost to intimidate both the print and electronic media; the possible underreporting of the early Watergate stories may have been the most significant consequence. While the Republican candidate was endorsed by the overwhelming number of newspapers, McGovern received the most support from the so-called "Eastern Liberal Press." The reduced importance of print in the popular dissemination of information was somewhat offset by the tendency of key newspapers to influence the agenda for television reporting.

In retrospect, it almost seems surprising that Nixon lost even one state. Massachusetts, along with the District of Columbia, gave McGovern a total of seventeen electoral votes. Nixon's 60.6 percent share, which represented 47,167,319 popular votes to McGovern's 29,168,509, was second only to Lyndon Johnson's 61.1 percent in 1964.

More significant for the long-run were the outlines of a realignment. At least for the moment, both political parties were more deeply polarized. The clearest change was confirmation that in presidential elections, the Republicans had reversed history and acquired a lock on the South. Nixon's sweep in the rest of the nation gave equally dramatic evidence of the change. He got the votes of slightly more than half of those who belonged to labor unions. He became the first Republican to win a majority of the Catholic vote, and he even cut into a sizable share of the Jewish and African-American vote that had gone to Humphrey in 1968. Most of the contours of Nixon's victory anticipated Ronald Reagan's 1980 accomplishment.

McGovern, in the end, seemed another Greeley rather than another Bryan. It was Nixon who was perceived as the antiwar candidate, and it was also Nixon who made the populist appeal, albeit a conservative one. McGovern passed into popular lore as a bumbler, whose ineptitude handed a major victory to one of the most unpopular of major American politicians. His failure hurt the credibility of the reform movement.

Democrats ran best in states with the highest incomes, culture, education, health, welfare, and civil awareness, capturing, in effect, the civil rights constituency. Legislative success in behalf of minorities cost them the support of many who viewed government assistance to the disadvantaged as the sacrifice of white middle- and lower-class workers. Nothing established Nixon's conservative credentials as much as his vigorous opposition to busing for school desegregation.

The congressional vote seems, at first glance, somewhat of an anomaly until one realizes that the pattern had, by then, become common. In 1972, in the face of the Nixon landslide, Democrats actually gained two Senate seats and Republicans picked up just twelve in the House, hardly a reflection of GOP strength on the local level. The presidency was clearly the most sensitive barometer of the national mood, which, by definition, left the Democrats in a wilderness they had not experienced since pre-New Deal days. Not even a flawless campaign could have won for McGovern. A more astute showing might have mitigated the deepening conservative trend, which was interrupted only briefly by the full, post-election impact of Watergate.

Pamphlet issued by the New York Conservative party.

354

Cardboard Indian headdress for Nixon.
The well-financed Nixon reelection
committee relied on television to
convey its message. Nevertheless,
the President's campaign
inspired many novelty items.

Ethnic-group buttons for Nixon and Agnew.

Poster for Nixon using a principal
slogan of the Republican campaign.

The New York Conservative party predicted the succeeding eight years would see an Agnew presidency.

Poster for Nixon. So many of these posters were printed for the campaign that they still can be found in large quantities.

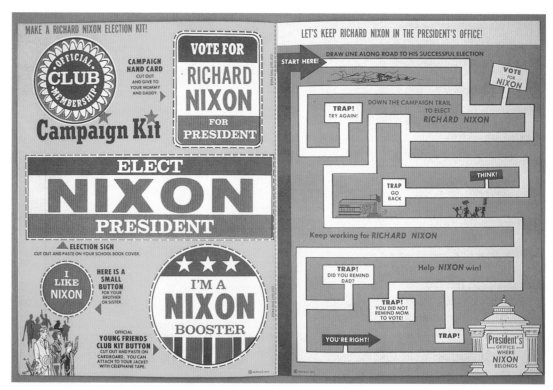

*Nixon and McGovern novelty items for the 1972 campaign.*

Anti-Nixon umbrella with one clear panel.

LET'S MAKE ONE THING PERFECTLY CLEAR

RE-ELECT THE PRESIDENT

Canvas Nixon book bag.

Rubber hand puppets of Nixon and Agnew.

Tin mechanical "theatre." The Nixon figure dances when it's wound up.

*Anti-Nixon poster and anti-Vietnam War button for McGovern and Shriver.*

McGovern for President

Poster showing McGovern at head of civil rights march.

"I hope the Nixon people
do to George McGovern what the
Democrats did . . . underestimate him.
If they do that
. . . WE'LL KILL THEM."

Gary Hart
McGovern Campaign Director
Washington Post May 14, 1972

*Sign for McGovern. Gary
Hart, who later became senator from
Colorado and was a contender for
the 1984 Democratic nomination,
directed McGovern's 1972 campaign.*

*The McGovern campaign committee
encouraged local groups to sell
their own items to raise funds.
The button at left was produced in
a limited and numbered edition.*

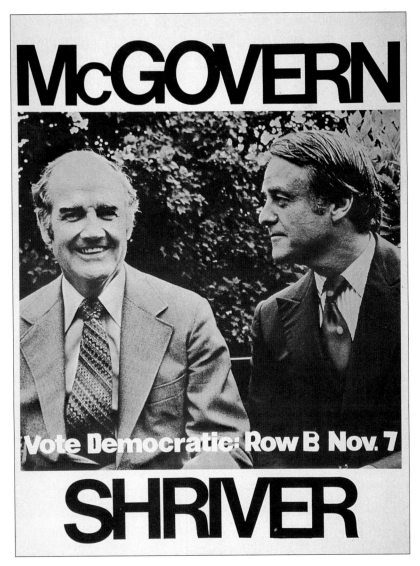

McGovern campaign items. The expanded role of young people in the 1972 campaign reflected not only their stake in the Vietnam War but also the Twenty-sixth Amendment to the Constitution (ratified in 1971), which lowered the voting age to eighteen.

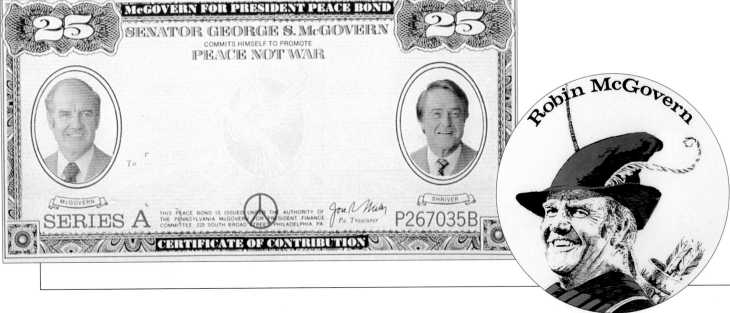

McGovern and
Nixon neckties.

McGovern campaign posters.

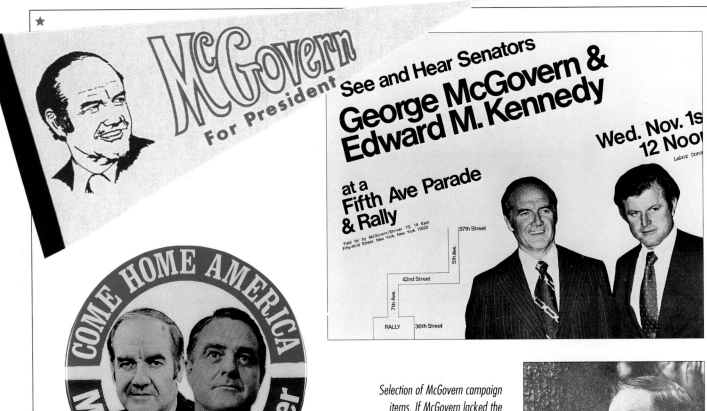

See and Hear Senators

# George McGovern & Edward M. Kennedy

## at a Fifth Ave Parade & Rally

Wed. Nov. 1st
12 Noon

Paid for by McGovern/Shriver '72, 19 East Fifty-third Street. New York, New York 10022

COME HOME AMERICA
McGovern ★ Shriver

*Selection of McGovern campaign items. If McGovern lacked the savvy of a professional politician, he possessed an antiwar record and a commitment to social reform that attracted the party's youthful new constituency.*

"He is so highly admired by all his colleagues, not just for his ability, but because of the kind of man he is."
Robert F. Kennedy

# In Concert at the Forum—April 15th · 8:30 PM

**Carole King**　　**Barbra Streisand**　　**James Taylor**

♪¾ McGovern
Use the Power 18 Register and Vote

## Quincy Jones and his Orchestra

Ushers: Warren Beatty · Jack Nicholson · Julie Christie · Sally Kellerman · James Earl Jones · Jacqueline Bisset
Michelle Gilliam · Mike Nichols · Shirley MacLaine · Goldie Hawn · Gene Hackman · Elliott Gould
Marlo Thomas · Burt Lancaster · Jon Voight · Raquel Welch · Michael Sarrazin · Britt Ekland and more

Campaign cigarette
packages for Nixon and McGovern.

*Less than two years after he won reelection by as huge a margin as any in
American history, Nixon resigned from office in defeat and humiliation.*

*After the exhausting Watergate ordeal, the good feelings of the first weeks of
President Ford's administration came as a relief. Ford's selection of Governor
Nelson Rockefeller of New York as vice president pleased Republican moderates.*

★

1976

50 STATES
IN THE UNION

*DEMOCRAT*
# Jimmy Carter
ELECTORAL VOTE 297, POPULAR VOTE 50.1%

REPUBLICAN
# Gerald R. Ford
ELECTORAL VOTE 240, POPULAR VOTE 47.9%

INDEPENDENT
# Eugene McCarthy
ELECTORAL VOTE 0, POPULAR VOTE 0%

LEO P. RIBUFFO
is professor of history at George Washington
University. He is the author of *The Old Christian
Right: The Protestant Far Right from the Great
Depression to the Cold War* (1983) and *Right
Center Left: Essays in American History* (1992).

The presidential election of 1976 was neither the first nor the last in which candidates, commentators, and voters expended great energy on trivial issues, but it was probably the first in which both major party nominees were widely regarded as figures of fun. President Gerald R. Ford was regularly asked whether he was smart enough to be President, and his falls on stairways and ski slopes, frequently satirized on network television, were taken as evidence that he was not. Democratic nominee Jimmy Carter, a "born again" Baptist who tried to explain his faith in *Playboy,* had to contend with what even his own chief adviser, Hamilton Jordan, called the "weirdo factor."

Curiously, neither Ford nor Carter was known for glad-handing, back-slapping, or wit, and the significant questions they addressed with comparable earnestness were unusually serious for a country enjoying relative prosperity and peace. The persistence of both inflation and unemployment—"stagflation"—suggested to some voters that underlying structural weaknesses afflicted the economy. Others, stung by the defeat in Vietnam, worried that the United States was losing the Cold War. The Watergate scandal fostered an amorphous sense that Americans were not so moral as they had thought, and Gerald Ford served as a flesh-and-blood reminder of their discomfort. Appointed by Richard Nixon to replace Vice President Spiro Agnew, who had resigned in disgrace, Ford succeeded Nixon in August 1974 and then, amid rumors of a deal, pardoned Nixon for all crimes related to Watergate.

Not only had the President come to office in unprecedented fashion, but the structure and style of national politics had changed significantly in recent years. Since the election of John F. Kennedy in 1960, presidential aspirants had tried to exude vigor and wit no matter how alien these traits were to their personalities. Questions of personal morality were now public issues, and candidates were expected to take positions on abortion as well as arms control. The social upheaval of the late 1960s had strengthened the conservative wing of the Republican party and shattered the Democratic coalition of hawks and doves, blacks and whites, ardent feminists and cultural traditionalists. The elections of 1964, 1968, and 1972 showed that party outsiders could drive incumbent Presidents from office and even capture the nomination. Federal funding of presidential campaigns, available for the first time in 1976, made such challenges easier to mount.

To an unusual degree, the races for the Republican and Democratic nominations influenced the general election. Ford suffered endless humiliation on his road to a narrow victory over former governor of California, Ronald Reagan. He had trouble finding a competent campaign manager, failed to recognize his party's drift rightward, and underestimated Reagan's political skill. Meanwhile, Reagan assailed Ford as a bumbling product of the Washington "buddy system," whose domestic policies strangled initiative and enriched "welfare queens." In foreign affairs, Ford's pursuit of *detente,* his approval of the Helsinki accords, and his renegotiation of the Panama Canal treaty proved that he lacked the "vision" to reverse the military and diplomatic decline Reagan postulated. In addition to costing Ford time and money, Reagan's challenge influenced his selection of a combative conservative running mate, Senator Robert Dole of Kansas.

Unlike Ford, Carter felt buoyed by his pre-convention efforts. A one-term governor of Georgia, he had defeated powerful Washington insiders by combining symbolic politics with careful planning and personal perseverance. Carter understood better than his rivals that the 1976 election was a referendum on American virtue. He would be elected, Carter had said in 1975, if he could "personify in my personal life the aspirations of the American people." His personality was, in fact, many-sided and he shrewdly emphasized different sides of himself to rival Democratic factions. Thus, he was variously a peanut farmer who studied nuclear engineering, an evangelical Protestant who read Reinhold Niebuhr, a white southerner who rejected racism, and a compassionate governor who still wanted balanced budgets. Above all, he was a self-conscious outsider who pledged to lead a government "as good as the people"—people who remained, in Carter's reassuring rhetoric, essentially virtuous despite Vietnam and Watergate.

Hamilton Jordan, pollster Patrick Caddell, and adman Gerald Rafshoon worked to "fine tune" campaign strategy (as Caddell liked to say). Carter attracted early attention by leading in the Iowa caucuses, won the New Hampshire primary with the help of a volunteer "Peanut Brigade" from Georgia, and courted influential politicians while building grassroots support. Rejecting the labels "conservative" and "liberal," he nonetheless ran to the right of all contenders except George Wallace. Nor did his campaign ignore the post-JFK politics of glamour. Carter adopted a fluffier hairstyle and advertised unlikely "friendships" with rock singers.

All of Carter's symbolism, planning, and perseverance would have counted for little if liberal Democrats had not been divided between avid cold warriors and their dovish critics. Eager for victory, however, all factions rallied around Carter at the national convention in July. Vice presidential nominee Walter Mondale balanced the ticket as a staunch welfare state liberal. Representative Peter Rodino, an ethnic hero of the Watergate scandal, nominated Carter, and Rev. Martin Luther King, Sr., the father of the civil rights martyr, suggested in the benediction that God Himself had ordained Carter to save America.

Despite this celebration, Carter's support was wider than it was deep. Northern working-class Catholics remained wary of his economic conservatism and evangelical demeanor. During the primaries, moreover, Carter's deliberate ambiguities and unintended slips-of-the-tongue had raised doubts about his integrity. According to one joke, Carter could never be honored on Mount Rushmore because there wasn't room for his two faces. Now, for the first time, he encountered in President Ford an opponent capable of exploiting these latent weaknesses.

Even after winning the nomination in August, Ford trailed Carter by more than twenty points in most polls. After several false starts, however, he put together a superb campaign team ranging from White House

Chief of Staff Richard Cheney to public relations specialists at Deardourff and Bailey. According to their analysis, Carter's strategy of displaying various sides of himself to different constituencies could be turned to Ford's advantage by painting the Democratic nominee as a devious opportunist. Conversely, voters liked the President's honesty but, prompted by Carter and Reagan, they questioned his intelligence. Accordingly, while stressing his restoration of good government and preservation of peace, Ford also needed to exude competence and underscore his opponent's inexperience. Blue-collar Catholics were especially susceptible to such appeals if Ford could overcome the issue of high unemployment.

The two nominees circled for position until late September. In his acceptance speech to the Republican convention, which he delivered with atypical fluency, Ford accused Carter of waffling on every major issue and challenged him to debate their differences. Thereafter, he retreated to the White House Rose Garden, hoping to distract attention from the deteriorating economy and the administration's misguided (and often satirized) effort to immunize all Americans against swine flu. Although Carter's strategy was formulated in Atlanta, safely distant from Washington insiders, the candidate's rhetoric was now fine-tuned to attract liberal Democrats. He kicked off his campaign at Franklin D. Roosevelt's little White House in Warm Springs, Georgia, compared himself to Harry S. Truman, and associated Ford with Herbert Hoover as well as Richard Nixon. Meanwhile, Republican and Democratic emissaries struggling to arrange the debates agreed on little beyond the exclusion of independent candidates Lester Maddox and Eugene McCarthy.

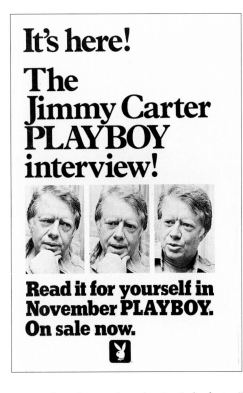

**It's here! The Jimmy Carter PLAYBOY interview!**

**Read it for yourself in November PLAYBOY. On sale now.**

*On September 20, 1976, Robert Scheer's interview with Jimmy Carter for Playboy was released to newspapers. While Carter outlined his views on a variety of subjects, what attracted attention was his statement that he often looked at women with "lust in his heart."*

In late September the "weirdo factor" flamboyantly surfaced in *Playboy*. Although Carter had granted the magazine an interview partly to demonstrate his own sophistication, his performance left the opposite impression. Warning against self-righteousness, Carter admitted having "looked on many women with lust" and "committed adultery in my heart." While supporters vainly pointed to the soundness of his theology, Carter's diverse detractors saw evidence of sin or political naivete. Reporters adapted "Heart of My Heart" to serenade him.

> Lust in my heart, how I love adultery;
> Lust in my heart, that's my theology.

Prudently sidestepping the lust imbroglio, both candidates reiterated their favorite themes during their first television debate on September 23. Carter indicted Ford for "lack of leadership" (a failing illustrated by persistent inflation and unemployment approaching 8 percent); promised "comprehensive" programs to restore government efficiency, balance the budget, and reform

**He's making us proud again.**

THE PRESIDENT FORD COMMITTEE, JAMES A. BAKER, III, CHAIRMAN, ROYSTON C. HUGHES, TREASURER.

*Poster for Ford. Republican campaign slogans stressed that Ford had restored dignity to the presidency.*

the tax system; and pledged always to draw "his strength from the people." Ford claimed credit for "turning the economy around" despite fiscally irresponsible congressional Democrats, denigrated Carter's gubernatorial record, and declared that true leaders never try to "be all things to all people." Neither candidate so much as smiled at the other during a twenty-seven minute interruption caused by a technological glitch. Ford sounded knowledgeable and looked dignified in a three-piece suit; benefiting from low expectations, he was judged the winner by most television viewers.

Buoyed by polls showing him within ten points of Carter, Ford escalated his attack. Even the name of his Illinois campaign train, the "Honest Abe," highlighted the integrity he ostentatiously advertised. Fearing that stridency might backfire, Caddell persuaded Carter temporarily to mute

personal attacks on Ford and stress the flaws of the "Nixon-Ford administration."

The candidates' families also brought substantive and symbolic messages to the electorate. Betty Ford, an outspoken feminist, had been a liability during the race against Reagan; now she became an asset in appealing to moderate Democrats, some of whom wore buttons declaring, "Keep Betty Ford's Husband in the White House." Carter's forthright and unpretentious wife, Rosalynn, helped him too; she hardly seemed the kind of woman who would marry a weirdo. Carter's mother, "Miz Lillian," (who combined humanitarianism with humor) and his brother Billy (who combined a beer belly with blue-collar irreverence) not only softened his prim image but also became celebrities in their own right.

The Republican resurgence faltered on September 30 when Ford learned that a vulgar joke about "coloreds" by Secretary of Agriculture Earl Butz was about to be reported in the media. Carter, impatient with rhetorical fine-tuning, compared this racist remark to an earlier bit of Butz humor about the pope and birth control. Equally troubling to Ford, a special prosecutor had begun to investigate his congressional finances. Thus, while Carter looked forward to resuming the attack, the President prepared less thoroughly for their next debate on October 6.

Carter attacked from both the left and the right. On the one hand, the Nixon-Ford administration betrayed American principles by conducting secret diplomacy, subverting foreign governments, and ignoring international human rights; on the other hand, the Republicans yielded to Arab economic pressure, weakened American defenses, and failed to stand "tough" against the Soviet Union. Though generally holding his own, Ford did himself irreparable harm by answering a question that wasn't asked instead of the question that was. Expecting renewed criticism of the Helsinki accords, the President had prepared to say that he did not *concede* the legitimacy of the Soviet sphere in Eastern Europe. Instead, responding to a question about Soviet expansionism, Ford said that there was *in fact* "no Soviet domination of Eastern Europe."

The issue was more complicated than it seemed because countries in Eastern Europe did enjoy varying degrees of autonomy, and American Presidents since Truman had tried to maximize that freedom. Carter understood the situation, but such nuances lost their customary appeal in mid-debate. He challenged Ford to persuade Polish-, Czech-, and Hungarian-Americans that "those countries don't live under the domination and supervision of the Soviet Union." Most pundits and reporters did not know that the nuances existed. Rather, they presented Ford's debate answer, stubborn refusal to recant, and inarticulate attempts to explain his policy as the latest examples of his chronic befuddlement. The acute phase of the crisis lasted until October 12, when Ford "bluntly" admitted making a "mistake." More important, the question of Ford's competence had been dramatically reopened, and a new round of jokes circulated until election day. After hearing Ford's debate answer, the Washington press corps chuckled, Polish Communist leader Edward Gierek had exclaimed, "Free at last, free at last!"

Discussion of Eastern Europe was one of several low points in the debate between the vice presidential candidates on Oc-

tober 15. Senator Dole not only accused Democratic Presidents of surrendering Eastern Europe to communism, but also attributed 1.6 million casualties to "Democrat wars" in this century. Senator Mondale responded that Dole had "earned his reputation as a hatchet man." Most television viewers agreed.

While the presidential nominees toured the country and held a third, lackluster debate in October, their favorite themes reached the electorate through print, radio, and (especially) television advertisements. In all media, the Republicans played variations on their slogan: "President Ford: He's Making Us Proud Again." A jauntier version of the message, "Feelin' good about America," graced posters, T-shirts, and a song. A biographical TV spot brought Ford from Eagle Scout to the White House and concluded, "Without seeking the presidency, Gerald Ford has been preparing for it all his life."

Democratic advertisements asked what there was to feel good about. The nation needed "Leadership for a Change" and Carter was the man to provide it. A biographical spot traced his rise from a farm boy in Plains, Georgia (where ads showed him in jeans still working the soil), to national leader. Since half the electorate still considered Dole unqualified for the presidency (according to Caddell's polls), the Democrats often highlighted Mondale as Carter's partner in statesmanship.

Family members played both offense and defense. Miz Lillian reminisced about Carter's youthful hard work; after the *Playboy* fiasco, Rosalynn Carter told viewers that there had never been "any hint of scandal" surrounding her husband. Ford's son Mike, a divinity student, underscored the

Carter, a former one-term governor of Georgia, was barely known to the country at the start of the 1976 campaign.

family's faith in God. At the end of the "Ford family" spot, one of the most effective on either side, the President gently kissed Betty on the cheek.

Advertising professionals adapted or supplemented the general messages for specialized audiences. Echoing a famous newspaper headline that appeared after Ford had rejected federal aid to New York, posters assured subway riders that Carter would "never tell the greatest city on earth to drop dead." In Carter's home region, ads slighted the liberal Mondale in favor of local pride, predicting that "on November 2, the South is being readmitted to the Union." Listeners to radio stations with predominantly black audiences learned that Carter's daughter, Amy, attended an integrated school. The Republicans customized their television ads for Hispanics of Cuban, Mexican, and Puerto Rican background, but none could match Carter speaking Spanish in his own spot.

By late October both media campaigns had mastered the techniques of denigration. In Ford's television spots, solid citizens in sequence called Carter "wishy-washy" and Georgians criticized his governorship. Exploiting a favorable cover story, a Ford newspaper ad advised: "One good way to decide this election. Read last week's *Newsweek*. Read this month's *Playboy*." The Democrats quoted Ronald Reagan's description of *detente* as a "one-way street." They also tested but ultimately rejected a TV spot explicitly criticizing Ford's pardon of Nixon, apparently realizing that repeated references to the "Nixon-Ford administration" served their purposes without overkill.

The election of 1976 was neither the first nor the last in which adversarial rhetoric obscured basic similarities between the major party nominees, but in this case the discrepancy between purported and actual differences was greater than usual. Both Ford and Carter were devout Protestants from solid middle-class backgrounds. Adapting to the changing political culture, both candidates made subtle religious appeals but both felt uncomfortable doing so. Although Carter rejected and Ford hedged on a proposed Right-to-Life Amendment, both personally opposed abortion and wanted the issue to disappear from presidential politics. Both valued integrity in government, and their occasional lapses into demagoguery were comparably inept. A moderate Republican, Ford was less hostile to the welfare state than he sounded; a fiscally conservative Democrat, Carter was less enthusiastic about the welfare state than he sounded. Though Carter held a deeper visceral commitment to international human rights, he agreed with Ford that containment of the Soviet Union was the central foreign policy concern.

The last week of the campaign was marked by vigorous personal appeals and massive television advertising highlighting the candidates' purported differences. In addition, an incident at the Plains Baptist Church where Carter taught his now famous Sunday school class threatened to undermine liberal and African-American support. Apparently seeking to embarrass Carter, a black minister tried unsuccessfully to attend services and then applied for membership. When the church reaffirmed its old ban on "Negroes and other civil rights agitators," Carter disagreed but declined to resign from the congregation. In telegrams to black clergy, the Republicans asked how Carter could advance the cause of civil rights nationally if he could not influence his own church.

By election eve Ford and Carter stood virtually even in the polls. Ford's last television appeal was primarily a pastiche of earlier ads plus conversations with such non-political friends as baseball announcer Joe Garagiola (who had played everyman in talk shows accompanying the final campaign tour). These conversations took place on *Air Force One,* where Ford, hoarse and tired, was almost inaudible. Finally, the plane flew into the sun to the strains of "Feelin' good about America." In his last television appeal, Carter, dressed in a conservative blue suit, answered canned questions from men and women selected to serve as flesh-and-blood symbols of important Democratic constituencies. In a curious turnabout, the Washington insider looked like a worn-out regular guy even though he spoke from the most consequential airplane in the world, and the outsider speaking from Plains, Georgia, looked presidential.

On November 2 Carter led Ford by 1.7 million votes and defeated him in the electoral college 297 to 240. The core of Carter's support came from groups that had voted heavily Democratic since the 1930s, including union members, blacks, and (despite misgivings) northern Catholics; many of them were affected by or worried about stagflation. Washington insiders—party professionals and their trade union allies—contributed to the victory by organizing impressive registration and get-out-the-vote drives. Even so, Carter would have lost if he had not attracted lukewarm Democrats and disenchanted Republicans. However weird his religion seemed to cosmopolitan critics, his born-again demeanor attracted Republican evangelicals, and he became the first Democrat since Truman to carry the South-

ern Baptist vote. Moreover, running against the man who had pardoned Nixon, Carter did manage to personify American aspirations for honesty and virtue in the wake of Vietnam and Watergate.

The narrow defeat prompted Ford and his campaign aides to ponder the might-have-beens. If Ford had taken Reagan seriously from the outset, he might have entered the fall campaign with more money and energy. If Ford had not bogged down in Eastern Europe, he might have preserved the look of competence created in the first debate. If the economic recovery begun earlier in the year had not stalled, Carter's incongruous identification with the New Deal tradition might have been less effective. If Democratic legal challenges had not removed Eugene McCarthy's name from the ballot in New York, he might have cost Carter that state as he did Oregon and Iowa. If Ford had picked a less conservative—or at least a less abrasive—running mate, he might have carried Ohio or Pennsylvania. Indeed, the election of 1976 was one of few in which the vice presidential nominees made a difference.

In his inaugural address, Jimmy Carter graciously thanked Ford for "all he has done to heal our land." This compliment eased the tension between the two men, who became good friends after Carter left the White House. By that point, their common traits and values were unmistakable, and their common experiences included a disastrous underestimation of Ronald Reagan.

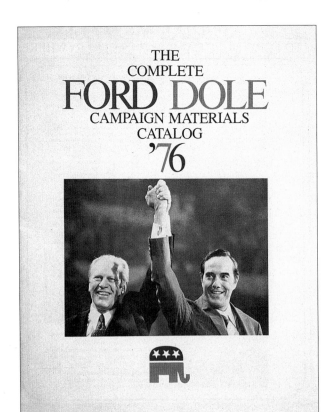

Ford and Dole campaign items. Ford's vice presidential choice of Senator Robert Dole was motivated by the need to heal ideological divisions within the Republican party.

Poster for Ford and Dole. Memories of Vietnam, Watergate, and the Nixon pardon haunted Ford throughout the campaign of 1976. His strategy was to be "presidential."

Ford campaign items. Ford and Carter had three televised debates, the first between presidential candidates since the Kennedy-Nixon exchanges in 1960. Although television was replacing traditional campaign materials, 1976 did see a variety of posters, buttons, and novelty items.

*Ribbon for Ford issued during the bicentennial celebration.*

*Group of Ford items. The Ford campaign spent three million dollars for fifty state campaign organizations, less than what Nixon had spent in California and New York in 1972.*

*Toy tractor-trailers for Ford and Carter.*

Carter-Mondale poster in Spanish.

Carter pamphlet showing him with Martin Luther King, Sr. Black voter turnout had a significant impact on the election.

The peanut became the Carter campaign symbol. Carter's 1975 autobiography, Why Not the Best?, gave an idyllic portrait of his youth and his religious and political life.

THE NEXT PRESIDENT 1976
PRESIDENT OF THE U·S·A·
JIMMY CARTER

I believe that our government
can be as great as our people are.
*Jimmy Carter*

JIMMY CARTER
for PRESIDENT in '76

TONY RUFFINO, LARRY VAUGHN & DON LAW
present

THE
ALLMAN BROTHERS BAND

IN A BENEFIT CONCERT FOR
Jimmy Carter
Democratic Presidential Candidate

TUES. NOVEMBER 25 at 8 P.M.
PROVIDENCE CIVIC CENTER

Tickets $6.50 Advance          $7.50 Day of Show

PAID FOR BY THE COMMITTEE FOR JIMMY CARTER. R.J. LIPSHULTZ—TREAS.
TICKET PURCHASE IS A CONTRIBUTION TO THE JIMMY CARTER PRESIDENTIAL CAMPAIGN.

A COPY OF OUR REPORT IS FILED WITH THE FEDERAL ELECTION COMMISSION, WASHINGTON, D.C.

*Selection of Carter items. The federal election law of 1974 limited expenditures by presidential candidates. Paradoxically, independent political action committees (PACs) proliferated. Therefore, the issuance of many campaign items shifted from central committees to the PACs.*

J C
CAN SAVE AMERICA

Right: Poster for Carter using the New York Daily News *headline of October 30, 1975.*
Below: Poster for Ford using the New York Daily News *endorsement of Ford, October 23, 1976.*

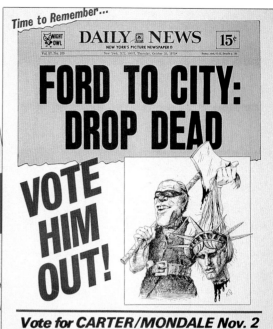

Transistor radio and wind-up toy satirizing Carter.

Silk bandanna for Carter.

Celluloid button for Carter
evoking the Watergate scandal.

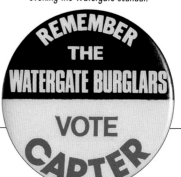

**1980**

50 STATES
IN THE UNION

*REPUBLICAN*

# Ronald Reagan

ELECTORAL VOTE 489, POPULAR VOTE 50.9%

DEMOCRAT

# Jimmy Carter

ELECTORAL VOTE 49, POPULAR VOTE 41.2%

INDEPENDENT

# John B. Anderson

ELECTORAL VOTE 0, POPULAR VOTE 7.9%

**JULES WITCOVER**
is a syndicated political columnist for the
Baltimore *Sun* and the author of eleven books,
including accounts of every presidential
election since 1976.

By 1980, the development of a cadre of career campaign managers, consultants, poll-takers, fund-raisers and media experts had reached full flower in presidential politics. These political technocrats had by now largely replaced the amateur advisers and professional politicians of old drawn to a presidential campaign essentially by personal association with the candidate or by party loyalty. The new breed was motivated not so much by friendship or party, or even ideology, as by a desire to build personal influence and personal wealth through the dispensing—and sale, at high rates—of their professional services.

These "hired guns," as they came to be called, looked upon the candidate who employed them in much the same way that a manufacturer looks upon a product he makes and then seeks to sell to the largest possible market. The basic approach had been evident in politics for a long time, particularly at the local and state levels in trendsetting states like California, but it had reached its most conspicuous implementation in the 1968 presidential campaign of Richard Nixon. Having lost one presidential race in 1960 despite campaigning at an exhausting pace, Nixon and his advisers set out in 1968 to analyze the challenge in terms of the new television era, as no campaigners had done before.

A former advertising executive, H. R. Haldeman, was a leading figure in masterminding a Nixon campaign sharply curtailing the traditional dawn-to-dusk retail campaigning that exposed the candidate to relatively few voters but to endless physical strain. While Nixon's Democratic foe, Hubert H. Humphrey, by tradition and by personal style slogged determinedly through eighteen-hour campaign days, Republican Nixon ran a much more disciplined, leisurely campaign designed by his professional advisers for maximum television exposure.

Each day by noon, Nixon would deliver one well-executed speech at or near a major airport from which film of his appearance could be whisked back to New York (these were pre-satellite days) in time for the network evening news shows. Then he would often disappear from public view, while aides fed "position papers" to the accompanying press. Humphrey meanwhile would make numerous appearances, with the networks capturing on film his best and worst performances, often using the worst. Then, observing "balance," they would use the only film of Nixon they had. In this and other ways, the Nixon political technocrats managed through most of the campaign to put their candidate's best foot forward.

In ensuing presidential elections, the Republicans particularly learned from the 1968 Nixon example and conducted controlled campaigns in the hands of professionals. The Democrats, meanwhile, more often than not campaigned in the traditional all-out fashion, with a mix of amateurs and professionals. The Nixon pros easily won again in 1972, their manipulations and abuses of the electoral process in the Water-

*Movie lobby card. In addition to being a film actor, Ronald Reagan was the first President to be a union member as well as the head of a union, the Screen Actors Guild (1947–52; 1959).*

gate scandal not fully realized by voters at the time. And in 1976, the "hired guns" laboring for President Gerald R. Ford came within an eyelash of beating the "amateur hour" team of Georgia-based political newcomers working for Democrat Jimmy Carter. The skills of the Ford pros made a race of it despite Ford's politically disastrous pardon of Nixon in the wake of the Watergate revelations that had driven Nixon from the presidency and elevated Ford to it.

In that 1976 campaign, Ford first withstood a serious challenge for the Republican nomination from Governor Ronald Reagan of California, who had assembled a team of some of the best young career political operatives, led by John Sears, a former Nixon law firm associate and political aide. After Ford's defeat by Carter, the Reagan team reassembled under Sears's direction and began planning for 1980. Sears believed he had the perfect candidate for the television

era—a former movie actor accustomed to taking direction. The stage was set, or so Sears thought, for the classic television-age presidential campaign, featuring the communications skills of a professional actor playing a role created for him by professional directors who knew as a result of their research and political experience what it would take to win.

At the same time, the incumbent President, Jimmy Carter, again turned to the friends and associates from Georgia, together with a few professionals with national presidential campaign experience, to help win re-election against the survivor of the Republican primaries. Six other Republicans vied with Reagan for their party's nomination: former congressman, United Nations ambassador, and CIA Director George Bush; Senators Howard H. Baker of Tennessee and Bob Dole of Kansas; former Secretary of Treasury John B. Connally; and Representatives John Anderson and Philip Crane of Illinois. Carter as the incumbent Democrat was challenged by Senator Edward M. Kennedy of Massachusetts and Governor Edmund G. (Jerry) Brown, Jr., of California.

All candidates in both parties had their "hired guns," but a phenomenon was already emerging that marked a clear difference in the two parties and was to have an increasingly important effect on their relative success in presidential elections. While the Democrats continued to depend on a mix of amateurs and professionals attracted to the candidate, the Republicans were well on their way to building a durable stable of political technocrats.

In the familiar if overworked parlance of horseracing in politics, Democrats more often than not were one-horse jockeys, signing up for a particular presidential campaign out of personal devotion to or belief in a single candidate. If that candidate lost, as Democrats were developing the habit of doing during this period (they elected only one of their own, Carter in 1976, over a period of six presidential elections through 1988), most of his campaign workers would go back to their private pursuits. Also, Democrats whose candidates failed to win the party nomination would customarily go home rather than sign on with the winner—often because the nominee did not ask them.

Republican operatives, by contrast, were more committed to the horse race than they were to the one horse they were riding in the primary elections. If their candidate lost the nomination, most of them stood ready to help the winner—and were asked to help by the Republican nominee. After the general election, win or lose, these Republican political technicians would be "warehoused" in well-paying positions with the national or state party committees or in Washington law, lobbying, and political consulting firms, against the time they would be needed for the next presidential campaign. For example, the man who managed the Ford campaign in 1976, James A. Baker III, in 1980 signed on as manager of the George Bush campaign. After Bush lost the nomination to Reagan, Baker accepted the assignment of negotiating the conditions of Reagan's television debates with Carter.

This distinction between Republicans and Democrats concerning the use and dominance of political technocrats was pronounced in the campaign of 1980. On the Democratic side, the contest essentially was

between the incumbent and his severest critic within the party, Kennedy, who saw Carter as indecisive and uncaring in a nation where the needs of the traditional Democratic constituencies—the poor, the blue-collar workers, and racial and ethnic minorities—were being neglected. The Carter-Kennedy competition took on a personal bitterness and although Carter disposed of Kennedy and Brown without undue difficulty, that personal bitterness extended to the staffs and suporters of both men. By the time Carter had won renomination by turning back an effort by the Kennedy camp to break Carter's hold on pledged delegates at the national convention, the chances of reconciliation for the general-election campaign were shattered. The Kennedy people went home and sulked, and Carter—faced with widespread public dissatisfaction with his leadership—was left to wage his reelection campaign largely

*Movie lobby card. Hellcats of the Navy (1957) was the only movie in which Reagan and Nancy Davis, his wife-to-be, appeared together.*

with the team that had narrowly won the presidency for him in 1976.

On the Republican side, Reagan at first encountered equally contentious opposition from the field of six challengers. But he was able to ride out that early adversity with a minimum of intra-party bitterness, and to recruit for the fall campaign many of the political professionals who had labored for the losers (except for supporters of Anderson, who persevered as a third-party candidate). The only real scare for Reagan came in the year's first precinct caucuses in Iowa, where Reagan (on Sears's advice largely) left the campaign to his hired guns and they miscalculated, enabling Bush to upset him there.

In advance of the caucuses, Sears had estimated on the basis of past turnouts how many voters would have to be produced at the small neighborhood meetings across the state on caucus night to win. He set his professional organizers to work and held his popular candidate out of the state until the final weekend, assuming he could keep him above the fray while the other six contenders in frustration went after each other. Bush, however, had his own professional—a young organizer named Rich Bond who

*Reagan was elected governor of California in 1966 and reelected in 1970.*

quietly put together his own network of supporters. The Bush team blindsided Reagan by swelling the traditional caucus-night turnout on which Sears had made his calculations, producing about three thousand more votes for Bush than Sears mustered for Reagan.

Overnight, Reagan fell from front-runner to question mark. In the next test, the New Hampshire primary, he was obliged to return to intensive street campaigning, dispensing his personal charm and appealing rhetoric about getting government "off the backs" of average voters. By so doing, Reagan rapidly restored himself as the candidate to beat, capping his comeback with a clever bit of stage-managing by Sears that ended Bush's brief "Big Mo" (for momentum, as the buoyant Bush liked to call the windfall from his Iowa upset). In a debate scheduled to be a two-man affair between Reagan and Bush, Sears on Reagan's behalf invited the other candidates to take part. When they appeared on the platform, Reagan demanded that they be seated, as Bush sat stonily and unwaveringly by. The other candidates, thus rebuffed, finally left, but Reagan came off as the hero and good sport, Bush as the villain and grouch, and Bush never recovered.

In spite of the dramatic turnaround for Reagan in New Hampshire, he fired Sears and two of his best professional associates, Charles Black and James Lake, in an internal squabble and brought in as his campaign manager New York lawyer William J. Casey, a heavy-handed former intelligence official of conspiratorial nature and suspicions. The Reagan campaign by now, however, had been set on its winning course and the candidate himself, by force of his personality and appealing (if simplistic) anti-government message, assumed the dominant role. In the remaining primary contests and in television commercials that gave voters their main exposure to him, Reagan was the featured player reciting his familiar script flawlessly.

By the time of the Republican National Convention in Detroit, the only question of much interest was Reagan's choice of a running mate. Bush seemed an obvious choice by nature of his second-place finish in the contest for delegates, but Reagan was unable to shake the highly unfavorable impression Bush's unbending behavior had left on him in the New Hampshire debate fiasco. So when one of his "hired guns," pollster Richard Wirthlin, reported surveys indicating that the strongest running mate would be the man who had beaten Reagan for the 1976 nomination—Gerald Ford—Reagan listened. With Bush the most obvious alternative, Reagan was not disposed to dismiss out of hand the notion that a former President might consider accepting the Number 2 job he had already once held.

There then took place at the convention a brief but fascinating circus that underscored the role that network television had come to play in the presidential-election process. As purely exploratory talks were underway between Reagan and Ford advisers on the possibility of a Reagan-Ford "dream ticket," and then between the principals themselves, Ford agreed to a live interview with CBS News anchorman Walter Cronkite. Talk of the "dream ticket" had now reached the convention floor and when Cronkite asked Ford about it, the former President proceeded to set out the conditions that would have to be met if he were

*Novelty dolls of Reagan and Bush.*

to accept. And when Cronkite cast Ford's view of the job as "something like a co-presidency," Ford did not demur. In a flash, the idea was sweeping through the convention—causing great consternation among Reagan advisers who began to wonder what might be given away in this bizarre striving for the strongest possible Republican ticket. Finally, by mutual acquiescence, the notion was abandoned, and Reagan somewhat reluctantly agreed to accept Bush as his running mate.

The Democrats, meanwhile, were discovering that for all the growing dominance of political technicians in presidential politics, all the masterminding by them based on their poll-taking, and all the slickness of their television advertising, events still could be controlling. The events that unfolded in 1979 and early 1980 worked heavily in favor of Jimmy Carter in his successful pursuit of renomination, but they then posed insurmountable barriers to his reelection in the fall campaign.

The first of these was the seizing of the American embassy in Iran in November

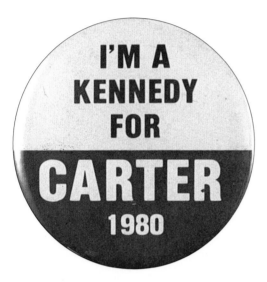

*Celluloid button for Carter.*

1979 and the eventual detention of fifty-two American hostages in protest against a decision to permit the deposed shah of Iran to enter the United States for emergency cancer treatment. Carter immediately focused on the hostage crisis and was preoccupied with it in December when Soviet troops suddenly invaded Afghanistan. Kennedy was already campaigning against Carter in Iowa and a televised debate had been scheduled there, also to include Brown. But Carter seized on the foreign policy crises as reasons to pull out of the debate and withdraw to a "Rose Garden strategy" for renomination.

Without the incumbent on the hustings offering a target, Kennedy and Brown could not get their campaigns off the ground. Kennedy already was struggling as a result of another episode that had demonstrated television's increasing influence in presidential campaigns. In a hard-hitting interview with Roger Mudd, then of CBS News, Kennedy had been unable to provide a lucid and persuasive answer to the most obvious question for which any White

House aspirant should be prepared: "Why do you want to be President?" He stammered and wandered through one of political television's most embarrassing moments for a candidate and never fully recovered, although he did run a more credible campaign once Carter, as a result of another event, abandoned his Rose Garden strategy.

A botched attempt in late April to rescue the hostages, which shook the American people's already sinking confidence in Carter, persuaded the President to resume campaigning. He managed to survive the Kennedy challenge, but not without severe political damage to himself and further alienation of the Kennedy faction and supporters. That alienation manifested itself in full view of the nation at the Democratic convention in New York. Kennedy kept the just-renominated Carter waiting for an interminable period on the platform and then offered him congratulations so perfunctory and distant as to be seen on television screens across the country as a contemptuous snub. Carter made it seem all the more so by following Kennedy across the stage like a supplicant as the senator turned his back and proceeded to greet other assembled Democrats.

In the fall, the hostage-taking that had enabled Carter to conduct his campaign through most of the primaries from the political sanctuary of the Rose Garden became a severe liability. The Reagan campaign hammered at the incumbent's ineptness, not only concerning the hostage crisis but also regarding the economic quagmire into which the country had sunk, with double-digit inflation and interest rates stifling growth and squeezing middle-income voters. Reagan himself deftly summed up the case against Carter with a remark in their one televised debate, asking the voters: "Are you better off than you were four years ago?" The answer came resoundingly on election day: Reagan won 51 percent of the popular vote to 41 for Carter and 7 for Anderson. He received 489 electoral votes in forty-four states to 49 for Carter in six states.

The results ushered in what came to be known as "the Reagan Revolution," in which the Republican winner moved, in his fashion, to get government "off the backs" of the voters. He slashed income taxes and deeply cut government services to many marginally surviving Americans, while sharply increasing military spending and imposing unprecedented federal deficits that made a mockery of his campaign pledge to balance the budget. In an election that was supposedly made to order for the new breed of political consultants—running a movie actor who would take direction easily and follow the script—the victory was fashioned as much as a result of events—the hostage crisis and the deplorable state of the economy, which together made Carter easy prey.

There was, however, one alleged aspect of the 1980 election that, if established to be true, would have been an outrageous excess of manipulation by Reagan's political professionals, rivaling even the campaign subversions of the Nixon operatives in Watergate. At the Republican convention, Casey told reporters of his concern that the Carter campaign might try to salvage the election by springing an "October Surprise"—somehow, managing the release

of the hostages. He said he was setting up an "intelligence operation" to keep an "incumbency watch" on the Carter campaign. Others confirmed later that a group of retired military officers had indeed kept an eye on airlifts out of domestic bases that might signal eleventh-hour shipments of supplies to Iran in return for the hostages' release. None was sighted and the hostages remained in captivity until moments after Reagan was sworn into the presidency on January 20, 1981.

The timing of their release, however, seemed most suspicious to some Democrats. A decade later, allegations surfaced that Casey or others in the Reagan campaign had conspired with Iranian officials, not to free the hostages but to delay their release until after the election in order to deprive Carter of the feared "October Surprise." It was alleged that Casey had promised to sell arms to Iran after Reagan's election and inauguration if this delay took place. By the time these charges were aired, Casey had died, but Democratic members of Congress forced an investigation that revisited the allegations. The public by now, however, had moved on to other concerns.

As farfetched as any such deal seemed to many, and as abusive of the whole American electoral process, it could not be dismissed out of hand in light of the dominant role that professional political operatives had come to exert in presidential elections, and the win-at-all-costs philosophy that seemed to guide them. With or without an "October Surprise," the election of 1980 demonstrated the continuing and increasing involvement of highly paid political technocrats in presidential politics, playing on real or imagined events of the day.

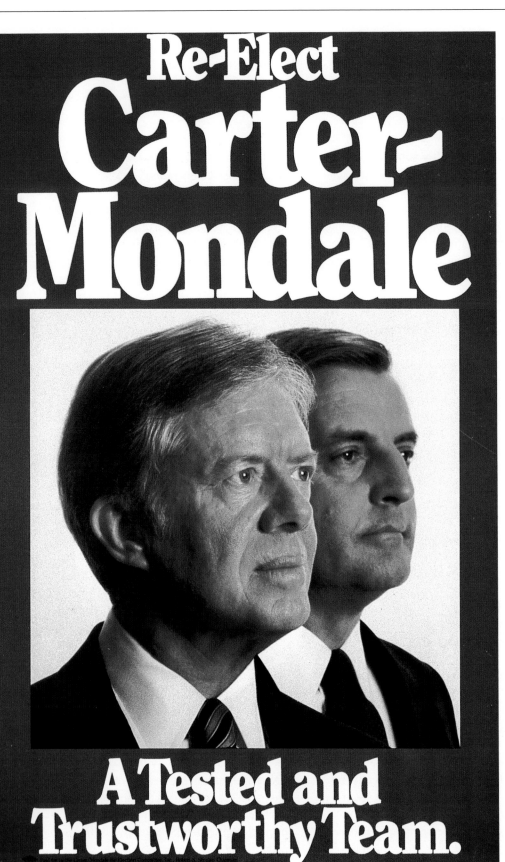

Poster for Carter and Mondale. This was the standard Democratic campaign poster.

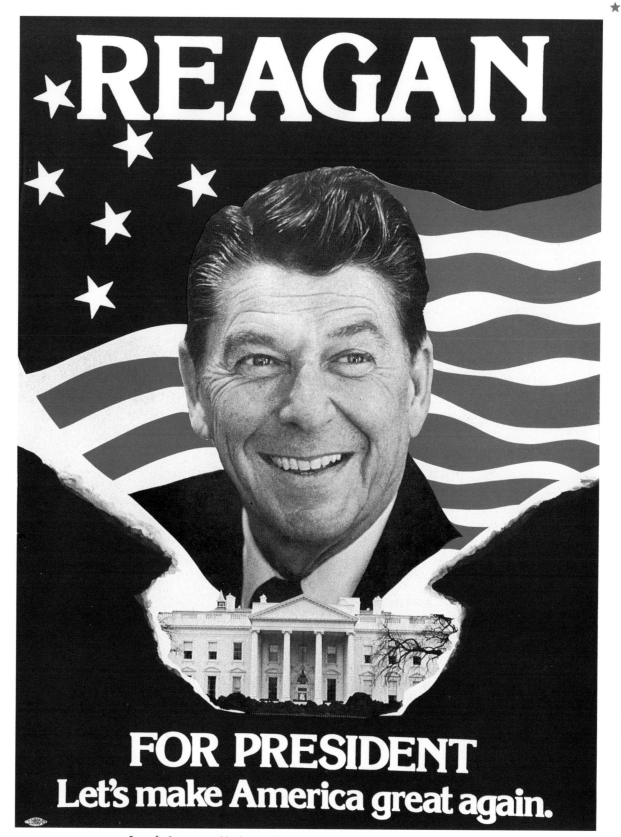

*Poster for Reagan issued by the Republican National Committee included Reagan's favorite slogan.*

A selection of Reagan
campaign buttons. Invariably smiling,
the sixty-nine-year-old candidate was projected as a virile westerner.

*Indiana campaign card for Reagan. Dan Quayle successfully ran for the Senate.*

*Metal badge for Reagan convention delegates from Iowa.*

*Celluloid button sold by New York City vendors.*

Suction cup novelties for Reagan and Carter.

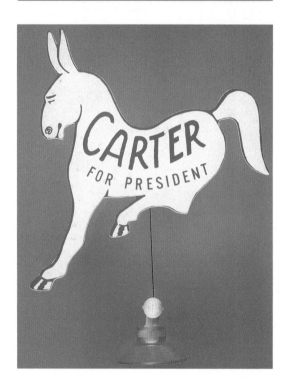

"Great Political Feud" mechanical bank. House Speaker Thomas P. ("Tip") O'Neill, Jr., raps Reagan with a gavel when coin is inserted.

Celluloid button for Reagan.

Castiron bank. Republican elephant holds a jellybean, Reagan's favorite candy. Campaign items for 1980 focused on Reagan's personality and avoided issue-oriented material.

Representative John Anderson and Wisconsin
Governor Patrick Lucey, both liberal
Republicans, ran on a third-party ticket.
Anderson called it a "NATIONAL UNITY
CAMPAIGN." They received 5.5 million votes.

"Straw vote" slate issued by General Cinema
Company for movie refreshment stands.

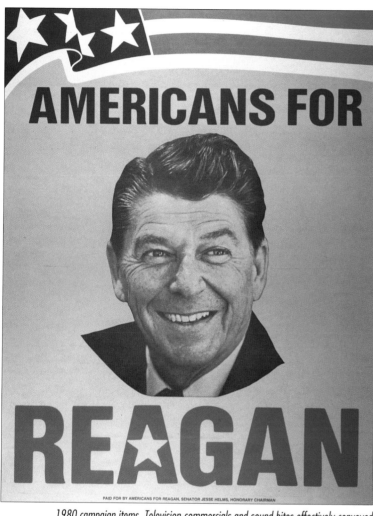

1980 campaign items. Television commercials and sound bites effectively conveyed the candidates' messages. Carter ephemera portrayed him as a solemn world statesman and Reagan material showed him as a personable, affable alternative.

★

A selection of Carter-Mondale campaign buttons.

Celluloid buttons of the candidates and their wives.

Two-sided cloth doll satirizing Reaganomics.

*Celluloid inaugural button, 1981.*

*Reagan campaign umbrella.*

*Celluloid button for Bush distributed at the 1980 Republican convention.*

★

1984

50 STATES
IN THE UNION

*REPUBLICAN*
## Ronald Reagan
ELECTORAL VOTE 525, POPULAR VOTE 59%

DEMOCRAT
## Walter Mondale
ELECTORAL VOTE 13, POPULAR VOTE 41%

Steven M. Gillon
is professor of history at Yale University.
He is the author of *Politics and Vision: The ADA
and American Liberalism* (1987) and
*The Democrats' Dilemma: Walter F. Mondale
and the Liberal Legacy* (1992).

Celluloid pin for
Reagan and Bush.

In his eerie prediction of life in 1984, George Orwell envisioned a sterile society presided over by a deified leader, Big Brother. "Nobody has ever seen Big Brother," Orwell wrote. "He is a face on the hoardings, a voice on the telescreen." The omnipresent telescreen—"an oblong metal plaque like a dulled mirror"—delivered regular catalogues of state achievements at the same time that it spied on the private lives of the docile public. Making effective use of "Doublethink," which gave people "the power of holding two contradictory beliefs in one's mind simultaneously, and accepting both of them," and Newspeak, which purged words that expressed free thought, the telescreen allowed Big Brother to maintain power by blurring the distinction between truth and fiction.

Many commentators believed that in the politics of 1984, television displayed the same hypnotic effect as Orwell's telescreen. "Television in modern politics has been as revolutionary as the development of printing in the time of Gutenberg," the journalist Theodore H. White observed. Television had a dual impact on campaigning in America. It nationalized issues by forcing candidates to seek themes that could appeal to a broad spectrum of the electorate. At the same time, by making the relationship between the voter and the candidate more direct, the media had an individualizing effect on politics. Voters no longer depended on party functionaries or interest groups for information about candidates. Instead, they received information and made decisions as individuals watching television in the privacy of their homes.

President Reagan, with his telegenic features and extensive experience in front of a camera, was a master of the new technology. Reagan had demonstrated the power of television during his first term as President. As one scholar observed, "No previous administration had devoted so many resources to managing the news or approached the task with so much calculation." The President's advisers, whom James Reston described as "the best public relations team ever to enter the White House," carefully orchestrated the media coverage. By controlling access to Reagan, the staff minimized the President's penchant for verbal slips, protected him against tough questions, and guaranteed that the public saw brief visuals that served to enhance his stature. These images, designed around a daily message, allowed the White House to focus public attention on Reagan's accomplishments—falling unemployment, lower inflation, and a growing economy—while ignoring failures—a potentially crippling two-hundred-billion-dollar deficit, tax cuts that had favored the rich, indifference to the poor, and an implacable hostility to the Soviet Union that had resulted in a dramatic increase in tension between the superpowers. "So far, he's proving Lincoln was right," observed a veteran reporter. "You can fool all of the people some of the time."

**REAGAN BUSH '84**

*President Reagan and Ethnic Americans*

"America is too great for small dreams"

With polls giving the President a commanding lead over any Democratic opponent, Republican strategists hoped for an electoral landslide that would assure Republican control of the White House for the rest of the century. Reagan's campaign strategy was simple: celebrate the President's identification with peace and prosperity, avoid a debate over specific issues, and identify his Democratic opponent with the "failed policies" of the Carter administration: high taxes, soaring inflation, and vacillating world leadership.

Reagan's challenger, former Vice President Walter Mondale, had won his party's nomination after a bruising primary fight against Colorado Senator Gary Hart. Mondale had little appreciation for media campaigns and little understanding of how they had transformed campaigning in America. A product of the Minnesota Farmer-Labor party, and a protégé of Hubert Humphrey, Mondale practiced an older style of politics. "Mr. Mondale is one of the few major figures on the American scene," observed a journalist, "whose political style and vocabulary fit comfortably in a world of Al Smith, Franklin Roosevelt and Harry Truman." Mass media allowed modern candidates to bypass traditional power structures and appeal directly to the anti-establishment sentiments of most voters. But Mondale practiced the politics of social cohesion and mediation. Believing that most voters looked to responsible community leaders for clues about how to vote, he courted interest groups, local officials, and civic figures rather than voters. Mondale's personal reserve and discomfort with the star qualities essential for media campaigns also limited his appeal. The camera accentuated his jowliness, focused attention on the pockets of fatigue which frequently surrounded his blue eyes, and highlighted the slightly beaked nose that protruded from his face. Television transformed him, according to some observers, "into a cruel caricature of a self-satisfied politician."

Mondale's hope was to arouse the enthusiasm of the party's traditional constituencies—blacks, Jews, union members, urban residents—while pulling back into the party the suburban white middle-class that had defected in recent years. As a first step in executing this strategy, Mondale needed to establish his credibility as a strong leader by proving that he was not a captive of "special interests." In July, he had surprised critics by selecting a woman vice presidential candidate, former Congresswoman Geraldine Ferraro of New York. A few weeks later, in his acceptance speech at the Democratic convention, Mondale had proposed raising taxes to pay for the deficit. He planned to continue the same combative style in the fall, forcing Reagan off the high road and into a debate on specific issues.

The candidates began their campaigns on Labor Day. Riding a wave of personal and organizational confidence, Reagan exhorted voters "to make America great again and let the eagle soar." At Republican rallies smothered with balloons and music, the President repeated the evidence of a booming economy and a safer world. With images that touched a deep chord of patriotism, Reagan invoked memories of the Soviets marching into Afghanistan and the Iranians holding fifty-two American hostages. He had a photo session with the Olympic team, held an an-

## Mondale / Ferraro: for the Family of America

niversary celebration of the invasion of Granada, and posed in front of a B-l bomber. "The essence of the Ronald Reagan campaign," ABC reporter Sam Donaldson observed, "is a never-ending string of spectacular picture stories created for television and designed to place the President in the midst of wildly cheering, patriotic Americans. . . . God, patriotism, and Ronald Reagan, that's the essence this campaign is trying to project."

About ten days after Labor Day, the Reagan campaign unfolded what *Time* magazine called "the slickest, most ambitious political ad ever made." Dissatisfied with traditional campaign agencies, the White House assembled its own "Tuesday Team"

*Poster for Mondale and Ferraro. In choosing Representative Geraldine Ferraro, Mondale had lowered a historic barrier against women participating at the highest level of national politics.*

of Madison Avenue allstars, including the wizards responsible for Michael Jackson's Pepsi commercials, the Gallo wine ad, and the Meow Mix singing cat. Their commercial, produced at a cost of $435,000 and originally shown at the Republican National Convention in Dallas, was studded with vignettes of American life—a smiling old couple, the sun rising over the horizon, a house under construction—and featured highlights from Reagan's political career. Without mentioning issues or programs, the film announced "America's back." The journalist William Henry commented: "It reminded the public, almost flagrantly, that Reagan was a televised image, distinct, serene. Like Big Brother, the leader in Orwell's *1984*, Reagan manifested himself chiefly as an electronic impulse, an ionized, ethereal stream."

On the stump as on television, Reagan was distinctly a nonthreatening individual. He never scolded a crowd; his style was always conversational, flavored with humorous and self-deprecating asides. Reagan communicated compassion. "He just sounds like a genuinely decent human being, always in control," observed one scholar. His soft voice made every word fit the natural cadence of his speech. Always the professional, he read smoothly from the TelePrompTer, without miscue. Each gesture was practiced until it appeared genuine and spontaneous.

While Reagan soared, Mondale stumbled. Hoping to score points by outlining the details of his "fair" tax proposal, Mondale used charts and statistics to show how he would raise $85 billion in taxes a year from corporations and families earning more than $25,000 a year. Critics charged that

Mondale's emphasis on substantive policy combined with his natural reserve and phlegmatic manner made him a perfect foil for Reagan's media politics. "One might think Mondale was running for director of the Office of Management and Budget," quipped Robert Kuttner. Mondale's staff pleaded with him to give fewer substantive speeches and spend more time crafting cameo spots for the evening news. Mondale had always resisted the advice in the past, but unable to make a dent in Reagan's commanding lead, he reluctantly agreed to try a few media events.

To dramatize his concern for struggling unemployed workers, he met with a young couple in Philadelphia who had lost their jobs. The instructions from his staff were clear: no new policy proposals, no speeches, just look concerned and let the camera roll. It seemed easy enough. "So I understand you lost your job," Mondale said, sitting in the comfortable suburban living room. "Yes," the woman responded, "but I got a new one that's even better!" Mondale's heart sunk. Willing to give the new approach a decent trial, Mondale then traveled to a paper factory to be pictured talking with average workers about their problems and concerns. Because of poor planning, he missed the shift change. Instead of seeing a concerned Mondale in touch with the problems of average Americans, viewers saw the plant manager present Mondale with a roll of toilet paper.

The Mondale campaign produced a number of high-quality ads, but poor organization and the candidate's discomfort with the media, diminished their effectiveness. One ad cited $1,800 as each voters "share of Mr. Reagan's deficit," and con-

cluded with the plea: "Let's stop mortgaging America." Another showed a long line of blue-suited corporate executives walking out of the Treasury building into waiting limousines. A stern voice identified the men as representatives of "profitable corporations that pay no taxes, defense contractors on bloated budgets, foreign interests who make money on our debt."

Television emphasized the contrast in styles between the two candidates. In Reagan's campaign, discussing issues was secondary, taking a back seat to invoking themes, creating visual images, and communicating shared values. Where Reagan appealed to values and underlying passions, Mondale spoke of programs and policies.

Reagan appealed to people's hearts, Mondale to their minds. Reagan understood that politics in a television age was a performing art, not political science. "Reaganism is politics-as-evangelism, calling forth a majority with a hymn to general values," George Will wrote. "Mondalism is politics-as-masonry, building a majority brick by brick."

On October 1, as the candidates prepared for their debates, Reagan held a commanding fifteen point lead in the polls. During his practice sessions, Mondale seemed to discover the power of television. Rehearsing his answers in front of a videocamera, he paused to watch and analyze his responses. After carefully studying the camera positions, an adviser had found that if Mondale stepped out from behind the podium, turn-

*Celluloid buttons for Reagan and Bush reflecting support by some ethnic Americans.*

ed toward the President, and confronted him directly, the cross-angles would provide a dramatic image of confrontation. Although at first reluctant to engage in such theater, Mondale acquiesced, practicing the crucial pivot and turn almost a dozen times. For his part, Reagan held a series of intense mock debates with Budget Director David Stockman playing the role of Mondale. The President was also forced to study a twenty-five-page briefing book full of possible questions, answers, and one-liners.

On October 7, the candidates met on the stage of the Kentucky Center for the Arts in the first of two nationally televised debates. From the opening question it was clear that Mondale was in control. The Democratic challenger began by saying that Reagan reminded him of what Will Rogers once said about Herbert Hoover: "It's not what he doesn't know that bothers me, it's what he knows for sure that just ain't so." Appearing sharp and confident, Mondale attacked a plank in the Republican platform that called for the appointment of judges who opposed abortion. In the most tense exchange of the night, Reagan, responding to a Mondale

charge that he would raise taxes if reelected, repeated his famous 1980 line: "There you go again." Mondale, anticipating the line, shot back. "Remember the last time you said that?" as he executed his well-practiced pivot and turn. It was, he charged, when Carter accused him of trying to cut Medicare. Once in office he had proposed a twenty-billion-dollar cut in the program. "When you say, 'There you go again,' people remember this," Mondale said. Forced on the defensive, Reagan responded with confused statistics and contradictory statements about his position on Social Security, Medicare, and student aid.

For the next week the President's age became a central issue of the campaign. The evening news replayed Reagan's most embarrassing moments—dozing off during an audience with the pope, being coached by his wife in response to a simple question about arms control. Fearing their candidate might be vulnerable, the Tuesday Team decided to refocus public attention on Mondale. Their efforts resulted in the most famous commercial of the season. In an obvious effort to highlight Mondale's weakness in dealing with the Soviets, the camera showed a grizzly lumbering over a hilltop, as a stern voice warned: "There's a bear in the woods. For some people, the bear is easy to see. Others don't see it at all. Some people say the bear is tame. Others say it is vicious and dangerous. Since no one can really be sure who's right, isn't it smart to be as strong as the bear?" As the bear reached the top of the hill, a solitary hunter with a rifle slung over his shoulder stood watching him.

Convinced that Reagan had "over prepared" for his first clash with Mondale, the President's handlers made sure their candidate appeared more relaxed and less burdened with facts in the second debate on October 21. In an early exchange, Reagan noted a Mondale commercial showing him on the deck of the *Nimitz* watching F-14s take off. "If he had had his way when the *Nimitz* was being planned, he would have been deep in the water out there, because there wouldn't have been any *Nimitz* to stand on," he said. He also effectively deflected the age issue. When asked whether he was youthful enough to stand the strains of office, Reagan responded: "I will not make age an issue of this campaign. I am not going to exploit, for political purposes, my opponent's youth and inexperience." Even Reagan's rambling closing statement about driving down the California coast did not hurt public impressions of his performance. Republican surveys showed Reagan opening up a lead of twenty points by the next night. "I knew when I walked off that platform after the second debate that the election was over," Mondale reflected.

In the final days both candidates sharpened their messages. Before a small black church in Memphis, Mondale spoke of the world portrayed in Reagan's commercials. "It's all picket fences and puppy dogs," he said. "When was the last time you heard the word decency, the word justice, compassion at the White House?" Complaining about the four million children removed from the school lunch program, he called the Reagan administration "an insult to American decency." They "can hear the faintest drum—but they can't hear the cry of a hungry child," he declared. The President concentrated his efforts on Democratic strongholds in the Northeast and Midwest. He warned voters in Iowa and Wisconsin that if they chose Mondale, the nation would be left wandering in "an endless desert of worsening inflation and recession." Confident of victory, he made a last minute trip into Mondale's home state of Minnesota in hopes of a fifty state landslide.

On election day, voters returned Reagan to office with 59 percent of the vote and the biggest electoral vote total in history: 525. Mondale, carrying only Minnesota and the District of Columbia, received 13 electoral votes. Reagan hailed the results as an endorsement of his economic and foreign policies, but his mastery of the media also played a role in his triumph. "The truth of the matter is that Ronald Reagan is the perfect candidate," said campaign manager Edward Rollins. "He does whatever you want him to do. And he does it superbly well." The campaign also forced Mondale to recognize the importance of mastering the media in modern elections. "Modern politics requires television," he reflected. "I've never really warmed up to television, and in fairness to television, it's never really warmed up to me."

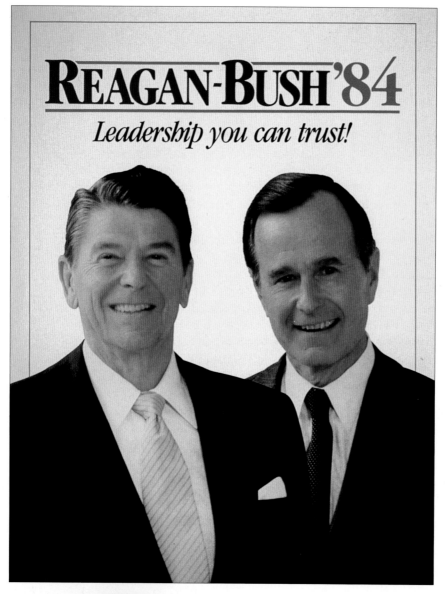

Celluloid button for Reagan and Bush.
This was the most common Republican button issued.

The National Federation of Republican Women issued many buttons to offset Reagan's sizable gender gap. Surprisingly, although Reagan opposed most feminist objectives, there were more items issued by women's groups for Reagan than for any other candidate in American political history.

Anti-Mondale button inspired by the movie Ghost Busters.

*Right: Poster of Reagan and Bush. The President, always shown smiling, conveyed an image of confidence and optimism. Below: Celluloid buttons for Reagan and Bush. Center button was used in Virginia senator John Warner's reelection campaign.*

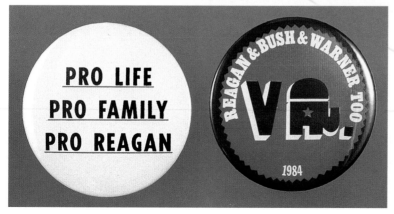

The 1984 Republican convention met in Dallas under ideal circumstances for the incumbent. The nation was at peace, the economy was booming. Reagan was popular and in complete command of his party.

Musical and flashing campaign buttons were introduced in 1984. Operated by computer chips and powered by tiny batteries, these novelties again showed the impact of technology on political ephemera.

Selection of Mondale and Ferraro items. Two successive misfortunes hit Geraldine Ferraro. The first involved her family finances. Then, in a bruising battle with New York Archbishop John J. O'Connor over abortion, the hierarchy of her church acted like an arm of the Reagan reelection committee. Ferraro was effectively undercut and neutralized.

*A moment in history.*
*A day to remember.*

# GERALDINE FERRARO
*Democratic Vice Presidential Nominee*

## Friday, November 2nd
## Noon
## San Francisco
## Drumm Street at
## the Embarcadero
### (in front of the Hyatt Regency)

PAID FOR BY MONDALE/FERRARO COMMITTEE, INC.

MONDALE
Democratic
National
Convention
nea

AMERICA NEEDS NEW LEADERSHIP
19 84
MONDALE-FERRARO

MEET
*Walter* **Mondale** &
*Geraldine* **Ferraro**

First
Public Appearance
RESERVED AREA

**NOON** Monday, July 16
Market & Powell Sts.
PAID FOR BY MONDALE FOR PRESIDENT COMMITTEE

VALID UNTIL 11:45 A.M.

JULY 16 1984 SAN FRANCISCO

GERALDINE FERRARO
FOR VICE-PRESIDENT

WOMAN
VP
NOW

*Eugene Delacroix's 1830 masterpiece "Liberty Leading the People" adapted for Geraldine Ferraro.*

'I WANT TO BE THE PRESIDENT WHO
PUTS AMERICA BACK TO WORK!'
WALTER MONDALE to the AFL-CIO
Oct. 6, 1983

HELP MONDALE GET
AMERICA WORKING!
Steelworkers for Mondale

Ronald Reagan won a sweeping victory in 1984, receiving 59 percent
of the popular vote compared to Mondale's 41 percent. He carried
Catholics (61 to 39 percent), women (55 to 45 percent), and a
majority in every age group. Reagan received an overwhelming mandate
in every group except for non-whites, blacks, and union members.
Mondale and Ferraro failed in their strategy of holding on to Carter's
1980 supporters and adding those who had voted for John Anderson.

To Protect Your Job...

Vote For
The Team
That Wants
To Limit
IMPORTS

WALTER                    GERALDINE
MONDALE & FERRARO

SHEET METAL WORKERS
Register & Vote for

MONDALE/FERRARO

Sheet Metal Workers' International Association Political Action League ★ 1750 New York Avenue N.W. Washington, D.C. 20006

Large union poster for Mondale and Ferraro. In seven of the eight presidential elections between 1952 and 1980, labor union families voted for the Democratic candidate over the Republican by an average of 28 percentage points. In 1984, Mondale received only 52 percent of that vote.

Selection of celluloid buttons for Mondale and Ferraro. On election day, Reagan achieved one of the great political triumphs of American history. He carried 49 states, losing only Mondale's home state of Minnesota and the District of Columbia.

1988

50 STATES
IN THE UNION

*REPUBLICAN*

# George Bush

ELECTORAL VOTE 426, POPULAR VOTE 53.4%

DEMOCRAT

# Michael Dukakis

ELECTORAL VOTE 111, POPULAR VOTE 45.6%

ROBERT SQUIER
is president of Squier-Eskew, Washington, D.C.
He has served as a political consultant to
the Democratic National Committee. Mr. Squier
received an Emmy award for his television
documentary series, *Sounds of Summer*.

I n the mythology of India two young men, vying for the love of a lady, lose their heads in a bloody sword fight. The heads are hastily sewn back, but on the wrong bodies. The Legend of the Transposed Heads is also the story of the 1988 U.S. presidential election.

Approaching the Democratic convention, Michael Dukakis was likened to Zorba the Greek facing Ronald Reagan's vice president struggling with the wimp factor that so often accompanies that job.

Zorba vs. the Wimp: The Democratic dream campaign. But it was not to be. The reputation of American presidential elections for volatility, unpredictability and drama was reconfirmed. In the course of three remarkable months in the fall of 1988 the two candidates, seemingly by mutual consent, transposed images. Michael Dukakis would return to his job as governor of Massachusetts and George Bush would become the forty-first President of the United States. Zorba became the wimp; the wimp became President.

This was the first American election in which paid advertising became central to the outcome of the campaign. It was also an election in which a political stranger played a key role. Willie Horton did not appear on the ballot in 1988 but he became the election's third man; as important as George Wallace had been to Hubert Humphrey and Richard Nixon in 1968.

The unpredictable and fluid nature of contemporary American presidential politics springs from a weak party system. Be-

fore the 1960s, what little organized party power that existed was centered in the courthouses of the South and the city halls of the North and East. When political bosses could find common ground, ad hoc national parties existed. This power was virtually wiped out by the convergence of two technologies: television and the automobile.

The mass production of the automobile made it possible for voters to drive out from under the machine politics of cities and towns and look their political choices directly in the eye through the new prism of television For good or evil, voters began to trust their own eyes.

Candidates started turning up on the television news. Political outsiders soon figured out that by getting free coverage and purchasing advertisements for themselves they could bypass not only the existing party machinery, but the scrutiny of journalists as well. A short circuit occurred in our politics: The direct experience of television produced a system based on campaigns and candidates.

Private political polling allowed candidates to listen to the voters; now television offered a way to talk back to them. The loop was closed. The electronic candidate was born, delivered through the narrow confines of the forty-five-second sound bite and the thirty-second spot. (Thirty years later paid advertisements were still thirty seconds long but the sound bite had shrunk to nine seconds.) To advertise themselves, politicians simply borrowed the existing and primitive forms of name-repetition con-

*Square celluloid button for Michael Dukakis.*

sumer advertising developed to move low-ticket items from store shelf to home shelf.

By the early 1980s the Gallup organization found that in state and local races most voters were relying on information from electronic advertising to make their electoral decisions. By contrast, in presidential campaigns, advertising was still at sea in a wealth of competing information. Voters could follow presidential races through network and local news broadcasts and in their newspapers and magazines. Also, conventional wisdom and tradition worked against taking money out of traditional campaign activities like brochures, bumper stickers, organization and street money to put much TV on the air. Political advertising was used in presidential campaigns, but it was not as important to the outcome as it was in statewide races.

In 1984, the Reagan campaign used advertising as an effective supplement to the candidate and his campaign. "Feel good ads" were sprayed like chloroform on the electorate to lull them into a happy sleep until their wake-up call on election day. These ads were even given the surprisingly honest title of "Morning in America." It was the perfect use of media for a front-running candidate campaigning on the strength of his personality; advertising playing in the background like a movie score.

President Dukakis. You could hear it everywhere at the 1988 Democratic convention as the candidate confidently sounded the theme of his campaign. He repaired to the well-worn but, in his mind, time-tested standard he had used to win the nomination. "I don't think I have to tell any of you how much we Americans expect of ourselves, or how much we have a right to expect from those we elect to public office. Because this election is not about ideology. It's about competence." It was the best speech of his life and the high point of his political career.

A week later, referring to a military procurement scandal, Dukakis surprisingly made an attack, not on his opponent, but on popular President Reagan, saying, "a fish rots from the head down." Within days rumors were swirling inside the Capital beltway questioning not only the wisdom of Dukakis's attack but—quite unjustly—his mental health. On August 3 the issue broke through to the surface when Reagan said, "I am not going to pick on an invalid," a remark he later retracted but not before it had done its damage. Nevertheless, pleased with the polls and unconscious of the bad start he had made, Dukakis coasted through August savoring what appeared to be an insurmountable lead.

The Bush team, behind by double digits in the polls, adopted a strategy to try to put Dukakis on the defensive and keep him there. On August 8 Bush accused Dukakis of being the "stealth candidate" whose policies "can be neither seen nor heard." Ten days later

Bush was nominated at the Republican convention in New Orleans and despite the controversial selection of Dan Quayle as his running mate his poll numbers began to rise.

Cynics hold that very few differences exist between the Democratic and Republican parties. In fact there are many differences, and they played a role in the 1988 election. If truth in labeling applied to American political parties Democrats would be called the Government party; Republicans the Anti-Government party. Democrats love government, both in theory and in practice. Republicans are by nature suspicious of government and are happiest campaigning against it. Ronald Reagan masterfully exploited this difference when he came to office in 1980 by campaigning against the Carter government: He was even reelected four years later campaigning against the very government he now headed. George Bush, ever the attentive pupil, would campaign against the government of Michael Dukakis.

When modern campaign technologies became available, Republicans, then out of office, were quick to adapt them to their needs. They moved swiftly to bring direct-mail fundraising, television, radio, and computers to the center of their party. Power may not always corrupt, but it can blind incumbents to the instruments of change. Democrats, mostly incumbents at the time, resisted the modern tools of the campaign trade.

Following the loss of the U.S. Senate majority in the 1980 Reagan landslide, Democrats were able to build back their strength at the state and local levels. How they succeeded explains another difference between the two parties. Republicans had successfully learned to nationalize elections for President. But they ran into trouble trying to impose national

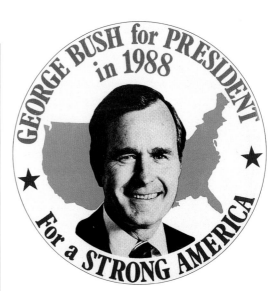

Celluloid button for George Bush.

strategies on local elections. As a result their local campaigns sounded like relay stations for homogenized messages broadcast from Washington. The Democrats had become adept at tailoring their campaigns to local circumstances but met failure when they tried to apply lessons learned from their successes at the local level to campaigns for President.

Republicans are fond of quoting their eleventh commandment: "Thou shalt not speak ill of other Republicans." It is especially effective against a Democratic party schooled in internecine warfare. Republicans also operate on what must be an unspoken twelfth commandment: "Rally round the party boys." Republicans know how to get the best people in their party to work together in general elections no matter how divisive the nomination battle. Republicans circle the wagons. Democrats circle a firing squad, faced inward.

James Baker occupied the Cabinet chair first held by George Washington's secretary of the treasury, Alexander Hamilton. Yet he was coaxed from the Reagan Cabinet, at the nadir of Bush's fortunes, to manage what promised to be a brutal campaign. Baker took the surest path forward in his party: He later became secretary of state.

In 1988 Republicans once again nationalized their presidential campaign, put aside their differences, and ran for the office of President as if it were the most important political office in the world; which, of course, it still is.

One axiom of conventional wisdom in American campaigns is that you never let your candidate do the attacking. Paid media (read "negative advertising") do the dirty work and the candidate rides above on the high road. For the Bush campaign this would have been the road to a respectable loss. Instead, the Republicans used paid advertising to debunk the Dukakis claim of "competence" but then assigned their candidate the task of convincing voters that he was "the better man." Bush bullied his opponent around the campaign, toughening up his own image while simultaneously putting Dukakis on the defensive.

Dukakis was in the ring for the heavyweight championship but he refused to don the gloves. He failed to answer damaging questions about himself and his abilities raised by Bush, the Bush advertising, and eventually by the press. "If Dukakis is so competent how is it that he has allowed America's historic Boston Harbor to turn into a sewer?" went one refrain. An answer, at least as politically responsible as the question, was available to Dukakis. Responsibility for the harbor obviously fell just as much on the Reagan/Bush administration as on Dukakis. Although Dukakis had said in a rare August appearance that he had finally found the money to clean up the harbor, the Bush ad went basically unchallenged and the rebuttal sounded defensive. This became a pattern in the campaign.

In mid-September, smarting from attacks on his lack of experience in foreign policy, Dukakis took the wheel of an M-l tank for a photo opportunity meant to show his support for a strong national defense.

*Satirical anti-Dukakis monopoly card.*

He did not look like a potential Commander-in-Chief. In fact, he looked so silly in his tank helmet that footage of the event became the basis of a Roger Ailes ad attacking him on the very issue he was trying to defuse: defense. On September 22 Bush picked up the endorsement of the Boston Police Patrolman's Association. Dukakis quickly cobbled together his own rally of Massachusetts law enforcement officers, but on television that night it was clear that he had barely fought Bush to a draw in his own backyard, and he had helped raise the saliency of an issue central to the Bush attack: law and order.

The questions kept coming. "If Dukakis is so competent how is it that he allows dangerous criminals, rapists, and murderers like Willie Horton to be let out of prison on furlough?" An effective counterattack could have neutralized the question and allowed Dukakis to move the argument to his own turf.(Years before, Bush had sponsored a halfway house in Texas, and a furloughed convict living there committed a crime against a young family that was at least as gruesome as anything done by Willie Horton, and it was a Republican governor who had initiated the furlough policy in Massachusetts.) Yet no rebuttal was issued.

The Horton issue attacked the Dukakis competence claim at a liberal Democrat's most vulnerable point: personal safety. Unchallenged, it was perceived to show personal weakness on the part of Dukakis and strength on the part of his accuser. It was an arrow, dipped in the poison of racism, aimed straight at the heart of the Dukakis candidacy. It was introduced in an officially sponsored ad which posed the furlough question without showing or mentioning Willie Horton. But soon candidate Bush was

*Celluloid button for Texas Senator Lloyd Bentsen. During the campaign, Bentsen became more popular than Dukakis.*

personally raising the specter of Horton and a second "unauthorized" commercial was aired by an independent committee supporting Bush. The second commercial used both the name and face of Willie Horton in a blatantly racist appeal. In the heat of the campaign the attack was not judged by the standards of right or wrong. Rougher justice prevailed: Did it work? It worked.

Dukakis refused to "lower himself" to Bush's level so the attack commercials went unanswered for weeks. In the absence of a rebuttal, the unanswered attacks eventually appeared to be agreed to by Dukakis.

Presidential debates are rare islands of unvarnished reality in contemporary presidential campaigns. Advancemen, speechwriters, spin doctors, handlers, pollsters, media consultants are all swept from the stage, and the candidates are left to stand alone answering to each other, and more important, to the voters. Debates have been the turning point in many presidential campaigns. JFK proved he was Nixon's equal in the 1960 debates, teaching Nixon a lesson

*Plastic press badge issued by ABC News.*

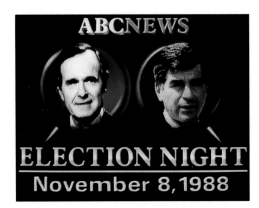

he applied to his next two opponents by refusing to debate them. President Ford, facing Jimmy Carter in their second debate, accidentally freed an iron curtain country and never recovered from the week spent trying to explain away his mistake. Carter in a 1980 debate admitted to seeking advice on nuclear policy from daughter Amy and soon regretted the confidence.

The 1988 debates played an even more important role. Jim Baker, heading the Republican debate negotiating team, obtained concessions that put Dukakis in a hole before he ever took the stage. The Democratic negotiators wanted four presidential debates and the Republicans two: they compromised at two.

The vice presidential debate on October 5 between Dan Quayle and Senator Lloyd Bentsen produced a flap that would haunt Quayle long after the election. He made the mistake of comparing himself favorably to President Kennedy. Bentsen moved in for the kill. "Senator, I served with Jack Kennedy. I knew Jack Kennedy. Jack Kennedy was a friend of mine. Senator, you're no Jack Kennedy." Voters watching the dumbstruck Quayle on television didn't need to have this event explained to them by an anchorman or a political boss.

The first 1988 presidential debate was fought to a draw: Both sides claimed victory. Expectations were high for the final debate because Dukakis desperately needed a win. The opening question came from moderator Bernard Shaw of CNN. Picking up on the Horton issue, he confronted Dukakis with a case study: the hypothetical rape of his wife Kitty. Instead of showing the instincts of a husband, Dukakis followed the advice he had gotten by phone from Governor Mario Cuomo just seconds before he stepped out on the stage; remain cool at all costs. Dukakis remained unruffled and cerebral; more Harvard Yard than backyard. Not only was the exchange devastating; it suited the Bush strategy perfectly, and set the tone for what was to follow.

The Republican campaign had been drawing up an indictment against Dukakis: Dukakis won't defend himself. He didn't defend Boston Harbor. He couldn't defend the citizens of his commonwealth from Willie Horton. He can't defend his country. And now on live television, with the whole country watching, he fails to defend his wife. It was a devastating lapse. Four days later the NBC News/*Wall Street Journal* poll found that Dukakis was now seventeen percentage points behind.

Why was the Dukakis campaign so paralyzed? In August they had set out on a front-runner's strategy: trying not to lose. No offense became the worst defense. Nature may abhor a vacuum but political opponents love them. The Republican campaign had filled in the Dukakis vacuum with their own version of the Dukakis record.

A new team was installed to handle the Dukakis advertising. Less than a week before the first presidential debate a retooled advertising campaign was presented to Dukakis and his top staff. It was introduced as being "not your typical aldermanic political media," and it wasn't. As one observer put it later, "No serious candidate for alderman would have used it!"

The campaign was presented in descending orders of importance. The top rung was devoted to a series of ads suspiciously reminiscent of the "Morning in America" commercials designed for the front-running Ronald Reagan in 1984. The most memorable storyboard featured a flower growing up through a crack in the ruins of an aging city: Democratic hope springing eternal.

The next level was devoted to a series of "talking head" ads to be delivered by Dukakis speaking directly to the camera. Following the presentation the campaign hierarchy approached the elaborate storyboards covering each wall for a closer look. In the copy block under each of the Dukakis talking heads were the words "Blah-blah-blah-blah-blah-blah." A metaphor for the campaign.

Still lower in priority was an idea the new group was especially proud of: "The Handlers." In this series they planned to take the voters to a fictionalized backroom of the Bush/Quayle handlers; as actors playing the Bush team cynically brag about how they plan to trick the voters into voting against their self-interest and for the Republican ticket. (One ad in this series was later screened for Vice President Bush but he found it baffling, he was unable to tell whether it was an ad made *for* him or *against* him!)

The job of responding to Bush and developing a counterattack offensive was given the lowest priority. This style of campaigning was clearly repugnant to the can-

didate, and no discussion of how it might work took place. In fact, few questions were asked at the presentation except by Dukakis finance director Bob Farmer who wanted to know why the campaign they had just seen wouldn't better suit the needs of the front-running Bush.

By 1988 it was commonplace in contested statewide campaigns for spot advertising to drive the race, but it had yet to be the case in a presidential election. Voters had become accustomed to a mini-debate of charge and counter-charge in political advertising. They told poll takers and the press that they didn't like these campaigns, but survey research made it clear that voters were using this information in making their political decisions. Now they had seen this same style of campaign for the highest office in the land: But it was a one sided electronic debate, and Dukakis lost it.

Election-eve polls showed Bush ahead by a margin of twelve percentage points or more. Dukakis probably found some consolation in what politicians are fond of calling "the only poll that counts": the election. He lost by eight percentage points, not by the landslide he dreaded.

In the course of three months, the two candidates for President had not only transposed their images but a quarter of the electorate. For the first time paid advertising had played a central role in the result of an American presidential campaign. An anomaly? Probably not. With news-gathering organizations all drastically cutting their coverage of campaigns following the 1988 election, it is likely that paid appeals will be just as important, if not more important, in future elections.

Stay tuned.

Poster for George Bush. He was one of the youngest naval pilots in World War II and received the Distinguished Flying Cross.

*Building on America's Strength*

GEORGE BUSH
PRESIDENT

Celluloid button issued to Pennsylvania delegates to the Republican convention.

Celluloid button for Bush issued in New Hampshire prior to that state's primary.

**George Bush for President**

Paid for by George Bush for President
733 15th Street, N.W. • Suite 800 • Washington, D.C. 20005 • (202) 842-1988

Poster of Bush and his family issued by the Bush for President Committee.

According to the Gallup Poll, perceptions of Dukakis deteriorated between the Democratic convention and election day. The percentage of voters saying he would make a good President fell from 42 to 36 percent while those thinking he would not rose from 12 to 31 percent.

**VICTORY '88**

President George **BUSH**

Vice-President Dan **QUAYLE**

Peace ★ Prosperity ★ Leadership
Continues
November 8, 1988

Bush 88 Quayle

**GUEST TICKET**

**VICE PRESIDENT GEORGE BUSH DAY**

**Friday, Sept. 2, 1988
11:00 a.m.**

Belmar, New Jersey

Entrance at 4th or 7th Ave.
9:00 A.M.

Paid for by Bush-Quayle '88

# BUSH
# QUAYLE

*Selection of Bush campaign items. The Bush lead over Dukakis remained constant between the end of the Republican convention and election day.*

*Satirical rubber doll with Dan Quayle being carried by Bush.*

Boston Herald, August 1988

# Gov 'gave pardons to 21 drug dealers'

# Will Dukakis Turn Gun Owners Into Criminals... While Murderers Go Free?

*The Most Soft-on-Crime Governor in Massachusetts History Is a Leading Advocate of Gun Control*

*Gun Owner Magazine* quotes Dukakis as saying in 1986, **"I don't believe in people owning guns, only the police and military. And I'm going to do everything I can to disarm this state."** In 1976 Dukakis supported a (losing) statewide referendum which would have done just that. Dukakis has called for **federal registration** of all concealable handguns and has written, "... the solution to the problem of gun-inflicted violence must come at the national level."

Michael Dukakis talks about fighting crime, but there is a big gap between the *rhetoric* and the *record*. Maybe that's why the **Boston Police Patrolman's Association unanimously endorsed George Bush for President.**

While trying to deny the citizens of Massachusetts the right to defend themselves, Dukakis has put more convicted criminals on the streets than any governor in his state's history.

- He has used his gubernatorial pardoning power to commute the sentences of *44 convicted murderers* — a record for the state of Massachusetts.

- He has vetoed and continues to oppose the death penalty *under any circumstances,* even for cop-killers, drug kingpins and traitors.

- He *opposes* mandatory sentences for hardcore criminals but *supports* mandatory sentences for anyone caught with an unregistered gun *of any kind.*

Dukakis has also presided over and actively endorsed the *most liberal prisoner furlough program in America,* the **only one in the nation** releasing prisoners sentenced to life without parole.

- On average, in the state of Massachusetts, one convicted first degree murderer was released *every day* over the last seven years.

- Since the beginning of Dukakis' second term as Governor, 1,905 furloughs have been granted to first degree murderers and at least 4,459 furloughs to second degree murderers. He has given 2,565 furloughs to drug offenders.

- In 1986 alone, Dukakis gave 1,229 furloughs to sex crime offenders, including 220 to persons charged with *six or more* sex offenses.

- Today **85 violent felons from Massachusetts are on the loose** in America — set free on furloughs, they never bothered to come back.

### Meet Willie Horton.

*Willie Horton was convicted in 1975 and sentenced to life in prison without parole for stabbing a 17-year-old to death during a robbery. In 1986, on his tenth release* under the Dukakis-supported furlough program, he escaped to Maryland where he stabbed and beat a man and then repeatedly raped his fiancee.

Horton was captured, but Maryland Judge Vincent Femia *refused to send him back to Massachusetts* saying, "I am not prepared to take the chance that Mr. Horton might be furloughed or otherwise released ...

I would strongly urge the people of Massachusetts not to wait up for Mr. Horton ... not to bother to put out a light for him because he won't be coming home." Judge Femia recommended that Horton, "should never draw a breath of free air again ... and should die in prison." Michael Dukakis *refused to even meet* with the parents of the couple Horton attacked, saying, "I don't see any particular value in meeting with people ... I'm satisfied ... we have the kind of furlough policy we should have."

*In a series of television commercials and posters, Lee Atwater, chairman of the National Republican Committee, created the most powerful image of the 1988 campaign. This poster showing Willie Horton appeared briefly in New Jersey and Maryland before being recalled.*

Cardboard movie
refreshment-stand straw holder.

Satirical anti-Dukakis pamphlet.

Matching pairs of novelty
items for Dukakis and Bush.

Celluloid buttons for Bush.

THE RIGHT CHOICE

Celluloid labor union
buttons for Dukakis
and Bentsen.

Automobile bumper sticker
for Bush and Quayle.

★

1992

50 STATES
IN THE UNION

*DEMOCRAT*

# Bill Clinton

ELECTORAL VOTE 370, POPULAR VOTE 43%


REPUBLICAN

# George Bush

ELECTORAL VOTE 168, POPULAR VOTE 37%


INDEPENDENT

# Ross Perot

ELECTORAL VOTE 0, POPULAR VOTE 19%

## JOHN CHANCELLOR

is one of the nation's foremost broadcast
journalists. His career as a reporter, foreign
bureau chief, and commentator for NBC has
spanned four decades. Mr. Chancellor has
covered every presidential campaign since 1952.

I n the four decades following the election of 1952, presidential campaigns were controlled by the rules of political television, and political television was controlled by specialists in advertising. The election of 1992 changed that. Something new and surprising happened. Candidates for President began to speak directly to individual voters. Person-to-person communication with citizens assumed an importance equal to mass-market television and radio advertising.

During the fall, all the presidential campaigns gave high priority to appearances on interview programs and call-in shows which featured Larry King, Katie Couric, Arsenio Hall, Phil Donahue, Paula Zahn, and dozens of other performers of national or regional prominence. Rush Limbaugh's radio call-in show attracts a huge audience. He was an overnight guest of President and Mrs. Bush at the White House. The political importance of cable television increased significantly in 1992. CNN, C-SPAN, and MTV became serious players in the presidential game.

The established press lost power and influence. After the election, Bill Clinton described the old, traditional relationship between candidates and political reporters in these words: "Anyone who lets himself be interpreted to the American people through intermediaries alone is nuts." The disciplined questioners of the Sunday-morning interview programs, journalists as knowledgeable as David Broder, Elizabeth Drew, and Bob Novak, were shunned during the 1992 campaigns.

The candidates preferred to talk politics with less-experienced interrogators on early-morning and late-night talk shows. Candidates had intimate chats with voters on telephone lines while other voters listened in. Talk-show America became party-line America.

In previous elections, programs of this kind had been *terra incognita* for presidential candidates. George Bush learned the hard way that entertainers who work at night play by different rules. The President's spokesman said Mr. Bush might appear on some talk shows, but not on *The Arsenio Hall Show* (where Clinton had recently played the saxophone). A few hours later, Hall began his program with these words: "Excuse me, George Herbert-read-my-lying-lipping, slipping-in-the-polls, do-nothing, deficit-raising, Quayle-loving-Bush! I don't need you on my show. My ratings are higher than yours."

D espite the roughness of this terrain, the candidates continued to campaign on talk shows. Political consultants call these programs "free media"; campaign treasurers like them because they don't cost money; and in 1992, campaign managers realized that talk shows were reaching huge numbers of voters. Credit for this discovery goes to Ross Perot, whose appearances on interview and call-in programs persuaded millions of voters to telephone his 800-number with pledges of support. Perot started it, and they all followed. The records of *Larry King, Donahue,* and the three morning network shows

*Celluloid Clinton button. In an appeal to younger voters, Clinton put on his Ray-Bans, got out his saxophone, and played "Heartbreak Hotel" with Posse on The Arsenio Hall Show.*

reveal that George Bush made sixteen appearances on those programs, Ross Perot made thirty-three appearances, and Bill Clinton was on a total of forty-seven times. Their efforts were not wasted. Clinton put on dark glasses and played the saxophone on Arsenio Hall's late-night syndicated, non-network program. The musical portion of his appearance was brief, but it became one of the icons of the political year. It was repeated endlessly on television. On NBC news programs, Clinton's saxophone performance was replayed twenty-five times. At his inauguration, many people wore saxophone pins.

After he became President, Clinton told reporters, "You know why I can stiff you on the press conferences? Because Larry King liberated me by giving me to the American people directly."

All the candidates were "liberated" in 1992 by changes in technology and demography which presented new opportunities for campaigning. The new technology of cable television was challenging the primacy of conventional news organizations, the newspapers, magazines, and networks. Younger voters were getting less political information from *Newsweek* or NBC and more from C-SPAN and MTV. According to the Times Mirror Center for the People and the Press, half of all Americans under thirty-five get their political news only from television, and MTV claims a large share of that audience. This cable network is basically a rock music channel, but it produces eighteen newscasts every twenty-four hours. Bill Clinton's first televised interview as President was given to MTV's Tabitha Soren, a young reporter who became a star in the political coverage of the 1992 election. MTV gave a party the night of President Clinton's inauguration; Vice President Gore told the guests, "Thank you, MTV, thank you for winning this election. You did it!"

Another phenomenon of this extraordinary year was Ross Perot, whose run for the Oval Office is one of the more remarkable narratives in American history. To describe it as politics is inadequate. A better way might be to analyze the Perot candidacy as a classic hostile-takeover bid, conceived and executed by an audacious entrepreneur. Perot wanted to win control of the Executive Branch of the government which would make him the CEO of the USA. He would do that by offering the stockholders a bold new plan for running the business, bringing down its debt, and making it a world-class competitor. The shareholders would approve the new management at the annual meeting of the stockholders of the USA on Tuesday, November 3, 1992 (known also as election day).

Perot had poll data which showed that an outsider had a chance of winning. He had performed well on a few talk shows, teasing his interviewers and his supporters with the possibility that he might run for President. Finally, he said on Larry King's television program that if the people put him on the ballot in every state, he would become President on their behalf. He had an explanation that might have come from a Frank Capra movie: This patriotic millionaire would *buy* the election for the American people because he had the money and they didn't.

He made this announcement on the evening of February 20. The date does not seem accidental. Two nights before, on February 18, in the primary elections in New Hampshire, Bill Clinton had come in a poor second in the Democratic contest. President Bush had won the Republican primary, but his victory had been tarnished; he had been humiliated by Pat Buchanan, who got 37 percent of the vote. The President was wounded, perhaps mortally; and it looked as though Clinton had been killed by accusations of adultery with a woman named Gennifer Flowers and allegations of draft dodging. Nobody else in either party looked strong. Perot jumped in.

To enter the race at that moment was a reasonable gamble for Perot. He became, instantly, a phenomenal success. His poll ratings increased and he attracted supporters in every state. In the next few months his prospects soared. Never before had an outsider without an organization, without a base, and without any advertising reached parity with the major-party candidates. At the end of the primaries in June, his standing in the polls was statistically equal to Bush and Clinton. They had run in thirty-two primary elections and had spent millions on advertising. Perot had run nowhere and had never bought a single ad.

One reason for Perot's astounding performance was a desperate desire for change on the part of the voters. He had not produced bulky books of positions and policies on foreign and domestic affairs. He had no party platform. Voters had no idea where Perot stood on many public issues. That was not important. Analysts at the Gallup Poll discovered that voters who supported Perot didn't care where he stood on issues, *as long as they perceived him as an agent of change.* He was like a man in a glider, flying without power, sustained by updrafts. While it lasted, it was remarkable politics. But it didn't last very long.

Perot's takeover bid had looked like a reasonable gamble in the shambles of February's politics, but it began to look less attractive in June. Clinton hadn't died, after all. On

Metal license plate attachments.

the Republican side, Buchanan had faded and Bush had become stronger. Late June was the critical period for Ross Perot. The political professionals he had hired to help with his campaign told him it was time to start spending big money on radio and television advertising. He was facing budgetary demands that could easily have reached $40 or even $50 million. They said if the money weren't spent, there was no chance he could win the political advertising contest that would take place during the fall campaign. Perot found himself in a three-way fight among equals. His takeover gamble began to look expensive and risky.

Too risky for a businessman, perhaps, but a politician would have read the situation

*Celluloid button evoking the Persian Gulf War. Bush is shown wearing a World War II naval flight jacket, undoubtedly to remind voters of his wartime service.*

differently. In the early summer, Perot had slipped a bit in the polls, his negatives had increased somewhat, but his popularity was amazingly strong. In early July, three national polls showed Bush, Clinton, and Perot neck and neck; the *Los Angeles Times*, Gallup/*Newsweek*, and CNN/*Time* polls said the race was a statistical dead heat.

No independent candidate in American history had done as well, the midsummer odds on a Perot victory were one in three, and the price of staying competitive was at least $50 million, which he could easily have afforded.

This was not, however, good enough for Ross Perot. Suddenly, he quit the race, with slippery excuses no one believed. Millions of his supporters were abandoned without a word. On July 16, the election became a Bush-Clinton contest.

Clinton had beaten off all Democratic challengers and his position in the public opinion polls was improving.

Bush was struggling to overcome a catastrophic drop in public support. At the end of the Gulf War in February, 1991, just twelve

months before the New Hampshire primary, the President had a record-breaking favorable poll rating of 89 percent. Desert Storm, the attack on Saddam Hussein's Iraq, had been a political triumph. The enemy had been defeated easily and American casualties were amazingly light. Bush was seen as a skilled leader who had forged a successful international crusade, a determined commander who had gone to war and won. Bush said then, "We have liberated a nation abroad and transformed a country at home." If he had added, "Here is my plan to continue the transformation of our country and strengthen our economy," and pressed vigorously for a program of tax cuts and spending on public works, the President would have been hard to beat.

Instead, the White House gambled that the economy would improve without government stimulus. The recession had actually ended in the spring of 1991; by election day, 1992, the economy had been growing slowly for a year and a half, but the administration could not convince the voters that things were getting better. The White House seemed complacent. There was an unusual lassitude about the reelection campaign. One senior official said the President's work was mainly done and the Congress might as well go home. Another said it didn't matter whether the United States made computer chips or potato chips.

The President's abilities as a campaigner didn't help. He had won in 1988 with the help of Ronald Reagan's skilled political handlers, but when he became President, he seemed not to listen to them. Relations between President Bush and ex-President Reagan were, at best, coldly correct. There were those who wondered if Reagan's Hollywood training, his insistence that every phrase and gesture be rehearsed to perfection, had somehow offended Bush. Did Bush view his predecessor's attention to dramaturgy as beneath the dignity of a President? Was there a touch-of-class warfare involved, Skull and Bones versus the Screen Actors Guild? In any case, the difference between Bush's campaigning style and Reagan's was the difference between the amateur and the professional.

The Clinton campaign, in contrast, seemed much better organized. Its main theme was summed up in a sign posted in its "war room" in Little Rock, which read, "The economy, stupid." (The *Washington Post* reported later that the sign was not a symbol of Bill Clinton's ability to stay focused on a central issue, but was "a constant reminder of how hard it was to keep the often-undisciplined Clinton campaign on track.")

The campaign had been knocked off the track in its very first contest, the New Hampshire primary. Clinton had been badly damaged by accusations of adultery and avoidance of military service. He dismissed it all as "a draft I never dodged and a woman I never slept with," but most forecasters declared him a ruined candidate before a vote was cast. They were wrong; they had not reckoned with Clinton's ferocious resolve. On the evening of February 18, as the New Hampshire votes were being counted, early returns indicated a close battle between former-Senator Paul Tsongas and Clinton. In an inspired, desperate, long-shot stratagem, Clinton seized the moment, called himself "the comeback kid", and the press picked up the phrase. When the final votes were tallied, Tsongas had won by a decisive eight-point margin, but it didn't matter. The "comeback kid" dominated the coverage. Clinton had stayed alive and would not be seriously challenged again.

Mary McGrory, the columnist, has written that Clinton goes through life crossing raging torrents on little rope bridges. His experience in New Hampshire showed how quick and agile a survivor he can be.

Clinton's performance for the rest of the year showed how well he understood the country's mood after a dozen years of Ronald Reagan and George Bush. Twelve years is a long time in presidential politics. The conservative coalition that had supported the Republican party was beginning to come apart; suburbanites and younger voters were developing doubts about the GOP. Reagan had been popular for most of his two terms as President. A few years later, his ratings in some polls were lower than Jimmy Carter's. One of Bush's problems was that he had committed the unpardonable presidential sin of saying never. He had trapped himself in a corner when he said, in 1988, "Read my lips, no new taxes." Bush was forced to break that pledge two years later, and among those most deeply resentful were Democrats who had supported Reagan and Bush. These middle-aged, working-class voters had many worries. Their standard of living had been either flat or in decline for almost two decades. In 1992, the economy was sluggish, jobs were scarce, the welfare system seemed out of hand, and social changes seemed threatening. Their children were living at home longer, marrying later, and earning less. In the eleven years from Reagan's election to 1991, median household income, adjusted for inflation, had increased only fifteen dollars a week.

Clinton presented himself to these disenchanted voters as a young leader who would return the Democratic party to a centrist, Trumanesque position. He would break the

*General Cinema conducted this nationwide straw vote. Although more than 17 million customers participated, voter eligibility was not a requirement—only the purchase of a soft drink.*

party's habit of tinkering with society through social programs. He said, "The best social program is a good job and a growing economy." He promised a fundamental reform of the welfare system; after two years on welfare, everyone who could work would have to accept a job, or go into training for one. In a confrontation that was widely publicized, and not lost on white working-class voters, Clinton faced down Jesse Jackson by attacking rap artist Sister Souljah for her provocative language about blacks killing whites.

It can be argued that the 1992 presidential election was won by the challenger. An equal case can be made that it was the incumbent who lost it. But in early October, before anyone won or lost, there was another surprise.

Ross Perot returned as an active, independent candidate for President.

He said politics in the United States was a mess. He said Americans wanted a system that did not attract, as he put it, "ego-driven, power-hungry people." Following his abrupt withdrawal in July, Perot had spent ten humiliating weeks in the wilderness. He was subjected to an endless barrage of public scorn and derision, critical magazine covers, mocking comedy routines, and savage editorial cartoons. Perot endured as much ridicule and disrespect as any political figure in memory.

Perot had also spent millions during this period, according to reports he had to file with the government, quietly maintaining Perot organizations in fifty states and discreetly stockpiling political advertising. He was well prepared for his return as a candidate.

In his second incarnation, Perot spent more money running for President than anyone had spent before. In the first two weeks of October, he spent more than George Bush and Bill Clinton *combined*, almost $2 million every day. It was nearly all his own money, and he predicted that his campaign expenses would total $60 million. The Bush and Clinton organizations each received about $55 million in public funds for their fall campaigns. That was the spending limit for their campaigns. Perot's campaign had no spending limit because it was his money.

Perot was allowed to participate in the presidential debates. His exposure in the debates, along with his huge advertising budget, caused his positive ratings in the polls to double. But his negative ratings were increasing as well. In fact, in October, the negative ratings of all the candidates were higher than their positive ratings. A typical survey was made by CBS and the *New York Times* in the second half of October; Bush showed a positive/negative rating of 35/45, Clinton's was 33/39, while Perot's was 29/32. In the history of polling, there had never been results of this kind. One pollster said of the voters, "There isn't anybody they're truly in love with."

In the end, Ross Perot didn't matter. Despite all his bluster and all his millions, Perot's presence on every state ballot did not affect the outcome of the election. Polls of voters on election day by Voter Research & Surveys, known as exit polls, indicate that the outcome in only one state might have changed had Perot not been a candidate. Ohio might have gone to Bush instead of Clinton. This still would have given Clinton 349 electoral votes to 189 for Bush.

There were other curiosities produced by the presidential election of 1992. An incumbent President lost his bid for a second term while his party *gained* seats in the House of Representatives. That has happened only twice before. Only once before has a sitting President gotten as low a percentage of the vote as George Bush received in 1992. That was in 1912, when President Taft, another Republican Yale man, lost a three-way race to Theodore Roosevelt and Woodrow Wilson. In modern times, no candidate who lost the New Hampshire primary, as Clinton did, has gone on to win the presidential elec-

tion. And not since 1912 has a winning candidate received as low a percentage of the popular vote as Clinton did.

There are two ominous conclusions to be drawn from the election of 1992.

The voters continued to ignore, or reject, the system of choosing presidential candidates in party primary elections. Never before had voter participation in primaries been as low. Turnout was below 20 percent. The voting-age population for the 1992 primary elections increased by nearly six million over 1988, but the number of people who voted in them dropped by 1.3 million. There were attractive and vigorous Democratic presidential candidates in the early primaries, but Democratic turnout dropped by 16 percent. 1992 was the twentieth anniversary of the modern system of presidential primaries, in which most states choose national convention delegates in primary elections. The 1992 results show clearly that this method has become unpopular, undemocratic, and almost unworkable.

Ross Perot won not a single state, but he demonstrated, as no candidate ever has, the power of unlimited private funding. He got almost twice as many votes as any independent candidate in American history. If Perot had not dropped out for two-and-a-half months with a fantastic explanation hardly anyone believed, the outcome of the election might have been quite different. Perot traveled a long way without the support of a conventional political party, a party convention, or a platform on which he could have been judged.

It was not Ross Perot's *plan* that failed him; it was his *execution* of it. Some day, another wealthy nonparty candidate might win with it. That should be a matter of concern to all who believe in political parties.

Left: Celluloid button commemorating Clinton's memorable appearance on late-night TV.
Below: Privately issued audio cassette tape containing pro-Clinton songs and ditties.

♪ IT'S TIME FOR ♫ ♫ THEM TO GO...♪

•WARNING•
CONTAINS EXPLICIT
PATRIOTIC LYRICS

MAY BE OFFENSIVE TO REPUBLICANS

Right: Democratic poster. During the campaign, Clinton was portrayed as "an average guy" who could effectively handle the economy. Clinton's "People First" stock speech scored three times higher in the polls than Bush's attack on Clinton as a tax-and-spend liberal.
Far right: Pamphlet containing the major campaign promises of the Clinton/Gore ticket.

Labor Supports
CLINTON GORE in '92

Putting People First
...For a Change
Bill Clinton and Al Gore

ELECT HILLARY'S HUSBAND in '92

Celluloid button. Clinton aides joked that his approval rating rose or fell whenever Mrs. Clinton changed her hair style.

**ARKANSAS' FAVORITE SON**

**Bill Clinton FOR PRESIDENT**

*Celluloid button distributed during the July Democratic convention in New York City.*

**WOMEN FOR DEMOCRATIC VICTORY '92**

**Clinton/Gore**

Light The Way For Change!

**Torchlight Parade**

For:
Jobs
Health Care
Education
AIDS Awareness
Supreme Court
Civil Rights
Choice

**WEDNESDAY, OCTOBER 28**

*Issue-oriented Democratic campaign buttons .*

**THE 1992 DEMOCRATIC TICKET!**

**BILL CLINTON**
★ FOR PRESIDENT ★
**ALBERT GORE, Jr.**
★ FOR VICE PRESIDENT ★

**A NEW COVENANT TO MAKE AMERICA WORK AGAIN!**

**PRO CHOICE**
**PRO FAMILY**
**PRO CLINTON**

*Above: Celluloid button. Tennessee Senator Al Gore had an excellent environmental record. In a three-way race with Bush and Perot, the idea of a southern vice presidential candidate appealed to Clinton and his campaign strategists.*
*Right: Wooden toy bus. The day after the Democratic convention ended in New York, the Clinton and Gore families began a 5-day, 1,000-mile bus trip deep into small-town America.*

On the Road to Change America   **CLINTON/GORE '92**

Paper fan. On the eve of the Republican convention, Gallup figures showed that 48 percent of all registered voters and 37 percent of registered Republicans thought that President Bush should choose another vice presidential running mate. While senior presidential advisors flirted with replacing Quayle, they concluded this would be a confession of error by the President.

Technology enabled supporters to be pictured immediately on celluloid buttons with the candidates of their choice. Jonathan A. Frent is between Bush and Quayle.

Celluloid buttons distributed during the Republican convention in Houston.

Celluloid button. During the campaign, resgistered Republicans rated abortion last in importance from a list of sixteen major issues presented in a poll.

Republican cotton bandanna with patriotic motif.

**STAND BY THE PRESIDENT 1992**

Celluloid buttons of all three candidates and their wives.

REBUILD AMERICA
BILL CLINTON   HILLARY CLINTON
FOR OUR CHILDREN

We Share Your Family Values
Barbara and George Bush

America's Favorite Family
Ross & Margot Perot

I SUPPORT
DESERT SHIELD
&
DESERT STORM

VETERANS FOR
BUSH ★★★ QUAYLE 92

Celluloid buttons. In March 1991, after the Persian Gulf victory, George Bush received the highest approval rating of any President (89 percent) since the Gallup poll began to track Presidents' performance in 1938. The previous record of 87 percent was accorded Harry Truman after the 1945 German surrender.

Nodding rubber-head doll of Bush.

Pamphlet. Perot's major criticism was of the governmental process that produced a $4 trillion national debt. Polls showed that a majority of Americans agreed with him.

Top: Celluloid buttons. After Ross Perot announced he would consider an independent presidential candidacy, messages of support inundated his Dallas offices. Over a million calls came in during a ten-day period in March. Above: Bumper stickers. The Gallup poll reported that between June 4–8, 1992, Perot, still an unannounced candidate, held a significant lead in a test election against President Bush and likely Democratic nominee Bill Clinton. No third party or independent candidate had ever run second in a Gallup poll, let alone first.

H. ROSS PEROT

JAMES BOND
STOCKDALE

THE SECOND COMING
WILL WIN IN '92!

*Left: Celluloid button. On October 1 Ross Perot reentered the presidential race, after abruptly withdrawing in midsummer. His running mate, Admiral James Stockdale, was a congressional medal of honor recipient and a Vietnam POW. Below: Popular troll doll outfitted in a Perot t-shirt.*

*Celluloid button. Perot had carefully cultivated the tough warrior image, willing to take on anyone who got in his way.*

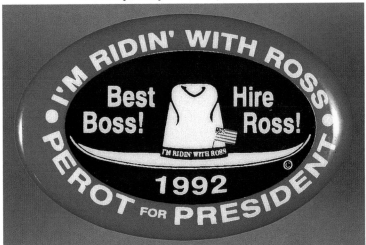

MORSELS OF
HISTORY

JONATHAN H. MANN

COLLECTORS of political Americana are indebted to Thomas Jefferson for providing the rationale for what may be irrational behavior. In an 1817 letter to John Adams, Jefferson wrote that "a morsel of genuine history is a thing so rare as to be always valuable." What a wonderful justification for acquisitive behavior! Those of us preoccupied with the search for campaign buttons, ribbons, and ferrotypes are helping in that cause of rescuing priceless "morsels of genuine history." Of course few would accuse the average collector of such selflessness—but there is an element of truth to Jefferson's thought. The reason so many artifacts of our electoral history still exist is because people have valued them. From George Washington's first oath of office in 1789, Americans have saved and treasured memorabilia that provide a direct link to those we elect to office. And while this link is often distant, it is material and very personal.

Whenever asked why I collect presidential campaign memorabilia, I respond: "Fix in your mind an image of Abraham Lincoln." I then reach into my wallet and remove a five-dollar bill. "Is this the picture you were thinking of?" The answer is usually yes. I then ask the person to think of another image of Lincoln. The image remains the same: that of a bearded, weathered, sixteenth president.

When I think of Lincoln, I visualize the Matthew Brady portrait taken a few hours before his 1860 Cooper Union speech in New York City. The truly rich portrait shows a warmth in the clean-shaven candidate that is missing from later photographs. Lincoln credited the photo with helping him to win the election. Those who value presidential ephemera appreciate all this, as well as the incidental knowledge that exactly 127 different pictures of Lincoln were taken from his first sitting in 1846 as a lawyer in Springfield to a postmortem picture taken nine days after the President's assassination. The historical knowledge required of collectors gives

them an appreciation of the real Lincoln, who was a wily, flawed, often manipulative politician, as well as our noblest statesman. The attribution "Honest Abe" is not a later creation of legend or demagoguery. Like the contemporary sound bite, it was a campaign slogan used on silk ribbons in his first national campaign. Collectors of political Americana relish the knowledge gained with each acquisition. The "morsels," therefore, are not just material. They include an understanding of who James G. Blaine was, why Samuel J. Tilden rightfully should have been President, how William McKinley was an executive with integrity who deserves to be remembered.

Each new election renews interest. The scramble for buttons from local party headquarters is mirrored by the continuing pursuit of artifacts from historic campaigns. Across the country, personal involvement in politics creates new collectors. Sociologists have coined the phrase "politicalization" to describe this process—the time when we each decide if we are Republicans or Democrats, active or passive, voters by candidate or by party. A collector, however, rises above those issues and worries about the lasting value of each campaign's artifacts. The collector considers value from the perspective of an archivist, curator, conservationist, and most certainly, historian.

Collections of political Americana take many forms and reflect personal tastes. From the simple campaign button to an elaborate silk ribbon of the nineteenth century, from a military commission signed by President Grant to a delegate badge worn by someone's grandfather at the 1940 Democratic Convention—the broadest definition of political Americana encompasses a staggering number of collectibles. Some of the most valuable pieces are from those candidates whom few recall—the losers.

Every four years, manufacturers help candidates define national interests, regional concerns, and local issues with ephemera that are often clever, sometimes crass, and generally far more imaginative than those seeking office. A short list would include:

- political textiles (bandannas, kerchiefs, banners, pennants, campaign flags)
- campaign ceramics (commemorative china, early whiskey flasks, glassware)
- lapel pieces (early brass badges, ferrotypes, celluloid buttons, ribbons)
- political paper (electoral tickets, campaign postcards, ballots, broadsides, sheet music, posters, newspapers, political biographies and almanacs, fans)
- clothing, hats, uniforms, parade lanterns, canes, torches, tobacco-related items
- novelties and games, puzzles, pocket mirrors, stickers, tabs, paperweights, stickpins and jewelry, serving trays, license plates, automobile attachments.

Collectors' preferences are shaped by innumerable areas of specialization. Some value graphic twentieth-century celluloid buttons. Others collect third-party or "hopeful" items from the primaries. Some relish "locals." There are those who treasure anything prior to 1896—the year the celluloid button was patented. Still, quite a number are concerned with the breadth of a.collection, seeking memorabilia from every campaign.

Few collections remain static; they evolve as the tastes and resources of the owner mature. But no matter what one chooses to collect, there are two rules that always must be remembered. The first is to collect what you like and like what you collect. Second, always know when you cross the line between collecting and investing.

There are many pragmatics to collecting political Americana. I would argue that it does not take a great deal of money to build a wonderful collection. More important is acquiring the knowledge required to collect. This knowledge is an understanding of why an item is important. Such understanding is precious and comes with time and experience. Fortunately, there are specific resources to consult while acquiring this acumen.

The American Political Items Collectors (APIC), started in 1945, is a non-profit organization with more than 4,000 members. It publishes a newsletter and journal and hosts bourses and conventions held throughout the country. There are also monthly newspapers for the hobby, not to mention a number of reference books.

And while nothing can substitute for knowledge gained from legwork in the search for hidden treasures, competent collecting requires an established base of knowledge. This includes an understanding of terms unique to the hobby, ability to judge the "condition" of a piece by accepted standards, knowledge of the best, and safest, ways to store and display a collection. This kind of information can be learned from the more experienced, most of whom are eager to share their passion. No matter what an individual collects, as a group we all have common interests: a love of history, an appreciation for the beauty of something uniquely American, a fascination for the design and graphics of a "classic" campaign button and the esthetics in a piece of political folk-art, a weakness for the quirky and unusual.

While random pins and buttons from recent campaigns have little meaning, a cohesive assembly of pieces with a common theme takes on a special significance—giving validity to the notion that the whole is more than the sum of the parts. This is why collections take on a life of their own and help define the personality of the owner. When a remarkable collection is assembled, its value outlives its creator. It helps us to recall what one person was able to build with love, passion, time, and concern. What a wonderful way to be remembered! As I always remind novices, no one really "owns" the artifacts we rescue from trunks and attics. We are all temporary custodians with a responsibility to preserve these "morsels of history." Long after we are gone, the artifacts will remain.

**GENERAL REFERENCE**

Levy, Leonard W., and Louis Fisher, eds. *Encyclopedia of the American Presidency*, 4 vols. 1994.
Schlesinger, Arthur M., jr., and Fred L. Israel, eds. *History of American Presidential Elections, 1789–1968*, Vols. I–IV. 1971; *1972–1984*, Vol. V. 1986.

**POLITICAL AMERICANA REFERENCE**

Collins, Herbert A. *Threads of History: Americana Recorded on Cloth, 1775 to the Present*. 1979.
Cunningham, Noble E., Jr. *Popular Images of the Presidency: From Washington to Lincoln*. 1991.
Earle, Alice M. *China Collecting in America*, repr. 1973.
Fischer, Roger A. *Tippecanoe and Trinkets Too: The Material Culture of American Presidential Campaigns, 1828–1984*. 1988.
Lawrence, Vera B. *Music for Patriots, Politicians, and Presidents: Harmony and Discord of the First Hundred Years*. 1975.
Lindsey, Bessie M. *American Historical Glass*. 1967.
McKearin, Helen, and Kenneth M. Wilson. *American Bottles & Flasks and Their Ancestry*. 1978.
Melder, Keith. *Hail to the Candidate: Presidential Campaigns from Banners to Broadcasts*. 1992.
Sullivan, Edmund B. *American Political Badges and Medalets, 1789–1892*. 1981.
Sullivan, Edmund B., and Roger A. Fischer. *American Political Ribbons and Ribbon Badges, 1825–1981*. 1985
Sullivan, Edmund B. *Collecting Political Americana*. 1991.

**THE ELECTIONS**

**1789–1792**
Freeman, Douglas Southall. *George Washington: A Biography*, Vol.VI, *Patriot and President*. 1954.
Jensen, Merrill, et. al., eds. *The Documentary History of the First Federal Elections, 1788–1790*. 1976.
McCormick, Richard P. *The Presidential Game: The Origins of American Presidential Politics*. 1982.
Mitchell, Broadus, *Alexander Hamilton*, Vol.II, *The National Adventure*. 1962.

**1796**
Lomask, Milton. *Aaron Burr: The Years from Princeton to Vice President, 1756–1805*. 1979.
Kurtz, Stephen G. *The Presidency of John Adams: The Collapse of Federalism, 1795–1800*. 1957.
McCormick, Richard P. *The Presidential Game: The Origins of American Presidential Politics*. 1982.
Malone, Dumas. *Jefferson and His Times*, Vol.III, *Jefferson and the Ordeal of Liberty*. 1962.

**1800**
Banning. Lance. *The Jeffersonian Persuasion: Evolution of a Party Ideology*. 1978.
Chambers, William Nisbet. *Political Parties in a New Nation: The American Experience, 1776–1809*. 1963.
Cunningham, Noble E., Jr. *The Jeffersonian Republicans: The Formation of Party Organization, 1789–1801*. 1957.
Peterson, Merrill. *Thomas Jefferson and the New Nation*. 1970.

**1804**
Chambers, William Nisbet. *Political Parties in a New Nation: The American Experience, 1776–1809*. 1963.
Cunningham, Noble E., Jr. *The Jeffersonian Republicans in Power*. 1963.
Johnstone, Robert M., Jr. *Jefferson and the Presidency*. 1978.
Malone, Dumas. *Jefferson the President: First Term, 1801–1805*. 1970.

**1808**
Cunliffe, Marcus. *The Nation Takes Shape, 1789–1837*. 1957.
Cunningham, Noble E., Jr. *The Jeffersonian Republicans in Power, 1801–1809*. 1963.

Ketcham, Ralph. *James Madison: A Biography*. 1971.
Rutland, Robert A. *James Madison: The Founding Father*. 1987.

**1812**
Brant, Irving. *James Madison: Commander in Chief, 1812–1836*. 1961.
Brant, Irving. *James Madison and American Nationalism*. 1968.
Kerber, Linda. *Federalists in Dissent: Imagery and Ideology in Jeffersonian America*. 1970.
Rutland, Robert A. *The Presidency of James Madison*. 1990.

**1816, 1820**
Ammon, Harry. *James Monroe: The Quest for National Identity*. 1971.
Heale, M.J. *The Presidential Quest: Candidates and Images in American Political Culture, 1787–1852*. 1982.
Livermore, Shaw, Jr. *The Twilight of Federalism: The Disintegration of the Federalist Party*. 1962.
McCormick, Richard P. *The Presidential Game: The Origins of American Presidential Politics*. 1982.

**1824**
Mooney, Chase C. *William H. Crawford, 1772–1834*. 1974.
Remini, Robert V. *Martin Van Buren and the Making of the Democratic Party*. 1951.
Remini, Robert V. *Andrew Jackson and the Course of American Freedom, 1822–1832*. 1981.
Remini, Robert V. *Henry Clay: Statesman for the Union*. 1991.

**1828**
McCormick, Richard P. *The Second American Party System: Party Formation in the Jacksonian Era*. 1966.
Remini, Robert V. *The Election of Andrew Jackson*. 1963.
Remini, Robert V. *Andrew Jackson and the Course of American Freedom, 1822–1832*. 1981.
Ward, John William. *Andrew Jackson: Symbol of an Age*. 1955.

**1832**
Chase, James Staton. *Emergence of the Presidential Nominating Convention, 1789–1832*. 1973.
Remini, Robert V. *The Life of Andrew Jackson*. 1986.
Remini, Robert V. *Henry Clay: Statesman for the Union*. 1991.
Vaughn, William Preston. *The Antimasonic Party in the United States, 1826–1843*. 1983.

**1836**
Cole, Donald B. *Martin Van Buren and the American Political System*. 1984.
Cooper, William J., Jr. *The South and the Politics of Slavery, 1828–1856*. 1978.
Latner, Richard B. *The Presidency of Andrew Jackson: White House Politics, 1829–1837*. 1979.
McCormick, Richard P. *The Presidential Game*. 1982.

**1840**
Gunderson, Robert Gray. *The Log-Cabin Campaign*. 1957.
Howe, Daniel Walker. *The Political Culture of the American Whigs*. 1979.
Schlesinger, Arthur M., jr. *The Age of Jackson*. 1945.
Watson, Harry L. *Liberty and Power: The Politics of Jacksonian America*. 1990.

**1844**
Niven, John. *Martin Van Buren: The Romantic Age of American Politics*. 1983.
Poage, George R. *Henry Clay and the Whig Party*. 1936.
Remini, Robert V. *Henry Clay: Statesman for the Union*. 1991.
Sellers, Charles G., Jr. *James K. Polk: Continentalist, 1843–1846*. 1966.

**1848**
Bauer, K. Jack. *Zachary Taylor: Soldier, Planter, Statesman of the Old Southwest*. 1985.
Hamilton, Holman. *Zachary Taylor: Soldier of the Republic*. 1951.
Rayback, Joseph G. *Free Soil: The Election of 1848*. 1970.
Smith, Elbert B. *The Presidencies of Zachary Taylor and Millard Fillmore*. 1988.

**1852**
Gienapp, William E. *The Origins of the Republican Party, 1852–1856.* 1987.
Holt, Michael F. *The Political Crisis of the 1850s.* 1978.
Nichols, Roy F. *Franklin Pierce: Young Hickory of the Granite Hills,* 2d ed. 1958.
Silbey, Joel H. *The American Political Nation, 1838–1893.* 1991.

**1856**
Gienapp, William E. *The Origins of the Republican Party, 1852–1856.* 1987.
Holt, Michael F. *The Political Crisis of the 1850s.* 1978.
Nevins, Allan. *Ordeal of the Union: A House Dividing, 1852–1857.* 1947.
Nichols, Roy F. *The Disruption of American Democracy.* 1948.

**1860**
Crenshaw, Ollinger. *The Slave States in the Presidential Election of 1860.* 1945.
Luthin, Reinhard H. *The First Lincoln Campaign.* 1944.
Nevins, Allan. *The Emergence of Lincoln,* Vol.II. 1950.
Potter, David M. *The Impending Crisis, 1848–1861.* 1976.

**1864**
Nelson, Larry. *Bullets, Ballots, and Rhetoric: Confederate Policy for the United States Presidential Contest of 1864.* 1980.
Sears, Stephen. *George B. McClellan.* 1988.
Trefousse, Hans. *The Radical Republicans.* 1969.
Williams, T. Harry. *Lincoln and the Radicals.* 1941.

**1868**
Benedict, Michael Les. *A Compromise of Principle: Congressional Republicans and Reconstruction, 1863–1869.* 1974.
Coleman, Charles H. *The Election of 1868: The Democratic Effort to Regain Control.* 1933.
Mantell, Martin Eden. "The Election of 1868: The Response to Congressional Resconstruction." Ph.D. Thesis, Columbia University, 1969.
Silbey, Joel H. *A Respectable Minority: The Democratic Party in the Civil War Era, 1860–1868.* 1977.

**1872**
Gerber, Richard Allen. "The Liberal Republicans in Historiographical Perspective." *Journal of American History,* 62 (1975).
Gillette, William. *Retreat from Reconstruction, 1869–1879.* 1979.
Ross, Earle Dudley. *The Liberal Republican Movement.* 1919.
Sproat, John G. *"The Best of Men": Liberal Reformers in the Gilded Age.* 1968.

**1876**
Current, Richard N. *The Terrible Carpetbaggers.* 1988.
Foner, Eric. *Reconstruction: America's Unfinished Revolution, 1863–1877.* 1988.
Polakoff, Ian. *The Politics of Inertia: The Election of 1876 and the End of Reconstruction.* 1976.
Woodward, C. Vann. *Reunion and Reaction: The Compromise of 1877 and the End of Reconstruction.* 1951.

**1880**
Clancy, Herbert J. *The Presidential Election of 1880.* 1958.
Doenecke, Justus D. *The Presidencies of James A. Garfield and Chester A. Arthur.* 1981.
Jordan, David M. *Winfield Scott Hancock.* 1988.
Reeves, Thomas C. *Gentleman Boss: The Life of Chester Alan Arthur.* 1975.

**1884**
Morgan, H. Wayne. *From Hayes to McKinley: National Party Politics, 1877–1896.* 1969.
Muzzey, David S. *James G. Blaine: A Political Idol of Other Days.* 1934.
Nevins, Allan. *Grover Cleveland: A Study in Courage.* 1932.
Welch, Richard E. *The Presidencies of Grover Cleveland.* 1988.

**1888**
Baumgardner, James L. "The 1888 Presidential Election: How Corrupt?" *Presidential Studies Quarterly,* 14 (1984).
Campbell, Charles S., Jr. "The Dismissal of Lord Sackville." *Mississippi Valley Historical Review,* 44 (1958).
Socolofsky, Homer E. and Alan B. Spetter. *The Presidency of Benjamin Harrison.* 1987.
Welch, Richard E., Jr. *The Presidencies of Grover Cleveland.* 1988.

**1892**
Dozer, Donald Marquand. "Benjamin Harrison and the Presidential Campaign of 1892." *American Historical Review,* 54 (1949).
Knoles, George Harman. *The Presidential Campaign and Election of 1892.* 1942.
Lorant, Stephan. "1892: The Twenty-Seventh Election," *The Glorious Burden.* 1968.
Rosenstone, H. J., et. al. *Third Parties in America.* 1984.

**1896**
Coletta, Paolo. *William Jennings Bryan: Political Evangelist, 1860–1908.* 1964.
Glad, Paul W. *McKinley, Bryan, and the People.* 1964.
Hofstadter, Richard. *The Age of Reform: From Bryan to FDR.* 1955.
Jones, Stanley. *The Presidential Election of 1896.*

**1900**
Coletta, Paolo. *William Jennings Bryan: Political Evangelist, 1860–1908.* 1964.
Gould, Lewis L. *The Presidency of William McKinley.* 1980.
Morgan, H. Wayne. *William McKinley and His America.* 1963.
Williams, R. Hal. *Years of Decision: American Politics in the 1890s.* 1978.

**1904**
Blum, John M. *The Republican Roosevelt.* 1954.
Broesamle, John M. "The Democrats from Bryan to Wilson," In *The Progressive Era.* Edited by Lewis L. Gould. 1974.
Gould, Lewis L. *Reform and Regulation: American Politics from Roosevelt to Wilson.* 1986.
Mowry, George W. *The Era of Theodore Roosevelt.* 1958.

**1908**
Coletta, Paolo. *William Jennings Bryan: Political Evangelist, 1860–1908.* 1964.
Koenig, Louis W. *Bryan: A Political Biography of William Jennings Bryan.* 1971.
Morgan, H. Wayne. *Eugene V. Debs: Socialist for President.* 1962.
Pringle, Henry F. *The Life and Times of William Howard Taft,* 2 vols. 1939.

**1912**
Cooper, John M., Jr. *The Warrior and the Priest: Woodrow Wilson and Theodore Roosevelt.* 1983.
Link, Arthur S. *The Road to the White House.* 1947.
Link, Arthur S. *Woodrow Wilson and the Progressive Era, 1910–1917.* 1954.
Mowry, George E. *Theodore Roosevelt and the Progressive Movement.* 1946.

**1916**
Link, Arthur S. *Campaigns for Progressivism and Peace.* 1965.
Link, Arthur S., et al., eds. *The Papers of Woodrow Wilson,* Vols. 36–38. 1966–1993.
Lovell, S. D. *The Presidential Election of 1916.* 1980.
Pussey, Merlo J. *Charles Evans Hughes,* Vol. I. 1951.

**1920**
Bagby, Wesley M. *The Road to Normalcy: The Presidential Campaign and Election of 1920.* 1962.
Downes, Randolph C. *The Rise of Warren Gamaliel Harding, 1865–1920.* 1970.
McCoy, Donald R. *Calvin Coolidge: The Quiet President.* 1967.
Russell, Francis. *The Shadow of Blooming Grove: Warren G. Harding in His Times.* 1968.

**1924**

Burner, David. *The Politics of Provincialism: The Democratic Party in Transition, 1918–1932.* 1986.

Leuchtenburg, William E. *The Perils of Prosperity, 1914–1932.* 1958.

Murray, Robert K. *The 103rd Ballot.* 1976.

Rice, Arnold S. *The Ku Klux Klan in American Politics.* 1962.

**1928**

Burner, David. *The Politics of Provincialism: The Democratic Party in Transition, 1918–1932.* 1986.

Handlin, Oscar. *Al Smith and His America.* 1958.

Perry, Elisabeth Israels. *Belle Moskowitz: Feminine Politics and the Exercise of Power in the Age of Alfred E. Smith.* 1987.

Silva, Ruth C. *Rum, Religion, and Votes: 1928 Re-Examined.* 1962.

**1932**

Farley, James A. *Behind the Ballots.* 1938.

Freidel, Frank. *Franklin D. Roosevelt: The Triumph.* 1956.

Hoover, Herbert. *Memoirs,* Vol. III. 1952.

Schlesinger, Arthur M., jr. *The Age of Roosevelt: The Crisis of the Old Order.* 1956.

**1936**

Allswang, John M. *The New Deal and American Politics: A Study in Political Change.* 1978.

Andersen, Kristi. *The Creation of a Democratic Majority, 1928–1936.* 1979.

Burns, James MacGregor. *Roosevelt: The Lion and the Fox.* 1956.

Schlesinger, Arthur M., jr. *The Age of Roosevelt: The Politics of Upheaval.* 1960.

**1940**

Donohoe, Bernard F. *Private Plans and Public Dangers: FDR's Third Term Nomination.* 1965.

Freidel, Frank. *Franklin D. Roosevelt: A Rendezvous with Destiny.* 1990.

Johnson, Donald D. *The Republican Party and Wendell Willkie.* 1960.

Parmet, Herbert S., and Marie B. Hecht. *Never Again: A President Runs for a Third Term.* 1968.

**1944**

Blum, John Morton. *V Was for Victory: Politics and American Culture during World War II.* 1976.

Burns, James MacGregor. *Roosevelt: Soldier of Freedom, 1940–1945.* 1970.

Polenberg, Richard. *War and Society: The United States, 1941–1945.* 1972.

Smith, Richard Norton. *Thomas E. Dewey and His Times.* 1982.

**1948**

Hamby, Alonzo L. *Beyond the New Deal: Harry S. Truman and American Liberalism.* 1973.

Markowitz, Norman D. *The Rise and Fall of the People's Century: Henry A. Wallace and American Liberalism, 1941–1948.* 1973.

McCullough, David. *Truman.* 1992.

Ross, Irwin. *The Loneliest Campaign: The Truman Victory of 1948.* 1968.

**1952**

Ambrose, Stephen E. *Eisenhower: Soldier, General of the Army, President-Elect, 1890–1952.* 1983.

Donovan, Robert J. *Tumultuous Years: The Presidency of Harry S. Truman, 1949–1953.* 1982.

Hamby, Alonzo L. *Beyond the New Deal: Harry S. Truman and American Liberalism.* 1973.

Martin, John Bartlow. *Adlai Stevenson of Illinois.* 1976.

**1956**

Ambrose, Stephen E. *Eisenhower: The President.* 1984.

Martin, John Bartlow. *Adlai Stevenson and the World.* 1977.

Pach, Chester J., Jr., and Elmo Richardson. *The Presidency of Dwight D. Eisenhower.* 1991.

Parmet, Herbert S. *Eisenhower and the American Crusades.* 1972.

**1960**

Ambrose, Stephen. *Nixon: The Education of a Politician, 1913–1962.* 1987.

Reeves, Richard. *President Kennedy.* 1993.

Schlesinger, Arthur M., jr. *A Thousand Days: John F. Kennedy in the White House.* 1965.

White, Theodore H. *The Making of the President, 1960.* 1961.

**1964**

Bornet, Vaughn Davis. *The Presidency of Lyndon B. Johnson.* 1983.

Cummings, Milton C., Jr., ed. *The Presidential Election of 1964.* 1966.

Lamb, Karl A., and Paul A. Smith. *Campaign Decision-Making: The Presidential Election of 1964.* 1968.

White, Theodore H. *The Making of the President, 1964.* 1965.

**1968**

Ambrose, Stephen. *Nixon: The Triumph of a Politician, 1962–1972.* 1989.

Hung, Nguyen, and Jerrold L. Schecter. *The Palace File.* 1986.

Nixon, Richard. *The Memoirs of Richard Nixon.* 1978.

White, Theodore H. *The Making of the President, 1968.* 1969.

**1972**

Ambrose, Stephen. *Nixon: The Triumph of a Politician, 1962–1972.* 1989.

McGovern, George. *An American Journey: Presidential Campaign Speeches of George McGovern.* 1974.

Parmet, Herbert S. *Richard Nixon and His America.* 1990.

White, Theodore H. *The Making of the President, 1972.* 1973.

**1976**

Glad, Betty. *Jimmy Carter: In Search of the Great White House.* 1980.

Ribuffo, Leo P. "Is Poland a Soviet Satellite? Gerald Ford, The Sonnenfeldt Doctrine, and the Election of 1976," *Right Center Left: Essays in American History.* 1992.

White, Theodore H. *America in Search of Itself: The Making of the President, 1956–1980.* 1982.

Witcover, Jules. *Marathon: The Pursuit of the Presidency, 1972–1976.* 1977.

**1980**

Dallek, Robert. *Ronald Reagan: The Politics of Symbolism.* 1984.

Drew, Elizabeth. *Portrait of an Election.* 1981.

Hargrove, Erwin. *Jimmy Carter as President.* 1988.

Wills, Garry. *Reagan's America: Innocents at Home.* 1985.

**1984**

Mayer, Jane, and Doyle McManus. *Landslide: The Unmaking of the President, 1984–1988.* 1988.

Noonan, Peggy. *What I Saw at the Revolution: A Political Life in the Reagan Era.* 1990.

Pomper, Gerald M., ed. *The Election of 1984.* 1985.

Speakes, Larry. *Speaking Out: The Reagan Presidency from Inside the White House.* 1988.

**1988**

Blumenthal, Sidney. *Pledging Allegiance: The Last Campaign of the Cold War.* 1990.

Drew, Elizabeth. *Election Journal: Political Events of 1987–1988.*

Germond, Jack W., and Jules Witcover. *Whose Broad Stripes and Bright Stars? The Trivial Pursuit of the Presidency, 1988.* 1989.

Runkel, David R., ed. *Campaign for President: The Managers Look at '88.* 1989.

**1992**

Duffy, Michael and Dan Goodgame. *Marching in Place: The Status Quo Presidency of George Bush.* 1992.

Levin, Robert E. *Bill Clinton: The Inside Story.* 1992.

Phillips, Kevin. *Boiling Point: Republicans, Democrats, and the Decline of Middle Class Prosperity.* 1993.

Pomper, Gerald M., et al. *The Election of 1992: Reports and Interpretations.* 1993.

Carter, Jimmy (continued)
nominations as Democratic presidential candidate
in 1976, 368
in 1980, 387-388
similarities to Ford, 372
and television debates, 428
Carter, Lillian (Miz Lillian), 370, 371
Carter, Rosalynn, 370, 371
Casey, William J., 388, 391
"Catholic and Patriot" (Proskauer), 147
Catholicism issue, and Smith as Democratic
presidential candidate in 1928, 147
Catholics
and Carter's campaign in 1976, 368
for Nixon in 1972, 352
and personal tax exemption issue in 1972, 347
prominence within Democratic leadership
in 1936, 187
for Stevenson in 1956 compared with
Kennedy in 1960, 297
see also Anti-Catholicism; Catholicism
issue; Roman Catholic Church
CBS, and coast-to-coast television in 1952, 260
CBS News, Mudd's interview of Edward Kennedy in
1980, Democratic primaries and, 390
Celebrities
and Corwin's radio show supporting
Franklin D. Roosevelt in 1944, 220
and Franklin D. Roosevelt's campaign in
1944, 227
at Nixon's election eve telethon, 296
participation in presidential election
campaigns, in 1920, 112
supporting Dewey in 1944, 222
use in Democratic party campaign of 1960, 295
Chafin, Eugene W., as Prohibition party
presidential candidate
in 1908, votes for, 47
in 1912, votes for, 67
Character issue, in presidential election campaigns,
and Johnson's campaign in 1964,
310-311; see also Scandals
Checkers (Nixon's pet dog), 262
Cheney, Richard, 368-369
Chennault, Anna Chan, 331
Chennault, Claire, 331
Chicago, Illinois, police attacks on antiwar
demonstrators during Democratic
convention in 1968, 330
Chicago Tribune, 220
headline announcing Dewey's victory in
1948, 239
Child labor issue, in Republican platform of
1924, 129, 130
Childs, Marquis, 293
Chisholm, Shirley, effort to win Democratic
presidential nomination in
1972, 349
Christensen, P.P., as Farmer-Labor presidential
candidate in 1920, vote for, 105
Church, Frank, 294
CIO
Political Action Committee of, and Dewey's
charges about Franklin D.
Roosevelt's link to communists,
226-228
unions, campaigning for Franklin D.
Roosevelt in 1936, 190
Civil Rights Act (1964), Johnson on, 312
Civil rights issue, 176, 241, 311, 312, 350
Clark, Champ, 69
Class privilege. See Privilege issue
Clay, Lucius D., 263

"Clear it with Sidney" slogan, in Dewey's
campaign in 1944, 227-228
Cleveland, Grover, 26
and reasons for Bryan's defeat in 1908, 55
refusal to run for President in 1904, 29
Clifford, Clark, and Truman campaign in 1948,
240-241
Clifford memorandum, as key strategy
document in Truman campaign
of 1948, 240-241
Clinton, Bill
as Democratic presidential candidate
adultery charges, 441,443
campaign organization, 443
campaign tactics, 443-444
polls, 442
social programs, 443
and use of late-night radio, 440
CNN, 428
Cold War
attitudes toward, and U.S. defeat in
Vietnam, 367
as issue in 1952, 263, 264, 265
and Reagan administration, 405
and Reagan's television advertisements in
1984, 410-411
and Stevenson, 257
Collective bargaining issue, in 1924, 129
College students
and changes in American society in 1968, 327
support for Wilson in 1916, 93
see also Antiwar movement; Columbia
University
Collier's, 91, 259
Colonialism, as campaign issue in 1900, 6-8
Columbia University
opinion poll during campaign of 1916, 95
student seizure of administration buildings
in 1968, 328
Committee of Arts and Sciences for
Eisenhower, 277
Committee of One, 187
Committee to Re-Elect the President (CREEP)
activities against Democratic primary
candidates, 348-349
role in Nixon's campaign in 1972, 352
Common man theme
and Coolidge's campaign in 1924, 130
in Franklin D. Roosevelt's campaign in
1940, 207-208
and Franklin D. Roosevelt's nomination of
Smith in 1928, 147
and Nixon's Checkers speech in 1952, 262-264
and Truman, 257
and Willkie, 203
Commoner, The, 50, 51
"Commoner Army," in 1908, 51
Communism. See Anti-communism issue;
Cold War; Communist party
Communist party
attitude toward Progressive party in 1924, 129
efforts to condemn at Republican convention
in 1964, 309
Franklin D. Roosevelt accused of links to,
226-228
Competency issue, in 1988, 426-427
"Confirming election," 1900 contest as, 3
Congress, United States
Democratic members of, exclusion as
delegates to Democratic
convention in 1972, 348
Eightieth, and Truman's proposals in 1948, 241
and Gulf of Tonkin resolution, 315

and investigation of arms-for-hostages
scandal, 391
presidential consultation with, as issue in
1940, 206
relationship with Johnson before 1964, 311
see also Congressional elections
Congressional elections
in 1900, 3
in 1904, 32
in 1956, 279
in 1968, 333
in 1972, 353
Connally, John B., efforts to win Republican
presidential nomination in
1980, 386
Conscience of a Conservative, The
(Goldwater), 309
Conservatism. See American conservatism;
Conservative Democrats;
Conservative Republicans
Conservative Democrats
in 1908
and Bryan's campaign platform, 50
and Bryan's defeat, 55
efforts to stop Franklin D. Roosevelt's
nomination at Democratic
convention in 1932, 164-166
and Wilson's stand for eight-hour day in
1916, 92
Conservative Republicans
and Goldwater's nomination in 1964, 309
and Liberty League activities in 1936, 188
opposition to New Deal labor legislation, 187
strengthened by social upheavals of 1960s, 367
Coolidge, Calvin
administration of, Hoover's influence
under, 146
announcement of decision not to run for
President in 1928, 145
nomination as Republican presidential
candidate in1924, 127
nomination as Republican vice presidential
candidate in 1920, 107
as Republican presidential candidate in 1924
electoral and popular votes for, 123, 131
and modern techniques of packaging,
125, 130
personality of, 127
as Republican vice presidential candidate in
1920, speaking tours by, 111
Cooperative marketing movement in
agriculture, 129
Corcoran, Thomas, 187
Corporate taxes, as issue in 1900, 9
Corruption issue, in presidential campaigns
in 1908, and Bryan's campaign, 51
in 1920, 112
in 1952, 265
and Nixon's Checkers speech, 262-264
in 1956, 277, 278
in 1964, and Johnson's reputation, 310
and Truman administration, 257
Corwin, Norman, 229
Cost of living issue, 107, 276
Coughlin, Charles, 183
Counterculture, and televising of Democratic
convention in 1972, 349-350
Counterdemonstrations
at Democratic convention in 1968, 329-330
at Goldwater rallies in 1964, 313
Couric, Katie, 439
Cowboy hats, and Theodore Roosevelt's
campaign in 1912, 74

Media
  and changes in campaigning in 1924, 130
  -made candidates, Willkie as in 1940, 206
  *see also* Newspaper photography; Newsreels;
    Press; Radio
Medicaid, Goldwater's opposition to in 1964, 309
Medicare issue
  in 1964, 309
  in 1984, 410
"Mess in Washington" slogan, in 1952, 258, 264
Methodist Episcopal Church, campaign
    against Smith in 1928, 150
Michigan Survey Research Center, 280
Middle class voters
  identification with Stevenson, 257
  and National Citizens Political Action
    Committee, 227
  white, backlash in 1968, 327
Middle East crisis in 1956, 278-279
Midwest
  beginning of movement against big business
    in 1900, 9
  Gallup in-depth survey in farm belt in 1956, 277
Military hero image
  of Eisenhower in 1952, 258, 262
  of Hoover, 145, 146
  of Kennedy, 293
  of McGovern, 348
  of Theodore Roosevelt, 4
Military spending issue
  in 1984, 410-411
  and "Reagan Revolution," 391
Minimum wage issue, in 1948, 241
Minor parties
  in 1908, 49
    total vote for, 54
  in 1920, votes for, 108
  in congressional elections of 1904, 32
  presidential nominees in 1920, 107-108
  Theodore Roosevelt's attack on, 87
  *see also* Populist party; Progressive party;
    Prohibition party; Socialist party
Minorities
  and reforms in Democratic party in 1972, 348
  voter perception of legislation on behalf of, 353
  *see also* Black Americans
"Missouri Compromise of 1944, 223
Mitchell, John, 329, 331
Mondale, Walter
  as Democratic presidential candidate in 1984
    background, 406
    campaign style compared with Reagan,
      406-407, 409
    and efforts to attract traditional Democratic
      party coalition, 407
    electoral and popular votes for, 403, 411
    image problems, 408-409
    in last days of campaign, 411
    need to establish credibility as strong
      leader, 407
    and performance as media campaigner,
      406-407
    selection of Ferraro as running mate,
      1984, 407
    strategy, 406-407
    televised debates with Reagan, 409-410
    television advertisements, 408-409, 411
  as Democratic vice presidential candidate
    in 1976
    and attitude toward Dole's qualifications, 371
    debate with Dole, 371
  effort to win Democratic presidential
    nomination in 1984, 406

nomination as Democratic vice presidential
    candidate in 1976, 368
  on role of television in modern elections, 411
Monetary policy issue, in 1900, 6
Moore, Edmond, 108
Morality issue, 1976 election campaign as
    referendum on, 367, 368, 369
"Morning in America" commercials for
    Reagan in 1984, 429
Mortgages, refinancing of, as issue in 1932, 166
Moskowitz, Belle, 147-148
Movie industry, influence of, 143; *see also*
    Celebrities
Movie newsreels. *See* Newsreels
Moyers, Bill, 313
"Mr. Harding, You're the Man for Us" (song), 112
MTV, 440
Mudd, Roger, 390
Mudslinging
  against Franklin D. Roosevelt in 1940, 209
  in campaign of 1944, 226
  and Cox's charges of Republican
    corruption, 112
  by Dewey campaign in 1944, 227-228
  and Willkie's campaign in 1940, 208-209
Murphy, Charles P., 50, 51
Muskie, Edmund S.
  in Democratic primaries in 1972, and trick
    played by Committee to Re-
    Elect the President, 348-349
  as Democratic vice presidential candidate
    in 1968, negative campaign
    against Agnew, 333
  nomination as Democratic vice presidential
    candidate in 1968, 330
Muskie, Jane, 348
Mussolini, 207
Mutual Broadcasting, 295

## N

NAACP, campaigning for Franklin D.
    Roosevelt in 1936, 190
National Association of Manufacturers, 54
National Citizens Political Action Committee, 227
National Colored Committee of the Good
    Neighbor League, rally for
    Franklin D. Roosevelt in 1936,
    187, 189
National debt issue
  in 1940, Willkie on, 204
  and "Reagan Revolution," 391, 405
National defense issue. *See* Defense policy issue
National Industrial Recovery Act (1933), 187
National Labor Relations Act (1935), 187
National medical insurance, Truman's call for
    in 1948, 241
National No-Third Term Day (1940), 204
National unity, and Johnson's second
    administration, 315
NATO
  Eisenhower as military leader of, 258
  Goldwater's call for authority over tactical
    nuclear weapons for
    commanders of, 310
NBC
  and coast-to-coast television transmission
    in 1952, 260
  coverage of 1960 campaign, 294
NBC News/*Wall Street Journal* poll, on
    Dukakis-Bush race in 1988, 428
"Negative advance". *See* Negative campaigning
Negative campaigning
  in 1964

Goldwater's attitude, 310-311
  and Johnson's campaign, 312-313
  in 1968
    by Democrats against Agnew, 332-333
    by Nixon, 331
    and Nixon's use of bombing halt issue,
      332-333
  in 1976, 372
  in 1988
    and Bush's campaign, 426-427
    and Dukakis's campaign, 424, 429
  *see also* Black propaganda
Neutrality Act (1935), 207
New Deal
  agencies, partisan use of radio in 1936 by, 185
  domestic policy initiatives of, impact on
    post-1936 campaigns, 183
  Hoover on, 169
  Landon's attitude toward in 1936, 191
  legislation, and growth of labor movement, 187
  New York state relief agency as model for, 164
  programs, and Franklin D. Roosevelt's
    "nonpolitical" appearances
    during campaign of 1940, 205
  radio skits ridiculing, 185
  relief agencies, and black voters in 1936, 190
  Franklin D. Roosevelt's claims about, 191
  and Franklin D. Roosevelt's "fireside chats," 184
  Franklin D. Roosevelt's 1932 proposal for,
    163, 166
  solidification of coalition in 1936, and future
    dominance of Democratic party, 183
  Willkie's positions on, 203
"New Freedom"
  and Jeffersonianism, 74
  in Wilson's campaigns
    in 1912, 71
    in 1916, 92
"New Nationalism" slogan
  and Hamiltonianism, 74
  as Theodore Roosevelt's campaign slogan in
    1912, 71
New Orleans, Louisiana, Johnson's 1964 speech
    on civil rights in, 312
"New Politics," and reform of delegate selection
    process by Democrats, 347-348
*New Republic*, 88
New York City
  attitudes toward in 1920s, 143
  hostility against, and Smith's campaign in
    1928, 150
  Franklin D. Roosevelt's automobile tour
    through in 1944, 229
  as site of Democratic party convention in
    1924, attitudes of delegates
    toward, 126
*New York Post*, 168
New York State
  governorship of, and presidential
    aspirations, 25-26, 149
  Theodore Roosevelt as governor of, and
    Republican nomination for vice
    presidency, 4
New York *Sun*, 27-28
*New York Times*
  advertisement for Hughes in 1916, 93-94
  opinion poll in 1916, 95
  on reasons for Harding's victory in 1920, 113
  report on Axis hope for Franklin D. Roosevelt
    defeat in 1940, 209
  on Franklin D. Roosevelt in 1932, 168
  and rumors on Franklin D. Roosevelt's link
    with Hillman, 227

and Truman's campaign in 1948, 241
Unemployment issue
   in 1976, 367, 369-370
   and Reagan's campaign in 1984, 405
Union members
   in Gallup in depth survey in 1956, 277
   and Mondale's campaign in 1984, 407
   *see also* Labor unions
Union Party, campaign in 1936, and use of
      radio, 183
*U.S. News & World Report,* 259
U.S.- Soviet relations, Goldwater's positions on
      in 1964, 310; *see also* Cold War
Urbanization
   in 1920 Census, 143
   influence on national politics, 144
Urban-rural conflict, in 1928, 150, 151

# V

Van Buren, Martin, 25
Vandenberg, Arthur H., 206
Vanzetti. *See* Sacco and Vanzetti case
Veterans' issues
   in 1920, 107
   and Hoover's eviction of Bonus marchers from
         Washington, D.C. in 1932, 167
Vice presidents
   and political liabilities for aspirants to
         presidency, 25-26
   succeeding fallen presidents, and efforts to
         win nomination and/or election
         to presidency, 25
Vietnam war
   Americans killed in action in, 327
   and call for bombing halt, 331-332
   and Gulf of Tonkin resolution, 315
   LeMay's proposed policies on, 328
   *see also* Vietnam war issue
Vietnam war issue
   in 1964, 313-315
      Goldwater's position on, 310
   in 1968, 330, 331
      and bombing halt issue, 331-332
      and Democratic party platform, 330
      and impact of Tet offensive, 327-328
      and Johnson's victory, 315
      and Nixon's campaign, 329
      and Nixon's negotiations with South
            Vietnamese, 331-332
   in 1972
      and Nixon's reelection, 352
         and public opinion of Watergate
               scandal, 351-352
      and perception of Nixon as antiwar
            candidate, 353
   in 1976, 367
Villa, Pancho, 91
Voter apathy
   in 1944, 224-225
      and CIO Political Action Committee,
            226-228
   in 1955, and Corwin's radio show, 229
Voter behavior
   in 1956, and choice between Eisenhower
         and Democratic party, 276
   factors influencing, 276
   and impact of television, 405
   and in-depth interviews by Gallup among
         key voter groups in 1956, 277-278
   and regionalism in 1916, 95
   and spot advertising, 429
Voter registration drives, by CIO Political
         Action Committee in 1944, 227

Voter turnout
   in 1900, decline in, 3
   in 1904, continued decline in, 32
   in 1928, 151
   downturn since 1960s, reasons for, 281
   downward trend in twentieth century, 3
Voters
   blocs, nonparty organizations and attempts
            to mobilize in 1936, 183
   influence of radio and press on, 222
   new, and Willkie campaign in 1940, 209
   reaction to George Wallace's program in
         1968, 328
Voting fraud
   Bryan's accusations in 1908 of, 53-54
   in Chicago, rumors of in 1960, 297
   Cox's charges against Republicans in 1920, 112

# W

Wagner Act. *See* National Labor Relations Act
Wald, Lilian, 187
Walker, James, 164
   Franklin D. Roosevelt and forced resignation
         of, 168
Wall Streeters, contributions to Hoover's
         campaign in 1928, 149
Wallace, George C.
   as American Independent presidential
         candidate in 1968
   and Agnew's nomination as Republican
         vice president, 329
   electoral and popular votes for, 325, 333
   hecklers at rallies for, 330
   opinion polls, 330, 331
   platform of, 328
      compared with Nixon's, 329
   assassination attempt against in 1972, 349
   effort to win Democratic presidential
         nomination in 1972, 349
   influence on Humphrey-Nixon campaign in
         1968, 423
Wallace, Henry A.
   creation of Progressive party in 1948, 239
      impact on Truman campaign, 240
   as Democratic vice presidential candidate
         in 1940
      campaign tours by, 205
      and mudslinging against Willkie, 209
   as Democratic vice presidential candidate
         in 1944, 223
   as Progressive party presidential candidate
         in 1948 campaigning by, 242
      votes for, 237, 245
Walsh, Thomas J., 127, 165
War and peace issue
   in 1916, 88, 94
   in 1956, 276
      and crises in Middle East and Eastern
            Europe, 279
   in 1964
      and Goldwater's campaign, 309-310
      and negative advertising by Johnson
            campaign, 313
   in 1972, and Nixon's victory, 372
   *see also* Vietnam war issue; World War II,
         American involvement in
War on Poverty, 309
Warren, Earl, as Republican vice presidential
         candidate in 1948, 242
Wartime elections, advantages to incumbent, 224
Washington, George, 262
Washington, D.C., riots after King's
         assassination in 1968, 328

Water rates issue, in 1924, 129
Watergate scandal
   and Carter's victory in 1976, 367, 373
   lack of press coverage, 351, 352
   and Nixon's campaign in 1972, 351-352,
         385-386
   and trend toward conservatism, 353
   underreporting of, 352
Watson, Thomas E, as Prohibition party
         presidential candidate in 1904,
         vote for, 32
Watterson, Henry, 50
"We Work Again" (pamphlet), 190
Welfare state
   Goldwater's attacks on in 1964, 309-310
   and Truman, 241, 257
Welliver, Judson, 109
West
   Franklin D. Roosevelt's tour of, in 1932, 168
   Socialist campaign in 1904 in, 32
Westmoreland, William, 327
Wet-dry issue. *See* Prohibition issue
Wetmore, Moses G., 50
Wheeler, Burton R., nomination as
         Progressive vice presidential
         candidate in 1924, 128
White backlash, and support for George
         Wallace in 1968, 328
White, Theodore H., 108, 292, 294, 296, 313, 405
Whittaker & Baxter, 261
*Why Not Victory?* (Goldwater), 309-310
Will, George, 409
Willkie, Wendell Lewis
   and Dewey's nomination as Republican
         presidential candidate in 1944, 219
   nomination as Republican presidential
         candidate in 1940, 69
   as Republican presidential candidate in 1940
      acceptance speech, 203
      advantages of, 203-204
      and American involvement in World War II,
            207-208
      attacks on Franklin D. Roosevelt, 206-207, 209
      blunders made by, 206-207
      electoral and popular votes for, 201, 209
      harassment during campaign, 208-209
      and influence of Time, Inc. on campaign, 206
      as "media-made" candidate, 203, 206
      and New Deal programs, 203
      personality of, 203
      and public opinion polls, 204
      railroad tours, 204
      reasons for loss of support, 205-206
      as Franklin D. Roosevelt's strongest
            opponent,209
      themes of campaign, 204
Williams, George Fred, 50
Wilson, Woodrow, 164
   appointment of Hoover as food
         administrator, 145
   attitudes toward, and Cox's campaign in
         1920, 111
   background, 33, 69
   and Bryan's innovations in campaign
         techniques, 52
   campaign contribution in 1920, 108
   and Conservative Democrats, 33
   and Cox's campaign in 1920, 108, 112
   as Democratic presidential candidate in 1912
      attacks on Theodore Roosevelt, 75
      and centrality of trusts issue, 70-75
      choice of McCombs as campaign
            manager, 70